Strategic Coupling

East Asian Industrial Transformation in the New Global Economy

Henry Wai-chung Yeung

Cornell University Press
Ithaca and London

Cornell University Press gratefully acknowledges receipt of a grant from the Faculty of Arts and Sciences, National University of Singapore, which aided in the publication of this book.

First published 2016 by Cornell University Press
First printing, Cornell Paperbacks, 2016
Printed in the United States of America

Library of Congress Cataloging-in-Publication Data

Yeung, Henry Wai-chung, author.
 Strategic Coupling: East Asian industrial transformation in the new global economy / Henry Wai-chung Yeung.
     pages cm—(Cornell studies in political economy)
 Includes bibliographical references and index.
 ISBN 978-1-5017-0255-6 (cloth : alk. paper)
 ISBN 978-1-5017-0256-3 (pbk. : alk. paper)
  1. Economic development—East Asia. 2. Globalisation—East Asia. 3. Manufacturing industries—East Asia. 4. Industrial policy—East Asia. I. Title. II. Series: Cornell studies in political economy.
 HC460.5.Y48 2016
 337.5—dc23
                                                      2015032272

Cloth printing   10 9 8 7 6 5 4 3 2 1
Paperback printing   10 9 8 7 6 5 4 3 2 1

Strategic Coupling

A Volume in the Series

Cornell Studies in Political Economy
Edited by Peter J. Katzenstein

A list of titles in this series is available at www.cornellpress.cornell.edu.

To Weiyu, Kay, and Lucas—
for accompanying me
throughout this long march

Contents

Tables

Figures

Preface and Acknowledgments

This book has taken me a very long time to write. But I have learned a great deal from the scholarship by writing it, and I am much happier with the work in this final form. It reflects my personal journey through East Asian development, first as a beneficiary, then as a student, and now an analyst. Growing up as a teenager in Hong Kong and Singapore during their formative decade of the 1980s, I experienced firsthand this transformative development in two of the four East Asian "tiger" economies. Still, I benefited much more than just being someone living in these rapidly developing city-states. I had the fortune of studying them as well!

My first encounter with the developmental state literature was in late 1992 when I embarked on my doctoral research under the supervision of Peter Dicken at the University of Manchester, England. Thanks to Peter's insightful knowledge of the then-emerging field of searching for the "miraculous" East Asian developmental model, I had the early advantage of reading writers who have since become giants in this field of the political economy of East Asian development. Looking at my well-worn copy of Robert Wade's *Governing the Market* (1990)—bought at the university bookstore in Manchester in March 1993—evokes in me a strong reminiscence of the early excitement as a keen student of East Asian industrial transformation. Then I read with intense interest all the other classics, such as Chalmers Johnson's *MITI and the Japanese Economic Miracle* (1982), Frederic Deyo's *The Political Economy of the New Asian Industrialism* (1987), Alice Amsden's *Asia's Next Giant* (1989), Stephan Haggard's *Pathways from the Periphery* (1990), and so on. Here, I pay tribute to all these thinkers for laying the solid intellectual foundation on which this book is predicated.

Since this early period of my interest in the East Asian developmental state, I have consistently followed this rapidly growing literature after my return to the National University of Singapore in 1995. Collectively, this enormous developmental state literature has prompted a heated debate on the role of the state in "governing the market" by "getting the prices wrong" and by promoting selective domestic firms as national champions. Authors in this literature have argued forcefully and demonstrated empirically that state-directed initiatives through industrial policy and credit allocation led these East Asian economies to industrialize rapidly, catching up with advanced industrialized economies in North America and Western Europe. As more books, book chapters, and journal articles were published in the second half of the 1990s and throughout the 2000s on this state-led industrial transformation, I began to witness at the same time a new dynamic mechanism of economic development at work in East Asia that went beyond this domestic statist force.

Since 2004, my research into the leading domestic firms in Singapore, Taiwan, and South Korea has pointed to a new direction of theorizing industrial transformation in an increasing interconnected world economy. Instead of being driven primarily by their home states, these national firms have taken over the leadership of industrial transformation through their dynamic articulation into complex global production networks—this is the mechanism of strategic coupling that forms the core focus of this book. Conceived as a major contribution to this debate on the changing role and continuity of the state in East Asian economies, this book aims to reshape the ways in which we understand the political economy of economic development and evolutionary state-firm relations in these three East Asian economies. I argue that the developmental statist approach to industrial transformation and economic development in these East Asian economies has often ignored the complex and dynamic coevolutionary nature of state-firm relations within the changing context of economic globalization. This work thus brings together the bottom-up approach in the developmental state literature with the more top-down perspective in the recent social science literature on global production networks and global value chains.

The theoretical and empirical research underpinning this book clearly benefits from my longstanding collaboration with different colleagues. My theoretical work on global production networks has its deep roots in the "Manchester school" originating in the early 2000s. I thank Peter Dicken, Jeffrey Henderson, Neil Coe, Martin Hess, and Jennifer Johns for their comradeship and support. Neil Coe, in particular, has recently rejoined my department, and our collaboration in this research has since deepened and led to our coauthored work *Global Production Networks* published in 2015 and our jointly directed Global Production Networks Centre (GPN@NUS). Philip Kelly, Weidong Liu, and Kris Olds are also my early partners in crime in this endeavor toward understanding complex production networks in the global economy.

My empirical work on the three East Asian economies has its origin in a major research project starting in 2004. I am very grateful to the more than one hundred top executives and senior government officials who acceded to our personal interview requests and shared generously their knowledge of

East Asian development. The promise of anonymity means that I cannot name any of them here. My two NUS collaborators in this project, Yong-Sook Lee and Jang-Sup Shin, have made fundamental contributions to my empirical analysis in this book. I am most indebted to their role in collecting the interview data on domestic firms and state institutions in South Korea. Our outstanding research assistant, Angela Leung, deserves a special commendation for her dedicated assistance throughout the several years of fieldwork in all three economies (plus Hong Kong). Liu Yi, my former Ph.D. student, also helped compile some of the statistics used in the book.

In Taiwan, Jinn-Yuh Hsu (National Taiwan University) and Tain-Jy Chen (Chung-Hua Institution for Economic Research) were very kind in hosting my multiple visits to Taipei and were most generous with their time and resources. Jinn-Yuh, Bruce Tan, Daniel Yang, Sue-Ching Jou, and their graduate students in NTU Geography kept me well entertained and in good spirits during extended field trips. All this empirical work would not have been possible without the sustained financial support of the National University of Singapore over the past ten years. In the second half of 2006, I spent several months of sabbatical leave in Hong Kong and Japan during which more empirical data were collected. I thank Eric Ramstetter at the International Centre for the Study of East Asian Development in Kitakyushu, Japan, and George Lin at the University of Hong Kong for their strong friendship and support in securing me generous visiting professorships in both institutions.

Translating this protracted theoretical and empirical research into an actual book has been a Herculean task that necessitates a whole new set of benefactors. The writing of this book started in 2010 when I was on the NUS Humanities and Social Sciences Faculty Research Fellowship for one semester. The book proposal was written in November 2012 when I was on the Residency Fellowship at the Rockefeller Foundation's beautiful Bellagio Study and Conference Center in Italy. I thank Kishore Mahbubani for nominating me to the foundation and Catherine Weaver and Eric Sheppard for their careful reading and constructive comments on my book proposal. Other fellow academic residents at the Bellagio Center offered very useful suggestions and stimulating discussions: Laurie Brand, Ruth Fincher, Helga Leitner, Valerie Preston, Anne Salmond, and Michael Webber. Pilar Palaciá, the Bellagio Center's managing director, and her dedicated team provided the most amazing hospitality that made Villa Serbelloni's tranquility and serenity just so heavenly for all of us. Working on my manuscript in the villa's private study overlooking the magnificent Lake Como was simply a once-a-lifetime experience. The finalization of the entire manuscript for first submission was completed during my sabbatical leave at the School of Geosciences, University of Sydney, Australia, in 2013. I thank the University of Sydney for its visiting professorship appointment that enabled this crucial preparation, and my two wonderful hosts, Jeffrey Neilson and Bill Pritchard. An extended discussion with John Mathews over coffee in Potts Point was most fruitful.

Publishing this book with one of the world's top university presses and its renowned book series is a dream that has indeed come true by the time you read this! Four individuals are positively implicated in this process, and I am forever grateful to them. First and foremost, I am immensely grateful to Peter Katzenstein for spending a significant chunk of his invaluable time to read different submissions of my manuscript and for offering critical and yet extraordinarily productive comments. His penetrating insights into theory, analysis, and readership are unparalleled and have certainly made the book much stronger. With the usual caveats, I can only hope this version befits in a modest way his prestigious Cornell Studies in Political Economy series that has already made enormous contributions to the developmental state literature over the past thirty years. Roger Haydon, my executive editor at Cornell University Press, is really a gem to work with. His generous support and sustained encouragement have kept this project on track. I thank him and Peter for their exceptional responsiveness, great patience, and steadfast commitment to this work. Finally, I thank Dan Breznitz and an anonymous reader for their interventions at the critical stages of this manuscript publication. Dan was very kind with his candid advice on manuscript publishing and introduction to Cornell. The detailed and constructive comments from the reader were highly useful to my revisions.

The broad ideas in this manuscript have been presented as lectures and preliminary papers in different occasions since 2006: the Asia Pacific Viewpoint Lecture at the International Geographical Union Regional Congress in Brisbane, Australia (2006); the Norma Wilkinson Lecture at the University of Reading, England (2007); Birkbeck College, University of London (2007); annual meetings of the Association of American Geographers in Boston (2008) and Las Vegas (2009); annual conferences of the Regional Studies Association in Leuven, Belgium (2009) and Pécs, Hungary (2010); Asia Centre of Seoul National University, South Korea (2009); the DIME Workshop in Utrecht, the Netherlands (2009); University College Dublin, Ireland (2010); McGill University, Canada (2011); the Jeremiah Lecture, University of Oregon (2011); the LSE-NUS Public Lecture, the London School of Economics and Political Science (2012); National University of Ireland, Maynooth (2012); Academy of International Business (UK and Ireland) Conference at the University of Liverpool Management School, England (2012); Third Global Lecture, University of Copenhagen, Denmark (2012); the Institute of Australian Geographers Conference 2013, Perth; and the Regional Science Policy and Practice Lecture at the North American Regional Science Council Conference, Washington, DC (2014).

I thank all commentators of my lectures and/or papers in these venues; their inputs were critical to my manuscript preparation. In particular, helpful and constructive comments were received in various ways and formats from these scholars: Stephanie Barrientos, Ron Boschma, Peter Buckley, Mark Casson, Riccardo Crescenzi, Fred Deyo, Mike Dowdle, Niels Fold, Michele Ford,

Doug Fuller, David Gerber, Gary Gereffi, Alexandra Hughes, Simona Iammarino, Bob Jessop, Andrew Jones, David Levi-Faur, Imelda Maher, Matthew Mahutga, Franco Malerba, Andrea Morrison, Ram Mudambi, Alexander Murphy, Warwick Murray, Khalid Nadvi, Rajneesh Narula, Jeffrey Neilson, Sean O'Riain, Sam Ock Park, Mario Davide Parrilli, Stefano Ponte, Jessie Poon, Bill Pritchard, Roberta Rabellotti, Michael Storper, Timothy Sturgeon, Ngai-Ling Sum, Linda Weiss, and Chun Yang. Several of my former coeditors at the *Review of International Political Economy* also contributed to my ideas in this book: Walden Bello, Mark Blyth, Juliet Johnson, Eric Helleiner, Len Seabrooke, and Catherine Weaver.

Back in NUS Geography, two former department heads—Victor Savage and Shirlena Huang—were particularly supportive of this project during their tenure. Past and current members and distinguished visitors of the Politics, Economies, and Space (PEAS) research group were very helpful in discussing earlier drafts of some chapters. I am grateful to comments and suggestions from Neil Brenner, Tim Bunnell, Chen Rui, Neil Coe, Stuart Elden, Jim Glassman, Carl Grundy-Warr, Lily Kong, Karen Lai, Liu Yi, Harvey Neo, Bae-Gyoon Park, Jamie Peck, Eric Sheppard, James Sidaway, Aidan Wong, Chih-Yuan Woon, Godfrey Yeung, and Zhang Jun. I thank Jun for lending me several key developmental state books on a long-term basis from his extended private collection. Other Singapore-based scholars were also helpful with their ideas and suggestions for this work: Sea-Jin Chang, Andrew Delios, Natasha Hamilton-Hart, Baogang He, Teck Hua Ho, Hong Liu, Ishtiaq Mahmood, Ted Tschang, Lai Si Tsui-Auch, and Poh Kam Wong. In revising the manuscript, I received particularly useful comments and suggestions from two key members of our GPN@NUS research team: Kurtuluş Gemici and Soo Yeon Kim. Kurtuluş's generosity in guiding me through the social mechanisms literature in sociology must be acknowledged here.

At the end of the day, my family members in Hong Kong and Singapore have provided the unwavering support that makes this work worthy of its weight and wait. My parents and my brother and his family in Hong Kong always cheered me up during the different phases of my fieldwork in Hong Kong (and when I traveled to/from Taipei). At home, my wife and two children have been most patient with me during this long march. It is to their love, joy, and companionship that I dedicate this work.

Abbreviations

A*Star	Agency for Science, Technology and Research, Singapore
CEPD	Council for Economic Planning and Development, Taiwan
CIECD	Council for International Economic Cooperation and Development, Taiwan
CPF	Central Provident Fund
CPHCI	Committee for the Promotion of Heavy and Chemical Industrialization, South Korea
CSBC	China Shipbuilding Corporation
CUSA	Council for United States Aid, Taiwan
DPP	Democratic Progressive Party, Taiwan
DRAM	dynamic random access memory
EDB	Economic Development Board, Singapore
EMS	electronics manufacturing services
EPB	Economic Planning Board, South Korea
EPC	Economic Planning Council, Taiwan
ERSO	Electronics Research Service Organization, Taiwan
ETRI	Electronics and Telecommunications Research Institute, South Korea
FDI	foreign direct investment
FSC	Financial Supervisory Commission, South Korea
FSS	Financial Supervisory Service, South Korea
FTA	free trade agreement
GLC	government-linked company
HCI	heavy and chemicals industries
HDB	Housing and Development Board, Singapore
HHI	Hyundai Heavy Industries
ICT	information and communications technology
IDB	Industrial Development Bureau, Taiwan

IDM	integrated device manufacturer
IMF	International Monetary Fund
IMG	intermediate manufactured goods
IPO	initial public offering
ITRI	Industrial Technology Research Institute, Taiwan
KIST	Korea Institute of Science and Technology
KMT	Kuomintang, Taiwan
GPN	global production network
GVC	global value chain
LIUP	Local Industry Upgrading Program, Singapore
MAS	Monetary Authority of Singapore
MITI	Ministry of International Trade and Industry, Japan
MOCIE	Ministry of Commerce, Industry and Energy, South Korea
MOEA	Ministry of Economic Affairs, Taiwan
MOFE	Ministry of Finance and Economy, South Korea
MOIC	Ministry of Information and Communication, South Korea
MOKE	Ministry of Knowledge Economy, South Korea
MOPB	Ministry of Planning and Budget, South Korea
MOSF	Ministry of Strategy and Finance, South Korea
MOTIE	Ministry of Trade, Industry and Energy, South Korea
MTI	Ministry of Trade and Industry, Singapore or South Korea
NBFI	nonbank financial institution
NSTB	National Science and Technology Board, Singapore
OBM	original brand manufacturing
ODM	original design manufacturing
OEM	original equipment manufacturing
PAP	People's Action Party, Singapore
POSCO	Pohang Iron and Steel Company
R&D	research and development
SHI	Samsung Heavy Industries
SME	small- and medium-sized enterprise
SOE	state-owned enterprise
SPIL	Siliconware Precision Industries Corporation
TFT-LCD	thin film transistor-liquid crystal display
TNC	transnational corporation
TSE	Taiwan Stock Exchange
TSMC	Taiwan Semiconductor Manufacturing Company
UMC	United Microelectronics Corporation
USPTO	United States Patent and Trademark Office
VLSI	very-large-scale integration
WTO	World Trade Organization

Strategic Coupling

Chapter 1

East Asian Development
in the New Global Economy

When the late Steve Jobs introduced the first iPhone to the world on January 9, 2007, he claimed that the revolutionary product was "literally five years ahead of any other mobile phone."[1] He was exactly right. It would take Samsung Electronics, South Korea's largest chaebol, or conglomerate, until the first quarter of 2012 to overtake Apple Inc. as the world's largest smartphone vendor.[2] As a key supplier of iPhone's core components, such as semiconductors and display panels, Samsung also ousted Nokia, a longtime market leader in mobile phones from Finland, to become the world's largest mobile phone vendor. By March 2015, Apple had shipped more than 700 million iPhones since it was first released on June 29, 2007. In contrast, Samsung sold more than 837 million phones in total (including 607 million smartphones) to end users worldwide during the 2013–2014 period alone.[3]

By all accounts, Apple and Samsung have attained phenomenal achievements in the modern electronics industry. We now have a better understanding of the factors underlying their accomplishments. In particular, Apple's success is predicated on the world-class manufacturing and organizational capabilities of its strategic partners in East Asia. These national firms in South Korea, Taiwan, and Singapore have assumed industrial leadership since the 1990s, and they are the main analytical focus of this book. The existing literature on the political economy of East Asian industrial transformation shows that domestic developmental states provided the initial political and institutional bases for the emergence of these firms. Subsequently, I shall argue, these East Asian firms have developed strategic alliances with lead firms in global production networks and taken advantage of the new opportunities involved in these national-global articulations. Organizationally fragmented and spatially dispersed production networks constitute a new form of economic structure, one that underpins today's complex global economy and its uneven developmental outcomes.[4]

1

A *New York Times* report in January 2012 tells this story succinctly. When US president Barack Obama asked Steve Jobs, "What would it take to make iPhones in the United States?" Jobs replied, "Those jobs aren't coming back!"[5] The task of assembling more than 700 million iPhones went to Foxconn Technology's industrial cluster located in the city of Shenzhen in southern China. The same report points to the immense scale of manufacturing operations and supply chain flexibility orchestrated by Foxconn. Apple's own executives conceded that switching from Foxconn would be time-consuming and costly.[6] Foxconn's parent company is Taiwan's Hon Hai Precision Industry, a family-owned electronics manufacturing service provider that happens to be the world's largest, with an annual turnover of US$135 billion and a market capitalization of US$45 billion at the end of 2014. Since its strategic partnership as *the* manufacturer of Apple's iPhones and, more recently, iPads, Hon Hai saw its revenues grow by more than 75 percent between 2008 and 2011, and its net profits increase from US$1.8 billion in 2008 to US$2.6 billion in 2011 and US$4.2 billion in 2014.[7] More important, Hon Hai is not the only East Asian firm to have benefited from the unprecedented success of smartphones. Other high-tech firms in the region are making semiconductors, memory chips, display panels, camera modules, and other parts that go into each smartphone.[8]

This anecdote about three industry leaders—Apple, Hon Hai, and Samsung—and their global production of the now ubiquitous iPhone tells us something significant about the evolutionary dynamics of East Asian firms, their developmental states, and the increasingly complex global networks of production. It showcases the enormous success of industrial transformation in these East Asian economies and the rapid growth of their national firms, defined as private or state-linked firms headquartered in and controlled by nationals from these economies. Not surprisingly, Taiwan's Hon Hai and South Korea's Samsung have become the largest industrial firms in their domestic economies.

Their success in the global information and communications technology (ICT) industry also underscores the longstanding track record of state-led industrial policy in promoting the industry since the 1970s. A huge yet diverse literature explains why and how various state initiatives can account for successful economic development.[9] Starting as a sugar and wool producer in the early 1950s, Samsung Electronics became one of the poster boys and a major beneficiary of the developmental state in South Korea. It certainly owes much of its initial success in semiconductors in the late 1980s to the relentless efforts of the South Korean state in promoting an export-oriented electronics industry. Since the late 1980s, however, these national firms have grown out of their home states or become globally competitive through their own initiatives. They are no longer dependent on state support. At the same time, the efficacy of the developmental state in steering industrialization has had to change in tandem with changing domestic politics and with new opportunities associated with economic globalization. The state's role has evolved, and it now provides new and more indirect types of support for national firms competing in the global economy.

As a result of this new development in the global economy, there is a significant lacuna in the existing scholarship on East Asian industrial transformation. This gap emanates in part from the primary analytical focus in earlier studies on state capacity and their variations across different national economies. In that literature, state types and institutional capacities, *the* independent variable, are used to explain the pace and pattern of industrialization and, more broadly, economic development.[10] According to Peter Evans (1995, 12), the efficacy of a developmental state hinges on its "embedded autonomy"—embedded sufficiently in the domestic private sector to understand its needs and aspirations, yet autonomous enough from the same domestic elites to avoid their rent-seeking behavior and other social pressures. National firms, as part of the dependent variable of industrialization, tend to be read as *outcomes* of state action: these firms and their home economies were successful because during their formative decades, particularly during the 1960s and the 1970s, the developmental state cajoled private capital to perform competitively in the global export market. Their high growth in subsequent decades was therefore a direct consequence of strong state capacity: export-oriented industrial policy manifested itself in the growing competitiveness of national champions.[11]

What has happened to these national champions and their new "siblings" since the early 1990s? How do they survive and compete without direct financial support from their domestic states, which are no longer as "developmental" as they used to be? What is the nature of state presence in this changing reconfiguration of state-firm relations? These are the key questions to be addressed in this book.[12]

A New Political Economy Approach to East Asian Industrial Transformation

This book is primarily concerned with the coevolutionary dynamics of states and firms in shaping industrial transformation, and the role of domestic and international processes in mediating these effects. I go beyond a statecentric view of industrial transformation to consider the interaction between domestic states and national firms in a world economy characterized by deep global economic integration. My aim is to show how the previously one-sided relationship between developmental states and their national firms has changed over time in favor of firms that work with extranational actors embedded in global production networks. In the classic developmental state period of the 1960s and the 1970s, domestic firms were driven primarily by state intervention; now, domestic firms join global networks and their strategy is facilitated by new state functions and industrial or sectoral support.

Revisit for a moment our opening vignette: Hon Hai's runaway success has less to do with direct policy intervention from the Taiwanese state than with its strategic positioning as a manufacturing partner for global lead firms and its world-class production and organizational capabilities. Its participation in global production networks extends beyond the territorial reach of any developmental state.[13] Similarly, Samsung's success in the global semiconductor and telecommunication handsets industries today cannot be attributed only to domestic state policies.[14] These leading East Asian firms serve as important conduits through which their home economies become part of the new global economy. Their success is evident not only in their enormous size measured in domestic sales or assets (a common legacy of state-directed development). More important, these East Asian firms have emerged as world leaders in their market segments and in industries that are highly *globalized*. The conventional wisdom of an all-powerful developmental state steering economic growth and "picking winners" must be reframed in order to take into account these new forces and processes associated with economic globalization and cross-border production.

My main theoretical contribution in this book is expressed in the concept of *strategic coupling*.[15] I use this concept to argue for a recasting of the dominant statecentric view of industrial transformation in South Korea, Taiwan, and Singapore.[16] By "strategic," I afford greater analytical significance to firm-specific initiatives, such as technological innovation, capability building, international market development, and so on. By "coupling," I refer to the dynamic relational process through which national firms decouple partially from domestic political-economic structures—developmental states or associated institutions—over time *and* couple with lead firms in global production networks. As a midrange concept that connects opportunities in the global economy (as embodied in global production networks) to development outcomes in national economies (e.g., the rise of domestic firms in different industries) through firm-specific initiatives, strategic coupling helps us understand industrial transformation and, ultimately, national economic development in an increasingly integrated global economy.[17]

We saw earlier how strategic coupling works in the articulation of Hon Hai and Samsung into Apple's global production network. Premised on the perspective of global production networks (GPN), this new political economy approach requires a reworking of the developmental state thesis and the reconsideration of both the micro and the macro—national firms *and* developmental states. Adding to this micro-macro link is the changing context of the global economy—the emergence of new forms of economic organization, such as global production networks and global value chains. This book thus seeks to bridge the conceptual gap between the bottom-up analysis of the states role in national development (conventional developmental state studies) and the top-down analysis of global industries and national economic development (global value chain studies).[18]

To a limited extent, this need to focus on national firms in understanding industrial transformation has been pointed out by some prominent scholars. In his influential book *Innovation in East Asia* published in the same year as Evans's *Embedded Autonomy*, Michael Hobday (1995, 2) notes that "The dominance of the market *versus* state debate has left little room for the study of the technology strategies of East Asian firms. The central competition question of how companies acquired and 'learned' technology is almost untouched in the literature on East Asian industrialization. This is a serious oversight as firms are the locus of competition, exports, wealth creation, innovation and productivity growth in East Asia as elsewhere."[19]

The growing importance of East Asian firms in global production networks has been accentuated by the demise of both Japan-led regional integration and developmental state-led industrialization. The old flying geese pattern in which Japan provided the technological leadership is no longer the integrating force for East Asia because, as Boyer et al. (2012, 334–35) note, "standardization and modularization, allied with unprecedented FDI [foreign direct investment] mobility, have created large production networks. Those networks have, in quite a few industries, disconnected the previous specialization of each national economy." This reconfiguration of production has compelled scholars of economic development to go beyond domestic political-economic dynamics and alliances within individual economies.

My analytical approach elucidates the reconfiguration of state-firm relations in the three East Asian economies since the early 1990s through two sets of evolutionary dynamics. The first set is the evolving political-economic dynamics in the state-firm-GPN assemblage. The second refers to a complementary set of coupling processes through which East Asian firms achieve dominance in different global industries: strategic partnership, industrial market specialization, and (re)positioning as global lead firms. Two important caveats are necessary. First, this book is not so much concerned with the political origins and choices of national economic development and its divergent trajectories.[20] While I will briefly describe the new kinds of economic policies and institutions appropriate for a more globalized context, my analysis may appear relatively "thin" on the state (e.g., domestic political change) and its institutions (e.g., business associations, public-private institutions).

Second, my argument about evolutionary state-firm relations in these East Asian economies does not imply a zero-sum relationship in which state power declines *because of* the rise of national firms. Instead, I show that the strategic coupling of these national firms with global production networks cannot be exclusively attributed to state power. During the same historical period that national firms moved outward, starting in the late 1980s, the developmental state itself underwent significant political transformations that led to a relative decline in its internal cohesiveness and bureaucratic rationality. In this coevolutionary transition in state-firm relations, the strategic coupling of "winners" (national champions) with global lead firms means that these winners no longer necessarily owe their new competitive advantages to direct steering by their home developmental state.

Developmental States in a Globalizing Context

A brief reprise of the developmental state in the three East Asian economies is necessary here to set the baseline for my contemporary analysis of the evolving state-firm-GPN assemblage. Historically, successful industrial transformation in a national economy takes place through a process of catch-up in some, but not all, sectors. As Malerba and Nelson's (2011) study of six high-tech industries shows, South Korea and Taiwan have attained premier positions in semiconductors, and South Korea in automobiles and telecommunication equipment. Like many other indicators of economic achievements by latecomer economies, these measurements of industrial attainment typically mask the important role of such economic institutions as national firms; we need to probe below the level of the developmental state and its political choices.

Moreover, a major gap remains in the developmental state literature because we know relatively little about how East Asian firms are articulated into global production networks and become major players in their respective industries on a global scale.[21] This lack of understanding of the evolutionary dynamics and emergence of East Asian firms reflects the general underestimation, particularly in the mainstream debates on the role of state and market in East Asian development during the past three decades, of the importance of firms as a key actor in the articulation of domestic economies into the global economy. The existing literature has been much more concerned with the transformations and adjustments of domestic institutions in economic governance. There is insufficient attention to the complex interplay between the competitive dynamics in these global industries and the coupling processes of East Asian firms.

While contemporary thought on the central role of the state in economic development has a long intellectual pedigree dating back to the mercantilist period at the dawn of modern capitalism (Hirschman 1958; Gerschenkron 1962), the role of East Asia in this developmental state debate is indeed central and reciprocal. To Bello (2009, 180), "If there is one theory or approach that might be said to be uniquely associated with the region, it is the theory of the developmental state. Indeed, one can say that theoretical innovation and empirical work in IPE [international political economy] in East Asia has been largely driven by the developmental state debate." Based on the successful experience of the state in guiding economic development in Japan and, later, South Korea, Taiwan, and Singapore, leading proponents of the developmental state thesis have consistently argued that deliberate state interventions via active industrial policy and selective financial support have enabled state-sanctioned domestic firms, known as "national champions," to overcome their latercomer disadvantages and to achieve economies of scale in domestic and international competition.[22]

Indeed, many innovative policy instruments were effectively deployed by the developmental state to provide "organized help" to private entrepreneurs.[23] Instead of pursuing market-based price mechanism, the developmental state intentionally distorted the market by "getting the prices wrong," to use the term made famous by Amsden (1989, 13–14; 2007, 87) and Wade (1990, 32), in order to induce private entrepreneurs to participate in the state-led industrialization program. Interventionist policy instruments included trade and foreign exchange controls, selective allocation of credits, export and tax incentives, public enterprises, and other subsidies. Industrial policy was sectoral or firm specific in order to target the development of selective industries and/or national firms, to promote their efficiency and productivity growth, and to overcome initial coordination failures in the domestic market.

In return, these entrepreneurs were subject to stringent performance and standards monitoring by state agencies. Amsden (1989, 94; also 2001) thus argues strongly that "what lay behind successful postwar industrialization was a monitored system of controls on subsidies. Neither import substitution nor export-led growth was a free-for-all. In many cases, especially that of Korea and Taiwan, exporting was made a condition for domestic protection." If these entrepreneurs were not forthcoming or capable enough, the state took on the role of entrepreneurs and readily stepped in with the establishment of state-owned enterprises that socialized the market or the industry in the hands of the public sector. This direct state involvement in the domestic economy was most significant in Taiwan during the 1950s and in Singapore during the 1960s.[24] If necessary, and urgently so in the case of Singapore, the state also opened its arms to embrace foreign capital to industrialize the nation. By the late 1960s and the early 1970s, all three developmental states had actively pursued sectoral industrial policy to promote export-oriented industrialization.

In order to fund this highly selective industrialization program, the direct control and allocation of *financial resources* became a necessary condition for the developmental state to incentivize private entrepreneurs and to engage in large state-led industrial projects.[25] Through a combination of control mechanisms during the 1960s and the 1970s, such as the strategic manipulation of geopolitics to rally American aid and support, the nationalization of financial institutions (e.g., military control over the Bank of Korea after 1964), and the rationing of policy loans and export credits to targeted industries and firms, the developmental state in South Korea managed the "race to the swift," in the words of Woo (1991), and developed a strong competitive position and exports in several major industries, such as shipbuilding, chemicals, machineries, and later, electronics.

Table 1.1 shows that between 1960 and 1980, South Korea's manufacturing sector and exports grew very rapidly at respectively more than 34 percent

Table 1.1 Key macroeconomic indicators on South Korea, 1960–2010

South Korea	Average annual growth rate (%)					Annual figures						
	1960–70	1970–80	1980–90	1990–2000	2000–2010	1960	1970	1980	1990	2000	2005	2010
Population (million)	2.3	1.8	1.5	0.6	0.4	24.9	31.4	37.4	43.4	46.0	47.0	48.0
GDP (US$billion)	—	—	—	—	—	3.9	7.5	63.8	230.5	533.3	722.0	1,519.0
GDP (billion won at current prices)	27.4	30.3	17.2	12.2	6.9	246	2,775	39,110	191,383	603,236	865,241	1,173,275
Manufacturing	35.9	33.7	18.3	12.7	7.7	21.9	469	8,557	45,920	152,177	213,646	319,275
Trade	—	28.6	16.9	6.5	9.6	—	415	5,135	24,471	45,920	82,470	114,859
Finance	—	43.1	16.8	13.2	5.5	—	53	1,909	9,028	31,135	53,395	71,847
Business	—	39.4	23.4	16.5	4.9	—	23	625	5,094	23,498	37,893	55,494
Other	—	28.8	16.7	12.6	3.1	—	1,816	22,885	106,869	350,507	477,838	611,800
GNP per capita (thousand won at current prices)	—	27.7	15.7	11.5	6.5	—	89.5	1,029	4,408	13,051	18,376	24,479
Gross fixed capital formation (billion won at current prices)	—	33.3	18.7	10.1	6.3	—	707	12,492	69,368	180,748	249,690	331,734
Exchange Rate (US$1)	17.3	6.9	1.5	4.8	0.2	63.1	311	659.9	716.4	1,264.5	1,011.6	1,134.8
Inflation rate (%)	—	—	—	—	—	—	16.1	28.7	8.6	2.3	2.3	3.0
Total exports (billion won at current prices)	—	41.2	15.0	16.7	9.3	—	366	11,551	46,577	217,832	287,718	529,252
Total imports	—	36.6	13.0	15.0	9.0	—	652	14,710	50,036	202,928	264,269	482,531
Total labor force (,000)	2.4	3.6	2.8	1.5	1.2	7,563	9,617	13,683	18,085	21,042	22,699	23,684
Manufacturing	12.1	8.9	4.1	2.3	0.7	275	861	2,015	3,020	3,775	4,130	4,028
Trade	—	—	—	—	—	—	—	—	—	2,493	3,746	3,580
Finance	—	—	—	—	—	—	—	—	—	614	745	808
Business	—	—	—	—	—	—	—	—	—	619	742	1,023

Sources: Korean Statistical Information Service, http://kosis.kr/eng and the Bank of Korea, http://ecos.bok.or.kr, accessed on November 20, 2014.

and 41 percent per annum. From about 9 percent of its GDP in 1960, the manufacturing sector became the largest contributor to GDP at 21.9 percent in 1980, and rose further still to more than 25 percent of GDP in the 2000s. Its annual GDP growth rates during the 1960s and the 1970s were very high at 27 percent and 30 percent during these successive decades. The massive state-led financing of industrialization is also evident in the high annual growth rate at 33.3 percent of gross fixed capital formation during the 1970–1980 period. As the developmental state's role in financing industrialization changed over time, this annual growth rate subsequently declined to 10 percent in the 1990s and 6.3 percent in the 2000s.

In Taiwan, the Kuomintang (KMT) state pursued a dual financial structure through various policies and measures. Through the provision of credit by state-controlled banks, the formal financial market supported Taiwan's industrialization program led by large firms and state-owned enterprises (SOEs). While covering a wide range of sectors, these SOEs were concentrated in what Wade (1988, 47) calls "the commanding heights of petroleum refining, petrochemicals, steel and other basic metals, shipbuilding, heavy machinery, transport equipment, fertilizer—in addition to the normal electricity, gas, water, railway and telephone utilities." Wu (2005, 41–43) describes the creation of a huge public sector during the 1950s when SOEs accounted for 50 percent or more of industrial production and the average share of the public sector in gross fixed capital formation between 1951 and 1980 was 30.9 percent.[26]

As shown in table 1.2, this fixed capital formation increased quite dramatically at the annual rate of 16.8 percent in the 1960s and 25 percent in the 1970s. To finance its import-substitution industrialization program in light industry, heavy industry, and machinery, the state controlled all banks during the 1950s through the Bank of Taiwan and a system of complex interlocking shareholdings of all other banks. By the early 1960s, the state was able to pursue financial policies to stabilize the economy by reducing interest rates in both the state-owned and privately organized financial markets. This led to an improvement in the availability of financial resources for the Third Four-Year Plan (1961–1964) and the subsequent successful export-oriented industrialization drive by small- and medium-sized enterprises during the 1970s (Wu 2005, 180–81).

More important, this direct control of the financial sector by the central bank greatly encouraged domestic savings that could be used to finance economic development. Still, compared to South Korea, Taiwan's average annual GDP growth and manufacturing development during the 1960s and the 1970s were relatively less impressive at the 10–15 percent range, as indicated in table 1.2. The heavy role of SOEs and the bifurcated banking system were apparently less conducive to rapid industrialization, setting an important and yet contrasting stage for the subsequent articulation of Taiwanese ICT firms into global production networks.

Table 1.2 Key macroeconomic indicators on Taiwan, 1960–2010.

Taiwan	Average annual growth rate (%)					Annual figures						
	1960–70	1970–80	1980–90	1990–2000	2000–2010	1960	1970	1980	1990	2000	2005	2010
Population (million)	3.4	1.8	1.4	0.9	0.1	10.6	14.8	17.6	20.2	22.2	22.7	22.3
GDP (NT$billion at 2006 prices)	10.0	9.7	4.4	9.5	3.9	390	1,008	2,549	5,317	9,731	11,612	14,214
Manufacturing	17.0	13.5	7.3	5.0	7.1	39.1	188	667	1,344	2,179	2,971	4,311
Trade and F&B	11.0	10.4	7.9	7.7	3.4	50.4	143	387	831	1,751	2,084	2,458
Finance and business	12.0	13.4	2.4	7.0	1.3	29.6	91.9	322	407	798	870	908
Other	8.0	7.2	1.5	13.9	2.7	271.1	584	1,173	2,735	5,003	5,687	6,537
GNP per capita (NT$ at current prices)	9.9	20.0	8.9	7.6	2.7	6,012	15,502	95,776	224,241	465,502	529,313	605,921
Gross fixed capital formation (NT$bil at 1990 prices)	16.8	25.0	8.6	9.2	1.6	10.4	49.3	458	1,049	2,524	2,635	2,960
Exchange Rate (US$1)	—	—	−3.1	1.5	1.1	—	—	36.7	26.8	31.1	32.1	34.6
Inflation rate (%)	—	—	—	—	—	—	—	19.0	4.1	1.3	2.3	1.0
Total exports (NT$bil)	25.3	27.5	8.7	10.1	6.2	7.2	68.8	783	1,808	4,729	6,374	8,657
Total imports	19.2	27.8	6.3	11.5	6.1	11.9	68.9	801	1,474	4,391	5,877	7,943
Total labor force (,000)	—	—	2.0	1.4	1.0	—	—	6,764	8,283	9,491	9,942	10,493
Manufacturing	—	—	—	0.0	0.8	—	—	—	2,653	2,655	2,732	2,861
Trade	—	—	—	2.9	−2.1	—	—	—	1,621	2,163	1,726	1,747
Finance and business	—	—	—	6.5	0.4	—	—	—	220	412	406	428

Source: National Statistics, Republic of China, http://eng.stat.gov.tw, accessed on November 20, 2014.

Prior to its self-rule in 1959, on the other hand, the city-state of Singapore had already benefited enormously from an almost one and a half century–long experience as a strategic entrepôt serving the British Empire in Southeast Asia.[27] A nascent financial system with the prominent presence of major foreign banks and local banks had been developed by the time Singapore became a republic in August 1965.[28] The existence of a favorable capital market, however, did not provide sufficient endowments and resources for private entrepreneurial activity to kick-start Singapore's industrialization program. By the mid-1960s, much of this financial capital had remained entrenched in trading activity. As evident from the data shown in table 1.3, Singapore's gross fixed capital formation grew modestly at an average annual rate of 10.7 percent in the 1970s and 5.5 percent in the 1980s. The problem of late industrialization was exacerbated further by the lack of industrial know-how among Singapore's small population of around 2 million residents in 1970. British investment was very significant then, albeit mainly concentrated in the trading and distribution sectors.

Faced with this dire situation of a weak industrial bourgeois and a trade-oriented financial system, the developmental state had to participate directly in the capital accumulation process through the provision of credits and loans, the subsidization of labor costs, and the expansion of land supply. This state-led effort resulted in a high degree of integration between the financial sector and the manufacturing sector in Singapore's early phase of industrialization. One important feature of Singapore's financial system was, and still is, the role of the mandatory state-sanctioned pension fund, known as the Central Provident Fund (CPF). The CPF played an important role in financing national development plans since the late 1960s by pooling a large share of potential investment capital from its members. Financing complementary social programs such as public housing,[29] this compulsory savings scheme enabled the state to accumulate budgetary surpluses quickly from 1965 to the late 1970s to finance infrastructural development, state-owned enterprises, and industrialization.

While state control and allocation of financial and other resources was a vital precondition to the feasibility of its policy goals of achieving rapid industrialization,[30] the developmental state in all three economies needed sufficient institutional capacity to develop and operationalize its highly selective industrial policy. The institutional platform through which active industrial policy and financial control was pursued in these states was none other than its *elite bureaucracy*—the champion of all "national champions." These pilot or nodal agencies played extremely critical role in conceiving, coordinating, and implementing sectoral industrial policy.[31] They not only centralized functions previously distributed across a wide range of ministries and state agencies but also developed laws and regulations steering industrial transformation with relative autonomy from party politics and other organized pressure groups.

Table 1.3 Key macroeconomic indicators on Singapore, 1960–2010

Singapore	Average annual growth rate (%)					Annual figures						
	1960–70	1970–80	1980–90	1990–2000	2000–2010	1960	1970	1980	1990	2000	2005	2010
Population (million)	2.3	1.5	2.4	2.8	2.3	1.6	2.1	2.4	3.1	4.0	4.3	5.1
GDP (S$billion)[1]	9.2	9.0	7.7	7.2	6.5	5.8	13.9	32.9	66.5	127	209	310
Manufacturing	27.5	10.9	6.9	6.0	7.2	0.29	3.3	9.3	18.0	32.1	57.0	64.5
Trade	14.1	7.0	6.6	7.3	10.0	0.72	2.7	5.3	10.0	20.2	35.5	52.3
Finance and business	25.2	9.0	9.7	6.8	9.5	0.27	2.6	6.0	15.3	29.6	49.7	73.4
Other	17.9	8.8	6.6	6.8	10.3	1.02	5.3	12.3	23.2	44.9	66.5	120
GNP per capita (S$ at 2005 prices)	7.9	13.5	8.5	5.8	4.1	1,334	2,860	10,135	22,868	40,090	45,654	60,009
Gross fixed capital formation (S$bil at 1990 prices)[1]	—	10.7	5.5	7.7	4.3	—	4.6	12.7	21.6	45.2	50.1	69.1
Exchange Rate (US$1)	0.0	-3.5	-1.7	-0.5	-2.3	3.1	3.1	2.1	1.8	1.7	1.7	1.4
Inflation rate (%)	—	—	—	—	—	0.3	0.4	8.5	3.4	0.4	0.5	2.8
Total exports (S$bil)[2]	5.6	21.8	10.5	9.5	7.6	2.8	4.8	34.1	92.5	229	432	479
Re-exports	—	16.9	8.9	10.5	10.1	—	2.9	13.9	32.5	88.0	204	230
Domestic exports	—	27.1	12.0	9.2	5.1	—	1.8	20.2	62.8	151	227	249
Total imports	8.0	20.0	9.0	7.0	7.0	3.5	7.5	46.5	110	215	379	423
Total labor force (,000)	3.3	5.5	3.3	2.2	5.1	472	651	1,115	1,537	1,912	2,594	3,136
Manufacturing	6.8	9.0	2.8	-0.9	2.5	74.1	143	339	447	409	—	524
Trade	2.9	4.8	3.3	1.8	2.1	114	153	243	338	405	—	500
Finance and business	1.7	12.7	7.0	6.5	7.7	21.7	25.8	85.0	167	315	—	659

[1] Data for the 1960–1970 period are calculated based on 1968 prices. Data for 1980, 1990, and 2000 are at 1990 prices. The rest are at 2005 prices.

[2] Data for 1960 refer to 1964. Data for 1964 and 1970 are at current prices. Data for 1980, 1990, and 2000 are at 1990 prices. The rest are at 2005 prices.

Source: Department of Statistics, http://www.singstat.gov.sg, accessed on November 20, 2014.

In South Korea, pilot agencies, such as the Economic Planning Board (EPB) and the Committee for the Promotion of Heavy and Chemical Industrialization (CPHCI), were coordinated by the Economic Secretariat reporting directly to President Park Chung Hee. In Taiwan during the 1950s and Singapore during the 1960s, similar elite agencies such as Taiwan's Economic Planning Council (EPC), renamed the Council for Economic Planning and Development (CEPD) in late 1977,[32] and the Industrial Development Bureau (IDB) of the Ministry of Economic Affairs, and Singapore's Economic Development Board (EDB) and the Ministry of Trade and Industry, were established to orchestrate industrialization programs, particularly since the 1970s.

The exact operationalization and efficacy of these pilot agencies, however, differed greatly among the three East Asian economies. One of the key factors was the industrial structure of their domestic economies, particularly in relation to firm size and openness to foreign direct investment. Pilot agencies were most effective in a highly concentrated industrial structure dominated by fewer but significantly larger firms. South Korea was a prime example. The influence of foreign capital also mattered because pilot agencies would find it much harder to impose discipline, selectivity, or even performance requirement if these investors were relatively "foot-loose" and could opt for other locational destinations. Singapore's weaker bargaining position vis-à-vis foreign investors during its early phase of industrialization illustrated this well.

Another important factor was political legitimacy and the politics of survival. A state with less political legitimacy would have to be more careful with its industrial policy that might not be welcomed by a significant proportion of the population. As an émigré regime, Taiwan's KMT-led state faced such a legitimacy crisis during the first two decades (1949–1969) of its minority rule over the majority indigenous people. On the other hand, a state facing an existential crisis was more likely to mobilize its citizenry to accept difficult policy interventions by its pilot agencies. Without a readily available hinterland after its separation from the federation of Malaysia in August 1965, Singapore's survival crisis pushed the newly founded state to adopt an unprecedented set of economic policies in the ensuring years. The ascent of the People's Action Party (PAP) to power since self-government in 1959 and its enduring power in politics and government meant that national economic development became consistently the primordial goal of the PAP state.[33]

With hindsight, the developmental statist approach described above has provided very important insights into the unique pathways of industrialization and economic growth in the three East Asian economies. It explains the institutional legacies and origins of some leading East Asian firms to be analyzed in this book (e.g., Samsung from South Korea and TSMC from Taiwan). This intellectual achievement is particularly notable in light of the dominance of neoclassical economics and dependency schools in the analysis of economic development prior to the onset of the developmental state thesis in the 1980s. We now know a great deal more about the central role of the developmental state in governing the market and industrialization in these three East Asian economies during much of the 1950s–1970s period. But does the developmental state thesis continue to inform us as much about the increasingly complex articulation of these economies into the global economy since the late 1980s when globalization began to take shape in East Asia? The answer to this question is important because there are two interrelated issues at stake here—one concerning the epistemology of state-centrism and another relating to the empirical realm of evolutionary state-firm relations.

First, the primacy of the state as *the* analytical lens in the developmental state literature has compelled most scholars in this genre to focus exclusively on the domestic nature and specificity of state-firm relations. In this statist perspective, private and public firms are analytically important only insofar as they matter to the state's grand strategy of rapid industrialization and economic growth; the former has therefore become the latter's "objects of desire," very much akin to the pawns (firms) in the hands of skillful grandmasters (states) vying for world chess championships.[34] Even though capitalists are considered in this approach, Perraton (2005, 102) points out that they "have often lurked in the shadows of developmental state theory. The developmental state proponents have often effectively portrayed a timid capitalist class, unable (or at least unwilling) to undertake risky investment projects and needing a whole set of inducements to get them to do so." As argued by Boyd and Ngo (2005b, 9), this statecentric approach to industrial transformation in East Asia has put far too much weight on the state as an independent variable explaining economic growth, the dependent variable. The capitalist firm has mostly dropped out of the analytical theorem of the developmental state thesis.

Reflecting on his *Governing the Market* first published in 1990, Robert Wade (2003, xvii) later acknowledges that "missing, though, is analysis of the external economies of human capital that are a major source of increasing returns to production in Taiwan and other East Asian countries—microanalysis of firm capabilities and corporate governance, and mesoanalysis of interfirm input-output networks, factor markets, and tacit knowledge."[35] I argue that it is precisely these missing micro- and meso-elements of East Asian firms and their strategic coupling with global production networks that, since the 1990s, have come to the forefront of an evolutionary understanding of the diverse development trajectories in East Asia. Filling this gap requires both a revision of its strong claim of the deterministic state influence on national firms, and a reorientation of its analytical focus away from state policies and capacities to evolving state-firm relations.

Second, if national firms are indeed important to our understanding of the changing position of these East Asian economies in today's global economy, we are still confronted with a thorny empirical issue of analyzing the complex relationships between these East Asian firms and the broader competitive dynamics in global industries. Before I introduce these changing state-firm relations in the next section, let me briefly probe further into the analysis of national firms in the developmental state literature. While Chalmers Johnson's (1982) seminal contribution focuses primarily on one particular state institution in Japan, the Ministry of International Trade and Industry, the firm does get some attention in the work by subsequent protagonists of the statist thesis. Being cognizant of the shop-floor level operationalization of the state's industrialization policies, Amsden (1989, 112, original italics) notes that "the translation of high growth rates of output into high growth rates of productivity depends on what happens *inside the unit of production*. Closing the loop between growth and productivity, therefore, involves an analytical shift, a change in the center of gravity from the state to the other key institution of industrialization, the firm."

Even if the firm is sometimes featured in the developmental state literature, however, it tends to be read off from the state's policy regimes. Amsden (2001, 193, original italics) thus describes the essence of national firms in the Global South, including those from the three East Asian economies, as the by-products of the developmental state: "National leaders in 'the rest,' private or public, all shared one characteristic: they tended to be a product of government promotion ('targeting'). In the case of the private leader, it tended to be either an affiliate of a *diversified business group* with a history of government patronage, or a '*state spin-off*.'" This statecentric view of leading East Asian firms, however, is rather unhelpful in understanding their evolutionary transformations over time. In particular, the nature of East Asian firms has been transformed since the late 1980s in tandem with globalization tendencies. Their changing identity and organization in relation to the emergence of global production networks cannot be adequately analyzed within the existing statist literature.

To sum up, the developmental state approach is becoming increasingly obsolescent in the post-1990 context of the dynamic articulation of East Asian economies into the global economy. Its predominant focus on state initiatives and capacities in early industrialization has rendered itself "locked-into" a conceptual path dependency premised on seeing the economy and its key agents (firms) through the state and its political choice. Its ability to provide insights into the rise of East Asian firms in the global economy becomes handicapped by its analytical baggage of state-centrism.[36]

Strategic Coupling with Global Production Networks

To understand how East Asian firms become the key conduits in the articulation of their domestic economies into the global economy, we need a theoretical perspective that accounts for the complex and evolutionary nature of state-firm relations within the changing context of economic globalization. As I elaborate empirically in chapters 2 and 3, since the late 1980s and the early 1990s, these East Asian firms have strategically disembedded from developmental state apparatuses and successfully reembedded in global production networks that constitute the book's first set of coevolutionary dynamics in the state-firm-GPN assemblage. At the same time, the key components, institutions, and policy instruments of the development state have evolved into new and more sophisticated types in tandem with supporting this national-global articulation of domestic firms since the late 1980s. This transformation in state roles is systematically discussed in chapter 2.

My conceptualization of these evolving state-firm relations is grounded in two emerging and interrelated research frontiers that call for more theoretical attention to translocal actors and processes, evolutionary dynamics of change, and institutional contexts. The first strand of conceptual work refers to the global production networks perspective developed in-depth in Coe and Yeung's *Global Production Networks* (2015). It is useful here to clarify briefly the nature and organization of global production networks that involve both business firms and national economies in organizationally complex and geographically extensive ways. To Henderson et al. (2002, 445–46),

> Production networks—the nexus of interconnected functions and operations through which goods and services are produced, distributed and consumed— have become both organizationally more complex and also increasingly global in their geographic extent. Such networks not only integrate firms (and parts of firms) into structures which blur traditional organizational boundaries—through the development of diverse forms of equity and non-equity relationships—but also integrate national economies (or parts of such economies) in ways which have enormous implications for their well-being. At the same time, the precise nature and articulation of firm-centered production networks are deeply influenced by the concrete socio-political contexts within which they are embedded. The process is especially complex because while the latter are essentially territorially specific (primarily, though not exclusively, at the level of the nation-state) the production networks themselves are not. They "cut through" state boundaries in highly differentiated ways, influenced in part by regulatory and non-regulatory barriers and local sociocultural conditions, to create structures which are "discontinuously territorial."

In this perspective, a global production network can be defined as an inter-organizational structure that is coordinated and controlled by a globally significant lead firm (usually a transnational corporation) and involves the geographically dispersed network of overseas affiliates, strategic partners, key customers, and nonfirm institutions. Unlike leading firms in East Asian economies, global lead firms refer to powerful firms that orchestrate and coordinate complex production networks in their respective industries, spanning different territories and regions in the global economy. These lead firms are often large transnational corporations that in turn are movers and shapers of the global economy.[37] They are market leaders in terms of their brand names, technology, products/services, and marketing capabilities. To compete effectively in an era of accelerated globalization, they tend to move toward market control via product and market definitions, rather than through leadership in manufacturing processes and technologies.

Since the 1960s, global lead firms from advanced industrialized economies have been increasingly taking their production activity or outsourcing their value-added functions across borders. Through this process of internationalization, they have become transnational corporations. These transnational corporations are not autonomous and vertically integrated organizations; rather, they resemble forms of intrafirm and interfirm networks comprising a large assortment of other actors and organizations.[38] As transnational corporations become much more global in their scale and scope of operations, their networks are also concomitantly global in nature, leading to the emergence of global production networks.

As I develop further in chapter 3, this body of theoretical work showcases the critical importance of understanding the *strategic coupling* processes that connect actors in East Asian economies with their counterparts in global production networks. These processes are particularly important because earlier versions of regional production network accounts have not elucidated the firm-specific initiatives through which East Asian firms actively acquire managerial and technological capabilities and grow from subservient suppliers or subcontractors to become the strategic partners of global lead firms.[39] In their critique of these earlier accounts, Mathews and Cho (2000, 15, original italics) argue that "the existence of such networks provides at best a set of opportunities for local technological upgrading; it offers no guarantee that such opportunities will be exploited or harnessed effectively. The critical issue is *where* the impulse for the upgrading effort comes from." Amsden (1989) and Amsden and Chu (2003) point to the rise of the network form of organizing localized industrial production and the role of the developmental state in embedding these networks. But their conception of networks refers primarily to local clusters of small- and medium-sized enterprises, that is, cooperative relations among localized networks of firms. They continue to subscribe to a statecentric view of industrial dynamics in which "networking in the latecomer case, and the creation of high-tech jobs and high-tech industries, may be said to have been 'state-led' " (Amsden and Chu 2003, 77).

In contrast, the perspective pursued in this book focuses on the strategic coupling of actors at multiple spatial scales—from local and regional to national and global. I eschew a primary concern with localized networks embedded in national territories and the state's policy regimes. Instead, my empirical analysis of East Asian firms focuses on the growing significance of translocal forces and processes that have shaped East Asian development since the late 1980s. By focusing on the complex translocal network relations between domestic firms and global lead firms in the context of global competition, I view the emergence of global production networks as opening up new opportunities and substantial challenges to industrial development in East Asian economies. In fact, growth is no longer restricted to either endogenous sources or foreign firms, as previously stipulated in the developmental state literature.[40] National firms and other economic actors can now "plug" directly into these global production networks, which in turn enable and sustain their growth efforts. For this strategic coupling to take place, East Asian firms have to disembed partially or completely from their earlier dependence on domestic state-led regimes over time in response to the changing international selection environment; they also reembed in another organizational structure, such as global production networks orchestrated by lead firms from advanced industrialized economies, through which they gain technology, knowledge, and market.

These processes of embedding, disembedding, and reembedding, however, cannot be fully understood without paying simultaneous attention to their evolutionary dynamics and changing institutional contexts. This calls for the second strand of emerging theoretical literature that deals with issues of path dependence, lock-in effects, and dynamics of change in evolutionary theories.[41] As argued by Cimoli et al. (2009a, 5; emphasis omitted), "the co-evolutionary account rests on the sorts of congruence conditions between ingredients (including state variables which influence the subsequent dynamics) and processes wherein feature prominently the matchings or mismatchings between capabilities accumulation and the institutions governing the distribution of information and the incentive structures of any one economy." These evolutionary trajectories are particularly relevant for analyzing the changing state-firm relations in East Asia from one of structural dependence in the early phase of industrialization and economic development to increasingly autonomy and independence in recent decades.

This evolutionary change arises primarily because these East Asian firms increasingly participate in globalization through their firm-specific initiatives, which favor strategic coupling with different global production networks. Here, I see globalization as a set of tendencies providing "external shocks" in the selection environment that compels states and firms to reposition themselves not just internally within their domestic economies but more important also externally in a much more open and competitive global economy of the twenty-first century. In their reassessment of the developmental state approach, Underhill and Zhang (2005, 53) link the "structural" rise of East Asian firms to this changing selection environment in an era of globalization: "The increasing integration of the national economy with the international financial and trade systems only served to reinforce the position of private industrialists as crucial economic agents and deepened the dependence of the state upon them for national development in an era of globalization."

As elaborated further in chapter 3, this strategic coupling of East Asian firms requires favorable *structural conditions,* of which renewed state efforts in the form of supportive policy initiatives remain an important one. Taken together, this shift in state-firm-GPN relations from state-firm to interfirm dynamics in global production networks has profound implications for our understanding of the present and future developmental trajectories of these East Asian economies. After my specification of the concept of "strategic coupling" in chapter 3, the remaining three empirical chapters proceed to elucidate in-depth its three component processes in relation to firm-specific initiatives in the context of East Asian industrial transformation. Here I make a necessary conceptual distinction between a *meso-level* network process (i.e., strategic coupling and its components operating through evolving interfirm network relations) and a *firm-specific* initiative (e.g., individual action of capability building and market development). What firms choose to do (e.g., technological and organizational innovations) are strategic initiatives that can activate coupling processes necessary for industrial transformation. But these firm-specific initiatives are not the same as network-level coupling processes (e.g., strategic partnership and industrial market specialization). Indeed, these initiatives enable individual firms to engage with certain coupling processes so that they can create particular type of ties with global lead firms, connect better with global production networks, and ultimately, compete successfully in the global economy.

My strategic coupling approach to industrial transformation offers a micro analysis of firm-specific strategic initiatives and a meso analysis of interfirm coupling processes embedded in global production networks. Based on detailed industry- and firm-level analyses, chapters 4–6 illustrate the three distinct coupling processes engaged by East Asian firms in the global electronics, semiconductors, shipbuilding, automobile, and service industries since the early 1990s.[42] This global articulation of development trajectories goes beyond the initial launch of industrialization through state-led efforts and incorporates *new* developments in the context of evolutionary state-firm relations. Three such component processes are particularly prominent in this global articulation: strategic partnership, industrial market specialization, and (re)positioning as global lead firms. These coupling processes are situated in intense interfirm competition for spatial, technological, and organizational fixes. These competitive dynamics have significantly reduced the scale and scope of the state's developmental roles in transforming the national economy.

In chapter 4, I show that through *strategic partnership* with global lead firms, domestic firms from the three economies, in particular Taiwan's Quanta and Hon Hai and Singapore's Venture Corp, could provide cutting-edge design and manufacturing services in the global personal computers and consumer electronics industry. During the 1960s and the 1970s, this industry received significant attention in the developmental state's core program of export promotion. But its transformation from a subservient role of subcontracting to a more technologically capable role of providing original design and manufacturing services took place only in the 1990s and beyond, when these domestic firms became more articulated into diverse production networks coordinated by global lead firms. While this articulation was facilitated by the state's new role in upgrading labor, technology, and infrastructure in the domestic economy, its crucial impetus came from the emergence of global production networks as a new organizational structure for global competition. East Asian firms were integrated into these networks not primarily through state-led initiatives or incentives. Through their firm-specific organizational efforts, they bring together components, skills, and knowledge from their key suppliers to design, engineer, and produce a wider range of sophisticated products for their global lead firm customers.

In more capital-intensive manufacturing industries, such as shipbuilding and semiconductors, this coupling process of strategic partnership did not work because of the tremendous scale economies required for East Asian "second movers" to catch up with "first movers" in advanced industrialized economies. In chapter 5, I examine the strategic coupling of East Asian firms with these global production networks through *industrial market specialization*. In both industries, the developmental state performed a classic role of the "big push" during the initial phase of their development in the 1970s and the 1980s. These initial public subsidies and state-directed investment could help domestic producers quickly upscale to low-cost leaders in the global market. Their eventual domination in both industries since the 2000s and beyond was no longer based simply on these scale economies, but rather on new advantages developed through firm-specific technological and organizational innovations. In both industries, leading East Asian firms have acquired unique competitive advantages on the basis of new in-house process and product technologies in shipbuilding (e.g., Samsung Heavy Industries and Singapore's Keppel Corp) and production specialization in semiconductors (e.g., Taiwan Semiconductor Manufacturing Company and Samsung Electronics).

Eventually, the industrial transformation initially induced by state-led efforts can only be completed with the rise of global brand name lead firms in these three East Asian economies. As discussed in chapter 6, this *repositioning as global lead firms* represents the arrival of national champions as global leaders in their respective industries and the ultimate success of economic development. Through this distinct coupling process, top East Asian firms, such as Taiwan's Acer; South Korea's Samsung, LG, and Hyundai; and Singapore's Singapore Airlines no longer serve as partners or specialists in global production networks controlled by other global lead firms. Instead, they have emerged as lead firms spearheading their own global production networks with not only strong technological and managerial competencies but also deep market knowledge and sustained investment.

Their emergence in the global economy also points to a new era in the politics of development when capitalist national firms have outgrown their domestic state institutions and become the main actors in subsequent rounds of industrial transformation. In the concluding chapter 7, I reflect on the evolving pathways of economic development in East Asia by revisiting the politics of industrial policy and the changing role of the state. Here I argue for a new global political economy of development that takes into account both the state and nonstate institutions in the challenging context of global capitalism. My approach situates the rapid growth and transformation of the three East Asian economies in the wider literature on the changing configuration of the international political economy.

In a nutshell, this book draws on the more recent experience of three East Asian economies and their national firms to show that national economic development cannot be understood independently of the changing dynamics of global production networks. My analysis illustrates that the strong role of the national state as the primary actor in industrial transformation is a historically and geographically specific, but not necessarily sufficient, condition for economic development to sustain and evolve over time. There is a need for us to study the complex strategic coupling of diverse economic actors, particularly business firms operating in specific national economies and territorial ensembles, with global lead firms governing transnational production networks on a worldwide basis.[43]

Chapters in this book take up this analytical task of examining the changing state-firm relations in the three East Asian economies. This new political economy approach in turn allows for a greater diversity of evolutionary adjustments and adaptation exercised by economic actors in response to their changing selection environment in an era of intensified economic globalization. Instead of reducing such relations to one of dependence and lock-in, my strategic coupling approach brings more contingency into the coevolutionary dynamics of developmental states, East Asian firms, and global production networks. It sheds important light on the growing spatial mobility of national firms that leverage critical resources located in different countries and regions in order to compete effectively in the global economy. As production networks become more spatially decentralized and territorially discontinuous, the developmental state is confronted with a heightened sense of its own spatial immobility that confines its policy effectiveness and limits its bureaucratic reach. In this globalizing context of mobile firms increasingly disembedded from territorially immobile states, a fuller understanding of industrial transformation necessarily entails the analysis of both domestic structures (state institutions and policy initiatives) and economic agency (firms as actors and their initiatives), and their dynamic interaction with global production networks through the process of strategic coupling.

Chapter 2

Transformation of State-Firm
Relations in the 1980s and the 1990s

By the late 1980s, the developmental state's direct role in steering economic development in South Korea, Taiwan, and Singapore had started to weaken gradually. In many ways, the developmental state in these economies became a victim of its own success—rapid industrialization had led to the emergence of a more assertive and diverse set of domestic actors in politics, business, and society that in turn pushed for a significant transformation of state roles. This chapter offers a systematic analysis of this evolutionary process through which domestic actors would become more disembedded from the transformed state. I argue that the emergence of global production networks (GPN) since the late 1980s has provided a critical structural condition for reshaping these state-firm relations in the three economies. Through their articulation into different global production networks, national firms have been increasingly able to disembed themselves from the instrumental imperatives of their domestic states and to reembed in dynamic interfirm networks that offer new sources of knowledge, power, and capabilities. Understanding this dynamic shift from state-firm to interfirm relations requires a political economy approach that takes into account not just domestic politics and state initiatives but also growing windows of opportunities and repertoires of resources beyond the domestic-national arena. The dynamic recombinant of both shifting state-firm relations and new globalized interfirm networks is therefore critical to our understanding of evolutionary change and adjustments in these three East Asian economies—a dynamic phenomenon encapsulated in the *state-firm-GPN assemblage.* As Sean O'Riain (2004, 223) concludes in his analysis of the developmental network state in *The Politics of High-Tech Growth,* "The international and domestic politics of capitalism shapes patterns of state developmentalism profoundly, but the regimes that emerge contain important 'recombinant' institutional and political innovations that cannot be simply read off from their founding conditions. Furthermore, the accumulation of such innovations can transform the world system. The rise of East Asian firms in global capitalism and the intensification of global competition have been crucial features of contemporary global capitalism."

To set the necessary stage for my empirical analysis of these national-global evolutionary dynamics later in this book, this chapter provides a theoretically informed treatment of changing state roles up to the late 1990s in three major sections. In the next section, I recap briefly the theoretical conception of the developmental state in the existing literature and the conceptual rationale for its rethinking in the changing contexts of the world economy. The following section examines shifting state roles in relation to its key components (e.g., autonomy and capacity), institutions (e.g., bureaucracy and pilot agency), and policy arrangements (e.g., industrial policy). My empirical evidence from the three East Asian economies points to significant variability in these state roles and functions in promoting industrial transformation in a globalizing world economy. By the late 1990s, the state and its bureaucratic institutions in these economies had become more diverse and fragmented with the result that political power and control was more diffuse and less cohesive than its founding conditions. The state itself had evolved from the earlier type of a strong developmental state toward a postdevelopmental state that took on new functions of catalyzing rather than directly steering economic transformation. In the last section, I show that such evolution in state power and capacity was concurrently accompanied by the emergence of firm-specific dynamic capabilities, as these national firms had accumulated sufficient organizational and technological resources through decades of export-oriented production for the global market. New national firms had also emerged to take advantage of different opportunities arising from the deeper integration of these national economies into the global economy. Economic globalization and its associated technological and organizational changes could provide wider incentives and opportunities beyond the developmental state such that the loyalties of private investors and national firms became more divided, leading to their gradual disembedding from home states in search of markets, technologies, and ultimately, profits outside their domestic economies.

Rethinking the Developmental State in its Changing Contexts

What exactly is the developmental state? Stubbs (2009, 5) points to considerable variation in its definitions. Jayasuriya (2005, 382) describes the developmental state as having " 'core' strategic capacities to plan, monitor and enforce key developmental objectives, which will shift the comparative advantage of national economies toward those sectors that are of strategic value in the global economy." These capacities are critical to distinguishing those states that want to be "developmental" and those that want *and* deliver developmental outcomes.[1] One of the key dimensions of state capacity, according to

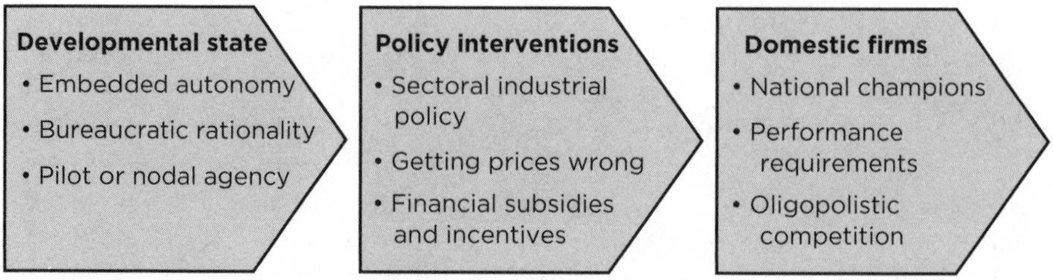

Figure 2.1. The developmental state and its relationships with domestic firms.

Evans (1995, 12, 57–58), is the state's embedded autonomy in society that insulates it from competing social interests and enables it to avoid rent seeking and predatory behavior of certain politicians and social groups.[2] With embedded autonomy, the developmental state could expand its institutional capacity to develop economic planning via associated institutions and state apparatuses in order to pursue its strategic industrial policy and other market-distorting measures. Figure 2.1 provides a summary of this causal link between the developmental state, its policy interventions, and domestic firms. One of the most powerful policy instruments of the developmental state was its highly selective industrial policy—the deliberate choice of developing specific firms or industries initially through import-substitution industrialization (ISI) programs and, since the early 1970s, through export promotion.[3] Wade (1990, 284–86) calls these "nudging policies" of directing firms' sourcing and technology practices. He further argues that "they have been going on across swathes of industrial sectors. They involved a mix of methods, including 'jaw-jaw' and promises of good will for future ventures, fiscal incentives, higher tariffs, and lengthening delays in permission to import (that had earlier been approved quickly and automatically)" (Wade 2003, xxii).

Building on this most important attribute of the developmental state—its embedded autonomy and institutional capacity—I now give a fuller description of its main characteristics. Although Johnson's (1982) "basic" model of Japan's developmental state was later expanded on and reformulated by many other protagonists of the developmental state theory,[4] Wade (1990, 25–26) provides the best overall summary of the expanded attributes of the developmental state:[5]

1. The top priority of state action, consistently maintained, is economic development, defined for policy purposes in terms of growth, productivity, and competitiveness, rather than in terms of welfare. The substance of growth and competitiveness goals is derived from comparisons with external reference economies that provide the state managers with models for emulation. The developmental state is fundamentally oriented toward catching up with advanced industrialized countries for nation-building purposes.

2. The state is committed to private property and the market, and it limits its interventions to conform to this commitment. Strategic selectivity is a gen-

eral feature of state interventions. Evans (1995, 71) argues that "without stringent attention to selectivity, overwhelmed bureaucracies deteriorate into developmental impediments or pools of patrimonial self-interest." Amsden (1989; 2001) points to stringent performance monitoring and state disciplining procedures known as "reciprocal control mechanisms" such that selected national firms had to meet performance targets, such as targets for exporting, local content requirements, or product specifications, in exchange for special favors.

3. The state guides the market with instruments formulated by an elite economic bureaucracy, led by a pilot or "nodal" agency or economic general staff who coordinates and resolves interagency conflicts and rivalries.

4. The state is engaged in numerous institutions for consultation and coordination with the private sector, and these consultations, defined as embeddedness by Evans (1995), are an essential part of the process of policy formulation and implementation.

5. While state bureaucrats "rule," politicians "reign." The function of the latter group is not to make policy but to create the economic and political space for the bureaucracy to maneuver in while also acting as a safety valve by forcing the bureaucrats to respond to the needs of groups on which the stability of the system rests. This mutuality between bureaucrats and politicians helps maintain the relative autonomy of the state while preserving political stability. This separation of ruling and reigning goes with a soft authoritarianism, when it comes to maintaining the needs of economic development vis-à-vis other societal claims, and with a virtual monopoly of political power in a single political party or institution over a long period of time. It also produces a particularly powerful form of institutional capacity necessary for state policies to be effectively implemented.

6. The state maintains internal cohesiveness or, what Chibber (2002) terms "bureaucratic rationality," by developing a strong commitment to norm and rule following by state agencies and by growing a culture of administrative bureaucracy through carefully selected career development and mobility among its elite officers.[6] State bureaucrats must know what they were doing and must share a common sense of purpose and mission. Their bureaucratic rationality must be sustained in order for policy to be formulated and implemented seamlessly and for control to be exercised over the international-domestic linkages.

By the late 1990s, the idea of the developmental state had become more than a theory of industrial transformation. Its wide circulation and acceptance in development studies and policy circles had produced an unintended consequence that the developmental state was unwittingly reified as a permanent fixture in the political economy of East Asian transformation.[7] This analytical stasis calls into question the dynamics of change that might punctuate the equilibrium in this state-business-society assemblage. Indeed, Evans's (1995, 228) own conclusion points to this need for a dynamic view of the developmental state: "Its transformative success threatens the stability of the state-society coalitions that made success possible to begin with. Re-examining the developmental state means rethinking embedded autonomy."[8] Before I discuss the shifting roles of the developmental state in governing state-firm relations since the 1980s in the next section, it is useful to reconsider briefly three analytical qualifications *for* the developmental state theory that might contextualize better my subsequent analysis: (1) the subject of analysis, (2) historical period, and (3) sectoral shift and selectivity. The first qualification refers to the exact *subject of analysis* in any study of East Asian development. There is no doubt that the original studies of the developmental state were specifically designed to explain economic growth and rapid industrialization.[9] Even though economic actors such as firms and industries were brought into their accounts, the most significant subject of analysis was the developmental state and its multitude of policy interventions. The dependent variable, whether firm growth or industrial transformation, did not require much analytical attention because it had indeed occurred in those economies, as illustrated in chapter 1.

Given this actual materialization of rapid corporate growth and industrialization, the analytical concern among the development state scholars was with its political economy. The independent variable, that is, the developmental state, was the primary focus of theorization and empirical work. This state-oriented approach carries a certain path dependency in both epistemological and empirical terms. Epistemologically, the state remains the center of attention in subsequent studies of East Asian development, even though the state itself is undergoing significant structural and institutional transformations. Following the early founders of the developmental state theory, these later scholars remain locked into a path-dependent mode of analyzing industrial performance and business actors by studying what the state does, as if these "targets" of state policies would necessarily translate state action into positive development outcomes.[10] Not surprisingly, these revisionist scholars continue to argue for the significant or even central role of the developmental state in governing the market. To a certain extent, this institutional fetishism has become an obstacle to developing a transformative view of evolutionary state-firm relations.[11] Empirically, the developmental state simply does not and cannot whither away completely in the East Asian economies. Even though it may undergo substantial institutional transformations, we can certainly observe different legacies, remnants, and fragments of its multifaceted institutions. There is thus a great deal of path dependency in the evolution of the developmental state itself.[12] A significant empirical question is whether these recombinant institutions of the state are still "developmental" and, if so, capable of realizing its developmental objectives. It is one thing for techno-industrial policymakers to continue to have an enduring developmental ambition; it is quite another for them to be able to cajole private sector actors to cooperate and to realize such an ambition over time. A reorientation in our subject of analysis toward these economic actors is necessary *not just* because the political power of the state might be somewhat diminished in a globalizing era but also because the previously dependent relationship of capitalist firms on the developmental state might be significantly transformed.

This observation on the evolutionary state-firm relationship points to the second qualification of the literature in order to reassess the role of the developmental state—*the historical period of research* chosen by the original proponents. The contentious issue here is whether the changing context over time has impacted on the original subject of analysis—the developmental state. In this sense, a critical take on the existing literature is not just about having to understand the historical context of the developmental state in East Asia: we should and must do so in order to avoid the analytical mistake well recognized by Woo-Cumings (1999b, 2) that "research into the political economy of Northeast Asia tended to privilege causal explanations (however spurious) at the expense of the history of economic growth and the context in which such growth occurred." Equally important, we should be aware of the limits of historical explanations so that we do not fall into the trap of historical determinism. Just because the developmental state used to work effectively and was configured as such does not mean that it will necessarily continue to exist in the same form and efficacy in the subsequent historical period. Much of its continual form of existence and causal power depends on the nature of change among its constituents. Indeed, most of the classic studies of the developmental state in South Korea, Taiwan, and Singapore have focused on the early period of industrialization starting in the 1960s through to the mid-1980s.[13] Some of them traced the developmental state all the way back to the colonial era during the 1930s and earlier with mixed assessments of the significance of colonial presence on the subsequent developmental states.[14] This choice of an earlier historical period is also evident in the later work by Evans (1995) and Waldner (1999), more recently, Kohli (2004), Wu (2005), Greene (2008), and Pirie (2008). Greene (2008, 9) goes one step further to argue that much of the literature "fails to consider the origins of this pattern of state behavior" and does not explain how the developmental state came into being and became developmental.

The central role of the developmental state in directing industrialization is therefore highly dependent on the historical period in which state policies and capacities are examined. In this sense, the efficacy of the developmental state should not been seen as a transcendental causal power but should rather be viewed as a historically and geographically contingent unfolding that worked particularly well in the earlier period of growth and industrialization in these East Asian economies. This early period of industrialization was also situated in a particularly favorable geopolitical environment in the international arena. As argued by Pirie (2008, 7), "The Korean state was a dirigiste state in a world of interventionist states. Korean elites were attempting to develop a distinctive Korean capitalism in a world of interconnected but still distinct national capitalism. . . . It must be understood as a child of its time." The developmental state theory should be viewed in its historically and geographically specific context as a critical intervention in certain "problem-spaces."[15] To Frangie (2011, 1185), "we need to grasp criticisms as a strategic form of intervention, implying that certain interventions could be critical in some contexts or periods, but might lose their 'critical purchase' in other contexts." When the contexts of this "problem-space" change over time, the relevance of these critical approaches, such as the developmental state theory, may be weakened.[16] By the mid-1980s, when these major studies have ended their historical narratives, significant changes and transformations had indeed been unfolding in the domestic and the international arenas. Described in the next section, these relatively recent trends during the past two decades do not automatically invalidate the key arguments and empirical findings offered by the classic works in the developmental state literature. But these trends do create a *different* problem-space for reconceptualizing the nexus of state-firm relations in a globalizing era that in turn compel us to rethink the role of the developmental state for understanding industrial transformation and economic development.

Third, *sectoral selectivity* is an important qualification that sheds critical light on the success of the developmental state. In the early period of industrialization during the 1960s and the 1970s, most developmental states in East Asia chose to promote and nurture heavy and chemical industries that served the relatively large domestic markets (except Singapore) and provided the foundation for industrialization to take off. This was the time when the argument for infant industries worked particularly well, and state-sanctioned protection was offered to carefully selected national champions, such as Hyundai Heavy Industries and state-owned POSCO in South Korea (Amsden 1989; Woo 1991), and Formosa Plastics and such state-owned enterprises as Chinese Petroleum Corporation, China Steel, and China Shipbuilding in Taiwan (Wade 1990, 90–112). Reflecting on the historical period between 1950 and 1985 when economic corporatism was practiced, Wade (1990, 284) notes that "Taiwan's industrial officials are engaged with the bigger industrial firms in relations that would be called 'administrative guidance' in Japan. They make suggestions as to suitable products or technologies, in line with a wider conception of where the industry should be going." This industrial shift and sectoral selectivity paid off in both economies. Between 1961 and 1974, the share of chemicals and machinery in manufacturing value-added increased from 23 percent to 39 percent in South Korea, and from 24 percent to 50 percent in Taiwan (Wade 1990, 88). In Singapore, state-owned enterprises in heavy industries, such as Singapore Petroleum Company, Keppel Corp, Sembawang Shipyard, and Natsteel, grew hand-in-hand with the rapid influx of foreign enterprises in light manufacturing industries, such as textiles, toys, and electronics (Rodan 1989; Huff 1994; Low 1998).

The dominant high-tech industrial players in these economies today (e.g., Samsung and Hon Hai as mentioned in chapter 1), however, were only infants or unborn entities during this early period of the developmental state. This reflects the sectoral selectivity of the developmental state in its historical context: state-directed industrialization was more effective and feasible in heavy and chemical industries. Thus the likes of Samsung Electronics from South

Korea and the Taiwan Semiconductor Manufacturing Company (and the United Microelectronics Corporation), undoubtedly the heavyweights in today's global semiconductor industry, were only briefly mentioned in Amsden (1989, 82–83), Wade (1990, 104–5), and Evans (1995, 176).[17] While the electronics industry did receive significant support from the developmental state in all three East Asian economies, these earlier studies did not go beyond an analysis of their domestic production for exports and thus underestimated the emergence of world-leading firms in the information and communications technology (ICT) industry from these economies. Since the late 1980s, the emergence of global production networks in high-tech industries have led to another major sectoral shift and selectivity in most East Asian economies.[18] This swift shift and its deep integration into the global economy in turn reduce the operating space for the developmental state to plan and implement its sector-specific industrial policy.

To summarize, the efficacy of the developmental state in the three East Asian economies was historically and sectorally specific. Focusing on state-led initiatives during the 1960s and the 1970s in a narrow range of light and heavy industries, pioneering studies of the developmental state have found strong empirical support for its "midwifery" and "husbandry" roles because the state was well embedded in private sectors and yet relative autonomous from social groups. By the early 1980s, however, the favorable historical-geographical contexts for this developmental state, such as colonial antecedents, authoritarian state control, and US-led geopolitical imperatives, began to change. Domestic political shifts and intensified pressures from international organizations and global competition started to reduce the state's institutional legitimacy and developmental capacity and to limit its policy options. Private firms were also growing out of their relationships with the paternalistic state to make their own inroads into the global economy through strategic coupling with global production networks. To a varying degree, the three East Asian economies were also much more integrated into the competitive dynamics of the global economy. These new contexts raise important questions about the evolving relations between the developmental state and national firms: Is the developmental state increasingly sidestepped by global articulations in this state-firm-global production network assemblage? Are state institutions transforming their roles in order to catalyze and promote firm dynamics and growth in a globalizing world economy? These questions point to the need for a critical examination of the changing nature of state presence in a globalizing era since the 1980s.

Transformation of State Roles in the 1980s and the 1990s

This section sets the political context for the book's in-depth analysis of the strategic coupling of national firms with global production networks in the

2000s and beyond. My approach here is both analytical and empirical. Analytically, this systematic presentation of the changing state roles in relation to its components, institutions, and policy instruments provides the necessary basis for a political economy perspective on the evolutionary dynamics in the state-firm-GPN assemblage in later chapters. Empirically, the section offers some evidence for the shifting nature of the developmental state bureaucracy, the weakened ability of state actors to formulate and implement strategic industrial plans, and the growing strength of private firms in taking on industrial development or in sidestepping state policy agendas.[19] Described by Castells (1992, 41) as "the rise of flexible capitalism under the guidance of an inflexible state," all these changes in the 1980s and the 1990s point to a transformed state that took on new functions for providing the necessary support and conditions in favor of the articulation of domestic firms and national economies into the competitive dynamics of global production networks.

Following Wade's (1990, 26–29) treatment of state roles in his "governed market" theory, I focus on the political arrangements of the developmental state, that is, its components and institutions, that provided the initial basis for governing the market through a specific set of policy instruments. While Wade and others (e.g., Evans 1995; Weiss 1998) described these political arrangements as corporatist and authoritarian in nature, I examine the changing domestic political dynamics and international conditions that reshaped these political arrangements in the 1980s and the 1990s. This shifting nature of state autonomy led to the dismantling or decline of pilot agencies and the redistribution of state power across multiple state and nonstate institutions. Instead of the developmental state taking strong leadership in governing the market and directing corporate development through firm- or industry-specific policies, this weakening of state autonomy and the decentering of developmental state institutions set in motion a major policy shift from sectoral- and target-specific industrial policy toward more horizontal and functional policies in support of domestic firms and industries taking advantage of growing global opportunities.[20] In short, domestic political and economic dynamics interacted with changing international contexts to redefine the state's roles in providing the political and institutional bases for strategic coupling. While these state roles may fall short of the defining nature of the classic developmental state in the earlier decades, it must be acknowledged that this postdevelopmental state remains substantially involved in economic development in ways far greater and deeper than the neoclassical ideal of the liberal market state.[21]

State Components

While a developmental state is commonly defined by its embedded autonomy, strong institutional capacity, and the lack of accountability conditional on its authoritarian control and weak social groups, these key components faced increasing domestic challenges and international pressures in the mid-1980s and thereafter. Domestically, changing political dynamics such as democratization and interparty competition and the greater leverage of private firms contributed to the weakening of the defining core of state autonomy—the state's internal cohesiveness or bureaucratic rationality. This rise of party politics and political cleavages in a more democratic system led to the greater subjugation of state bureaucracy to political interests. Compared to the earlier periods, the state's economic bureaucrats no longer ruled, but rather followed the factional interests of politicians and their electoral maneuvering. These politicians became the masters of state bureaucrats. Meanwhile, private firms became more powerful because democratization and money politics had ironically placed greater demand on patron-client relationships between political parties and wealthy business groups. Reflecting on this weakened bureaucratic autonomy and governance, Lim (2009, 103) observes that "a dysfunctional bureaucracy has been captured by businesses, crippled by electoral competition and corruption, and become inefficient in planning. In this case, politicians reign, but business rules."

In the three East Asian economies, democratization through direct election and constitutional reforms and economic reforms through liberalization and deregulation began to take shape since the late 1980s—the democratization decree in South Korea in 1987 and the lifting of the martial law in Taiwan the same year. South Korea and Taiwan are perhaps two of the best examples of how political democratization and financial liberalization since the late 1980s and the 1990s has significant bearings on the reduced role of the state and its "developmental" capacities.[22] The developmental state in Singapore, however, managed to buck the trend toward institutional decline in the midst of democratization and liberalization. But it too had to loosen its grip on the domestic economy and private interests. At the end of the 1980s, Singapore was going into the "next lap" of its development with a change of guard in the leadership of the ruling People's Action Party (PAP), the privatization of former state-owned enterprises, and the continual growth of private enterprises. These changing political dynamics brought about dramatic shifts in state-firm relations and major economic challenges (e.g., the Asian financial crisis in 1997–1998).[23]

More specifically, South Korea's democratization started in 1987 when the incoming president Roh Tae Woo (1988–1993), chosen by the authoritarian president Chun Doo Hwan (1980–1988) who took over from the strongman Park Chung Hee after his assassination in 1979, unexpectedly announced direct presidential elections in December 1987 and legislative elections in the spring of 1988. Roh took cues from the decline of the ruling Democratic Justice Party (DJP) in the 1985 legislative elections in which the DJP won only 54 percent of seats (Slater and Wong 2013, 725). The mobilization of the *minjung*, or "common people's" movement, in the 1980s also signaled the emergence of a broad-based coalition of middle-class activists, students, religious leaders, and workers who demanded more democratic rights and fair electoral processes.[24] The 1987 democratization decree led to intensified domestic political conflicts that saw weak political parties increasingly divided along regional lines and organized around cliques (Lim 2009, 92; Kim 2014, 81–84). Roh's attempt to rein in the chaebol in 1991 in response to rampant corruption during the Chun regime was also ineffective because the state did not have the political power and institutional capacity to direct or even discipline the chaebol. State technocrats were more content with preserving their bureaucratic power and the status quo than with developing new initiatives to steer economic growth.[25] This bureaucratic weakness can be further attributed to the strong role of the largest chaebol in the Federation of Korean Industries (FKI), which had a systematic influence on Park's policies in the 1970s. By the late 1980s, the FKI had developed significant influence over financial policy because of its extensive organizational clout premised on the massive industrial concentration dominated by the chaebol. It had enormous institutional resources to engage in collective action to advance the chaebol's particularistic interests. Through the FKI, the largest chaebol gained powerful leverage over public policy, such as financial market deregulation (Zhang 2002, 424).

By the early 1980s, the Kuomintang (KMT) state in Taiwan had also evidently passed the apex of its authoritarian rule. The emergence of opposition (non-KMT) candidates in the 1980 supplementary elections was unprecedented (Slater and Wong 2013, 723; Rigger 2014, 114). From capturing 8 percent of the popular vote in the 1980 elections, these non-KMT candidates won some 20 percent of the vote, and the KMT share declined further to 69 percent in 1986. Since then, Taiwan experienced rapid democratization and market liberalization during the late 1980s, a period known as the "Great Transition" (Tien 1989), and changing international relations associated with the rapid rise of mainland China.[26] Democratization also proceeded swiftly apace since the establishment of the first opposition party, the Democratic Progressive Party (DPP), in September 1986, the lifting of the martial law (imposed since 1949) before President Chiang Ching-kuo's death in January 1988, and the succession of Chiang by the first native Taiwanese president, Lee Teng-hui, between 1988 and 2000. Since the beginning of the 1990s, the Legislative Yuan has emerged from its historically inactive role in domestic governance to become a powerful body in the policymaking process: the first batch of newly elected members in 1991 represented their constituent interests, and these included 31 percent of seats held by the DPP (Nathan 1993). As argued by Haggard and Zheng (2013, 452), this change in electoral politics contributed to the need of the ruling party to seek support from new voters and constituents that went beyond its traditional "mainlander" core in the military and the government. A variety of private sector groups began to play a greater role in KMT politics, resulting in a power shift from insulated technocratic agencies toward elected officials. The Taiwanese state in the 1990s and the

2000s was no longer the highly centralized and relatively autonomous developmental state led by such economic strongmen as Yin Zhongrong (K. Y. Yin) and K. T. Li in the 1960s and the 1970s. State autonomy began to give way to special interests from social groups and private sector actors (Mattlin 2011, 56–57).

In Singapore, the PAP state also met with greater domestic opposition.[27] Still, the PAP state was committed to its primordial developmental goals. In comparison with South Korea and Taiwan, the PAP state's institutional capacity remained strong in several key aspects that partly reflected Singapore's small size as a city-state, with less population and land area than the capital cities of South Korea (Seoul) and Taiwan (Taipei). Politically, the PAP enjoyed its uninterrupted and overwhelming majority rule between 1959 and 2014.[28] It held all seats in the Singapore Parliament and won 60 percent to 75 percent of all votes in each of the four general elections between 1968 and 1980. While it lost, for the first time, one seat in Parliament to the opposition party in a by-election in 1981, the PAP continued to secure a vast majority of votes and parliamentary seats in the next eight general elections between 1984 and 2015. The founding prime minister Lee Kuan Yew was able to enjoy unparalleled political autonomy from social groups and the private sector. When he passed on the baton to his deputy, Goh Chok Tong, and the second-generation political leaders in the 1991 general election, the PAP won "only" 61 percent of the popular votes. However, Goh ended his premiership on a high note. In his last general election as prime minster in November 2001, the PAP won 75.3 percent of the total votes.[29] In short, the PAP's uninterrupted success as the ruling party between 1959 and 2015 has given the state enormous political "reign" to ensure its autonomy from society.

Internationally, the stable and enduring international-domestic linkages necessary for the state's autonomy were under pressures from changing geopolitical environments and global competitive dynamics. First, geopolitics took a different turn in the late 1980s, with the fall of the Berlin Wall and the opening of mainland China to the global economy.[30] During the first three decades of state-led industrialization in these three economies, the international economy was indeed overshadowed by geopolitical imperatives under America's "First Empire" (1950–1980). This was a period of unfettered access to export markets and technological licensing for these latecomers to play their catching-up games. This stable international environment allowed the developmental state to work out its policy interventions without much international pressure and domestic resistance. All three economies were favorably supported by the foreign policy imperatives of the United States and its allies in Western Europe. The end of Cold War geopolitics made it much harder for the developmental state to steer the domestic economy because these advanced industrialized countries could not tolerate market distortions and protectionist industrial policy practiced by the developmental state. The defeat of communism in Eastern Europe and the opening of China reduced the geopolitical significance of strong East Asian states and their capitalist economies. Through its influence in the International Monetary Fund and the World Bank, the United States also intensified its pressure on South Korea and Taiwan to liberalize their domestic markets in order to sustain growth potential, enable foreign market access, or redress bilateral trade imbalances (Pirie 2008, 69; Gray 2011, 579). These external pressures worked in tandem with domestic political changes that led to divergent economic reforms and market liberalization.

State autonomy was also challenged by the emergence of new regimes of global economic governance. For example, the reregulation of global trade under the auspices of the World Trade Organization (WTO) since its inauguration on January 1, 1995, led to the establishment of new trade rules that nullified countervailing practices, such as export subsidies and local content requirements. These practices were critical policy tools of the developmental state during its earlier phase of industrialization. In particular, WTO rules made it much harder for these, or any other, economies, to practice sectoral industrial policy because they are deemed trade distorting (Perraton 2005, 105–6). Export subsidies for domestic firms and industries and local content requirements were banned under such WTO rules.[31] Moreover, the WTO rules governing intellectual property rights, such as the Agreement on Trade Related Aspects of Intellectual Property Rights (TRIPS), made it much more difficult for latecomers to catch up through reverse engineering of advance technologies developed in industrialized economies. These international pressures served as the broader structural context in which the developmental state experienced greater erosion of its institutional autonomy.

State Institutions

As the developmental state experienced decreasing autonomy from domestic politics and international pressures and engaged in market-oriented reforms, its developmentalist bureaucratic institutions were put under the spotlight for restructuring or reorganization. This decentering of institutional capacity weakened the ability of state actors to formulate plans and changed the nature of public-private consultation (e.g., weaker embedding of the state in the private sector). Two core dimensions of this institutional restructuring are particularly significant for this study: the dismantling or shifting nature of pilot agencies and the rise of multiple institutional arrangements. Both processes contributed to the reduction of bureaucratic control and policy coordination— the critical institutional capacity that had characterized the developmental state in the earlier phase of industrial transformation.

First, the dismantling of the pilot agency was most visible in South Korea. At the beginning of his administration, the civilian president Kim Young-Sam (1993–1998) ordered his economic aides to draft a five-year plan removing direct state controls and promoting market liberalization (Chung 2007, 89).[32]

In 1993, the Economic Planning Board—the elite pilot agency so central to defining South Korea's developmental state—was abolished. The EPB was absorbed into the Ministry of Finance (MOF) to form the super Ministry of Finance and Economy (MOFE) in 1994. This merger marked the withdrawal of the state from sectoral industrial policy, active coordination of private sector investment decisions, and direct financial supervision of the banking sector. With the abolishment of selective industrial protection under the Industrial Development Law in 1995, the state had essentially given up its deployment of target-specific industrial policy as a directive instrument for steering economic development.[33] Both the MOF and, subsequently, the MOFE were dominated by US-trained neoliberal economists. The EPB's function in formulating strategic industrial policy was decentralized to different ministries. Industrial development was taken over by the new Ministry of Trade, Industry and Energy (MOTIE) through a merger of the Ministry of Trade and Industry and the Ministry of Energy and Resources in 1993. In 1998, the MOTIE was reorganized again to become the Ministry of Commerce, Industry and Energy (MOCIE).[34] International trade policy was also transferred from MOTIE to the Ministry of Foreign Affairs, signaling a shift in the state's conception of international trade as a matter of diplomatic relations and negotiations rather than a fundamental element of sectoral industrial policy.[35]

In Taiwan, despite the active role of the KMT state in industrialization, Wade (1990, 226) acknowledges that Taiwan's elite economic bureaucracy, such as Council for Economic Planning and Development (CEPD) and the Industrial Development Bureau (IDB) of the Ministry of Economic Affairs (MOEA), was "less preeminent" and not as powerful as their counterparts in Japan (MITI) and South Korea (EPB and MTI). During the 1980s, the CEPD was subject to immense challenges from different segments of society (Wu 2005, 245). In the 1990s, the CEPD played an advisory role to the cabinet where the real power resided. Various ministries formulated and implemented their own economic policies without going through the CEPD. Meanwhile, the much greater autonomy of the central bank and its priorities of macroeconomic stability and low inflation meant that Taiwan's banking system was very conservative. The state's industrial policy was not funded through discretionary state allocation of bank credits during much of its export-oriented industrialization. The Ministry of Finance was "more of an implementing agency" of monetary and foreign exchange policies set by the Central Bank of China (Wade 1990, 208; Lim 2009, 96–98). The bank exercised broad authority over monetary management and financial regulation and was subject to limited legislative oversight of its budgets and operations. This high degree of central bank autonomy in conducting its macro and micro policy functions also made it difficult for the economic bureaucracy to influence bank credit allocation.[36]

Second, the shift of bureaucratic authority and control from the pilot agency to different state institutions contributed to institutional fragmentation and multiple policy arrangements. This loss of internal cohesiveness of the development state and its key institutions resulted in frequent and significant conflicts among different state institutions over the direction and implementation of specific industrial policy. In South Korea, for example, while the Ministry of Commerce and Industry opposed Samsung's entry into the automobile industry in 1992 because of overcapacity, excess competition, lack of economies of scales, and high exit costs among existing producers, the other "camp" of the state—comprising the Blue House, the Fair Trade Commission, and the EPB—thought that after three decades of unsatisfactory state-led development of the auto sector, market conditions should be allowed to determine the viability of Samsung and other existing producers in the sector. Trade liberalization should condition such a competitive field and produce the desired rationalization (Ravenhill 2003, 116–22; Lee 2013, 69–71).[37] Similarly, the Ministry of Information and Communication (MOIC) was renamed the Ministry of Communication in 1994 and reconceptualized as a more specialized quasi-pilot agency for promoting the domestic telecommunications sector.[38] This decentralization and fragmentation of the key pilot agencies in turn made it even harder for the state to coordinate industrial policy in the face of mammoth chaebol dominating the domestic market. Frequent jurisdictional disputes occurred between the MOIC and other ministries, indicating the lack of clear policy coordination in the ICT sector (Lim 2010, 199).

In Taiwan, the state became far too insular to keep pace with private sector developments. Recent empirical research has shown that there was indeed intense rivalry, incoherence, and nationalist politics in its key state agencies.[39] Fields (1995) questions the developmental role of the Kuomintang state because of the strong and ultraconservative influence of the Central Bank of China. To him, Wade's (1990) characterization of the Industrial Development Bureau's (IDB) role in industrial policy may be exaggerated. Chu (1989, 666) also notes that the IDB "enjoys little clout in the overall economic bureaucracy, and has limited influence over fiscal and credit policy."[40] Drawing on declassified archival materials on Taiwan's state agencies and ministerial meetings, Ngo (2005, 83) argues that "instead of manifesting a high degree of unity, the state machinery in Taiwan was plagued by factionalism and intrastate rivalry. State apparatuses were constantly in conflict with one another." To him, the strong and unitary state depicted in Wade (1990) was in reality a diverse network of bureaucratic kingdoms and crony enterprises. Similarly, my field research shows that the different resource endowments and status of agencies within the MOEA, for example, were detrimental to interagency coordination.[41] The Industry Development Bureau (IDB), the Department of Industrial Technology (DIT), and the Board of Foreign Trade (BoFT) were all full units within the MOEA and had executive authority power. Their size and administrative authority were much greater than the Department of Investment Services (DIS), known as a "step unit."[42] This phenomenon of overlapping agencies and authorities clearly contradicts the idea of a pilot agency taking charge of target-specific initiatives within the developmental state.

The frequent rotation, typically between two to five years, of directors general among different departments and bureaus also contributed to instability and inconsistency in policy directions and initiatives. Instead of directing and guiding new industries, economic planning officials fell behind the private sector and other interest groups, and became increasingly reliant on consultative groups (Chu 2007; Haggard and Zheng 2013).[43]

Among the three East Asian economies, it might be argued that only Singapore's developmental state has achieved a fairly consistent internal coherence and bureaucratic rationality between the 1960s and the 1990s. This institutional consistency was largely predicated on Singapore's unique postindependence conditions. The PAP's high degree of political legitimacy was absent in both South Korea and Taiwan. The city-state nature of Singapore also saved the PAP state from having to deal with interregional and other forms of local politics that gradually destabilized the developmental state in both South Korea and Taiwan. Elite agencies in Singapore, such as the Economic Development Board (EDB) under the Ministry of Trade and Industry (MTI), not only did not experience reorganization and restructuring but remained politically powerful and bureaucratically coherent into the 2010s. By the late 1980s, these state agencies had gained much credibility and legitimacy through their success in industrializing the nation. Their key bureaucrats had emerged as highly influential economic planners and strategists in the PAP state. Between the 1980s and the first half of the 2000s, the EDB was led by two of Singapore's best-known bureaucrats: Philip Yeo (chairman, 1986–2006) and Tan Chin Nam (managing director, 1986–1994).[44] These bureaucrats were well connected to the PAP leadership and enjoyed significant political clout and support for their economic development initiatives. Under their "rule," the EDB worked closely with the MTI to develop and implement new directions for the Singapore economy since the 1985 recession.[45] Despite this unusually strong capacity of the PAP state in Singapore, the political nexus between the PAP and the elites in civil service, known as the Administrative Service, was too porous for embedded autonomy to work out fully in Singapore. The EDB, in particular, produced a number of alumni who have served as political appointees in the PAP state since the 1980s.[46] This close alliance between the ruling party and elite state bureaucracies, such as the EDB and other statutory boards, has rendered the notion of bureaucratic autonomy from political interest a rather problematic concept.[47]

Policy Instruments

The above discussion of changing state autonomy and institutional fragmentation necessitates a systematic analysis of the different policy instruments and options available to the postdevelopmental state that remains committed to developmentalist goals in a globalizing world economy. While the developmental state in the earlier period could coordinate production and investment decisions by exercising its financial leverage over private-sector firms (credit allocation and policy loans), establishing state-owned enterprises, and targeting industrial policy through sectoral subsidies and selective trade and investment management, the postdevelopmental state has responded to its declining autonomy and growing fragmentation by switching to new roles through developing *catalyst* policies for supporting and facilitating economic promotion in general. These new state functions include promoting science and technology, facilitating trade and investment, enforcing market-based rules and regulation, supporting for small- and medium-sized enterprises financially, and continuing corporatist initiatives involving firms and labor unions. In particular, the practice of industrial policy, long hailed as the defining attribute of the ideal developmental state, has evolved from targeted firm- or industry-level support to meso-level network support in favor of market competition, capability development, and global articulations.

Fraught with definitional problems, "industrial policy" is a term in need of conceptual elaboration.[48] In its broadest sense, Cimoli et al. (2009b, 1–2) define it as not only policies affecting "infant industry" support but also trade policies, science and technology policies, public procurement, policies affecting foreign direct investment, intellectual property rights, and the allocation of financial resources. A more useful way to differentiate these policies and their relevance to promoting economic development is to divide industrial policy into two basic types: sectoral/vertical and functional/horizontal. The former tends to be highly selective (i.e., "vertical," or top down) and therefore firm or industry specific, requiring strong state interventions into the domestic economy through investment coordination, tax and other incentives, policy loans and credit rationing, technology transfer, and trade and investment protectionism.[49] Functional industrial policy refers to more general (i.e., "horizontal") policies promoting overall industrial development and economywide effects without favoring particular firms or industries. It entails "industry-selection neutral" support through R&D tax benefits, research institutes, start-up supports, incentives for returning technopreneurs, public-private R&D consortia, productivity enhancement through skill development and industrial automation, energy efficiency and environmental protection, market development through international branding, and so on. In short, functional industrial policy tends to support a more market-led industrial development. But it does require state involvement far beyond what is considered appropriate for the liberal market state.[50]

In the three East Asian economies, this shift from sectoral to functional industrial policy began with the weakening of industrial targeting underpinned by less favorable international-domestic linkages. The state's financial resources were also limited by other competing demands from different fragments of society—for instance, social and welfare spending.[51] As discussed in the next section, the private sector also became more resourceful in financial means, technological capability, and market access, reducing its desire for direct state support and performance-based discipline. In particular, this shift toward functional industrial policy entails promoting industrial upgrading and innovation and facilitating trade and investment. In the first place, functional industrial policy addresses *industrial upgrading and innovation* through inducing domestic firms to enlarge their scale of production and fostering innovation and knowledge accumulation through investment in R&D (Di Maio 2009, 134). While the former can be achieved through incentives for small- and medium-sized enterprises (SMEs) and mergers among larger firms, the latter requires a range of related policies, such as the liberalization of technology transfer policies to enable collaboration between domestic and foreign firms, greater R&D funding to reduce imitative reverse engineering, and a shift in innovation policy from the promotion of strategic industries to the support and development of strategic activities within sectors, in particular innovation-related ones.[52]

Apart from promoting industrial upgrading and R&D capabilities, the state also strengthened *trade and investment policies* in order to facilitate the articulation of national firms into global production networks. But their implementation through the state bureaucracy was more market following than market leading, particularly in Taiwan and South Korea. Prior to the 1990s, these horizontal policies used to be restrictive and protectionist in nature. But due to changing international-domestic linkages described earlier, they became more open and internationally oriented, described by Haggard and Zheng (2013, 451) as "open economy industrial policy." This trade- and investment-facilitating industrial policy focused on creating conditions favorable for both foreign and domestic investors to invest in more capital- and technology-intensive sectors.[53] Of the three economies, Singapore's developmental state has achieved the strongest performance in promoting industrial transformation through trade and investment facilitation. Singapore's early decision to open its domestic economy to the full vagaries of the global economy since its self-government in 1959 meant that its elite pilot agency, the Economic Development Board, was and continues to be particularly focused on attracting foreign direct investment.[54] Singapore was much more open to and reliant on foreign capital, and the state's industrial policy was thus less directive and more cooperative toward foreign investors.[55]

With hindsight, my analysis of shifting state roles during the 1980s and the 1990s points to an evolutionary process through which the developmental state evolved from its role as *the* leader in industrial transformation to a catalyst of the dynamic articulation of domestic firms into global production networks. In his *Innovation and the State*, Breznitz (2007, 31) argues that such an evolutionary change tends to occur once this articulation becomes stronger and the networks more international. Meanwhile, the postdevelopmental state has taken on a wider range of economic and noneconomic functions, including the separation of policy from operation through contracting out services, the creation of new and autonomous regulatory institutions such as independent central banks, the increasing role of the state as the regulator, and the shift from a discretionary to rule-based mode of governance in a range of economic and social policy areas (Jayasuriya 2005, 384). The state's previously embedded relationships with private firms (e.g., policy consultation and coordination) have also evolved into a more disembedded form, as these firms have developed greater internal capabilities and direct access to domestic and international resources.

Emerging Dynamic Capabilities of Firms by the 1990s

Since the late 1980s, leading East Asian firms have graduated from their initial role as the "chosen winners" to become globalizing firms; they have grown up from adolescence and become less dependent on their developmental state "parents." Other new "kids" have also emerged in sectors and industries previously not on the state's favored list. A much more diverse group of capitalist firms have occupied the developmental space in East Asian economies, leaving less instrumental policy space for the postdevelopmental state. Understanding this evolutionary process of domestic firms disembedding from changing domestic states requires an analysis of their emerging dynamic capabilities. For latecomer catching up to take place, East Asian firms must learn the existing production and management know-how from incumbents or "first movers" in advanced industrialized economies, which includes different kinds of firm-specific capabilities, such as capabilities to access complementary assets, absorptive capabilities, and innovation capabilities (Malerba and Nelson 2011, 1648).[56] Once acquired, these initial "foreign" capabilities can be further developed, enhanced, or recombined to become a new form of capability peculiar to these domestic firms in East Asian economies. In the changing competitive domestic and international contexts, this evolutionary and creative process involves indigenous learning-by-doing, adaptation and modifications, and incremental or new innovative activity. The resultant new products, technologies, and organizational processes are generally embedded in emerging *dynamic capabilities* defined as "the firm's ability to integrate, build, and reconfigure internal and external competences to address rapidly changing environments" (Teece et al. 1997, 516). Tracing and explaining the emerging dynamic capabilities of capitalist firms in the three East Asian economies requires a firm-based perspective that takes into account their internal and external resource endowments and their processes of organizing these endowments in ways that enhance their competitive advantage over time.[57]

While resource endowments, such as capital, technology, and labor, can be readily borrowed, acquired, or developed, organizational processes of coordinating and managing different activities are much harder to develop because norms, values, and routines in firms take much more time and costs to evolve. The developmental state literature tends to emphasize the acquisition of such resource endowments as capital and technology, particularly through state-directed interventions and policy preferences. In doing so, it underestimates the competitive significance of superior organizational processes that can only be developed through learning and knowledge accumulation *within* capitalist firms.[58] Once developed though, these firm-specific initiatives can serve as one of the most important platforms for firm competitiveness and industrial upgrading. As argued by Teece et al. (1997, 518), "The essence of competencies and capabilities is embedded in organizational processes of one kind or another. But the content of these processes and the opportunities they afford for developing competitive advantage at any point in time are shaped significantly by the assets the firm possesses (internal and market) and by the evolutionary path it has adopted/inherited. Hence organizational processes, shaped by the firm's asset positions and molded by its evolutionary and co-evolutionary paths, explain the essence of the firm's dynamic capabilities and its competitive advantage."

The changing selection environment in the three latecomer economies since the late 1980s has facilitated or expedited the development of the organizational and technological capabilities of their domestic firms. I argue below that East Asian firms, particularly those from South Korea and Taiwan, have benefited enormously from five major evolutionary changes that allow them to accumulate and develop firm-specific assets and organizational processes: (1) learning from production for exports; (2) acquiring technologies in the international markets; (3) building firm-specific capabilities through reverse "brain drain"; (4) intensifying in-house R&D activity; and (5) leveraging on global finance. First, *production for exports* has been extremely important in enhancing firm-specific learning. In her classic study of South Korea, Amsden (1989) calls this mode of catching-up "industrializing through learning." When all three East Asian economies had switched to export-oriented industrialization by the 1970s, domestic firms were incentivized to engage in learning-by-doing and to experience through international subcontracting arrangements. One of the most significant beneficiaries of such arrangements was the electronics industry.[59] Through the original equipment manufacturing (OEM) arrangement, East Asian firms initially served as low-cost subcontractors to their OEM customers located in North America, Western Europe, and Japan who were looking for alternative locations to reduce production cost in their labor-intensive assembly manufacturing.

Compared to the earlier phase of import-substitution industrialization during the 1950s and the 1960s, such organizational arrangement gave East Asian firms the initial opportunity to engage in learning and catching up and to articulate into an emergent form of globalizing production networks. The stringent demands of exporting to international markets led to greater knowledge accumulation through "learning-by-exporting" that was simply not available in the earlier period when these firms were oriented toward domestic and "closed" markets. While the developmental state, particularly in South

Korea, was instrumental in monitoring the export performance of its national firms, it should be noted that this firm-specific learning-by-exporting went well beyond production capacity (i.e., scale), sometimes financed by state-directed industrial policy, to knowledge acquisition and technological innovation over time. To Hobday (1995), the OEM arrangement led by international customers offered a training platform for latecomer firms to overcome their initial entry barriers in international markets and to assimilate manufacturing and design technology that was transferred from their OEM customers to local engineers and technicians in East Asian firms.

By the late 1980s, leading East Asian firms had accumulated two decades of OEM-based export experience and some had graduated from this arrangement to become innovative firms in their own right. Other new entrants in these East Asian economies tended to leapfrog by skipping the OEM stage. Hobday and Colpan (2010, 767–68) thus observe that "the first business groups to enter electronics (for example, Samsung of South Korea) tended to graduate from simple to advanced learning over a period of two decades or so. Later entrants began at the more advanced stages, missing out early phases. The OEM system became a training school as firms entered new sectors, secured a market channel, and acquired technology." This OEM arrangement evolved into original design manufacturing (ODM) by 1989. In an ODM arrangement, East Asian firms become much more involved in product and process design in accordance with a general design layout supplied by their international customers. In a more advanced form, this ODM arrangement entails complete product design by East Asian firms on the basis of their own knowledge of the international market and technological capabilities. To Hobday (1995, 37), this more sophisticated form of "ODM signifies the internalization of system design skills, and sometimes complex production technologies and component design abilities on the part of the latecomer." It also allowed these firms to achieve enormous economies of scale so that they could rapidly ramp up production volume later on when they developed their own brand name products.[60] As their firm-specific capabilities evolved over time, East Asian firms tended to rely less on domestic sources of technological know-how because OEM and ODM arrangements provided important technological conduits for them to achieve speedy market-technology progress.

While this learning through exporting explains the initial evolution of emerging dynamic capabilities of East Asian firms, however, *acquiring technologies in the international markets*, often led by large-scale state initiatives, was critically important in the early founding of these firms and major industries. There are two competing views on the importance of these technological acquisitions. The first view refers to the accumulation of foreign technologies through direct transfer or reverse engineering by East Asian firms. This view sees little and no new dynamic learning originating from these recipients. East Asian firms benefited essentially from technological development through second-mover advantages and exploitation of mature technologies. As argued by Wong (2011, 27), "High-tech industrialization in Korea, Taiwan, and Singapore was afforded by the accumulation of existing knowledge rather than the assimilation of completely new knowledge bases; in short, they copied." On the other hand, a more dynamic and evolutionary view believes in the assimilation of foreign technologies that in turn gives impetus to new capability development in East Asian firms. While state-financed or state-facilitated licensing and acquisition in the international markets had been important in the 1970s and the 1980s, leading East Asian firms were successful in developing dynamic capabilities in both technological and organizational frontiers by the early 1990s that enabled them to rely less on foreign technologies and state-financed initiatives.[61]

This assimilation view is echoed in Mathews and Cho's (2000) pioneering study of the critical success factor of leading East Asian firms in the semiconductor industry, such as Samsung Electronics (South Korea), Taiwan Semiconductor Manufacturing Company (TSMC), and Chartered Semiconductor (Singapore).[62] They argue that by the late 1990s, these three East Asian semiconductor firms were able to acquire technological competences through a process of technology diffusion management known as developmental resource leverage. In this "technology leverage as latecomer strategy," East Asian firms "acquired technological capabilities by engineering various kinds of linkages with advanced firms, through contract manufacturing, licensing, joint ventures and other forms of interfirm collaboration, while maintaining a fiercely competitive approach to winning markets and rapidly developing copies of products introduced by leading firms elsewhere such as in Silicon Valley" (Mathews and Cho 2000, 3). For example, through the state-funded Industrial Technology Research Institute (ITRI), Taiwan's TSMC licensed its first VLSI IC fabrication technology from Philips in 1986. By July 2000, TSMC was technologically advanced enough to license its own process technologies to National Semiconductors and became the first independent foundry house in Taiwan to license to an integrated device manufacturer (IDM) in the United States.[63] In the flat panel display (TFT-LCD) market,[64] major Taiwanese makers such as AU Optronics, Chi-Mei, Quanta Display, and Chunghwa Picture Tubes initially sourced their technologies from Japan in the early 1990s. Full technology transfer was achieved by the end of the 1990s when Japanese makers such as Mitsubishi faced serious financial trouble and had to give up their TFT-LCD business.[65] These Taiwanese display makers thus acquired the proprietary ownership of these technologies and emerged to be the world's biggest players in the 2000s, only to be rivaled by Samsung and LG from South Korea.

East Asian firms in other sectors also leveraged successfully on foreign technologies to develop their own dynamic capabilities. For example, South Korea's Hyundai Motor relied on in-house R&D to supplement or supplant their foreign purchases by the late 1980s. Hyundai's first foray into self-made machines in its domestic plants was made through its machine tool division established in 1978. It initially licensed its Computerized Numerical Control (CNC) technologies from Cincinnati Milacron (United States) and Kashifuji (Japan) during the 1980s. After a period of in-housing learning and improvisation, Hyundai began manufacturing its own CNC turning center in 1986 and a CNC gear-hobbing machine in 1988 (K. Lee 2000, 176–78). Other more recent studies of technological innovation in East Asia also found the decreasing reliance of East Asian firms on advanced industrialized countries for technologies and the increasing regionalization of knowledge flows within East Asia. In their study of patent citation patterns in East Asia since 1990, Brahmbhatt and Hu (2010) observe that intraregional flows of patent citations rose rapidly since the 1990s, and East Asian innovations relied less on knowledge flows from the United States and Japan. Between 1990 and 2004, Taiwanese inventors cited South Korean patents much more frequently than American and Japanese patents, and South Korean inventors cited Taiwanese patents more often than American patents and as often as Japanese ones (Hu 2009, 1474). This intraregional trend in patent citations indicates the emergence of a strong national and regional knowledge base to sustain firm-based innovation.

To assimilate foreign technologies and develop new firm-specific capabilities, East Asian firms benefited from a process of reverse *"brain drain"* through which cohorts of overseas returnees, having learnt their trade and honed their skills in the world's most competitive and technologically advanced markets such as Silicon Valley, returned to their home economies to establish the next generation private enterprises. While initially attracted by developmental state incentives and direct support in the early 1980s, these returnee technologists and entrepreneurs played an instrumental role in building the dynamic capabilities of East Asian firms.[66] Their critical role in developing high-tech industries in the three East Asian economies during the 1990s and the 2000s reflects not so much the initial importance of state-led incentives and industrial policy, but rather the personal technological and organizational prowess of these technopreneurs derived from their deep embeddedness in globalized innovation and production networks. Since the late 1990s, the rise of these technopreneurs as leaders of major East Asian firms has heralded an evolutionary shift in the state-firm-GPN assemblage toward the strategic disembedding of domestic firms from the postdevelopmental state. National champions are now gradually decoupled from state initiatives and industrial policy to become formidable competitors in the global economy.

In South Korea, around eighty Bell Labs alumnus and hundreds of others from Caltech, MIT, and other leading US technology centers could be identified by 1994 (Hobday 1995, 49). More specifically, overseas returnees were absolutely vital to Samsung's initial start in DRAM during the mid-1970s (Chang 2008, 34–35). When Samsung's founder Byung-chull Lee acquired Korea Semiconductor to mark his foray into the semiconductor business in 1974, he did not have the right expertise and technology to succeed in this capital-intensive, high-tech industry. The Park Chung Hee regime was not able to provide the necessary technological support either. By the late 1970s, Samsung's semiconductor division was almost out of business had it not been saved by importing Japanese semiconductor engineers who traveled over the weekends to South Korea to transfer technology to Samsung's own engineers. Still, Samsung was not able to make significant technological breakthroughs based on Japanese technology. By the early 1980s, Lee decided to go into the VLSI semiconductor business and built factories in Giheung to achieve economies of scale in producing DRAMs. To kick-start its 64K DRAM development in 1983, Chairman Lee hired US-trained Korean-American semiconductor engineers from leading US firms, paid them up to three times his own salary, and appealed to their nationalist pride (Mathews and Cho 2000, 107). Its initial 64K DRAM technology was licensed from an American semiconductor firm Micron Technology that was facing financial difficulties. But to develop its own 256K DRAM technology, Lee brought in highly trained South Korean engineers and researchers who had been schooled in the United States and had worked for American semiconductor firms.[67] With these returnees, Samsung finally made its breakthrough in the DRAM business. In July 1990, Samsung's 16MB DRAM semiconductors presented at conferences in the United States were ahead of market leaders from Japan, the United States, and Europe.[68] Samsung maintained the same technological leadership, again ahead of Japanese and US firms, with its latest 64MB DRAM developed in 1992 under the leadership of Oh-Hyun Kwon. Its global market dominance was clear by the time of its successful construction of the world's first 1-gigabyte DRAM prototype in November 1996.[69]

In Taiwan, these overseas returnees were as significant to the development of its high-tech industries and firm-specific capabilities as their counterparts in South Korea. During the 1960s and the 1970s, Taiwan suffered from serious "brain drain." The annual number of returning students hardly exceeded a dozen. But this trend was reversed by the late 1980s due partly to state encouragement throughout the 1980s in order to maintain informal connections with other countries. This strategic "utilization of overseas Chinese scientists in R&D projects" was first explicitly announced in the 1979 Science and Technology Development Program of the Republic of China proposed by the Science and Technology Advisory Group and approved by the Executive Yuan on May 17, 1979 (Greene 2007, 139). From an initial number of 250 in 1985, these returnees increased substantially to 750 in 1989 and to more than 1,000 in 1991 (Hobday 1995, 38). In 1988 alone, more than 7,000 Taiwanese studied abroad. In 1992, the Taiwanese Bell Systems Alumni Association had some 120 members. This reverse "brain drain" accelerated rapidly during the 1990s. During the 1989–1993 and the 1994–1999 periods, respectively, 1,139 and 1,963 foreign-trained Taiwanese semiconductor technologists returned to Hsinchu

Science-Based Industrial Park, totaling 3,102 in ten years (Keller and Pauly 2003, 149). Between 1990 and 1995, the total number of returning students in all industries increased dramatically to 30,238 (Greene 2007, 137).[70]

To a certain extent, this dramatic surge of returnees reflects the rapid growth of Taiwan's information and communications technology (ICT) industry during the 1990s and beyond.[71] Macronix's chairman and CEO Miin Wu is a good example. Before establishing Macronix, he had held senior and managerial positions in VLSI Technology, Intel, Rockwell, and Siliconix in Silicon Valley. During the emerging stage of Taiwan's semiconductor industry in the late 1980s, Wu brought home several of his fellow Taiwanese engineers working in the United States to found Macronix in 1989.[72] Macronix's president, Chih-Yuan Lu, had a Ph.D. from Columbia University and worked as a researcher in Bell Labs before returning to Taiwan.[73] Other top executives at leading Taiwanese high-tech firms had also worked in the United States before returning to Taiwan. AU Optronics' David Su, for example, joined General Electric in 1986 and was responsible for its TFT-LCD project for avionics application. He came back to Taiwan in 1990 to join Unipac Optoelectronics, a subsidiary of United Microelectronics Corporation (UMC), and set up Taiwan's first TFT-LCD fab. In 2001, Acer Display Technology was merged with Unipac and renamed as AU Optronics, and became a part of the BenQ group.[74] As argued by Chuang (2008), interfirm flow of technologists and engineers was at least as important in firm-specific capability building as personnel flow from such state-funded R&D organizations as ITRI.

With this large presence of overseas returnees and technopreneurs, particularly in South Korea and Taiwan,[75] the role of state-funded national science and technology institutes in steering high-tech development had been reduced by the late 1980s and the early 1990s. Instead, we witness the rapid *intensification of in-house R&D activity* among leading East Asian firms that have taken over the leadership role in technological innovation in South Korea and Taiwan. As pointed out by Kim and Nelson (2000b, 5), "The innovation drive of newly industrializing economies in selective industries in the 1990s is marked by intensified in-house R&D activities and participation in global alliances and reflects their aspiration to become members of the industrially advanced community." As these newly industrialized economies approach the frontier of technological innovation in high-tech industries, the state's leading role becomes increasingly replaced by private sector initiatives. This shift is partly explained by the rapidity in technological innovation that outpaces the learning capacity of the state bureaucracy and research institutes. To Pack (2000, 86), "The limited role of public research institutes is not surprising. In sectors in which there is a rapidly evolving technology frontier and knowledge is proprietary, the public sector is likely to learn the proprietary knowledge in OECD firms with a significant lag. But it was hardly useful to learn to produce a 256K chip when the world standard changed to one or four megabytes. In other sectors with more slowly evolving technologies, public institutions would seem a fifth wheel given that much of the information is not proprietary and can be identified and purchased by individual firms."[76]

The significant decline in the role of state-sponsored R&D and research institutes in South Korea has occurred since the mid-1980s. The ratio of government-private R&D expenditure dropped dramatically from the peak of 97:3 in 1970 to 25:75 in 1985 and 19:81 in 1990 and 1995. Measured in the total number of researchers, it is clear that the private sector outstripped government research institutes and universities respectively by 1985 and both combined by 1990. In 2008, almost 55 percent of South Korea's 436,228 research personnel came from the private sector. State-funded institutes accounted for less than 7 percent of these personnel.[77] L. Kim (2000; 2003) attributes this declining role of state-funded research institutes vis-à-vis university laboratories and corporate R&D centers to two factors. First, such state-funded institutes as the famed Electronics and Telecommunications Research Institute (ETRI) and Korea Institute of Science and Technology (KIST) were far less dynamic and attractive to star researchers because of their bureaucratic control by the state. Second, these institutes suffered from many rules and regulations unfavorable to stimulating creativity and innovation. State-funded institutes also found it hard to retain strong R&D personnel who were attracted either to universities for prestige or to private sector R&D laboratories for better remuneration.

Meanwhile, the role of private firms in commercializing technologies through their in-house R&D institutes has been significant since the early 1990s. For example, Samsung's Advanced Institute of Technology was established in the October 1987 (Hobday 1995, 57, 83). In 1989, only about 10 percent of funding for Samsung's DRAM venture with other companies came from the state-funded ETRI, whereas the core efforts and investment was in house. Few, if any, of Samsung engineers interviewed in Hobday's (1995, 93) study mentioned any role of ETRI. As the group's central lab, the institute employed around 450 researchers and 150 support staff in 1993 and spent around US$50 million annually (much more than most state-funded institutes at that time). By then, Samsung's twenty-six companies had already had a total of a thousand researchers, plus thirteen thousand development engineers. The same happened to Goldstar's (LG) central research lab that employed some two hundred staff and was headed by an ex-employee of Digital Equipment Corporation (DEC) in the United States. This trend continued throughout the 2000s in the telecommunications sector. The South Korean state found it hard to play a developmental role in setting the indigenous mobile broadcasting standard because its efficacy in developing new firms was circumvented by the dominance of large chaebol (S. Y. Kim 2012, 161; see also Jho 2007). While the state has attempted to nurture upstream, high-tech start-ups specializing in core components and solutions, the dominance of such chaebol as Samsung and LG in downstream areas, that is, handsets and services, has made them the technological and market centers for such small start-up firms founded, ironically, by former researchers working in these chaebol's own laboratories.

Because of their intimate knowledge of these chaebol's customers, these small firms are strategically more aligned with the interest of the large chaebol than with state-sponsored institutes or policies.

In Taiwan, a similar trend of declining significance of publicly funded research institutes and state agencies has occurred since the early 1990s. The share of private enterprises in Taiwan's R&D expenditure grew rapidly from 21.8 percent in 1978 to reach 52.8 percent in 1990, 64.9 percent in 2000, and 71.2 percent in 2010.[78] The pioneering role of these public R&D institutes has significantly diminished since the early 1990s.[79] As described by Chu (2007, 166), "Before 1990, virtually all consortia were forms of direct provision of technology services by quasi public R&D institutes. Firms provided only funds to the projects, most of which were highly subsidized by the MOEA [Ministry of Economic Affairs]. After about 1990, the consortia were transformed from simultaneous subsidized technology transfer to genuine consortia with horizontal and vertical dependence among firms, and a significant degree of cooperation among competitors." The pioneering role of these public R&D institutes has significantly diminished since the early 1990s. In the semiconductor industry, Mathews and Cho (2000, 181) observe that while "ERSO [a part of ITRI] was the vehicle for technology transfer and adaptation in the 1970s and 1980s, in the final phase of development of the semiconductor industry the private sector has itself become involved in a series of technology import measures." Similarly, Breznitz (2007, 142) observes that "ITRI, especially its Computer and Communication Lab (CCL), changed from being the leader and initiator of the industry, especially in semiconductors, into being a supporting actor in the 1990s, particularly as the main provider of R&D services in the industrial system, as well as an important channel for foreign technology."

In addition to this changing role of state-sponsored research institutes toward technology channeling through their technology-transfer programs, my own interviews with engineers and executives in state agencies and leading semiconductor firms in Taiwan further show that the developmental role of the state during the 1970s and the 1980s was delivered mainly through spin-offs from ERSO and ITRI rather than through direct state allocation of credits to the industry. These spin-offs, such as UMC (1980), TSMC (1986), Winbond (1987), and Vanguard (1994), were clearly subject to market forces because their survival was entirely dependent on business cycles in the global semiconductor industry.[80] As noted by my interview with senior officials from the MOEA, the state did not believe in offering a direct subsidy: "The principle of the government to help the market is to use the strategy of spin-off. That's the key point. So when TSMC/UMC were spun off from ITRI, the IC/semiconductor industry began to prosper and develop. . . . Our strategy is that we refrain from giving funds directly to the industry, but we encourage the institute to spin off new companies. The new companies can cluster together and form a new industry."[81] As more technological initiatives involved alliances with global lead firms, there were also firm-specific limits to the strong role of the state in steering high-tech development.[82]

By the turn of the new millennium, large firms in Taiwan's electronics industry were much more active than state-sponsored institutions in pursuing independent R&D work and thus received more patents from the United States Patent and Trademark Office (USPTO).[83] In 2001, ITRI received only 219 US utility patents, whereas TSMC (including its subsidiary Vanguard), UMC, and Hon Hai Precision posted respectively 691, 629, and 309 US utility patents. More specifically, while TSMC was perhaps the most celebrated success of ITRI's four spin-offs, the vital role of Philips as a source of both the initial technology and capital investment must be acknowledged. Indeed, Philips remained as the largest shareholder of TSMC until the mid-2000s, gradually reducing its ownership stake from the initial 40–50 percent to about 20 percent in 2000 and 13.6 percent in 2003. Ironically, the initial technology from Philips was not cutting edge. The catching-up in world-leading wafer fabrication process technology was only achieved at least ten years later by the late 1990s through TSMC's internal R&D efforts.[84] By the mid-2000s, the role of ERSO-ITRI in the semiconductor field was to provide supporting initiatives, such as environmental concerns. But these were no longer core technology in the industry: "ITRI provides environmental protection research and this is very good, e.g., how to enhance power efficiency and so on. ITRI does a lot of things. But in terms of core technology, even if we need it, they can't do it."[85] In the ICT industry, state-sponsored research institutes are neither the technology-creating agent nor the main provider of R&D services and technology channeling. Domestic firms have developed strong internal R&D capabilities to access such cutting-edge technologies.

As the three economies became more industrialized and diversified in their economic structures over time, the state's capacity in financing further expansion plans across different industries was limited. *Leveraging on global finance* served as the primary source of capital for leading firms from these economies. By the late 1980s, private sector firms from South Korea and Taiwan had relied much less on state funding and state bank credits to finance the deepening of their in-house R&D efforts and firm-specific development plans. They increasingly turned to capital markets in their home economies and in major international financial centers, such as New York and London. Since the 1990s, the growing accessibility of global finance has significantly strengthened the efforts of these leading East Asian firms in building their dynamic capabilities in technology, management, marketing, and other organizational know-how. Global finance has also undermined the developmental alliance between state-controlled domestic financial institutions and major industrial firms. Global financial integration has worked hand in hand with financial opening and market liberalization sanctioned, ironically, by the same developmental state to enable private firms to cut the umbilical cord that had previously nurtured them.

In South Korea, the liberalization of official controls on outward investment by domestic firms in 1986 had allowed South Korean chaebol to take on globalization as their raison d'être. When the Ministry of Finance under Roh Tae Woo's regime allowed local securities houses to raise funds directly in foreign capital markets in 1988, the regulatory chain on the chaebol's reckless globalization drive based on short-term foreign debt financing was finally unleashed. In the 1990s, President Kim Young-Sam pushed for globalization, or *segyehwa*, by loosening regulatory control over short-term capital inflows. With their dominant control of nonbank financial institutions (NBFIs) by the late 1980s, the chaebol could now bypass the state's regulatory regime and raise new funds abroad through their in-house financial vehicles or through issuing stocks in domestic and international capital markets. In 1990, South Korea had only six foreign-affiliated merchant banks. By 1996, some twenty-four newly licensed merchant banks had been established to undertake most of the domestic commercial paper issuing and discounting business. Sixteen of them were owned by the chaebol (B. K. Kim 2003, 63).[86] The chaebol became more dependent on their NBFIs and the global capital market for corporate financing. Endowed with both financial and human resources, the chaebol were able to benefit from the still imperfect market-supporting institutions and to increase further their investment size and business scope (H. Kim 2010, 165).

In Taiwan, the domestic capital market was not well developed until the late 1980s and the domestic banking sector failed to put Taiwan's high levels of savings into productive capital for industrial development. Private sector firms had to rely mostly on debt-financing to fund their business development. While large firms tended to borrow from state-owned banks, SMEs went to the informal curb market (Thurbon 2007, 94; Leou 2011, 125–26). The domestic banking and nonbank financial sectors were not liberalized until the first "Big Bang" through the new Banking Law in 1992 that prompted the emergence of sixteen private commercial banks mostly tied to business conglomerates (Wu 2007, 985). Meanwhile, a new breed of high-tech firms had emerged, and their technopreneurs were more financially savvy than entrepreneurs in traditional family firms and domestic business groups. Their experience in working for high-tech firms in the United States during the 1970s and the 1980s gave them solid knowledge and access to financing through capital markets. Between 1988 and 2000, a large number of today's leading ICT firms from Taiwan were publicly listed on the Taiwan Stock Exchange (TSE) after its liberalization in the late 1980s.[87] When it had completed its first full year of operation in 1963, the TSE had only 24 listed firms with a market value of NT$19 billion. By 1986, the number of listed firms had increased to 130 and the market value had grown to NT$548 billion. The lifting of martial law and the rapid appreciation of the New Taiwan dollar in 1987 resulted in massive increase in the trading value and total market value of these listed firms. During the 1980–1987 period, only 38 new firms were listed on the TSE. Between

1988 and 2000, however, the number of listed firms increased more than threefold from 163 to 531, and the total amount of capital increase also expanded more than ninefold from NT$41.6 billion to NT$389 billion. The successful IPOs of high-tech ICT firms on the TSE during this period therefore transformed the structure of corporate financing from a bank-led to an equity-based endeavor and rapidly expanded the market capitalization of firms listed on the Taiwan Stock Exchange. These "globalizing" firms could engage in their own technological acquisition and production expansion without necessarily conforming to the state's industrial planning and financial incentives.

As an international financial center, Singapore presents a rather different case from South Korea and Taiwan. While financing has always been a major obstacle to the growth and development of domestic small- and medium-sized enterprises, the developmental bottleneck can be attributed more to the conservative lending policy of domestic private and government-controlled banks. For large domestic firms, Singapore has been a gateway to a wide range of financial services almost since the beginning of its industrialization in the late 1960s. Domestic firms did not face the kind of financial restrictions imposed on private firms in South Korea and Taiwan. The developmental state in Singapore also did not practice discretionary allocation of bank credits to finance industrialization projects.[88] However, despite its political dominance, the PAP-led state is not well insulated from the interests of the banking community. In fact, Hamilton-Hart (2000; 2002) argues that Singapore's state bureaucracy has little autonomy outside the financial sector and the political leadership is quite entwined with leading members of the financial community.[89] Unlike the substantial autonomy enjoyed by central banks in South Korea and Taiwan since the mid-1980s, Singapore's central bank, the Monetary Authority of Singapore (MAS), can hardly be seen as independent of the PAP state.[90] Given the relatively small pool of top leaders in the PAP state, this close relationship between cabinet ministers and top civil servants and local banks contributes significantly to a form of institutional capture of the state bureaucracy by interest groups in the financial sector.

Before the 1990s, this institutional capture allowed the emergence of major domestic banking institutions under the protectionist policies of the state, an irony of Singapore's continuous effort to be a global financial center and a major player in financial globalization. But this relatively stable relationship between domestic financial institutions and the state did not last long. Primarily because of the intensification of global competition and the state's recognition of the need to develop Singapore as a leading international financial center, financial market liberalization was initiated through formal state policies before and in the aftermath of the 1997–1998 Asian economic crisis (Yeung 2000; Chong 2007). The financial liberalization program started in 1990 when MAS raised foreign shareholdings of Singapore banks from 20 percent to 40 percent. Foreign banks could compete freely with local banks in wholesale domestic banking, offshore banking, and treasury and capital market activities. They accounted for more than one-third of resident deposits, 45 percent of loans to resident borrowers, and about 90 percent of business with nonresidents (*Straits Times*, May 17, 1999, 38). What makes the Singapore case different from South Korea and Taiwan is that this financial market liberalization proceeded gradually under the close supervision of such state institutions as the Ministry of Finance and MAS. As former prime minister Lee Kuan Yew has stated, "What we did was out of our own convictions, but it coincided with the IMF and US Treasury prescription on how to develop a financial free market" (Lee 2000, 552–53).

Conclusion

In this chapter, I have argued that a strict conception of embedded autonomy may well explain the *initial* origin of certain state-initiated industrialization projects in the three East Asian economies during the 1960s and the 1970s. But this statist view cannot adequately account for the evolutionary dynamics of key actors emerging from these state-led projects and rapidly growing new firms and industries during the next two decades in the 1980s and the 1990s. Changing international geopolitical contexts and a greater desire for democracy and pressures for welfare from domestic interest groups and social movements compelled the state in these economies to adjust and adapt to a new political economy in which the state could no longer wield unlimited and autonomous power in governing the market and in directing the growth trajectories of national firms. This chapter has shown the significant transformation of state involvement toward more catalytic roles since the late 1980s. Successful industrial transformation in the preceding decades did change the basis of subsequent state involvement in relation to core state components, institutions, and policy instruments. My analysis thus adds important political economy dynamics to Evans's (1995, 225) comparative institutional approach that "offered some ideas about how states might affect industrial transformation but had relatively little to say about how this transformation would change the basis of subsequent state involvement."

Between the late 1980s and the 2000s, the developmental state in these East Asian economies experienced varying degrees of decline in political autonomy and growing institutional fragmentation. The state's shift toward functional industrial policy also varied in relation to its changing domestic-international linkages. In South Korea, the state had started to change by the early 1980s and has since been reconstituted as a postdevelopmental state. The deregulation and liberalization of the domestic economy in successive political regimes gave the chaebol an unprecedented opportunity to increase their dominance in the domestic market and to venture rapidly into the global economy. The state's elite agencies were dismantled and reorganized into different and even competing loci of policy making. In Taiwan, the state was more fragmented during the late 1980s and the 1990s. While the state's industrial policy in high-tech development was relatively more cohesive and developed during the 1980s, its effectiveness was critically dependent on the emergent capabilities of private sector firms and new technopreneurs who willingly took on these projects. Political upheavals in the late 1990s and throughout the 2000s created further instability in state bureaucracy. Electoral politics came to trump sound economic policies as the principal concern of different political parties and weakened state agencies. Of the three economies, only the Singapore's PAP-led state was able to weather the relative decline in institutional capacity in an era of globalization and liberalization. The Singapore state maintained its developmental posture through its domination of domestic politics, its continual renewal of political leadership, and the bureaucratic rationality in its elite pilot agencies. Since the late 1990s, however, even the PAP state has begun to concede more to demands from domestic capital and social groups. New national strategic plans have been developed and implemented to foster technological development, nurture domestic firms, and expand its national economy through direct investment abroad.

Meanwhile, the changing international environment during the 1990s created tremendous opportunities for latecomer firms in the three economies to upgrade their firm-specific capabilities and to upscale their capacities. Three decades of successful policy interventions by the developmental state had produced a whole army of leading national firms that could compete on their own feet in the global economy. In key manufacturing sectors, leading domestic firms accumulated substantial experience through producing for exports and moved rapidly toward original design and branding. Others emerged from imitators to become original innovators. These firms developed firm-specific capabilities and new organizational processes through reverse "brain drain" and overseas returnees whose presence led to the intensification of their in-house R&D activity and their success in gaining access to global finance. By the turn of the new millennium, these East Asian firms were no longer "junior partners" to a postdevelopmental state. Disembedding from their earlier dependence on the state for capital and technologies, these East Asian firms took on a more direct role in steering their respective industries and sectors, a role previously occupied by the developmental state. The successful articulation of national firms into global production networks also rendered state planning in such areas as developing sectoral industrial policy and picking national champions increasingly difficult and ineffective. In the next chapter, I offer a conceptualization of this reembedding of domestic capital and national firms in global production networks since the late 1990s.

Chapter 3

Strategic Coupling

East Asian Firms in Global Production Networks

Building on the previous chapter's analysis of changing state roles and emerging firm capabilities in East Asian economies, this chapter develops *strategic coupling* as an integrative midrange concept and elucidates its structural conditions and meso-level operationalization in dynamic network relations. This conceptualization paves the way for analyzing the empirical dynamics of national-global articulations in shaping industrial transformation and its divergent outcomes in the next three chapters.[1] I argue that the successful articulation of domestic firms from these economies into global production networks is dependent on the necessary process of strategic coupling through which these latecomer firms' emergent capabilities and organizational choices must couple with the evolving strategies and intents of global lead firms in their coordination and orchestration of production networks across different territorial ensembles. Strategic coupling is therefore defined as a mutually dependent and constitutive process involving particular ties, shared interests, and cooperation between two or more groups of economic actors who otherwise might not act in tandem to achieve a common strategic objective.[2] In the East Asian context, these actors refer to domestic firms and global lead firms in different industries. Their translocal and transnational interactions involve both material flows in transactional terms (e.g., components, modules, and finished products) and nonmaterial flows (e.g., capital, information, intelligence, services, and practices). While the statist political economy approach might explain the initial preconditions for state-selected national champions to grow and prosper in their home economies, it is inadequate in illuminating how these existing national firms break away from their structural dependence on the developmental state and articulate gradually into global production networks over time. Nor is it dynamic enough to account for the rise of *new* domestic firms originating from the postdevelopmental state era in these economies.

This chapter begins with the first section offering an evolutionary perspective on strategic coupling. I conceptualize briefly the processes of national firms disembedding from domestic states and reembedding into global production networks. Thereafter, my strategy is to highlight in three further sections the structural conditions and dynamic operationalization favorable to strategic coupling, before presenting the East Asian national contexts in which such coupling has taken place since the 2000s. Specifically, the second section analyzes three favorable conditions for strategic coupling. As strategic coupling requires East Asian firms to venture beyond their domestic economies and to participate directly in the global economy, its realization is generally premised on the emergence of transnational communities, dynamic changes in industrial organization, and domestic institutional support. The third section focuses on the operationalization of strategic coupling in interfirm relations, as the key conceptual roadmap for subsequent empirical chapters. I outline three such coupling processes of strategic partnership, industrial market specialization, and (re)positioning as global lead firms. Taken together, these two sections offer a broad-based global production networks perspective on the emergence of domestic firms from East Asian economies and the dynamics of their industrial transformation.[3] The final section extends the discussion of changing state roles and emergent firm capabilities in the previous chapter to recast the dominant position of leading domestic firms in each of the three East Asian economies since the 2000s.

The Nature of Strategic Coupling

As the overarching concept for this book, strategic coupling illustrates how East Asian firms *can* become articulated into the competitive imperatives of lead firms in global production networks over time; it is about dynamic relational processes that mediate their common interests and collective action. In general, this strategic coupling process exhibits several distinctive attributes. First, it is strategic because the process does not happen without active involvement and intentional action on the part of the participants (e.g., firms and states). Actor-specific initiatives are important because they activate these relational processes that connect individual initiatives eventually to intended or unintended developmental outcomes. Moreover, these actor-specific initiatives are strategic because actors choose certain courses of action in relation to their particular objectives and constraints. As argued by Mathews (2006), strategizing is most useful and profitable in a market condition of disequilibrium because such condition allows for the arbitraging of different opportunities.[4] This view of strategizing as an intentional act is consistent with the Schumpeterian conception of entrepreneurship, which postulates the function of the entrepreneur as someone serving as a disruptive force in an economy that has reached a static equilibrium. Through carrying out "new combinations"

(Schumpeter 1934, 66), the entrepreneur disrupts an existing static equilibrium in the economy and forces it into disequilibrium. This disruptive process, popularly known as creative destruction, allows for our reconsideration of leading East Asian firms as the primary actor in the transformation of their home economies.

Second, strategic coupling is time-space contingent because the coupling process is not permanent and is therefore subject to change. This contingent view does not seek to ascribe universal causality for such a coupling process to take place. Indeed, a typical strategic coupling resembles the formation of a temporary coalition among different actors and institutions within specific global production networks; it is historically emergent and geographically mutable. But as the strategies and intents of actors in these networks evolve and change in response to new selection environments, such as changing market conditions, technological shifts, or state interventions, this temporary coalition may be reconstituted to sustain and reproduce the network as a whole. As detailed in the following chapters, the component processes of strategic coupling are an empirical matter and can only be ascertained in relation to particular sets of firms, industries, and economies situated in their historical-geographical contexts. Third, the convergence process of strategic coupling transcends territorial boundaries and geographical scales, as actors from different spatial sites (firms, states, regions, and economies) converge and their practices radiate out to diverse geographical scales—some global and some highly local. The role of the state in a particular national economy is constrained by the simultaneous operation of this process at multiple geographical scales. In short, no single state or nonstate institution, no matter how internally cohesive and institutionally autonomous, can dominate and control this process.

In figure 3.1, this process of strategic coupling is illustrated with reference to East Asian firms, their home states, and global lead firms that are incorporated into an evolving state-firm-global production networks assemblage. As a starting point in the upper left box, the *embedded relationship* between the autonomous developmental state and the chosen national firms in East Asia was primarily developed when the state was institutionally strong (in bold), particularly during the early phase of industrialization in the 1950s through to the early 1980s. This strong state-firm developmental coalition worked well until the late 1980s when the changing domestic and international dynamics of state developmentalism made it much harder for the state to impose its political will and discretionary policy on national firms. As its domestic firms had grown up to become increasingly significant industrial players in the domestic and international markets, an evolutionary shift occurred in the state's role from "midwifery" or "husbandry" to that of a "nursing" or "catalyst" role. Since then, these domestic firms have become increasingly articulated into global production networks.

There are two mutually constitutive moments in this process of strategic coupling. The first moment (lower left box) refers to the *disembedding* of domestic/

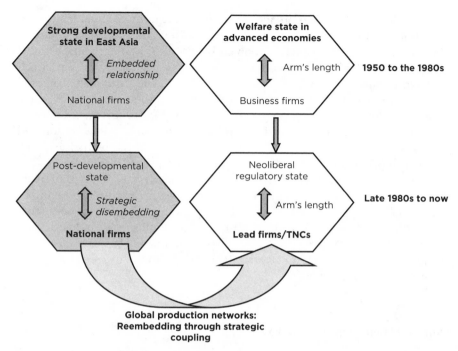

Figure 3.1. From embedded autonomy to strategic coupling: the evolutionary dynamics of the state-firm-global production networks assemblage.

national firms (in bold) from the postdevelopmental state since the late 1980s in response to the changing selection environment discussed in chapter 2. As the global economy no longer represents, in Kohli's (2004, 417) words, "bottlenecks to sustained profitability," these national firms have evolved to become more economically powerful and politically potent in the face of the postdevelopmental state in their home economies. The second moment points to the *reembedding* of these national firms in global production networks coordinated by lead firms from advanced industrialized economies. Both types of firms (in bold) have emerged as the principal economic actors in their national economies since the 2000s. While not necessarily a mirror image of each other, these two moments are often intertwined. The growing disembedding of domestic firms from home states may precipitate the reembedding of these economic actors in another organizational platform, such as global production networks, through which these national firms can gain access to resources, technology, knowledge, and markets.

As illustrated in the right hand boxes in figure 3.1, the profound transition from the Fordist welfare state to the neoliberal regulatory state in advanced industrialized economies during the same historical period has also produced a new regime of capitalist accumulation in which flexible specialization and production globalization have emerged as the quintessential features of the dominant paradigm of industrial capitalism.[5] In *The Second Industrial Divide*, Piore and Sabel (1984) describe this episodic shift in organizing global capitalism as a form of post-Fordism or flexible specialization through which industrial transformation was manifested in flexible intrafirm relations, rapid vertical disintegration of production processes, and the emergence of extensive hybrid forms of organizing production, such as subcontracting, outsourcing, and offshoring. From this debris of post-Fordist deindustrialization and capitalism's incessant drive for innovation, major lead firms and their expanding global production networks have emerged in different propulsive industries, such as automobiles, electronics, semiconductors, machinery, and so on. Lead firms from advanced industrialized economies have actively reorganized their production on a global basis.[6] This expanding set of global production networks spearheaded by lead firms in different high-growth industries has provided East Asian firms, already gradually disembedded from their less interventionist home states, an unprecedented opportunity to seek growth and development in the global arena.

Structural Conditions for Strategic Coupling

By the end of the 2000s, a variety of domestic firms from the three East Asian economies had emerged to be major regional and/or global players in a wide range of production networks in different industrial sectors. A handful of South Korean chaebol firms had become major global firms in the information and communications technology (ICT) and automobile industries. Such global significance can also be observed in the case of a larger number of ICT business groups from Taiwan. Almost without exception, private-sector capitalists led all of these globally competitive firms from South Korea and Taiwan, a clear reflection of the evolutionary shift in state-firm relations in these two economies since the late 1980s. The case of Singaporean firms points to a different developmental trajectory because both government-linked companies and private firms had grown beyond their domestic role and emerged to become major regional and global firms. This divergence in the evolution and sectoral specialization of leading firms from the three economies reflects their differential strategic coupling with global production networks. The *domestic* significance and capabilities of these East Asian firms, described more in the last section of this chapter, should be viewed as both an enabling condition for and an outcome of their successful coupling with global production networks. While domestic factors, such as a strong developmental state and its sectoral industrial policy, were critical to the early founding and development of *some* of these East Asian firms, their strategic coupling since the 2000s required substantial firm-specific initiatives and resources and favorable internal and external conditions that went well beyond the institutional capacity of the postdevelopmental state.

To understand better this emergent process of national-global articulations, it is necessary to analyze the structural conditions that transcend the domestic arena and favor the articulation of particular national firms into the global economy. At the conceptual level, strategic coupling is premised on three structural conditions: (1) the emergence of transnational communities, (2) dynamic changes in industrial organization, and (3) more sophisticated state-firm relations and supportive industrial policy. To begin, the critical role of communities and social capital in economic development is now well recognized. One such community refers to the transnational elite professionals and entrepreneurs who constantly shuttle around the globe.[7] To Malerba and Nelson (2011; 2012), these *transnational communities* are critical to firm-specific learning, access to global knowledge and technologies, and skilled human capital development. Exemplified fully in Saxenian's (2006) *The New Argonauts*, these transnational elite communities have rewritten the concept of international knowledge formation, from one of "brain drain" to a two-way process of "brain circulation." Through their constant movements between different regions of the world, these technologists and entrepreneurs have formed a transnational community of informal "brain networks" characterized by a certain common social identity and, sometimes, ethnic or nationalistic sentiments. As described further by Levy (2008, 953), global production networks "exist within the 'transnational space' that is constituted and structured by transnational elites, institutions, and ideologies. . . . Within this space, transnational communities emerge with economic systems, relations of power, and institutional forms that are distinct from, though interacting with, national or region-bound forms."

Indeed, the business practices of these transnational communities have contributed to the formal coupling of firms and institutions from the three East Asian economies with lead firms in global production networks through a variety of organizational arrangements. As argued by Saxenian (2002, 183, 186), "these communities have the potential to play an increasingly important role in the evolution of global production networks. Transnational entrepreneurs and their communities provide a significant mechanism for the international diffusion of knowledge and the creation and upgrading of local capabilities." In terms of knowledge flows, transnational technopreneurs can serve as the critical bridge for firms in domestic innovation systems and global production networks. Leveraging on their previous managerial and/or technical positions in global lead firms, these transnational technopreneurs can also bring about important business opportunities for strategic coupling with global lead firms.[8] Once this transnational community has been developed, their key members are often involved in leading some of the largest ICT firms from the three East Asian economies that have emerged to be both powerful competitors to and strategic partners with global lead firms in North America and Western Europe.

The second structural condition refers to *changing industrial organization*. For transnational communities to work effectively in coupling domestic firms with global lead firms, there must be favorable industrial dynamics that are structurally open to such coupling possibilities. In other words, the mere existence of these transnational technopreneurs and their actor-specific initiatives does not necessarily guarantee the strategic coupling of domestic firms with global production networks. These networks must be structurally reorganized and reconfigured in ways amenable to these meso-level coupling processes. Driven by greater cost pressures, market development imperatives, and intense financial discipline, global lead firms are often compelled to adopt organizational and technological innovations in order to fix their competitive problems.[9] These competitive fixes are implemented primarily through increasing fragmentation of production and vertical specialization in global industries that create a new form of industrial organization. This in turn provides a crucial condition for East Asian firms to articulate into evolving global production networks and, in doing so, for their home economies to experience continuous industrial transformation that can no longer be directed by the domestic state. This industrial-organizational view of the historically specific window of opportunity is important for my analysis of its strategic exploitation by East Asian firms through coupling with different global production networks. As noted by Hobday (1995, 195; my emphasis), "The form, depth and breadth of East Asian organizational innovations were new to the marketplace and to the world and therefore constitute innovation in the most meaningful sense of the word. Indeed, the manner in which regional development occurred under OEM and sub-contracting with foreign firms is a significant departure with no obvious historical parallel. It is a *new large-scale feature* of economic development only witnessed in the latter part of the 20th century."

In particular, the rise of vertical specialization engaged by brand name and/or original equipment manufacturing (OEM) firms in many global industries is linked to the vertical (intrafirm) disintegration of value chain activity within individual lead firms and the subsequent horizontal (interfirm) reintegration of this activity in geographically dispersed locations. This process of vertical disintegration and reintegration provides a structural platform for East Asian firms to connect with global lead firms and to develop strong interfirm partnerships on the basis of mutually beneficial exploitation of firm-specific advantages, such as market access and product development (global lead firms) and manufacturing capabilities and quality of services (East Asian firms).[10] As exemplified in later chapters, this interfirm coupling process can be effective in both manufacturing and service industries. Moreover, this changing industrial organization is greatly facilitated by technological changes, such as the modularization of production in the ICT and automobile industries. Technological advancement in production facilities through continuous investment is equally significant in the development of firm-specific capability among East Asian firms. Primarily because of their capability, flexibility, response time, and cost competitiveness, East Asian firms in particular industrial districts and high-growth regions bring significant benefits to global lead firms in various industries and sectors. To a large extent, they have developed strong firm-specific capabilities to serve as "systems integrators" who put together different suppliers of technologies and products to serve the strategic imperatives of their global lead firm customers.[11] These emerging organizational-technological capabilities of East Asian firms thus enable their strategic coupling with global production networks.

As these East Asian firms become more articulated into global industries under the favorable conditions of expanding transnational communities of technopreneurs and changing industrial-organizational dynamics, it is important for us *not* to forget the *continual supportive role* of the state and its multifarious institutions. While the central role of the state in steering and directing economic development has somewhat diminished over time, the availability of these transnational communities and organizational-technological capabilities of domestic actors can still be complemented by the renewed efforts of postdevelopmental state institutions in paving way for this strategic coupling to take place. In other words, favorable domestic state initiatives are structurally important for East Asian firms to couple with global lead firms. But the state and its policy efforts are not efficacious if the first two conditions do not exist or are not effective. In short, the state cannot do it alone. The successful articulation of domestic economies into the global economy therefore requires the favorable conditions of transnational communities and industrial dynamics whose positive recursive effects can be further strengthened through supportive state initiatives. In this sense, the evolving political economy of state-firm relations and the broader shift toward horizontal or functional industrial policy during the 1990s and the 2000s can be viewed as the state's renewed efforts in grounding and localizing transnational flows of economic activity orchestrated by global lead firms in different high-growth industries. Developmental or otherwise, the state matters because its initiatives can *condition*, though not determine, the ways in which domestic firms are strategically coupled with global lead firms. Generally, the state's horizontal industrial policy is well manifested in terms of incentives and investments in physical infrastructure, research capacity, entrepreneurial start-ups, and human resources.

In the three East Asian economies, the state has been actively promoting the ICT industry as the key growth sector since the 1970s, although they have taken different pathways to achieve such an aggressive objective. Whereas South Korea and Taiwan rely mostly on domestic firms in collaboration with foreign high-tech companies from the United States and, later, Japan, Singapore is much more open to the local presence of global lead firms in the ICT industry. All three states have aggressively invested in infrastructures (e.g., science parks), research institutes (e.g., Korea Electronics Technology Institute; Taiwan's Industrial Technology Research Institute; and Singapore's Agency for Science, Technology and Research), and sometimes, high-tech, capital-intensive start-ups (e.g., TSMC, UMC, and Chartered Semiconductor).[12] These states have also provided generous incentives to attract returning technopreneurs who have developed successful careers in Silicon Valley and elsewhere.[13]

Unlike Taiwan, however, South Korea's developmental state was directly involved in picking industrial winners and subsidizing their investment up to the
late 1980s. Lacking indigenous capability in the manufacturing industry, the
state in Singapore has been active in attracting world-class electronics companies, such as Hewlett-Packard, Philips, General Electric, Seagate, Toshiba, and
Matsushita, to locate their high-value activities in Singapore. The rise of some
leading domestic firms is directly linked to the kind of global industries and
global lead firms brought into Singapore through such pilot agencies as the
Economic Development Board (EDB).[14]

The role of state institutions in these three economies has also been important in enhancing human resources and physical infrastructure in respective
industrial districts and growth regions. In 2002, for example, the total cost of
an integrated circuit chip engineer in East Asia was only 10 to 20 percent of
that in Silicon Valley (Ernst 2005, table 3; 2009, 29). This is no doubt a direct
outcome of state involvement in developing human resources and physical infrastructure. The consequence for economic development is staggering, as a
result of the growing cost competitiveness of leading East Asian firms in chip
design and engineering capabilities, it stimulates both the relocation of chip
design work from Silicon Valley and elsewhere in developed economies to
leading high-tech clusters in East Asia. Another role of state institutions in
the strategic coupling of domestic firms with global lead firms has to do with
the rapid growth of public-private R&D consortiums. In Taiwan and Singapore, these consortiums are strategically developed in high-growth industries,
and they serve as a direct conduit to couple the strategic interests of both
local high-tech firms and global lead firms. They also represent a form of
state-sponsored collective action to reduce excessive competition among participating firms and to develop path-breaking technologies.[15]

State agencies in Taiwan, for example, play an active role in matching global
lead firms with local firms by inviting and sponsoring the former's R&D centers
to be established in Taiwan: "We have a well developed supply chain. So we get
the order to engage in OEM production for MNCs [multinational corpora-
tions], and then they think that if they can set up R&D centers in Taiwan, they
can shorten the manufacturing time. Also some of them can let Taiwanese
companies and industry be involved in their R&D activity."[16] In the optoelectronics (TFT-LCD) industry, for example, twenty-three global lead firm R&D
centers of companies such as Intel, Sony, and IBM, and seventy local firm
R&D centers were established in the first three years of the launch of the Challenge 2008 six-year development plan in 2002. As argued by Fuller (2008,
254), the fact that this program went beyond one presidential term (2000–
2004) indicates the heavy influence of the economic bureaucracy in terms of
planning and execution. While Taiwan was strong in the mid- and downstream
parts of the industry (i.e., panel production and applications) by the mid-
2000s, it still had to rely on importing foreign technology in upstream material
supply for the industry.[17] The Industrial Development Bureau thus engaged

trade and investment firms to identify and target specific foreign firms that were subsequently invited to invest in R&D activity in Taiwan.

These state-led initiatives, however, should not be seen as the only, or even the most important, determinant of the successful articulation of domestic economies into the global ICT industry since the 2000s. Following my earlier analysis of changing state roles in chapter 2, I view these initiatives as part of the state's broader catalyst role in stimulating such articulation and coupling of domestic firms through its "spurring" efforts and functional industrial policy in favor of domestic firms supplying higher-value key components to global lead firms or providing more sophisticated manufacturing and design services for global lead firms. In this more complicated scenario of national-global articulations, a statecentric view of industrial transformation cannot encompass the divergent goals and strategies of domestic firms in their pursuit of competitive success in and through global production networks. The strategic goals of, and their implementation by, these domestic firms also do not necessarily align or reconcile with the state's policy goals. As we will find out in the next three empirical chapters, many leading East Asian firms have defied the logic of state planning and policy goals and developed a unique set of business models and growth trajectories that couple with the strategic imperatives of their major partners and customers in different global production networks. This divergent outcome of domestic firms participating in global industries and its implication for rethinking industrial transformation requires us to identify explicitly the specific component processes of strategic coupling.

Dynamic Operation of Coupling Processes

The deeper articulation of East Asian firms into global production networks since the late 1990s is premised on the simultaneous presence of both domestic evolutionary state-firm relations and favorable competitive dynamics in the global economy. Without the transformation of the developmental state since the late 1980s (described in chapter 2), East Asian firms might never have been "allowed" to venture out on their own and to participate in different global industries; these domestic firms also might not have grown out of their role as dependents or junior partners of the developmental state. While this changing domestic political economy is a necessary condition, it is insufficient to ensure the strategic coupling of East Asian firms with global production networks. Without favorable competitive dynamics on a global scale, such as vertical disintegration and flexible specialization, different global lead firms might not have taken advantage of the emerging organizational-technological capabilities of these East Asian firms, and strategic coupling might not have occurred. And without successful strategic coupling, industrial transformation in these economies might have been halted or locked into a particular historical "low road" of economic development.

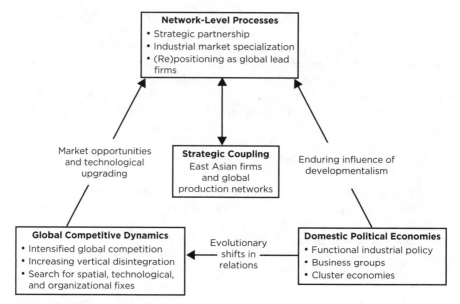

Figure 3.2. Conceptual framework for analyzing the strategic coupling of East Asian firms with global production networks.

As the analytical roadmap for the subsequent empirical chapters, figure 3.2 consolidates this book's conceptual discussion so far in relation to *domestic political economies* (home base advantages) and *global competitive dynamics* (vertical disintegration). Both sets of institutionalized conditions shape the developmental trajectories of East Asian firms through the enduring influence of capitalist developmentalism and the new opportunities for market access and technological upgrading. Nevertheless, I argue that *meso-level* network processes are as, if not more, important in determining the nature and efficacy of this strategic coupling in different sectors or different segments of the same sectors—South Korea in consumer electronics, semiconductors, shipbuilding, and automobiles; Taiwan in electronics and semiconductors; and Singapore in electronics, transport, marine engineering, banking, telecommunications, and trading. Political-economic and industrial-organizational dynamics, while becoming more conducive to these national firms over time, remain as *external* conditions influencing intra- and interfirm strategic relations. They do not directly enable us to understand why global lead firms choose these East Asian firms as their strategic partners and/or how these East Asian firms emerge to become leading specialized industrial players in their own right. In other words, these changing domestic political economies and global competitive dynamics are useful for us to situate and contextualize the effectiveness of dynamic coupling processes engaged by different East Asian capitalists through their firm-specific initiatives.

In figure 3.2's top box, I draw analytical attention to three such network-level component processes that collectively constitute strategic coupling. The first component process refers to *strategic partnership* through which East Asian firms develop strong firm-based competence and work with global lead firms as network partners in order to gain access to technology and market. As latecomers lacking technological and market know-how, many East Asian firms started off as subcontractors for global lead firms by engaging in a kind of organizational relationship generally known as OEM suppliers. In this mode of international subcontracting, East Asian suppliers to OEM firms experienced a limited scope for technological upgrading, as their global lead firm customers often controlled product specifications, manufacturing equipment, process technologies, and pricing and marketing. East Asian manufacturers pursuing this supplier role faced tremendous competitive pressures, as the barriers to entry in the OEM subcontracting market were relatively low.[18] Some East Asian firms have therefore chosen to bypass this low-cost approach of being OEM suppliers by engaging with a competence-based coupling process that enables them to emerge as strategic partners of global lead firms. Through continuous firm-specific investment in R&D capabilities and production efficiency, these East Asian firms have become original design manufacturing (ODM) firms and providers of integrated electronics manufacturing services (EMS). As ODM and EMS providers, they are much better positioned in value chain activities because they are seen as strategic partners in these global production networks. Global lead firms not only rely on these East Asian ODM and EMS providers for their manufacturing services, but more importantly engage their original design and research capabilities for new product development. These East Asian firms thus become strategic partners rather than merely subcontractors in the global production activities of brand name lead firms.[19]

The second coupling process engaged by leading East Asian firms is *industrial market specialization* on a regional and, sometimes, global basis. Instead of moving along the OEM-ODM continuum, these East Asian firms have taken particular initiatives to gain specialization in certain market or industrial niches and to develop sophisticated and proprietary expertise in these value chain activities. These activities can be specialized components, integrated modules, and full-scale services. In each type of value activity, these leading East Asian firms have accumulated substantial knowledge and experience in relation to their presence in the domestic market, as outlined in chapter 2. Over time, some of them have also developed "first-mover" advantages through new technological and organizational innovations that are difficult for their competitors or lead firm customers to imitate. In short, they have become world leaders in these highly specialized industrial markets for intermediate or finished goods. This coupling process of industrial market specialization therefore enables East Asian firms to play an integral role in diverse global production networks across a wide range of industries and markets.

The third coupling process, often the most difficult to succeed in, is for East Asian firms to *(re)position as global lead firms* through developing their own brand names and organizing service excellence. Transforming organizationally from OEM/ODM to global brand manufacturers or global service providers requires a quantum leap in strategic initiatives and high demand on firm-specific resources and competences. While leapfrogging in technological development in a latecomer situation might be possible through a process of "upscaling" of production capacity and capital investment—an important argument advanced in Amsden and Chu's (2003) *Beyond Late Development*—growing a globally recognizable brand name can be a daunting task. Still, some leading East Asian firms have successfully pursued this pathway to develop their own global production networks and win market shares in global competition. This strategic (re)orientation requires not only technological and managerial competencies but also market knowledge. As latecomers to the global economy, many East Asian firms are relatively slow in their globalization efforts. Those few East Asian firms that are at the forefront of globalization tend to become significant global players over time through establishing their own brand names and winning substantial market shares.

For these three component processes of strategic coupling to work, East Asian firms need to capitalize on emerging opportunities made available because of changing global competitive dynamics. The capacity of these East Asian firms to articulate into global production networks is also significantly shaped by the supportive institutional contexts of their domestic political economies. Taken together in figure 3.2, these three pillars underpinning the developmental trajectories of East Asian firms—appropriate network-level coupling processes, favorable global competitive dynamics, and supportive home bases—must be interactively present for them to compete effectively in the global economy. The evolutionary shift from embedded state-firm relations in domestic political economies toward dynamic interfirm relations embedded in global production networks constitutes a new state-firm-GPN assemblage. In short, *strategic coupling* takes place (middle box) when this reconfigured state-firm-GPN assemblage and network-level processes are complementary and mutually reinforcing. Even though not all East Asian firms march in lockstep to a particular set of coupling processes, I believe there is a fairly generalizable pattern in the empirical evidence to be presented later in this book. While not meant to be completely exhaustive, these three component processes are characteristic of the ways through which *most* leading East Asian firms have articulated into diverse production networks in global industries. Before I elucidate these coupling processes through detailed industry- and firm-specific analyses, I need to establish an up-to-date baseline of the role and significance of these East Asian firms in their domestic economies since the 2000s.

National Firms in East Asian Economies since the 2000s

During the 2000s, we witnessed not only the proven maturity and sophistication of East Asian firms, but also their crucial developmental role exercised through their strategic coupling with various global production networks spanning different high-growth industries. In the manufacturing sector, one proxy to measure such network embeddedness of East Asian firms is the value of trade in intermediate manufactured goods (IMG) in a particular national economy.[20] These goods are necessary parts, components, and partially manufactured modules in the global production of any final manufactured product. As indicated in table 3.1, South Korea, Taiwan, and Singapore experienced rapid growth in their exports of IMG between 1988 and 2006, a period during which these domestic states began to change their roles toward the functional support of firm-specific initiatives. Their individual share in world trade in IMG in 2006 was also much more significant than other developing countries, except China.[21] This proxy points to the central role of these East Asian *economies* as the geographical loci of manufacturing IMG in different global industries.

While the international trade data in table 3.1 are useful as a proxy indicator, it really tells us little about the significance of East Asian *firms* in their domestic economies and global production networks. We need to conduct a careful firm-based analysis to shed light on such a critical issue. Table 3.2 provides some data on the top business groups in South Korea, Taiwan, and Singapore in 1997 and 2003. These data represent the outcome of the restructuring and growth of these groups after the 1997–1998 Asian financial crisis. Two observations are relevant for my empirical analysis of the strategic coupling of East Asian firms.[22] First, the state's role as a dominant source of ownership capital has declined, particularly in South Korea and Taiwan. Two of South Korea's largest business groups in 1997, Korea Electric Power and POSCO, were state-owned, but they became independent by 2003. Several state-owned or state-linked banks also became independent. In Taiwan, a large number of state-owned banks in 1997 were restructured and privatized into independent financial holding institutions after the July 2001 reform in the financial sector under the Finance Holding Company Law. In Singapore, however, the role of government-linked companies in the top business groups remained mostly unchanged between 1997 and 2003.

Second and more important, high-tech manufacturing groups have rapidly emerged as the dominant business groups in South Korea and Taiwan.[23] In the ICT industry, Samsung and LG became the largest groups of electronics-related firms in South Korea in 2003. In Taiwan, twelve high-tech ICT firms dominated its twenty-seven largest business groups in 2003, which included seven financial institutions. Most of these ICT firms were established in the late 1980s when the state started to experience significant transformation in its developmentalist role. In 1997, only four of them (TSMC, UMC, Acer, and

Table 3.1 The role of East Asian economies in global production networks measured by value of total trade in intermediate manufactured goods (IMG), 1988–2006 (in US$billion and percentage)

Economy	World rank	Total IMG trade in 2006	Share of world total in 2006	Cumulative average growth rate, 1988–2006
Tiger economies				
South Korea	12	286.4	3.0	10.6
Taiwan	14	246.2	2.6	14.3
Singapore	11	289.6	3.0	17.2
Hong Kong	6	372.3	3.9	17.7
Total	—	1,194.7	—	14.9
China	3	807.9	8.5	24.0
Mexico	15	228.8	2.4	23.3
Malaysia	17	162.3	1.7	12.5
Thailand	18	121.1	1.3	13.2
India	21	114.1	1.2	11.7
Japan and North America	—	1,928.4	—	6.9
Western Europe	—	3,377.1	—	6.7
Top 50 economies	—	9,110.9	—	12.4

Source: Based on UN COMPTRADE data presented in Whittaker et al. (2010, 449, table 1).

Winbond) were ranked among the top thirty business groups. Hon Hai Precision, one of the two East Asian firms in the opening vignette in chapter 1, did not even make the top thirty list in 1997. But it rose swiftly to top five in 2003 and went on to become Taiwan's largest industrial firm since 2007. In the automobile industry, South Korea's Hyundai and Taiwan's Yulon emerged to be the leading automotive business groups in their economies. By the mid-2000s, these high-tech manufacturing firms and business groups had developed rapidly from their earlier role as followers and subcontractors to become market leaders and global players in their respective industries. The following three subsections analyze briefly the emergence of these firms in their changing domestic political-economic contexts since the 2000s.

South Korea: Growing Domination and Concentration of Chaebol Power

Since the 1997–1998 Asian financial crisis, the gradual transition toward a postdevelopmental state in South Korea, once arguably the strongest and most dictatorial among the three East Asian economies in steering national champions, has given the chaebol virtually a free hand in the domestic and international economies. Since the early 2000s, the chaebol groups have not only flouted directive policies initiated by the state but also have dominated the public discourse about the country's economic future.[24] The largest chaebol groups, such as Samsung, LG, Hyundai, and SK, have become the lead institutions steering industrial transformation in South Korea. The state has been turned into a mere follower of the strategic initiatives of these large business groups.[25] As evident in S. J. Chang (2003) and H. Kim (2010), this enormous concentration of corporate power in *fewer* chaebol groups was particularly pronounced in the 2000s. By the end of 1999, eleven of the top thirty chaebol in 1997 had gone bankrupt or been dissolved. Some of them were acquired by other chaebol (e.g., Kia by Hyundai Motor). Others were disaggregated and sold to different investors. For example, the Daewoo group was dissolved in 2000 through the disposal of intragroup companies previously owned and managed by Daewoo Corporation, the group's holding company.[26] Its automobile firm was sold to General Motors to become GM-Daewoo. Other Daewoo companies in construction and shipbuilding became independently owned by new investors.

On the other hand, the successful restructuring of the four largest industrial groups led to their further consolidation and domination of the domestic economy during the 2000s. Samsung Electronics became the leading group in South Korea in 2006. Together with the fourth-ranked chaebol, LG Electronics, it has joined the ranks of global lead firms in the ICT industry since then. With five of its affiliated companies on the top thirty list, Hyundai Motor became the second largest group.[27] The Hyundai group has attained global leadership in automobiles (Hyundai Motors), semiconductors (Hynix), and shipbuilding (Hyundai Heavy Industries).[28] Gaining its independence from the state, POSCO remains a major player in the global steel industry. Other large chaebol groups have emerged to be dominant players in telecommunications (SK), chemicals (SK and LG), shipping (Hanjin), and retail (Lotte). Overall, Samsung, Hyundai (Hynix), and LG had become not only the largest chaebol groups in the domestic economy, but also leading players in the global ICT industry by the mid-2000s.

This increasing domination and concentration of chaebol power can be attributed to two important historical episodes related to financial opening and corporate restructuring since the late 1990s. First, *financial opening* in the post-1997 crisis era took the form of the unprecedented growth of foreign direct investment (FDI) in all sectors and the massive foreign ownership of the financial sector that was once the most powerful leash for the developmental state to control its unruly chaebol groups. This opening was greatly prompted by the landmark Foreign Investment Promotion Act (opening 98 percent of all business sectors) and an amendment to the Foreigners' Land Acquisition Act in 1998 (Bello 2009, 197). In general, FDI plays a useful role in promoting corporate restructuring and reembedding the chaebol in global production networks. Among the three East Asian economies, South Korea used to be the least dependent on foreign investment for its industrialization program. The actual cumulative FDI between 1962 and 1990 was a fairly small amount of US$5.9 billion (Kim and Lee 2007, 23–25). While FDI inflows accelerated in

Table 3.2 East Asian domestic business groups in *Businessweek's* Emerging Market 200 and Global 1000 in 1997 and 2003 (in US$million)

Firm name	Market value in 1997	Group name	Firm name	Market value in 2003	Group name^Y
South Korea					
Korea Electric Power	19,361	State-owned	Samsung Electronics	44,188	Samsung
Samsung Electronics	8,801	Samsung	SK Telecom	13,343	SK
POSCO	6,172	State-owned	KT	11,321	Independent*
Daewoo Heavy Industry	3,125	Daewoo	Korea Electric Power	10,589	Independent*
SK Telecom	2,552	SK	Kookmin Bank	9,309	Independent
Hyundai Motor	1,998	Hyundai	POSCO	7,303	Independent*
			Hyundai Motor	5,992	Hyundai Motor
			LG Electronics	4,971	LG
			Woori Finance	3,610	Independent
			KT Freetel	3,548	Independent*
			Samsung SDI	3,036	Samsung
			KT&G	3,001	Independent*
			Shinhan Financial	2,970	Independent
			Samsung F&M Insurance	2,756	Samsung
			KIA Motors	2,722	Hyundai Motor
			LG Chem	2,541	LG
			Shinsegae	2,517	Shinsegae
			Samsung Electro Mechanics	2,259	Samsung
			Chohung Bank	2,174	Independent
			S-Oil	1,976	Independent
			Hyundai Mobis	1,967	Hyundai Motor
Singapore					
Singapore Telecom	27,524	SingTel^T	Singapore Telecom	15,209	SingTel^T
OCBC Bank	12,526	OCBC	United Overseas Bank	10,057	UOB
Singapore Airlines	10,946	SIA^T	DBS Bank	8,298	DBS Group^T
United Overseas Bank	9,842	UOB	OCBC Bank	6,843	OCBC
DBS Bank	8,655	DBS Group^T	Singapore Airlines	6,742	SIA^T
City Developments	7,381	Hong Leong	Singapore Press Holdings	3,526	SPH^T
HongKong Land	7,267	Jardine M			
Singapore Press Holdings	6,748	SPH^T			
Jardine Matheson	5,018	Jardine M			
Overseas Union Bank	4,662	UOB(merged)			

Firm name	Market value in 1997	Group name	Firm name	Market value in 2003	Group name[Y]
Taiwan					
Cathay Life Insurance	16,020	Cathay	TSMC	28,713	TSMC (87)
TSMC	11,381	TSMC	Chunghwa Telecom	13,846	Independent*
First Commercial Bank	11,194	State-owned	UMC	9,722	UMC (80)
Hua Nan Bank	10,336	State-owned	Cathay Financial H	9,696	Cathay (61)
Chang Hwa Bank	10,216	State-owned	Hon Hai Precision	6,903	Hon Hai (73)
UMC	7,930	UMC	Fubon Financial H	6,475	Fubon (01)
China Steel	7,855	Independent*	Nan Ya Plastic	6,465	Formosa (54)
Nan Ya Plastic	7,214	Formosa	Formosa Plastics	5,946	Formosa (54)
China Devt Financial H	6,979	Independent	China Steel	5,431	Independent*(71)
Formosa Plastic	5,681	Formosa	Mega Financial	5,126	Independent(02)
Shin Kong Life	5,299	Shin Kong	Quanta Computer	4,931	Quanta (88)
Tatung	4,829	Tatung	Asustek Computer	4,666	Asustek (90)
Int'l Commerce Bank	4,351	State-owned	Formosa Chemicals	4,494	Formosa (54)
Acer	4,099	Acer	China Devt Financial H	3,911	Independent
President Enterprises	3,246	President	Chinatrust Financial H	3,869	China Trust (02)
Formosa Chemicals	3,236	Formosa	Taiwan Cellular	3,231	Pacific Elec(50)
ASE	3,032	ASE	Compal Electronics	2,922	Kinpo (73)
Mosel Vitelic	2,992	Mosel Vitelic	Hua Nan Financial H	2,736	Independent
Far Eastern Textile	2,963	Far Eastern	AU Optronics	2,504	BenQ (84)
Taiwan Cement	2,553	Taiwan Cement	First Financial Holding	2,269	Independent
Evergreen Marine	2,528	Evergreen	China Motor (CMC)	2,243	Yulon (53)
Taipei Business Bank	2,459	State-owned	Acer	2,127	Acer (79)
Winbond Electronics	2,396	Walsin	Winbond Electronics	2,117	Walsin (66)
Asia Cement	2,369	Far Eastern	Yulon Motor	2,114	Yulon (53)
Hualon Teijran	2,343	Hualon	Nanya Technology	2,090	Formosa (54)
Cathay Construction	2,196	Cathay	BenQ	1,981	BenQ (84)
Fubon Insurance	2,111	Fubon	Lite-On Technology	1,942	Lite-On
Pacific Electric W&C	2,080	Pacific Electric			
Taichung Business Bank	2,010	Independent*			
China Airlines	2,004	Independent*			

*Formerly state-owned.

[T]Majority-owned by Temasek Holdings, a state investment holding company.

[Y]Numbers in brackets refer to year of establishment.

Sources: S.J. Chang (2006a, Appendix 1.1, 18–20) and Chung and Mahmood (2006, 77, table 4.1).

the 1990s prior to the 1997 financial crisis, they became colossal during the 1998–2005 period. The actual amount of FDI between 1998 and 2005 was US$59.5 billion, ten times more than the *entire* 1962–1990 period. This relatively high inflow of foreign investment has continued since then. By the mid-2000s, it would not be an exaggeration to claim that South Korea was no longer an indigenous economy driven primarily by domestic capital. FDI had deeply integrated South Korea into the global economy. Foreign investors had bought more than 40 percent of the market capitalization of the Korea Stock Exchange and accounted for 46.5 percent of shares in the top ten chaebol groups in 2004 (Chang 2006b, 64; Crotty and Lee 2007; 81–82; Pirie 2008, 137–39).[29]

Meanwhile, the shift of FDI into the service sectors points to a more significant issue—foreign ownership of the banking sector (Kalinowski and Cho 2009; Kang 2009; Lim 2009 and 2010). The post-1997 period witnessed a massive growth in the share of service sectors in FDI from 29.3 percent in 1998 to 72.4 percent in 2007 and the corresponding decline in manufacturing share of FDI from 65.9 percent to 25.6 percent during the same period. The foreign takeover of South Korea's banking system has undoubtedly contributed to this overwhelming share of service sectors in total FDI.[30] As presented in table 3.3, this foreign ownership and control of commercial banks in South Korea became very significant by December 2005. While foreign ownership share of the eight large urban banks was only 12 percent in 1998, it grew rapidly in the first half of the 2000s. By the end of 2005, six of the eight largest commercial banks were majority-owned by foreign investors. In 2006, foreign-controlled banks accounted for 65 percent of all bank assets in South Korea (Mo 2008, 261; Kalinowski and Cho 2009, 234). This significant presence of foreign ownership of the domestic banking sector weakened the intermediary role of banks in corporate financing. Foreign-owned banks are particularly aggressive in expanding consumer and mortgage loans at the expense of more risky corporate loans. Consequently, external financing in the private corporate sector dropped from 67.5 percent in 1997 to 22.4 percent in 2005, and internal financing within private firms increased dramatically from 25 percent to over 80 percent (Kalinowski and Cho 2009, 240; Kang 2009, 258–60). Financial liberalization and foreign ownership of domestic banks have effectively compelled the chaebol to move away from a bank-financed model of industrial growth endemic in the earlier developmental state regime to a firm-specific capital accumulation model of growth through retained earnings and reinvested profits.

This continual strength in the strongest chaebol groups brings us to the second historical event—their successful postcrisis *corporate restructuring.* Pirie (2008, 146–75) offers some useful evidence on the relative success of this restructuring. In 2002, the average net profit of manufacturing firms was 3.7 percent and the highest since 1974. This profit rate grew further to 7.8 percent in 2004 (highest since 1965) on the back of a growth rate of 3.6 percent. The most significant issue in this corporate restructuring, however, was the leader-

Table 3.3 Foreign ownership and control of commercial banks in South Korea, December 2005

Banks	History	Foreign ownership (%)	Foreign control
Kookmin	Kookmin + Housing (2001)	85.7	No
Hana	Hana + Seoul (2001)	72.3	No
Shinhan	Shinhan + Choheung (2003)	57.1	No
Woori	Hanil + Commerce (1998)	11.1	No
Korea Exchange Bank	Lone Star (2003)	74.2	Yes
Citibank (Korea-America)	Citibank + Hanmi (2004)	100.0	Yes
SC Cheil (Korea First)	Standard Chartered + Cheil (2005)	100.0	Yes

Source: Mo (2008, 261, table 12.6). Based on newspaper reports.

ship role exercised not by the state but by the leading chaebol groups and foreign investors. Known as the Big Deal Program, this process was initiated by President Kim Dae-Jung (1998–2003) with the view of "creating a few lean and highly competitive players in strategic industries" (Weiss 2003b, 252; Kalinowski and Cho 2009, 235–36). This program was designed to be implemented in nine industries facing severe overcapacity and inefficiency. Ironically, these problems were themselves the unintended consequences of Park Chung Hee's heavy and chemical industries drive in the late 1970s during which some chaebol were specifically selected and generously induced with policy loans to enter into these new businesses. The Kim administration wanted to undo the state's earlier mistakes by forcing the weaker chaebol to give up certain industries or to sell their affiliates to other stronger chaebol. As argued by S. J. Chang (2003, 207; 2006b, 61–62), this Big Deal business restructuring was as big a failure as the plan itself because it was based on political rather than economic motives, that is, to demonstrate quick and visible results.

By the mid 2000s, the strongest chaebol had fully recovered from their financial woes. They have since been disembedded from the home state and taken direct initiatives to participate in and develop international linkages through global production networks. They are much less reliant on the home state for financing, policy guidance, market information, and technological know-how. The national economy had become more mature and more enmeshed in globalization. For example, my interviewee from LG Electronics did not think the state was capable of guiding the chaebol in its strategic decisions during the 2000s:

It doesn't work anymore. Nowadays, the liberal market economy is dominant so the government should let companies follow their own principles. In the past, government officials were the ones who held the most information. The situation is the other way round now. Companies have more information

Table 3.4 Economic significance of the top 100 business groups in Taiwan, 1973–2006 (in US$billion)

Economic significance	1973	1977	1981	1986	1990	1994	1998	2002	2006
Number of member firms	724	651	719	746	815	1,021	1,362	4,825	6,038
Group sales	3.5	6.3	13.4	23.7	62.3	102.1	150.6	248.9	468.1
National GDP	10.8	21.8	46.9	80.5	158.9	246.3	277.4	282.2	363.9
Group/GDP (%)	32.4	28.8	28.6	29.4	39.2	41.5	54.3	85.4	128.9
Group employment (,000)	272	306	318	335	396	467	730	894	2,438
Total employment (,000)	5,327	5,980	6,672	7,733	8,283	8,939	9,289	9,454	10,111
Group/total employment (%)	5.1	5.2	4.8	4.3	4.8	5.2	7.9	9.5	24
Group sales growth (%)	NA	23.5	10.9	18.1	10.8	20.6	27.8	1.13	14
Group return on assets (%)	NA	5.2	2.5	6.9	4.9	6.1	3.5	0.6	3.8

Source: Chung and Mahmood (2010, 188, table 7.2). Based on data from the biennial directory *Business Groups in Taiwan* compiled by the China Credit Information Service (CCIS).

and technology since they are sharing a lot of information and technology with each other. LG Electronics has compiled plenty of information and experience by working as an ODM and OEM with global leading enterprises such as IBM and HP so that it is well aware of how this world is operating. However, the government doesn't have such an experience. What we want for the government is just to let us work in our own way.[31]

This transformed role of the state toward supportive functions can also be observed in such heavy industries as construction, automobiles, and chemicals.[32] In the automobile industry, the domestic competitiveness of postcrisis South Korea has deteriorated due to escalating labor costs and declining labor productivity. Other business costs have also increased significantly. Major automobile firms such as Hyundai have to relocate their production activity abroad in order to grow their international market shares and to regain their competitiveness. In this globalization of chaebol's production networks, the state's role has shifted from directorship to economic diplomacy and indirect assistance through functional industrial policy.

Taiwan: The Rise of ICT Business Groups

As argued in chapter 2, Taiwan's Kuomintang (KMT) state was never as powerful and effective in governing the market and picking national champions as the state in South Korea. This weaker embedding of domestic firms in Taiwan's developmental state was already acknowledged in Amsden (1989) and Wade (1990). The successful emergence of leading Taiwanese firms in the global ICT industry since 2000 has therefore created a favorable condition for them to disembed further from the increasingly fragmented state bureaucracy in search of new strategic partnership with global lead firms. Table 3.4 describes the rapid growth and economic significance of the top one hundred business groups in Taiwan between 1973 and 2006. The significance of these groups grew rapidly after the 1997–1998 Asian financial crisis. Between 1998 and 2006, the combined sales/GDP ratio of these one hundred groups more than doubled to 129 percent. Their share in total employment also tripled from 7.9 percent in 1998 to 24 percent in 2006. This greater proportion of employment share by large business groups led to both the centralization of economic activities and the relative decline of small- and medium-sized enterprises. For example, Hon Hai Precision alone hired 4.7 million employees in 2006, and that figure exceeded the total employment by all top one hundred business groups in any year (Chung and Mahmood 2010, 189). These large business groups had undoubtedly emerged as the main driver of Taiwan's economy since the 2000s.

Moreover, the sector shift in these large business groups toward the ICT industry during the 2000s was even more pronounced. In 1973, the top ten business groups were in fairly diversified and heavy industries, such as plastics, chemicals, transport, and machinery. Only two groups, Pacific Electric and Sampo, were in electronics and electronic products (Chung and Mahmood 2006, 76). The pattern remained similar in 1994. In 2002 and 2006, some sixteen out of the top thirty groups were in electronics and electronic products. The main difference between 2002 and 2006, though, is that these ICT business groups were rapidly moving up the ranking. In 2006, eight of the top ten groups were in the ICT industry. This rapid emergence of leading ICT firms in Taiwan by the mid-2000s bodes well with my argument for the critical role of private firms in Taiwan's articulation into different production networks associated with the global ICT industry. Most of these ICT firms have already developed strong firm-specific dynamic capabilities described in chapter 2. Different from traditional family businesses and diversified groups, these high-tech firms are less interested in developing personal ties with high- ranking state officials and more interested in sector-based collective action for cooperation and coordination, for instance, forming R&D consortia, joint development of key components and parts, or generating sector-based collective goods through information-sharing, standardization, training, testing and certification, joint marketing, and so on. As noted by Chu (2007, 170), "The owners of the established diversified groups have already locked up all the strategic positions in the existing state-prescribed corporatist arrangements. As a result, most of the industrial associations in the high-tech sector have been able to operate on the basis of self-governance with a minimal degree of government control and KMT manipulation: the leadership role usually rotates among leading firms, rather than being the captive of one business group."

The corollary to this private sector-led industrial development has been the retreat of the state from direct policy intervention and picking national champions to functional support and indirect assistance in the 2000s. The Democratic Progressive Party (DPP)–led state between 2000 and 2008 clearly lagged behind the pace of industrial development spearheaded by the top

ICT business groups. This trend started as early as in the mid-1990s. As observed by my interviewee from the Industrial Development Bureau (IDB) of the Ministry of Economic Affairs (MOEA), "In the 1980s was electronics. At that time, government stood in front of the companies and pulled them along. But in the last 10 years [since the mid 1990s] in the development of electronics, companies are in front of the government. So our strategy now is providing a sound investment environment, rather than telling the industries what they should do. We do not preselect certain industries . . . because they [private firms] see a better picture than us."[33] My interviewees with leading semiconductor firms from Taiwan tend to concur with this self-recognition by the IDB of the state's follower role in promoting Taiwan's industrial transformation.[34] For example, my interviewee from Macronix notes that "I think the reason why the [ICT] industry bloomed in the last ten years was due to the liberalization policy, not the government's participation. Actually, less government intervention is better for Taiwan's industries. The problem is when the government exercises tight control and they know nothing about everything. But they try to control, and they look like they are running the companies. That's bad."

During this DPP-led regime, frequent change in top leadership and political brinkmanship led to not only serious clashes and confrontations in domestic politics, but also policy short-termism and bureaucratic inconsistency that were detrimental to state-led development. As observed by the CEO of one publicly listed firm, "The government is playing politics. People are worried about the election and there is no consistency. On average under Chen Shui-bian [president from 2000 to 2008], ministers survival rate is two years. Nobody cares because your survival rate is so low. How do you have a long-term plan? Every four years you have an election and every decision is about how to get more votes."[35] In this political environment unfavorable for sectoral industrial policy, state agencies took an adaptive position toward a relatively back seat role in economic development. Instead of directive state interventions through targeted industrial policy and financial support, the various state agencies were involved in promoting a more conducive business environment through deregulation, information sharing, persuasion, and engaging different institutions. Even the once-powerful IDB had to confront the challenge of having to communicate and negotiate with other agencies and institutions in its much scaled-down pursuit of industrial promotion.[36] Still, the IDB finds it impossible to sustain its industrial policy incentives in a globalized economy in which its domestic firms are major players and less reliant on state support. My IDB interviewee laments that "now we have fewer industrial policy tools, such as incentives. We have already given what we can afford and there is nothing else more we can give."[37] Lacking the institutional means and financial capacity to lead industrial development, state agencies in Taiwan's MOEA turned their attention to serving as intermediaries through information sharing, "nudging," and persuasion in the 2000s.[38]

Singapore: Increasing State Privatization and Emerging Local Capital

Unlike South Korea and Taiwan, Singapore's developmental state had chosen to work with foreign capital since its inception in 1965 and produced a class of domestic private capitalists who depended less on, if not indeed alienated by, the state's economic priorities. Still, the state deliberately intervened in the domestic economy by establishing a wide range of state-owned enterprises (SOEs) for the provision of public infrastructure and for the revitalization of industrial assets formerly controlled by the British colonial government.[39] Certainly much more pervasive in different sectors and long lasting in duration than in South Korea and Taiwan, these enterprises came to the forefront of global competition in the 2000s (e.g., Singapore Airlines, Keppel, and Semb-Corp, as will be analyzed in chapters 5 and 6). Since the late 1980s and the early 1990s, the developmental state has embarked on the difficult task of corporatizing and privatizing major SOEs to become government-linked companies (GLCs).[40] During this first wave of disembedding national firms from the state, Temasek Holdings, the state's financial holding vehicle, began to shed its stake in nonstrategic and viable companies through public listing and other forms of divestment. The main purpose of divestment was to promote marketization and to allow the private sector to play a greater role in the Singapore economy. Through privatization and corporatization, the assets of many former large, state-owned enterprises were transferred to Temasek Holdings, which in turn listed these enterprises on the Stock Exchange of Singapore.

The domestic political role of such an initiative toward privatization and corporatization was critical. As argued by Rodan and Jayasuriya (2009, 30), Singapore's state capitalism was a form of political strategy to reproduce authoritarianism at the expense of private capitalists and the middle class—"this structural relationship to the state brings with it systematic exposure to an institutionalized ideology that champions the role of technocratic political elites at the expense of ideas of representation and citizenship rights." But this structural relationship began to change in the aftermath of the 1997–1998 Asian financial crisis. As noted by Low (2001, 425–26) and Worthington (2003, 200), considerable restructuring and rationalization had already taken place among the GLCs prior to the crisis. This reorganization was further accelerated and given a policy and operational framework by the Ministry of Trade and Industry's (1998) report on Singapore's competitiveness.[41] Table 3.5 lists companies divested by Temasek Holdings between 1985 and 1999, and between 1999 and 2010. Six GLCs had a combined market capitalization of S$164 billion by the end of 1999. Some of these GLCs are world-class competitors in their respective industries today: SingTel (telecommunications), Keppel Corp and SembCorp Industries (shipyards and marine industries), CapitaLand (property development), DBS Group Holdings (banking), Singapore Airlines (air transport), Neptune Orient Lines (shipping), and Singapore Technologies Engineering (aerospace and high-tech

Table 3.5 Summary of divestments and holdings by Temasek Holdings in Singapore, 1999 and 2010 (in S$billion)

Companies	Date of divestments	Share by TH (%)			Market capitalization	
		Before divestment	End 1999	March 2010	End 1999	March 2010
Cerebos Pacific	November 1985	45.0	0.0	0.0	—	—
Natsteel	September 1986	19.7	8.2	0.0	—	—
United Industrial Corporation	September 1986	10.9	0.0	0.0	—	—
SNP Corporation (1st listed on SESDAQ)	January 1987	100.0	63.0	0.0	—	—
	Nov 1988–Dec 1993	63.0	49.0			
Neptune Orient Lines	May 1987–June 1993	62.0	32.6	66.0	18	5.2
Singapore Airlines	December 1985	77.0	63.0	54.0	21	18.1
	June 1987	63.0	56.3			
Chemical Industries (FE)	July 1987	22.9	0.0	0.0	—	—
Acma Electrical Industries	January–March 1988	12.2	0.0	0.0	—	—
Hitachi Electronic Devices	August 1988	15.0	0.0	0.0	—	—
Yaohan Singapore Pte Ltd	November 1988	15.0	0.0	0.0	—	—
Philips Petroleum Singapore Chemicals	December 1988	25.0	0.0	0.0	—	—
Keppel Corporation	Jan 1989–June 1993	58.5	31.7	21.0	30	14.6
Denka (S) Pte Ltd	March 1989	20.0	0.0	0.0	—	—
The Polyolefin Company	April 1989	25.0	0.0	0.0	—	—

Company	Date					
Ethylene Glycols (S) Pte Ltd	April 1989	50.0	0.0	0.0	—	—
Petrochemical Corporation of Singapore	April 1989	20.0	0.0	0.0	—	—
Singapore Telecom	November 1993	100.0	89.2	54.0	38	50.5
	July 1996–March 1998	89.2	78.2			
SembCorp Industries			57.9	49.0	29	7.4
DBS Groups Holdings			15.5	28.0	28	32.6
PSA Corporation			100.0	100.0	—	8.0
Singapore Technologies Engg			100.0	50.0	—	9.6
Singapore Technologies Telemedia			—	100.0	—	2.1
Media Corporation of Singapore			100.0	100.0	—	0.53
Singapore MRT			100.0	54.0	—	3.1
Singapore Power			100.0	100.0	—	6.8
CapitaLand Ltd			—	39.0	—	16.9
Mapletree Investments			—	100.0	—	5.1
Fraser and Neave Ltd[1]			—	15.0	—	6.7
STATS ChipPAC Ltd			—	84.0	—	2.3
Singapore Airport Terminal Services Ltd			—	44.0	—	2.9

[1] Sold to Japan's Kirin Holdings Company for S$1.34 billion in July 2010, about 49% increase in value for a stake bought for about S$900 million in December 2006 (http://www.asiaone.com, accessed on September 21, 2014).

Sources: Straits Times (June 25, 1999, 74; April 29, 2000, 62); Temasek Review (2010, 80–85).

manufacturing). This corporatization and privatization marks a significant turning point in the primary role of Temasek Holdings in controlling state assets embedded in domestic economic development. Since the 2000s, Temasek Holdings has become more strategic in its investment focus. Its strategic plan is committed to investment in new strategic or risky ventures (e.g., life sciences and water resources), in companies that would bring foreign skills and technology and access to foreign markets, and in nurturing global or regional leaders from its stable of companies or other non-Temasek Singapore firms (Dhanabalan 2001).

Apart from the state's divestment efforts, some of these GLCs also experienced a drastic change in their corporate governance through the growing presence of outside directors. For example, SingTel and Keppel Corp moved from no outside directors in 1997 to a significant presence in 2006 and beyond. In 2006, five out of the eight leading GLCs had more than 30 percent of outside board directors, ranging from 30 percent in Singapore Airlines to 44–54 percent in SembMarine, SingTel, and NOL (Tsui-Auch and Yoshikawa 2010, 280–81). My interviews with four of these GLCs indicate a relatively low level of direct state control. For example, while Temasek Holdings holds 21 percent of shareholding in Keppel Corp, it has only one member on Keppel's board of directors, and its influence on Keppel's business and strategy reflects its role as a shareholder. In fact, an interviewee from Keppel argues that state intervention can be detrimental to its business because of the political nature and objective of such an intervention: "We do not enjoy any preference. The Singapore government does not intervene. In our foreign business, whether the government helps? I don't think so. To be very frank, government intervention is not good. Any government has purposes and the business suffers."[42] Many CEOs of these GLCs have been working in the same GLCs for decades. Even though they came from the developmental state bureaucracy before joining the GLCs, they have acquired strong professional management capability and business acumen to take these GLCs from their humble origin as Singapore-based SOEs in the 1980s or earlier to highly globalized industry leaders since the 2000s. My finding therefore supports Gourevitch's (2008, 86) observation that "like France, Singapore has a cadre of professional manager-bureaucrats that moves back and forth between the public and private sectors, and many of these individuals can be found on the boards of both private and privatized SOEs on the SSE [Singapore Stock Exchange]."

Because of the persistent dominance of Temasek Holdings and its stable of companies, the state's role in Singapore's economic development since the 2000s has remained quite strong in comparison with South Korea and Taiwan. The substantial state ownership of a large number of GLCs also means that Singapore's articulation into global production networks is not entirely driven by private capital but also comes through state-mediated corporate vehicles. The paradox, though, is that these vehicles (GLCs) are as globally competitive as private firms from Singapore or elsewhere in East Asia in their respective industries. In many ways, these highly competitive GLCs should be envisaged as strategically and organizationally similar to private sector firms competing for dominant positions in different global industries. The state has become a strategic shareholder of these GLCs rather than a key driver of their firm-specific initiatives. As these GLCs become globally competitive and increasingly privatized, the role of the state in steering industrial transformation is partially transferred to leading private sector firms in different sectors such as banking (UOB and OCBC), real estate (Far East, Hong Leong, and Wing Tai), ICT (Creative Tech, Venture Corp, WBL, and MMI), trading (Olam and Wilmar), transport (Pacific International Lines), and so on.[43] Instead, the state focuses on trade and investment facilitation and developing public infrastructures, such as training, educational, and research institutes, in support of economic transformation toward a knowledge-based economy.

Conclusion

This chapter has developed the midrange concept of strategic coupling as a critical theoretical interface for understanding industrial transformation in an era of global production networks that have come to dominate a wide range of high-growth industries. Articulating into these networks has enabled domestic capitalist firms to disembed from their home state and to reembed into this newly institutionalized form of organizing the global economy. By now, it should be clear from my analysis that state-firm relations in the three East Asian economies have evolved into different degrees of structural *inter*dependence since the late 1990s. In this evolutionary shift from embedded autonomy in domestic state-firm relations to the strategic coupling of domestic firms with global production networks, we observe different pathways of development in the three economies. Whereas South Korea has experienced much greater domination and concentration of chaebol power in major industrial sectors, Taiwan's top business groups in the ICT sector have become the leading force in the domestic economy and its articulation into the global economy. In contrast, the much smaller and yet more globalized city-state of Singapore has witnessed the growing diversification of its domestic economic sectors and state-private capital formation. While foreign firms are still very significant in Singapore, various former state-owned enterprises and established private businesses have grown rapidly alongside new private-led business ventures. Taken together, leading domestic firms from these East Asian economies have emerged to be the dominant force in transforming their home economies. They have also shed their reliance on state-led developmental initiatives and grown into key actors in different global industries.

This evolutionary shift in the state-firm-GPN assemblage from territorial embeddedness in domestic political economies to organizational embeddedness in global production networks, however, does not necessarily take place in all latecomer economies and occur to all of their domestic firms. For example, Breznitz (2007) compares state choices and innovation policies in steering the divergent articulation of Israel, Taiwan, and Ireland into the global ICT industry. His own analysis of these different models of articulation points to the state's political choices and selective industrial policy. While his neostatist approach embraces the dynamic processes in global production networks, Breznitz (2007, 23) remains far too focused on the state and its industrial policy: "If we can analyze these processes to gain an understanding of how different emerging countries' industrial policies give these countries advantages in specific stages of production, we will have the beginning of an answer."[44] As I have argued hitherto in this book, the state's political capacity and choices can only offer a partial understanding of the divergent articulation of latecomer economies and their domestic firms into the global economy because of two critical missing links—the emerging strategic capabilities of domestic firms and the competitive dynamics of global production networks. Without situating these East Asian firms in global production networks, we cannot understand fully how these political choices, made on the assumption of an embedded-autonomous state, are actually translated into development in an era of economic globalization.

This chapter has conceptualized how such strategic coupling with global production networks is made possible through the interactive effects of three structural conditions of expanding transnational communities of technopreneurs, favorable industrial-organizational dynamics, and the continual supportive role of state institutions. More specifically, I have outlined three network-level coupling processes of strategic partnership, industrial market specialization, and (re)positioning as global lead firms that provide the concrete nexus through which industrial transformation in East Asia can be better situated in an era of global economic integration. In the next three empirical chapters, I will explain in detail each of these component processes in relation to original firm- and industry-specific material. While the coupling process of strategic partnership tends to be more effective for East Asian firms to articulate into the global electronics industry (chapter 4), industrial market specialization is more feasible among East Asian firms in the more capital-intensive global industries, such as marine engineering and semiconductors (chapter 5). Those East Asian firms (re)positioning as global lead firms confront the most challenging process of strategic coupling because of immense demand for corporate leadership and firm-specific resources (chapter 6). Each component process is premised on a peculiar combination of structural conditions that will be introduced at the beginning of the following three chapters.

Chapter 4

Strategic Partnership in Global Electronics

In retrospect, the successful industrial transformation of South Korea, Taiwan, and Singapore can be viewed as intimately linked to the globalization of the electronics industry. In all three economies, electronics has become the most economically significant manufacturing industry since the early 1990s. As major producers in the global electronics industry, these three East Asian economies have played an integral role in the rapid development of the digital era described by Zysman and Newman (2006) as the "second great transformation." This digital era can be understood in relation to three fundamental segments: information, networks, and equipment. While global lead firms in advanced industrialized economies, particularly the United States, have dominated in all three segments, leading East Asian electronics firms have emerged as major strategic partners in the *equipment* segment of this digital era. Much of the developmental state literature has ascribed the emergence of the electronics industry and these East Asian firms to state-led developmental initiatives.[1] This statist view of economic development in a highly globalized industry, however, has generally been couched in static and domestic terms rather than grounded in the evolutionary national-global dynamics analyzed in the previous chapter. To Zysman and Newman (2006, 278), while the state plays a vital role in the evolution of this digital era across the globe, "The emergence and evolution of the digital era have not been the products of purely neoliberal strategies, on the one hand, nor of purely interventionist strategies, on the other hand. Governments have acted simultaneously to subsidize infrastructure development, extract themselves from direct market control, and forge new rules to promote economic transactions. Framing the role of the state in ideological terms confounds the multitude and seemingly contradictory strategies governments undertook."

In this first empirical chapter, I analyze how through *strategic partnership* with lead firms in the electronics global production networks since the late 1990s—

the first of the three coupling processes conceptualized in the previous chapter—East Asian firms have evolved from their initial role as low-cost subcontractors to become key players in the global electronics industry and the critical conduits for articulating their domestic economies into the global economy.[2] Having grown out of the earlier developmental initiatives led by their home states, these leading national firms are no longer dependent on the transformed state described in chapter 2. Instead, their relationship may be conceived as reversed, whereby the postdevelopmental state depends to a greater extent on these major domestic firms to sustain the continual growth and competitiveness of its national economy. The success of these firms in global electronics also reflects their enormous market prowess and firm-specific capabilities in a globalized industry that requires significant manufacturing excellence, cost competitiveness, technological know-how, and organizational resources. In all three economies, the electronics industry is now the leading contributor in the manufacturing sector through value-added activity, exports, employment, and R&D expenditure. As pointed out in chapter 3, most of the leading industrial firms in these three economies are related to the electronics industry. In each of them, a number of domestic electronics firms are global leaders in their respective market segments, such as computers, consumer electronics, and semiconductors: South Korea's Samsung, LG, and SK Hynix; Taiwan's Hon Hai, Taiwan Semiconductor Manufacturing Company (TSMC), and Quanta; and Singapore's Venture Corp, WBL, and Creative Technology.[3]

More specifically, the strong foothold in the global electronics industry held by all three East Asian economies has been facilitated by the three structural conditions for strategic coupling specified in the previous chapters. First, the transformation of state roles has led to the shift toward a more functional support of this strategic partnership in the electronics global production networks. Not surprisingly, all three states have historically been very active in promoting the electronics industry during different time periods. The industry initially grew as a part of the state's program of export promotion in the 1960s and the 1970s, when the new international division of labor began to take shape in these economies. In *Race to the Swift*, Woo (1991, 144) describes the electronics industry as "really a deus ex machina for the upstarts of the late twentieth century—like Taiwan and Korea—because it so neatly fills the lacuna between the light and heavy phases of industrialization. It is a bridge between the two phases, and offers the best advantages while avoiding the worst pitfalls of a lead-off industry such as textiles." Together with shipbuilding and transport equipment, the electronics industry continued to receive significant state promotion in the 1980s and the 1990s.[4]

Second, the changing industrial organization in global electronics in favor of global outsourcing has created an unprecedented window of opportunity for East Asian firms to "plug" into emerging global production networks. This positive structural condition of globalizing electronics is underpinned by a wide range of factors, such as rising cost and financial pressures and the modularization of production. The next section will elaborate on these two structural conditions that favor the strategic partnership of East Asian firms in the electronics global production networks.

Third, a relatively large community of transnational technopreneurs has emerged after over four decades of rapid industrialization in East Asia. These "new Argonauts" have gained experience and knowhow through their work in advanced economies and/or through business transactions with global lead firms. The specificity and efficacy of this structural condition will become evident in many of the selected East Asian firms in my empirical analysis. Based on my original material, the detailed case studies in the second and third sections will focus explicitly on the emergence and role of these East Asian firms as strategic partners in two different electronics global production networks— notebook computers and consumer electronics. In these two sets of corporate cases (e.g., Quanta, Hon Hai, and Venture Corp), entrepreneurial domestic firms have emerged from East Asian economies primarily because of firm-specific competitive advantages and global articulation in which the home state serves as a subsidiary, albeit positive, factor. In all three economies, we witness different competitive dynamics at work that offer useful comparative insights into the differential strategic coupling of these East Asian firms with global production networks. In lieu of a detailed historical description of the emergence of the electronics industry in the three East Asian economies[5], this chapter offers a comparative analysis of how their leading national firms have taken advantage of opportunities in global electronics within the broader contexts of changing state roles and industrial organization.

The Globalizing World of Electronics

In now well-known cases of national champions from East Asia (e.g., Samsung and TSMC), the developmental state used to be highly instrumental in its sectoral industrial policy, targeted promotion of these handpicked electronics firms, and played a significant role in their early emergence and corporate transformation. But by the late 1990s, this state-led developmental role had been significantly reduced, as more domestic electronics firms had become much stronger through their strategic partnership with global lead firms, and they had begun to grow out of the state's industrial plan. As the electronics industry became more globalized, the role of the developmental state in ushering the strategic partnership of domestic firms with global lead firms was more important in the *earlier* phases of industrial development in two ways. First, the state laid the early foundation of the "manufacturing experience," in the words of Amsden (1989, 105), among domestic electronics firms. This manufacturing experience was embodied in the labor force, salaried management, production and engineering know-how, and project execution skills. By providing strong financial and nonfinancial incentives to attract the establish-ment of foreign-owned production facilities in their economies during the late 1960s and the 1970s, the developmental state was also instrumental in providing the initial condition for its domestic economy to secure a place in the evolving international division of labor in the global electronics industry.[6] Second, the state in all three economies was crucial in picking the "right" champions to lead the development of the electronics industry during the 1970s and the 1980s: the chaebol in South Korea, spin-offs of state-funded research insti-tutes in Taiwan, and foreign original equipment manufacturing (OEM) firms and local state-owned and private firms in Singapore.[7] This divergent form of state policy and institutional contexts significantly influenced the subsequent strategic participation and competitive outcomes of East Asian firms in global electronics. In particular, the semiconductor segment of the industry reflects this divergent state selectivity, but the "long arm" of the developmental state is much less visible and effective in the original design manufacturing (ODM) and the electronics manufacturing services (EMS) segments. Compared to South Korea and Taiwan, for example, Singapore does not have an indigenously owned and fully integrated value chain in the global electronics industry.

Despite significant state interventions in the early decades, the electronics industry in all three economies was ironically seen as facing a major competitive crisis by the late 1980s. Pointing to this crisis in their *Dragons in Distress*, Bello and Rosenfeld (1990) critically note that as late as in 1989, South Korea's elec-tronics industry was still heavily dependent on Japan for more than 70 percent of its components. To them, "Electronics had been designated as the decisive arena in Korea's drive to achieve advanced-country status. The chaebol and the government trumpeted R&D advances, but on a closer examination, these claims were flimsy. Indeed, the Koreans' decision to take on the United States and Japan in high-tech electronics as the key to industrial advance was begin-ning to shape up as a *strategic mistake*" (164; my emphasis). Applying their argu-ment further to Taiwan and Singapore, they extend this pessimistic assess-ment of the difficult, if not impossible, transition to a high-tech export economy on the basis of developing a domestic electronics industry. To put in perspective these early forms of state interventions and their differential pol-icy outcomes, table 4.1 summarizes the performance of the electronics indus-try in all three East Asian economies between 1991 and 2011. As of 1991, elec-tronics output in South Korea and Taiwan remained relatively modest in total manufacturing, hovering around 10–14 percent. Only in Singapore was elec-tronics already a dominant industry at the beginning of the 1990s, contribut-ing to over 46 percent of total manufacturing output. Yet, by 2009–2010, the share of electronics in total manufacturing output had reached 24 percent in South Korea, and 44 percent in Taiwan and Singapore.[8] Over a period of two decades, the alleged "strategic mistake" made by the home state in all three East Asian economies have been turned into a major success of industrial transformation and competitive reality.

Table 4.1 The electronics industry in South Korea, Taiwan, and Singapore, 1991–2011

East Asian economy	1991	1996	2001	2006	2009	2010	2011
South Korea							
Total manufacturing value added (million won)	86,366,421	174,214,797	206,647,453	304,133,706	374,500,730		
Electronic components, video, audio, apparatuses & ICT products	8,491,517	23,848,785	39,667,659	68,843,917	89,870,355		
Electronics (percent of total manufacturing)	9.8	13.7	19.2	22.6	24.0		
Taiwan							
Total manufacturing value added (NT$million in 2006 constant price)	6,590,547	8,780,125	10,419,602	14,482,005	13,836,619	17,065,026	
Electronic parts and components manufacturing	266,653	590,808	1,468,369	3,731,243	4,263,039	5,736,929	
Computers, electronic and optical products	266,892	555,497	824,364	1,063,787	1,007,540	1,291,662	
Electrical equipment manufacturing	374,294	545,070	514,706	497,884	386,287	465,588	
Electronics (total)	907,839	1,691,375	2,807,439	5,292,914	5,656,866	7,494,179	
Electronics (percent of total manufacturing)	13.8	19.3	26.9	36.5	40.9	43.9	
Total exports (US$million)			126,314	224,017	203,675	274,601	308,257
Electronic products			21,210	36,773	31,286	42,719	44,503
ICT products			8,201	4,957	4,546	5,720	6,920
Electronics/ICT (percent of total exports)			23.3	18.6	17.6	17.6	16.7
Total imports (US$million)			107,971	202,698	174,371	251,236	281,438
Electronic products			21,210	36,773	31,286	42,719	44,503
ICT products			8,201	4,957	4,546	5,720	6,920
Electronics/ICT (percent of total imports)			27.2	20.6	20.5	19.3	18.3
Singapore							
Total manufacturing output (S$million)	65,000	124,000	137,000	132,991	253,765	217,642	260,011
Computer, electronic & optical products	30,000	60,000	62,710	75,277	74,418	95,274	85,289
Electronics (percent of total manufacturing)	46.2	48.4	45.8	56.6	29.3	43.8	32.8

Sources: Korean Statistical Information Service, http://kosis.kr/eng; Taiwan National Statistics Bureau, http://eng.stat.gov.tw; *Singapore Manufacturing Yearbook 2001–2011*, http://www.singstat.gov.sg; accessed on October 15, 2014.

This industrial transformation since the 1990s has occurred at the time when domestic firms have become more articulated into global production networks. The role of the state has also shifted from a directive approach to a more supportive and facilitating function. During this period, the state power that provided the political capacity for the developmental state to engage in interventionist development strategies and sectoral industrial policy has been transformed by a combination of international pressures (e.g., geopolitical change) and domestic politics (e.g., democratization and liberalization). To maintain its "degraded" developmentalist posture,[9] the state in the three East Asian economies has pursued functional or horizontal industrial policy by promoting industrial upgrading and innovation and facilitating trade and investment. Instead of directly steering domestic firms to couple with global lead firms, the state plays a more indirect role in facilitating this strategic coupling process. On the one hand, state institutions have been actively involved in the rapid growth of public-private R&D consortiums in all three economies (Noble 1998; Bae 2011). On the other hand, more liberal trade and investment policies are implemented in order to create a conducive environment for domestic firms to import intermediate goods crucial for their strategic partnership with global production networks and for foreign firms to invest in domestic firms in order to improve their production capacity and technological capabilities. Still, this functional industrial policy for promoting domestic R&D capacity in the electronics industry is increasingly superseded by private firm initiatives as these firms have found new conduits for developing such capabilities through their expanding global production networks. In South Korea, Samsung, LG, and other chaebol began to disembed from state-sponsored R&D consortiums in the 1990s and accelerated their own inhouse R&D activity and technological advancement in order to catch up with global lead firms. By the early 2000s, these chaebol had effectively taken over the control of both R&D and production activity in the domestic electronics industry and become the leader in steering the industry's high growth during the ensuring decade.

In Taiwan, the previously well-defined division of labor between public research institutes and private electronics firms in technological development and industrial upgrading also began to break down.[10] State-sponsored institutions were no longer the best avenues for private firms to source for cutting-edge technologies in global electronics. As private firms were much more experienced in developing second-generation innovation in production processes and in working with global lead firms, they were more inclined to source for new and novel technologies directly from these global lead firms (and their competitors). Moreover, existing and new private firms began to develop in-house R&D capabilities in order to move away from the weaker position of captive suppliers to become strategic partners of these global lead firms. Lacking strong experience in working with global lead firms, state-funded research institutes became more insulated from industry need.[11] The process of state-centered R&D and technology transfer in the 1980s was now internalized and transformed into an intrafirm activity, particularly in the area of applied technologies. The state became less able to drive directly technological shifts among Taiwan's largest electronics firms. Its role was transformed into funding basic research in a conventional manner through universities and public institutes and providing good R&D infrastructure, such as science parks.[12]

In Singapore, the state has been consistently supportive of the presence of OEM lead firms and their direct investment to kick-start Singapore's industrialization. Among different manufacturing industries, the electronics industry stood out as the most significant recipient of these foreign investment flows.[13] This unique approach to rapid industrialization explains why electronics had emerged as Singapore's dominant manufacturing industry by the late 1980s, much earlier than in South Korea and Taiwan (see table 4.1). Apart from generous incentives offered by the state (e.g., tax and land), these OEM lead firms also benefited from Singapore's well-developed technology and transport infrastructure and its important logistical position in the electronics global production networks (Bowen and Leinbach 2006, 155). By the 2000s, a new form of international partnership had begun to develop between domestic firms and global lead firms in Singapore, facilitated by an indigenous community of transnational elites and new entrepreneurial firms. As evident in the final section, some domestic electronics firms (e.g., Venture Corp) were emerging to be major strategic partners of global lead firms.

The above analysis of the changing state role in facilitating firm-specific strategic coupling with electronics necessitates the discussion of the second critical structural condition that has positively influenced the emergence of East Asian firms in this global industry. This condition has to do with the *organizational transformation* of the global electronics industry since the late 1960s in favor of internationalization and, later on, production fragmentation and modularization orchestrated by large transnational corporations (TNCs).[14] To Hobday (2000, 161), the electronics industry "is an example of a fast-growing internationally traded industry in which the division of tasks across national boundaries is both technologically possible and advantageous to TNCs."[15] Without this historically contingent drive toward international subcontracting or outsourcing by first movers or OEM firms, the three East Asian economies would probably have never made their first break into this risky and yet highly lucrative and multifaceted global industry. As such, it is important to appreciate how the globalization of the electronics industry has offered a crucial opportunity for domestic firms from the three East Asian economies to plug into different global production networks, initially as low-cost suppliers and allowed these firms to upgrade continuously their market positions within these networks through strategic partnership with global lead firms.[16]

During this complex and overlapping process of globalizing electronics production networks since the 1960s, particularly in the personal computer and semiconductor sectors, different periods of opportunities have emerged for budding East Asian manufacturers (Yeung 2007a, 7–8). At the initial stage during the 1960s and the 1970s, few East Asian manufacturers were articulated into these globalizing production networks that remained fairly vertically integrated. Much of international production taking place during this period was low-value, labor-intensive assembly work well described in Amsden (1989) and Wade (1990). The global production networks of lead firms then, particularly those from the United States, were much more vertically integrated, involving few external firms and institutions.[17] Leading American, European, and later, Japanese OEM firms first established their wholly owned production facilities in East Asian economies in order to take advantage of cheaper labor and infrastructure costs and host state investment incentives. Between 1965 and 1968, these foreign firms set up the first in-house electronics assembly operations in South Korea (Komi in 1965, and Fairchild, Motorola, and Signetics in 1966), Taiwan (General Instrument in 1965, Philips in 1966, and Texas Instruments in 1968), and Singapore (Texas Instruments, National Semiconductor, and Fairchild in 1968).[18] In some instances, joint ventures were established with local firms to benefit from investment incentives offered by the developmental state.[19]

Throughout the 1970s, the manufacturing capabilities of domestic firms in all three economies were relatively weak. Most of them could only serve as low-end component suppliers to OEM firms from advanced industrialized economies, particularly the United States and Japan.[20] As low-cost suppliers to OEM lead firms, these East Asian manufacturers were merely subcontractors and followers of the production demand controlled by their OEM customers. No domestic firms in these three economies had yet developed advanced technologies and/or organizational competencies to cooperate with, let alone compete against, these OEM lead firms from the United States and Japan. The home state in these economies was in various stages of their industrialization and developmental postures. Industrial transformations in South Korea and Singapore were clearly led by their respective developmental states to achieve Park Chung Hee's drive toward heavy and chemical industries and Lee Kuan Yew's ambition of achieving full employment through attracting foreign investment in the electronics industry. In Taiwan, the state was not even developmental until the late 1970s when its vision for the electronics industry was finally articulated.

By the early 1980s, some East Asian firms had accumulated sufficient production know-how to take on more complex subcontracting work from established OEM lead firms in the electronics industry. As the global economy was moving toward a post-Fordist flexible production regime, leading OEM firms began to accelerate their product development cycles and to keep in-house production of only the latest generation of electronic products. This shift in the competitive strategy of many OEM firms led to a dramatic increase in opportunity for international outsourcing through interfirm transactions and technology transfer.[21] In the personal computer (PC) industry, Dedrick and

Kraemer (1998, 49–50) argue that "while the heroes of the U.S. PC industry were twenty-something hotshots who designed the hardware and software and were featured on magazine covers, most of the people in charge of manufacturing were veterans of the electronics industry who knew how to build and run factories. Many of them had spent time in Asia working for companies like Fairchild, Texas Instruments, General Instruments, and IBM, and they were familiar with the capabilities of the Asian companies and workers. This familiarity led U.S. companies to look across the Pacific, rather than to other parts of the world, as they globalized production in the PC era."[22] When IBM launched its first PC in August 1981, it outsourced the monitors to Taiwan's Tatung, which was able to achieve high-volume production and sold its excess capacity to new IBM-compatible PC makers from the United States (e.g., Compaq) and Taiwan (e.g., Acer). Meanwhile, a new generation of East Asian engineers and production managers, previously employed in such leading OEM firms as Hewlett-Packard, Texas Instruments, Motorola, Fairchild Semiconductor, National Semiconductor, and IBM, became entrepreneurs in their own right and established manufacturing facilities to partake in the rapidly growing outsourcing markets.[23]

As the global electronics industry had become intensely competitive by the late 1980s, particularly in the personal computer (PC), consumer electronics, and semiconductors sectors, financial pressures, time-to-market, and value chain efficiency had emerged as prime considerations of OEM lead firms. The world of electronics entered into the second phase of changing industrial organization, leading to even greater fragmentation of value chain activity. Internationalization of the *entire* value chain became the competitive tool for these OEM firms to lower their "cost to capability" ratios on the basis of productivity improvement, reduction in production costs, and sustained quality.[24] As noted perceptively by my interviewee from Singapore's Venture Corp, one of the world's largest EMS providers to these OEM firms,

> The only reason why they globalize their operations is to attain an overall achievement of the ratio distributed throughout the value chain. By doing that, can you push this ratio? That's what drives globalization. People don't come out here for no reasons. Among the OEMs here we've got HP, IBM, and Motorola. They all come to Asia because they want to improve their cost-to-capability ratio so that they can compete better against NEC, Dell, and so on. The way we view this is about stretching out the value chain. Initially it's about spreading the value chain around the world, using their own subsidiaries for the setup. And then they find that it's very troublesome, difficult, and challenging to do this everywhere, and that's too much to follow. So they find it's better to make a wise decision—outsource and work with strategic partners in Asia. That's the second phrase.[25]

In order to focus on developing new cutting-edge technologies and to shorten further their product development cycles, many of these global lead firms began to consolidate their global production networks, leading to further outsourcing of a significant portion of their manufactured products in the forms of specialized components and integrated modules. Some OEM lead firms (e.g., Apple and IBM) began to specialize in upstream R&D activity and downstream marketing, distribution, and services, and left the entire manufacturing segment of the value chain to East Asian manufacturers from the three economies. This changing industrial organization from OEM-led vertical integration to high levels of production fragmentation created an extremely important and favorable condition for the emergence of domestic electronics firms in South Korea, Taiwan, and Singapore. Enhanced by firm-specific technological innovations and, sometimes, spatial proximity to suppliers, this move toward greater specialization and fragmentation of value chain activity in different segments of the global electronics industry facilitated the rapid rise of a large number of specialized component suppliers, manufacturing services providers, and modular manufacturers from these East Asian economies.

In the computer equipment segment, for example, the decline of the mainframe market in favor of the explosive PC market since the late 1980s led to an unprecedented opportunity for East Asian manufacturers, which had now developed firm-specific competence in manufacturing excellence, production flexibility, and cost competitiveness, to serve as ODM partners for brand name lead firms.[26] This remarkable shift in industrial organization prompted a complete restructuring of the global computer industry, and no single firm nor state institution could have anticipated its wide-ranging impact on the rise and fall of different national firms and economies. As illustrated in table 4.2, by the mid-1990s, this horizontal segmentation in the entire global PC industry had created vast production networks spanning the United States, Japan, and the three East Asian economies, each establishing a unique position in the rapidly growing industry.

Since the early 2000s, the world electronics industry has experienced another "revolution" with the emergence of contract manufacturing and turnkey production as the key organizational platform to achieve maximum production efficiency through enormous economies of scale and highly sophisticated supply chain management.[27] In this most recent mode of industrial organization in global electronics, brand name lead firms engage large and highly globalized contract manufacturers as their strategic partners to take over their entire spectrum of manufacturing activities, while they specialize in the higher return premium product markets and/or higher value-added activities, such as R&D, production development, marketing, and sometimes, distribution. This phenomenon of vertical specialization has been particularly significant in all three segments of the electronics industry.[28] In PCs and consumer electronics, global lead firms now outsource the lion's share of their computers, communication devices, and electronic products to contract manufacturers in East Asia and concentrate on their core

Table 4.2 The global production network of personal computers by the mid-1990s

Economy	Leading firms	Role in the global production network
United States	IBM, Microsoft, Intel, Compaq, Hewlett-Packard, Dell, Seagate	Leading supplier of PCs, microprocessors, software Lead market
Japan	Fujitsu, Hitachi, NEC, Toshiba, Sharp, Canon	Supplier of cutting-edge components and peripherals Mature semiconductor industry Leader in notebook PCs
South Korea	Samsung, Hyundai, Daewoo, and LG Electronics	Major supplier of DRAMs Producer of monitors and flat panel displays Significant semiconductor industry
Taiwan	Acer, Mitac, Inventec, FIC, Tatung, Delta, Compal	Major producer of a wide variety of components and peripherals OEM supplier to global industry Significant semiconductor industry
Singapore	Creative Technology, IPC, and Aztech	Production platform for disk drive industry Large PC assembly operations Growing semiconductor industry Regional business hubs for foreign firms
Hong Kong	VTech and Legend	Gateway to China; conduit for trade, technology, and capital flows Business management for production operations in China

Source: Adapted from Dedrick and Kraemer (1998, 72, table 2-12).

products (e.g., computer servers and specialized equipment) and other high value-added activities (e.g., software, networks, and solutions). These East Asian manufacturers have grown up from their earlier role as low-cost suppliers to OEM lead firms to serve as ODM partners and/or systems integrators, such as EMS providers.[29]

Strategic Partnership through ODM in Notebook Computers

While the above two favorable structural conditions of state functional support and changing opportunities in the global electronics industry have provided a conductive selection environment for East Asian firms to evolve and excel in their delivery of value services to global lead firms, a complete analysis of this evolution in strategic coupling requires a more in-depth elucidation of firm-specific initiatives. As the first of my three coupling processes, the *strategic partnership* between global lead firms' greater demand for manufacturing partners in East Asia and the growing capability of these Asian manufacturers to fulfill this demand can be observed since the late 1990s.[30] This new industrial dynamic also points to the opening up of new market avenues and opportunities for technological upgrading that was not available in the evolving international division of labor during the earlier decades. A central feature of this strategic coupling refers to the development of East Asian firm-specific dynamic capability in systems integration. To Hobday et al. (2005), the core capability of the modern high-tech firm is defined by its capacity to design and integrate different systems while managing networks of component and modular suppliers. As leading East Asian firms have gained massive manufacturing experience from their earlier phase of subcontracting work for OEM lead firms and have since developed sophisticated in-house production and management capabilities, they can now offer a much wider range of design, technological, and logistical solutions to their global lead firm customers. East Asian firms no longer manufacture according to the proprietary specifications of their OEM customers. Instead, ODM firms move up the value chain and engage directly in proprietary product design and specifications, and integrated turnkey solutions in order to secure large orders from their brand name customers.[31] In contract manufacturing, leading EMS providers offer large-scale and highly automated manufacturing production systems. Responsible for process innovation, these providers have to incur large capital investments in production systems and to control the entire supply chain of specialist materials and equipment vendors (Hobday 2001, 16). These two modes of industrial partnership are distinctive as ODM firms are more specialized in their product categories (e.g., notebook computers), whereas EMS providers cover the entire value chain of most consumer electronics, from design and manufacturing to logistics and fulfillment. Domestic firms from Taiwan and, to a certain extent, Singapore, are particularly strong in these two market segments of ODM and EMS in the global electronics industry.

In this and the next sections, I examine this coupling process of strategic partnership through several original case studies of leading East Asian firms in the ODM (Taiwan's Quanta and Compal) and the EMS (Taiwan's Hon Hai and Singapore's Venture) segments of global electronics manufacturing. As top players in both market segments, these East Asian firms have actively pursued technological upgrading and capability enhancement in order to engage strategic partnership with global lead firms. By pursuing a *competence-based strategy*, these case study firms have chosen to bypass the strategy of serving as low-cost OEM suppliers and emerged as strategic partners of global lead firms. Through continuous investment in R&D capabilities and production efficiency, these ODM firms and EMS providers are much better positioned in value chain activities. Their design, engineering, and manufacturing capabilities are also highly integrated into the product and market development and brand management capabilities of their lead firm customers. Global lead firms not only rely on these East Asian firms for manufacturing services, but more importantly also engage their original design and research capabilities for new product development. These cases therefore illustrate how leading East Asian firms have evolved to become systems integrators that bring together components, skills, and knowledge from their key domestic and international suppliers to design, engineer, and produce a wider range of sophisticated products for their brand name lead firm customers. While these East Asian systems integrators still depend on global lead firms for their brand management, market access, and downstream services (e.g., retail and postsale services), their partnership relationship is mutually interdependent because these brand name lead firms rely on their East Asian manufacturing partners to achieve lower cost-to-capability ratios and to retain their edge in a highly competitive global industry.

To date, Taiwan's ODM firms have developed unique firm-specific dynamic capabilities that are absolutely essential to sustaining the competitiveness of their brand name partners' global production networks. In 1995, Taiwan's share in the global shipment of around 3 million notebook computers was less than 20 percent (Kawakami 2009, figure 2). As shown in table 4.3, leading ODM firms from Taiwan accounted for as much as 52 percent of the global shipment of 24.2 million notebook computers in 2000. Within a decade, this share increased sharply to 95 percent in 2010. This rapid growth represents the success of Taiwanese ODM firms in the more technologically challenging and profitable segment of the global market for computer manufacturing. The world's top brand name computer firms, such as Dell, Hewlett-Packard, Apple, Toshiba, and Lenovo (formerly IBM ThinkPad), depend on these ODM firms for the production of a large proportion of their notebook computers. Through partnership agreements with leading Taiwanese ODM firms, such as Quanta, Compal, and Wistron, these brand name lead firms can speed up their product innovation and time-to-market in order to compete effectively in this highly globalized industry. In 2010, these three relatively unknown Taiwanese ODM firms collectively accounted for some 68 percent of the world's total notebook shipments of 187 million units. While the growing partnership opportunities for these ODM firms have provided favorable conditions, we need to examine carefully firm-specific behavior and initiatives in order to understand fully their successful coupling with lead firm partners in different global production networks.

The story of Quanta Computer epitomizes this book's broad argument for the evolutionary shift from embedded state-firm relations in the earlier phase of Taiwan's industrial transformation to the strategic coupling with lead firms in global production networks.[32] Founded in 1988 by Shanghai-born Barry Lam, Quanta started off as an ODM niche player specializing in the production of computer notebooks. Lam's background in calculator manufacturing is interesting (Amsden and Chu 2003, 41). After graduating from the National Taiwan University with engineering degrees, he and classmates co-founded Kinpo Electric in 1973. Through its subsidiary Calcomp, Kinpo became the

Table 4.3 Shipments and market shares of notebook ODM manufacturers from Taiwan, 2000–2010

Company	1999 shipment (,000)	2000 shipment (,000)	2004 shipment (,000)	2010 shipment (,000)	Largest client (mil units)	Second largest client (mil units)	Third largest client (mil units)
Quanta	2,150	2,506	11,626	52,100	HP(24)	Lenovo(6.0)	Apple(5.5)
Compal	1,100	1,804	7,666	48,100	Acer(18)	Dell(11)	Toshiba(8)
Wistron	1,526	1,800	—	27,500	Dell(10)	Acer(8.5)	Lenovo(7)
Inventec	1,200	—	—	16,150	Toshiba(12)	HP(3)	Lenovo(1.5)
Pegatron	—	—	—	15,450	Asus(8.5)	Apple(3)	Dell(2)
Hon Hai	—	—	—	10,000	Asus(4)	Dell(3)	HP(2)
Taiwan total	—	12,707	33,340	177,600	HP(40.3)	Acer(33.5)	Dell(30)
World total	—	24,224	46,110	187,600			
Taiwan share	39%	52%	72%	95%			

Note: These figures include notebooks manufactured in China by Taiwanese-owned production facilities.

Sources: Amsden and Chu (2003, 30, 33, tables 2.6–2.7) for 1999 data; company annual reports; www.researchinchina.com, accessed October 1, 2014.

world's largest supplier of calculators to OEM firms in the early 1980s.[33] In 1984, Calcomp established Compal to assemble desktop computers.[34] As part of the Kinpo group that specialized in component manufacturing (e.g., monitors), Compal did not go into the notebook business until 1989.[35] In 1988, Lam was frustrated by the reticence of Kinpo's other major shareholders to venture into the notebook PC business. He left Compal with several of his colleagues to establish Quanta as a dedicated ODM firm specializing in notebook computers.[36] Beginning with the modest revenue of US$133 million in 1991, Quanta's annual sales grew rapidly to US$1.1 billion in 1997 (Amsden and Chu 2003, table 2.9). This figure increased dramatically to US$5.7 billion in 2002 and US$16.5 billion in 2006. In 2011, Quanta achieved record sales of US$37.4 billion and doubled its market capitalization from US$4.9 billion in 2007 to eclipse US$10 billion for the first time.

From an initial production volume of tens of thousands, Quanta's rapid rise within a span of two decades to become the world's largest ODM producer of some 53 million units of notebook computers is legendary. Its compounded annual growth rate of 32.6 percent between 1991 and 2011 is phenomenal in a highly competitive and dynamic industry. The case deserves deeper analysis in relation to one of the three component processes of strategic coupling—its strategic partnership with brand name global lead firms. First, the adolescent nature of the notebook computer industry in the late 1980s provided a favorable window of opportunity for Quanta and other ODM firms from Taiwan, allowing them to avoid entering into a captive mode of OEM-supplier relationship described by Gereffi et al. (2005). Quanta was established at the time when the technologies for notebook computers were emerging, and no dominant industrial player was established. Unlike the desktop IBM-compatible PCs that were standardized since IBM's first PC introduced on August 12, 1981, no industrial standard for notebook computers was firmly in place.[37] By the late 1980s, the basic technology for flat-panel displays (TFT-LCD) was also quite mature, and these displays were crucial to the portability of notebook computers.[38] While Sony and Compaq had already established their notebook PC divisions by the late 1980s, others OEM lead firms, such as Apple, IBM, Fujitsu, and Siemens, also possessed strong engineering know-how and were ready to enter into this new business.

But as the notebook industry was still evolving and the market remained highly volatile, a latecomer such as Quanta could still enter into this potentially lucrative market. As noted by my Quanta interviewee, "If you look back now, it's essentially just something you can grab. With a couple of companies having capabilities, the industry was not defined. Everybody had their own visions, very different. And then I think we pretty much grew on it. Obviously you look at some of the things other people do when they present ideas. Pretty much, I think, is not standardized. You could essentially come up with something good and establish yourself." This lack of industrywide standardization gave Quanta the initial opportunity to break into the ODM business as a strategic partner, rather than as a captive supplier, of global lead firms. Because a notebook computer was an all-in-one device rather than a set, such as a desktop computer and its necessary peripherals, its internal layout and key components were highly variable, and thus design could play a decisive role in the functionality and market success of each generation of notebook computers. Once established by the late 1990s, Quanta and other ODM firms from Taiwan became the de facto product designers *and* manufacturers for brand name lead firms that had now restructured their businesses and leveraged increasingly on the design and manufacturing excellence of these ODM firms to sustain or improve their market positions in the rapidly evolving global industry.

Second, Quanta's evolving technological capability in ODM has greatly promoted its strategic partnership with lead firm customers. The manufacturing experience of Lam and his cofounder C. C. Leung in Kinpo and, later, Compal taught them how to design power supply and functionality into lightweight packages, such as notebook computers. Right from the beginning, Quanta was established as a design-oriented manufacturer of notebook computers. Reflecting on its initial focus on ODM, my interviewee observes that "Quanta started differently from other companies, for the notebook PC was not even available in other countries. So there's nothing we could learn from others. Our company was similar to those foreign [start-up] companies. We were an ODM from day one. Quanta's competitive advantage was product design. From 1988, for the first seven to eight years, we're in design." By 1990, Quanta was able to showcase a new notebook product at a trade show in Germany and attracted Siemens and Philips as its early customers. Still, notebook computers used to be a niche and expensive product until its mass adoption in the late 1990s.[39] To stay ahead of other ODM firms over time, Quanta has continued to invest substantially in its design and technological development in the successive generations of notebook computers. Its unique production capability combines both design flexibility and production speed. Quanta can customize its notebook designs for different lead firms in innovative ways and ramp up its production capacity for the chosen design within a short period of time. As Barry Lam said in an interview with *Businessweek* in June 1999, Quanta's role as an ODM is to provide different combinations of notebook features, akin to menu design by the top chef in a gourmet restaurant: "The chef can be very innovative, but the decision is made by the customer. We have to make them feel we're giving them the best choices."[40] This offer of innovative choices of notebook design works in tandem with Quanta's unique capability in turning the chosen design of new, high-quality models into volume production. As noted further by Lam, "If we can do that, our customers will be very profitable and they will continue to do business with us."

Third, Quanta's evolving economies of scale and scope since the late 1990s has further contributed to its strategic partnership with brand name lead firms. By the time its annual sales exceeded US$1 billion in 1997, Quanta's market power began to increase in relation to its customers and component suppliers. It moved from dependency on a few customers, such as Dell, at the beginning in the early 1990s to leveraging on up to ten major customers in the late 2000s (see table 4.3). This incremental approach to leveraging on partnership with more top customers paid off in Quanta's rapid expansion during the 2000s. As noted by my interviewee, "We had better companies coming in, giving big orders, and we became very big. The customers came in and made us bigger. As a result, we didn't start with many customers, but we decided to add a couple more customers over time and it's gone very well. It's not all of a sudden we got ten customers, but one by one. . . . It's very different as we're not beholden to one company like Dell or HP or whatever. HP came in and said, 'This is what we would like.' . . . We started out independently. So we take on this and that business on more equal terms." For example, Hewlett-Packard becomes more dependent on Quanta for its ODM work in notebook computers. As shown in table 4.3, Quanta designed and shipped some 24 million units or up to 60 percent of Hewlett-Packard's notebook computers sold worldwide in 2010. Their partnership relationship is reciprocal and relational in nature, with Quanta providing the production excellence and Hewlett-Packard defining and dominating the global notebook market.

To handle its large number of top customers, Quanta has developed sophisticated ways of organizing its ODM business into different divisions on the basis of its major brand name customers. Each of these divisions is explicitly tied to one major customer, and their staff work closely with marketing and R&D personnel from the customer. Quanta employees in different divisions do not interact, and no staff transfer between these divisions is allowed.[41] Because of this intrafirm divisional setup, Quanta has been able to preserve the top secrets of its key customers, such as pricing and marketing plans, proprietary know-how, and production targets. For example, Quanta has been working closely with Apple Inc. to design and manufacture its successive generations of PowerBooks and MacBooks.[42] But it has never leaked any confidential information about these Macintosh notebooks. The world of Mac fans could only get to know the look and specifications of these notebooks when the late Steve Jobs unveiled them at his press conferences. In organizational terms, these ODM divisions operate like different firms because each of them is tightly coupled with the technology, product, and market development departments of their key customers. These organizational capabilities and production technologies are hard to imitate because the key to their right mix and combination is very much a matter of tacit knowledge. My interviewee describes this tacit knowledge as "kind of like a black box. A lot of people ask what's your key advantage, and I think the way to look at it is like Tiger Woods playing golf. Everybody can play golf, and just like everybody can really manufacture notebook PCs. But can you play golf like Tiger Woods?"

Quanta's knowledge and capacity in optimizing production within given time and financial constraints affords significant product flexibility to its customers and yet allows it to maximize volume discounts from its key suppliers of major components (e.g., processors and memory chips) and modules (e.g., storage disks and power supply). As its production capacity becomes fully developed in Taiwan and China, Quanta is able to combine organizationally its advanced design capabilities in Taiwan with production efficiency in China and global supply chain management capability to create a total system solution for its brand name customers.[43] In addition, Quanta has developed significant intragroup integration of key component manufacturing, such as TFT-LCD displays (Quanta Display) and storage devices (Quanta Storage). In 1999, Quanta established Quanta Display Inc. (QDI), based on technology transferred from Sharp in Japan, and sourced up to 30 percent of its notebook displays from QDI.[44] This intragroup vertical integration can speed up considerably volume production and offer a one-stop service to its key customers because testing these key components can be done in-house: "Quanta Computer is able to leverage its relationship with its subsidiaries. When we design a notebook computer, we test it with Quanta Display and Quanta Storage to make sure it would be perfect. But if somebody gets the Quanta Computer bare bone, he may then spend a week or two to go to Samsung or AU Optronics for the panel, and HLDS [Hitachi-LG joint venture] or Toshiba for the drive. We do like to offer a completely packaged product to the customer." Focusing on excelling in its ODM strategy, Quanta contributes significantly to new product development and specifications of its global lead firm customers, thereby mitigating the switching risks associated with the typical OEM business. Playing this integral role in the notebook business of its global lead firm customers, Quanta Computer has emerged as a key strategic partner of its global brand name customers in the fiercely competitive global market. Its production organization has become a critical link in the global production networks of this sector, and it has evolved to be a global market leader in spearheading continuous innovations in organizing this transnational production of computer notebooks.

With hindsight, Quanta's story is not the only successful one underpinning Taiwan's dominance in the global production of notebook computers. As shown in table 4.3, Quanta has been joined by a number of other top ODM firms, such as Compal, Wistron (a spin-off from Acer Computer), Inventec, and Pegatron. This market segment in the global electronics industry is perhaps the best illustration of the strategic partnership between Taiwan's ODM firms and their global lead firm customers. The rise of these ODM firms to prominence in the global computer industry within two decades, however, was neither anticipated by the developmental state nor well analyzed in the statist literature. As noted by Hobday (1995a, 37), Taiwan's prevalent system of being latecomer suppliers in the early 1980s was known as OEM subcontracting (or "captive" suppliers in Gereffi et al. 2005). Only in 1988 and 1989 did an emerging system of latecomer firms taking charge of the design, specification, and manufacturing of more sophisticated electronic products, such as computers, begin to be called ODM in Taiwan, and the term was not even used in South Korea, Singapore, and Hong Kong. The ODM system in notebook computers was critical to Taiwan's latecomer firms gaining market access through their global brand name customers.[45]

The founding of Quanta Computer in 1988 as a niche player initially making small quantities of computer notebooks and the venturing of Compal into notebook production in 1989 can be seen as the most significant milestone in the rise of ODM systems integrators from Taiwan. This was the time when the developmental state had almost completed its core mission of steering the initial launch of Taiwan's semiconductor industry. ODM firms, such as Quanta, Compal, and Inventec, did not depend on the state for resources and strategic directions in their growth trajectories. Even in their formative years during the early 1980s, these ODM firms forged close working relationships with global lead firms. As argued by Fuller (2005, 148), the barriers to entry into the OEM supplier market were relatively low, and the Industrial Technology Research Institute (ITRI) and its Electronics Research Service Organization (ERSO) "did not play as critical a role in the development and diffusion of technology as it did in the IC [integrated circuits] industry." Instead, these ODM firms are strategically coupled with lead firms in global production networks through which they derive their firm-specific resources and capabilities. Their critical success factor is not a strong developmental state at home, but rather a tight and interlocking coupling relationship with these global lead firms. My argument does not negate the supportive role of the state in, for example, human resource development and other trade-facilitating policies. The state's success in promoting the integrated circuits industry also provides positive spillovers to these ODM firms that in turn serve as the "domestic" market for local IC design firms (e.g., MediaTek) and semiconductor foundries (e.g., TSMC).[46] By the 2010s, these leading ODM firms from Taiwan have fully matured as world-class manufacturers through their ongoing strategic partnership with brand name global lead firms in notebook computers.

Strategic Partnership through EMS in Consumer Electronics

The coupling process of strategic partnership and growing interdependence between ODM firms and global lead firms in notebook computers described above is also evident in a broader market segment of the global electronics industry. In this mode of industrial organization known as contract manufacturing, large EMS providers have emerged to become the movers and shapers of the global electronics industry. While the EMS model was first developed in the United States in the late 1980s with the rise of independent contract manufacturers and, later on, spin-offs of manufacturing facilities previously owned by global lead firms (e.g., Apple and IBM), the dominance of US-origin EMS providers in the late 1990s has been challenged by several world-leading

EMS providers from Taiwan (Hon Hai and Foxconn) and Singapore (Venture and WBL) since the 2000s.[47] Listed in table 4.4, these East Asian EMS providers have become serious competitors to the market dominance of US-origin EMS providers, such as Flextronics (acquired Solectron in 2007), Jabil Circuit, Celestica (spun off from IBM in 1996), and Sanmina-SCI (which acquired Apple's manufacturing facility in 1996). In this EMS category of global electronics production, the role of East Asian firms goes well beyond notebook computers to cover the entire range of electronics products, from computers and peripherals to consumer electronics, telecommunications equipment, medical instruments, automotive devices, and so on. As the global production networks of these electronics products are reorganized continually, East Asian firms that have developed strong partnership relationships with brand name lead firms have grown further to become large contract manufacturers and systems integrators. Electronics manufacturers in Taiwan and Singapore are particularly quick in capitalizing on their established market positions and production know-how to grow rapidly as major manufacturing partners in the global electronics industry.

In Sturgeon's (2002, 460) original study, all of the world's top five EMS providers in 1995 were based in North America. He notes that ODM firms from Taiwan, including Hon Hai and others, had a much narrower product focus on computers, generated more revenue from design services, and demonstrated a greater penchant to compete with their customers in end markets than these "unknown" American EMS providers. These Taiwanese ODM firms were therefore not expected to grow rapidly and expand globally vis-à-vis their American EMS counterparts. By the mid-2000s, it became clear that this pessimistic view was mistaken. The four largest ODM firms (Quanta, Compal, Inventec, and Wistron) had revenues comparable to or exceeding these US-origin EMS providers. Meanwhile, three leading firms from Taiwan and Singapore have emerged among the top seven EMS providers in 2010 (see table 4.4). More important, they were much more profitable throughout the 2000s than the four US-origin EMS giants in Sturgeon's (2002) study—Flextronics, Solectron, Celestica, and Sanmina-SCI. These four "first-mover" EMS providers suffered from record losses while the three East Asian latecomer EMS providers grew their revenues and market share. By 2010, Taiwan's Hon Hai alone had revenue in excess of US$100 billion and eclipsed the combined total of all other EMS providers in the top ten. To account for this dramatic change of fortune in favor of East Asian EMS providers during the 2000s, it is useful to bear in mind that they were neither a major target nor a key beneficiary of state-led development during their formative years in the late 1980s and throughout the 1990s.

The key to these East Asian EMS providers is their capability in organizing and managing the *entire* value chain of an electronic product, from its design to manufacturing and fulfillment. These EMS providers are not low-end subcontractors for OEM lead firms that govern in a form of captive relationship

Table 4.4 World's top ten providers of electronics manufacturing services (EMS) by revenue, 1995–2010 (net income in parentheses and in US$billion)

Name (year of founding and geographical origin)	1995	2000	2002	2004	2006	2008	2010
1. Hon Hai Precision[1] (1974, Taiwan)	0.50 (0.14)	2.8 (0.32)	7.1 (0.49)	17.2 (0.94)	40.7 (1.84)	65.4 (1.68)	100.4 (2.66)
2. Flextronics International[2] (1990, US based in Singapore)	0.40 (−0.02)	12.1 (−0.45)	13.4 (−0.08)	15.9 (0.34)	19.3 (0.51)	30.9 (−6.09)	28.7 (0.60)
Solectron (acquired by Flextronics in 2007)	2.1 (0.08)	14.1 (0.50)	11.0 (−3.11)	11.6 (−0.18)	10.6 (0.13)	—	—
3. Jabil Circuit[3] (1966, US)	0.56 (0.01)	3.6 (0.15)	3.5 (0.04)	6.3 (0.17)	10.3 (0.16)	12.8 (0.13)	13.4 (0.17)
4. Foxconn International[4] (1990, Taiwan)	0.16 (−0.06)	0.87 (0.02)	0.31 (0.01)	3.4 (0.18)	10.4 (0.72)	9.4 (0.12)	6.8 (−0.22)
5. Celestica[5] (1996, Canada)	3.2 (−0.05)	9.8 (0.21)	8.3 (−0.45)	8.8 (−0.85)	8.8 (−0.15)	7.7 (−0.72)	6.5 (0.10)
6. Sanmina-SCI[6] (1980, US)	0.17 (0.02)	4.2 (0.21)	8.8 (−2.70)	12.2 (−0.05)	7.6 (−0.14)	7.2 (−0.49)	6.3 (0.12)
7. Venture Corp[7] (1984, Singapore)	0.18 (0.02)	0.8 (0.06)	1.4 (0.11)	2.0 (0.12)	2.7 (0.16)	3.8 (0.12)	2.7 (0.15)
8. Benchmark Electronics[8] (1979, US)	0.10 (0.01)	1.7 (0.02)	1.6 (0.04)	2.0 (0.07)	2.9 (0.11)	2.6 (−0.14)	2.4 (0.08)
9. Plexus[8] (1979, US)	0.28 (0.01)	0.75 (0.04)	0.88 (−0.01)	1.0 (−0.03)	1.5 (0.10)	1.8 (0.08)	2.0 (0.09)
10. Kimball International[8] (1939, US)	0.90 (0.04)	1.2 (0.05)	1.2 (0.03)	1.1 (0.02)	1.1 (0.02)	1.4 (−0.01)	1.1 (0.01)

[1] Hon Hai's revenue in 1995 refers to 1996. All figures are standardized to US dollars using the December 31 exchange rate for that year. It has been profitable every year since 1996.

[2] Flextronics' revenues in all years refer to the financial year ending on March 31 the following year and are separate from Solectron that it acquired in October 2007 after the latter's two years of record losses in 2002 (−US$3.1 billion) and 2003 (−US$3.5 billion). Flextronics incurred losses in 2001–2004 and 2008–2009, with the biggest loss in the industry's history in 2008 (−US$6.09 billion).

[3] Since 1988, Jabil Circuit only suffered from one year of major loss in 2009 at US$1.17 billion.

[4] Foxconn's revenue in 1995 refers to 1997. Its revenues prior to 2004 refer to Foxconn Technology that was previously known as Q-Run Technology established in Taipei in 1990. All figures are standardized to US dollars using the December 31 exchange rate for that year. Since public listing in 2000, Foxconn only suffered from one year of loss in 2010.

[5] Celestica's revenue in 1995 refers to 1998. It was spun-off from IBM Canada in 1996. Celestica incurred losses in 2001–2008.

[6] Sanmina-SCI's revenue in 1995 refers to Sanmina before it was merged with SCI Systems in December 2001. Sanmina-SCI incurred losses in 2002–2009, with record losses in 2002 (−US$2.7 billion), 2005 (−US$1.0 billion), and 2007 (−US$1.1 billion).

[7] Venture has been profitable every year since 1986, except in 1988 just before it was merged with Multitech Systems to form Venture Corp. All figures are standardized to US dollars using the December 31 exchange rate for that year.

[8] Benchmark has been profitable every year since 1987, except in 2008. Plexus has been profitable every year since 1984, except in 2002–2005. Kimball has been profitable every year since 1983, except in 2008.

Sources: Some 1995 data are from Sturgeon (2002, 461, table 1); the rest are from company reports in OSIRIS database, osiris.bvdinfo.com, accessed on September 4, 2014.

well described in Gereffi et al. (2005). Rather, they provide the entire manufacturing solution on a "turnkey" and global basis to their strategic customers. Their mutually constitutive relationship resembles a mode of strategic partnership that benefits both parties on a complementary and sustained basis. First, these EMS providers procure all the necessary components from key suppliers or their own in-house manufacturing facilities. These EMS providers are thus different from systems integrators, such as ODM firms, because they often manufacture key components internally. In short, economies of scale enjoyed by EMS providers can help drive down the final cost of electronics products sold by their lead firm customers. Second, these EMS providers have increased their global presence through the complementary processes of acquiring the existing manufacturing facilities of their major customers and/ or establishing new plants abroad. As such, EMS providers tend to handle a much greater range of electronic products and have their factories located in different parts of the world, from Asia to Europe and the Americas. They are the quintessential transnational corporations from East Asian economies. This globalization of production facilities enables EMS providers to be highly responsive to market volatility in the global electronics industry. Their customers can also benefit from their operational flexibility, as the EMS providers can rapidly adjust their production capacity for specific products in different markets and locations. The economies of scope offered by EMS providers can help their key customers manage different time-to-market pressures. Third and most important, the success of an EMS provider is critically dependent on its ability to organize and manage the ever more complex task of handling multiple and often complex relationships with their lead firm customers and major suppliers in different markets and global locations.

As introduced at the beginning of this book, Taiwan's Hon Hai Precision is perhaps the most extraordinary case of a family-owned firm that grew rapidly in the 2000s to become Taiwan's largest industrial firm and the world's largest EMS provider.[48] Founded by Terry Gou in 1974 as a family-owned company making plastic parts, such as channel-changing knobs for black-and-white television sets, Hon Hai did not experience exponential growth until the late 1990s. During most of its formative years in the 1980s, Hon Hai was a large diversified electronics parts manufacturer, specializing in a range of connectors and cable assemblies for desktop and notebook PCs and PC peripherals. As recent as in 1996, Hon Hai's revenue was only half a billion US dollars (see table 4.4). Measured in annual revenue, it was smaller than Taiwan's top ODM firms, such as Quanta and Compal, until after 2000.[49] But by 2010, Hon Hai had achieved US$100 billion in sales for the first time (and US$135 billion in 2014), and its compounded annual growth rate since 1996 was a whopping 46 percent. How then did Hon Hai grow from an unknown component maker in the 1980s to become a US$135 billion company with several million employees in 2014? The key lies in its adoption of the EMS model of strategic partnership with such global lead firms as Apple, Dell, Hewlett-Packard, Intel,

Motorola, Nokia, Sony, and Toshiba. Its competitive advantages are predicated on its ability to combine discretion with a solid record of quality control and competitive pricing. Established in China's southern city Shenzhen in 1988, its "Foxconn City" is well known for guarding the identities of Hon Hai's key customers and strategic partners. And yet its optimal production operation and in-house manufacturing of many parts for its EMS products have significantly reduced its per unit cost.

Hon Hai's first major breakthrough in its strategic partnership with global lead firms came in 1995 when Terry Gou met Michael Dell in southern China. On their way to the airport, he took the unexpected opportunity to detour and bring the thirty-year-old founder of Dell, then still not yet ranked among the world's top five PC vendors, to his Shenzhen factory. Gou was able to offer a one-stop solution to Dell's predicament arising from managing its hub-and-spoke manufacturing system. At that time, Dell and other PC companies would buy parts from their suppliers and assemble them in their own factories. But Hon Hai had created a full production line integrating most of these parts and processes, from the raw steel for PC casings and electrical connectors to the final assembly. Since the visit, Hon Hai has become Dell's largest EMS provider. Working closely with PC lead firms, such as Dell and Hewlett-Packard, Hon Hai had emerged by 2004 as the world's largest EMS provider in desktop PCs and PC servers for worldwide global lead firm customers. By 2005, its strategic partnership with Motorola and Nokia paid off when it became the world's largest mobile handset EMS provider with handset-related revenue of US$6.3 billion. Hon Hai is also the major manufacturer for Sony's PlayStation and Nintendo's Wii videogame consoles. In 2003, Hon Hai entered into the TFT-LCD business through joint ventures with Taiwan's panel producer Chi Mei Optoelectronics and United Keys from the US. By 2009, Hon Hai's was ready to take on a partnership with Sony to produce its LCD TVs for the Americas region. To strengthen further its production capacity and technologies in LCD TVs, Hon Hai merged its in-house display panel firm Innolux with Chi Mei Optoelectronics, then Taiwan's largest panel producer, in March 2010 to become a vertically integrated LCD TV producer. As the LCD panel typically accounts for 70 percent of the production cost of a LCD TV, this vertical integration serves Hon Hai extremely well as the one-stop strategic partner of leading brand name TV lead firms, such as Sony.[50] In February 2012, Hon Hai was financially strong enough to acquire a 10 percent stake in Japan's Sharp, a loss-making world leader in LCD-LED TV technologies. By August 2012, Hon Hai was operating jointly Sharp's two major plants in Osaka, Japan, that manufactured large LCD-LED TV panels. In November 2014, Hon Hai became the strategic partner of Nokia Technologies and gained the design licensing rights to be the dedicated manufacturer of its Nokia tablet (Thomas 2014). It has also been involved in such new partnerships with other brand name lead firms, such as Blackberry (phones) and Google (robotic operating systems).

Of all these strategic partnerships with global lead firms, Hon Hai's EMS work for Apple Inc. is the most significant (see the opening vignette in chapter 1). Through its China-based company Foxconn International established in 2000, Hon Hai has been serving as Apple's EMS provider in the almost-exclusive production of iPhones (since its launch in 2007) and iPads (since its launch in March 2010) and one of the few manufacturers of Apple's iPods (since its launch in November 2001). Hon Hai's competitive strength in EMS is phenomenal and highly critical to Apple's success since the launch of its iPhones. When the late Steve Jobs announced the first iPhone on January 9, 2007, the time-to-market was about six months.[51] The first shipment of iPhones came on June 29, 2007. Five years later, the time-to-market of new iPhones was reduced to less than two weeks. The new iPhone 6 and 6 Plus were announced on September 9, 2014. Nine days later on September 19, they were available for purchase in the United States, Australia, Canada, France, Germany, Hong Kong, Japan, Puerto Rico, Singapore, and the United Kingdom.[52] This extremely quick time-to-market is a key competitive strength of Apple and accentuates the great success of many of its products. Its rivals in smartphones, such as Samsung, Nokia, and Motorola, often take one to several months to deliver their newly launched handsets. In the quarter ending in September 2014 (before the new iPhone 6), the iPhone was synonymous with Apple's success when it accounted for 56 percent of Apple's US$42.1 billion revenue from all products.[53] As the key manufacturer of over 500 million units of the iPhone since its launch, Hon Hai's EMS capability has become a critical part of Apple's success. While Hon Hai's profit margin from such EMS provision is smaller relative to the profitability of brand name lead firms such as Apple,[54] its EMS capabilities in speedy ramping up of production volume, high quality control, and competitive pricing should not be underestimated because of their critical role in the competitive success of Hon Hai's strategic partners.

Unlike many other high-tech firms from Taiwan, Hon Hai's story is perhaps unique. Its founder Terry Gou is not a transnational technopreneur who has spent time working in world-class high-tech companies. His company was not a "national champion" on Taiwan's state list for favorable incentives and promotion policies in the 1980s. The timing of Hon Hai's rise to global leadership in EMS is also peculiar because it grew rapidly during the 2000s when the state's developmental efficacy was in decline, and its industrial policy shifted toward horizontal or functional roles. In short, Hon Hai's emergence as Taiwan's largest industrial firm owes neither to direct state-led industrialization efforts nor to indigenous industrial capabilities derived from the "brain circulation" of transnational technologists and elites. Its success as the world's leading EMS provider is conditioned by the changing industrial organization of global production networks that offers a critical moment of opportunity for it to emerge as a strategic manufacturing partner of global lead firms. As its economies of scale and scope have increased since the 2000s, Hon Hai's EMS model of industrial production has outdone all of its North American rivals, such as Flextronics, Jabil Circuit, Celestica, and Sanmina-SCI. During this period, it has developed strong manufacturing capabilities through continuous innovations. In 2005, it filed 3,346 domestic patent applications and ranked second only after TSMC among the top thirty Taiwanese innovative groups (Mahmood and Zheng 2009, table A1). In the 2010s, it has maintained this high quantity of patent applications.

In contrast, Singapore's Venture Corp has become one of the top ten EMS providers through a combination of transnational technopreneurship and focused strategic partnership.[55] Its successful strategic coupling with global lead firms, particularly Hewlett-Packard and its spin-off, Agilent Technologies, is not premised on the deliberate policy interventions of Singapore's developmental state. It is rather predicated on the existence of a transnational community of elite professionals and entrepreneurs who serve as the relational bridge between domestic firms and global lead firms. As a transnational technopreneur receiving his education at the University of California, Berkeley, Venture Corp's chairman and CEO, Wong Ngit Liong, was recruited by Hewlett-Packard in California to establish its factories in Malaysia and Singapore during the early 1970s.[56] After twelve years with Hewlett-Packard, he struck out on his own in 1986 to join Venture Manufacturing Singapore (VMS), then a new start-up founded in 1984. In 1989, VMS merged with Multitech Systems, founded by a former employee of IBM India in 1986, to become Venture Corp. Under Wong's leadership, Venture Corp has grown into a world-class EMS provider with a turnover of around US$2 billion in 2013. It remains as the only Singapore-origin EMS provider among the world's top ten, as shown in table 4.4.[57]

From an evolutionary perspective, the developmental state in Singapore might well be credited with attracting Hewlett-Packard to relocate its manufacturing operations to Singapore at the beginning of the 1970s and for inviting the private venture capital firm, South East Asia Venture Investment (SEAVI), established by Advent International, to invest in the initial founding of Venture in 1984. But the state and its bureaucrats were much less significant in Venture's subsequent growth and transformation, which has depended mostly on the entrepreneurial judgment and business acumen of Wong and his team of dedicated senior executives, many of whom came from Hewlett-Packard as well.[58] Their collective action within the firm and their strategic coupling with Hewlett-Packard and other global lead firms provided the main conduit through which Venture's rapid growth and competitive strength can be understood. When we move beyond Venture's origin in the mid-1980s, the analytical lens of the developmental state is less relevant for understanding its articulation into the global economy during the 1990s and the 2000s. Throughout its growth during these two decades, Venture focused on strategic partnership with key lead firm partners. In 1993, no single client accounted for more than 10 percent of Venture Corp's still modest sales. But by 2005, more than 80 percent of its revenue had come from its top twelve customers, such as Hewlett-Packard, Iomega, Agilent Technologies, Emulex Corp, IBM, Motorola, and Cisco. In 2005, Hewlett-Packard was Venture's top customer and contributed to about 25 percent of its revenues. In 2011, the two top customers in its EMS segment continued to account individually for more than 10 percent of Venture's group revenue. As one of the most profitable EMS providers given in table 4.4, Venture is able to corner a large share of the EMS market, such as Hewlett-Packard's printers, Iomega's storage devices, and Agilent Technologies' networking devices.

Venture's focused strategic partnership during the 2000s was based on several interrelated approaches. First, Venture has been careful and selective in partnering with specific global lead firms. From its initial ODM work in printers for Hewlett-Packard and the establishment of its greenfield plants during the second half of the 1990s, Venture expanded into EMS by acquiring the manufacturing facilities of its major customers, such as Agilent's plant in Spokane, Washington, and Iomega's plant in Penang, Malaysia. Its strong partnership with top customers was evident during Hewlett-Packard's restructuring in 2001 through which the number of its global suppliers was reduced from more than twenty to less than five strategic partners. Venture was retained as one of Hewlett-Packard's major EMS providers. To assure Hewlett-Packard and to avoid conflicts of interest, Venture would not work with its competitors, such as Kodak, Canon, or Lexmark, and produce their printers. Because of this trust embedded in longstanding interpersonal and interfirm relationships, their strategic partnership has evolved to become reciprocal in nature. In August 2002, Venture launched an entrepreneurial start-up in the United States, known as VIPColor Technologies, to market its own VP2020 digital color label printer for the industrial printing and packaging industries. Venture Corp manufactured this own brand printer, but Hewlett-Packard supplied its print heads and ink. Hewlett-Packard became a core component supplier for the new printer developed and manufactured by its EMS partner.[59] Their synergistic relation as strategic partners went well beyond the usual customer-supplier relationship.[60] Reflecting on the need for strong but carefully selected partners, my interviewee from Venture argues that "I may be very strong in manufacturing. But if I don't have design, then you have to find some companies to design, and then they have to work with me. Two big companies along this value chain is very difficult to manage because there's knowledge transfer, confidential information, inefficiency, gaps in between, time delay, and the time-to-market is slow. So there're a lot of inefficiencies that can occur if we have too many partners. In other words, if you form too long a chain with too many rings in the chain and you happen to find a weak one, then the whole chain becomes screwed."

Second, Venture has developed firm-specific design and manufacturing capabilities that are well complemented by its fulfillment services. Its EMS capability is underpinned by its "seamless transition" from R&D to manufacturing and its strong design capability since inception. This "seamless transition" is a critical competitive advantage in the EMS business, as global lead firm customers require strong product design support, manufacturing capability, and delivery efficiency from its EMS providers. Third, Venture has moved beyond its manufacturing expertise through continuous investment in design and service capabilities. Compared to other EMS providers, Venture Corp has developed strong expertise in design and manufacturing capabilities. The origin of its key executives from Hewlett-Packard has provided the most important impetus to its continual interest in expanding its ODM capabilities. This design capability has in turn provided the critical "glue" that cements its strategic partnership with key customers. As noted by my interviewee, its partnership with Hewlett-Packard and Agilent Technologies is strongly based on Venture's deep involvement in designing and manufacturing their products: "This kind of partnership, once it's established, it's very hard to change. If you don't want to work with someone who designs your products, then you're going to have a big problem. To build this neat trust, you need confidence. Let's say if I build a certain product and it's complicated. It will take a long time for somebody new to learn. And to shift from A to B, a lot of knowledge transfer and a lot of cost and time will be wasted. So it's not easy to do so." To strengthen further its value chain capabilities, Venture has also built forward and backward linkages into its EMS business. It has developed technology alliances with other high-tech firms in networking and printing products and invested in key suppliers of plastic molds and components and metal tools. All these evolving intrafirm organizational processes have enabled Venture to engage in production capacity building and to consolidate its leading role as a strategic partner of global lead firms.

Conclusion

This empirical chapter has provided an in-depth analysis of strategic partnership as an important meso-level process for East Asian firms to couple with lead firms in global production networks. Focusing primarily on the global electronics industry, I have illustrated that the competitive success of leading East Asian firms in this industry needs to be put in an evolutionary perspective in which the critical factors to their growth and development vary over time. In the early phase of industrialization in all three East Asian economies, the developmental state had played an important "husbandry" role in shaping the industrial trajectories of this sector. Some of today's leading East Asian firms in the electronics industry, particularly those in the semiconductor segment to be documented in the next chapter, were clearly early beneficiaries of the developmental state's "picking the winners." Going beyond this husbandry role effective in the early phase of the electronics industry up to the late 1980s, however, the state becomes less significant as the steward of this increasingly diverse and complex global industry. As East Asian firms become more articulated into global electronics, they are no longer dependent on the state for capital, finance, know-how, and market channels. Instead, these firms have developed strong strategic relationships with their lead firm partners in global production networks. It is through these globalized network relationships that East Asian firms and their home economies increasingly gain and sustain their dynamic competitive advantages.

More specifically, my detailed case studies of Taiwan's Quanta Computer, Compal Electronics, and Hon Hai Precision Industry; and Singapore's Venture Corp have shown the relative importance of the three sets of structural conditions underpinning strategic coupling in figure 3.2. While changing state roles and industrial organization have indeed provided favorable structural conditions for the initial founding of these firms in the 1980s, their emergence as the world's leading ODM firms and EMS providers is predicated on firm-specific initiatives enabling their strategic coupling with global lead firms. In particular, the continual pursuit of strategic partnership by these leading East Asian firms with their key brand name customers represents one such coupling process for understanding the articulation of their domestic economies into the global electronics industry. Through their firm-specific initiatives boosting manufacturing excellence, supply chain capabilities, and timely fulfillment services, these East Asian firms have developed a unique set of competitive advantages that couple well with the strategic reorientation of brand name lead firms in different global production networks.

Since the 2010s, these East Asian firms have firmly established their dominant positions in the global manufacturing of electronics products, and their home economies have become major players in the global electronics industry. Their enormous size and geographical reach have given them the necessary economies of scale and scope to work closely with strategic partners in different networks. They have come a long way from the major competitive crisis identified in Bello and Rosenfeld (1990). These leading East Asian firms have also graduated from the need to depend on or benefit from state-led initiatives in a globalized world of electronics. In short, they have become masters of their own destiny. One may argue, however, that the globalized nature of the electronics industry tends to allow for a firm-based competence strategy to excel, and this industry-specificity may not be applicable to heavy industries that have much higher sunk costs and require greater state intervention in the form of "big push" initiatives in order to activate and realize the dynamic processes of latecomer catching up and strategic coupling. The next chapter will consider this important argument in the context of shipbuilding and offshore rig production as a heavy industry in which leading East Asian firms have earned their legitimate place as world leaders. It will also analyze semiconductor manufacturing in which industrial specialization is required to achieve competitive success in the global economy.

Chapter 5

Industrial Specialization and Market Leadership in Marine Engineering and Semiconductors

Instead of following the strategic partnership process pursued by original design manufacturing (ODM) firms and electronics manufacturing services (EMS) providers to couple with brand name global lead firms, a handful of capital-intensive East Asian firms have focused on building *new* technological and organizational capabilities in heavy industries (e.g., shipbuilding and rig production) and high-tech products (e.g., semiconductors). Unlike ODM firms and EMS providers manufacturing for final consumers, these industrial leaders specialize in the production of intermediate goods for other industrial users in different global production networks. In their early developmental periods, many of these industries required substantial investment to achieve scale economies and cost efficiency in order to catch up with pioneering first movers in advanced economies that had possessed superior technological and organizational capabilities. This longer time-horizon in initial investment prompted the developmental state in the three East Asian economies to involve themselves directly in the early founding of these industries as an integral part of their state-led industrialization program.

While this "husbandry" or "demiurge" role of state-directed industrial development was crucial in the 1970s and the 1980s,[1] heavy state ownership, management control, and performance requirements became harder to sustain over time in a more liberalized and interconnected global economy, partly because of the significantly transformed state roles and the evolutionary dynamics of the state-firm-global production networks assemblage described in chapter 2. Since the late 1990s, this firm-led initiative toward strategic coupling with global production networks has been facilitated by the two favorable structural conditions of evolving state functions and industrial dynamics. First, the state has shifted from its initial role as a direct owner planning and steering these capital-intensive industries to become an institutional supporter of firm-led industrial development. Since the early 1990s, the financial resources and political legitimacy possessed by the state have generally decreased, and its direct developmental role in these national firms and industries has correspondingly diminished. Some of these national firms have been privatized in order to stimulate their market leadership and continuous investments in new technologies and organizational know-how. The postdevelopmental state has turned to horizontal industrial policy to promote firm-based innovation and R&D activity and to strengthen the broader industrial ecology system.

Second, changing industrial dynamics due to new market entrants means that the initial scale economies in favor of these East Asian firms are no longer sufficient for them to succeed in global competition in these capital-intensive industries. As more and larger developing countries, such as China, Brazil, India, and resource-rich countries from the Middle East have joined the "race to the swift" in these heavy and/or high-tech industries,[2] the competitive success of leading East Asian firms can only be sustained through well defined and highly specialized technological and organizational capabilities in industrial markets and niche products. Former state-owned enterprises are now fully professionalized in order to strengthen their organizational capabilities and market repositioning. In lieu of state directives and financial support, we witness the rise of firm-specific, capability-building and coupling initiatives in different global industries. Finally and different from the case of electronics manufacturing examined in the previous chapter, the role of transnational communities in facilitating this coupling process is relatively less significant because interfirm coupling relationships in these capital-intensive industries are based more on the sophisticated industrial requirements and performance of their capital goods, such as ships and chips, than on the global lead firm's tacit knowledge of product designs, consumer preferences, and final markets in the electronics industry.

To elucidate this important process of strategic coupling operating through industrial and market leadership at the firm level, I examine in depth multiple case studies of the world's largest shipbuilders and offshore rig makers from South Korea and Singapore and the world's largest semiconductor foundries and integrated chipmakers from Taiwan and South Korea. By dedicating themselves to specialized industrial products in global markets, these leading East Asian firms have not only surpassed second-mover advantages in their respective industries but also have become increasingly disembedded from their home states to emerge as global leaders in their industrial segments. These case studies show that state-led industrialization through equity ownership or policy directives in both industries has produced contrasting outcomes in all three economies. The more successful cases point to the critical importance of technological and organizational innovations. Before I analyze this emergence of East Asian firms as industrial market leaders in the marine industry (second section) and semiconductors (third section), it is necessary first to revisit the conceptual underpinning of second-mover advantages in order to understand better the dynamic catching up of these latecomers with their competitors in advanced industrialized economies and the role of new state functions and industrial dynamics in this process.

Beyond Second-Mover Advantages

The idea of "catching up" and "leapfrogging" has been a luring and enduring concept in the study of East Asian development.[3] Many of these studies have focused on the active and direct role of the developmental state in steering this process of catching up through which its national firms gain second-mover advantages vis-à-vis global market leaders from advanced industrialized economies. These latter economies, such as Britain and the United States and, later, France and Germany, are known as "early industrializers," and their national firms are deemed to possess unique first-mover advantages, such as superior technologies, strong organizational capabilities, and market control. In his *Scale and Scope*, Alfred Chandler (1990) makes a convincing case for the development of first-mover advantages by early industrializers through their three-pronged investment in scale economies, managerial capabilities and proprietary knowledge, and marketing and distribution channels. In the Schumpeterian sense, these firms were the original innovators who first introduced disruptive products or services based on new technologies and/or know-how, and successfully created new industries in their own image. To Schumpeter (1934), these first movers achieved the advantage of scale in relation to production cost, innovation, and international production. As first movers pioneering new markets and industries, these global lead firms enjoyed a substantial amount of entrepreneurial rents or profits from their new products or services. Once established, they tended to dominate these new markets and industries, coordinating their own global production networks.

Through highly selective sectoral policy interventions and the specific promotion of "chosen winners," the developmental state in East Asian economies has decidedly groomed a new generation of latecomer firms that can now compete effectively against first movers in the global economy. These East Asian firms are generally known as "latecomers" because they are not the original innovators prompting the development of new markets or industries. Instead, they have managed to catch up with first-mover firms in more mature industries. The key analytical and policy question is: What kind of second-mover advantages possessed by these East Asian firms has enabled them to compete against first-mover firms in these increasingly mature industries? In *Beyond Late Development*, Amsden and Chu (2003, 3) argue that the most distinctive element of such second-mover advantages is *upscaling* that refers to the attainment of economies of scale within a short period of time: "A latecomer must exploit unique types of scale economies and manufacture in large volume. Even if a firm starts small, it must ramp up very rapidly to achieve a high output level, a process that requires building assets related to project execution, production engineering, and a form of R&D that straddles or falls somewhere in between applied research and exploratory development (integrative design in the case of electronics)."

This second-mover advantage requires substantial investment in order to achieve both scale and speed in three ways (Amsden and Chu 2003, 7–10). First, product maturity is necessary for latecomer firms to achieve scale economies through production-related economies or learning-by-doing. East Asian firms usually enter into the production of mature products through acquisition of foreign technologies originally developed by first-mover firms. This process of technological acquisition is often described in the literature as copying or reverse engineering.[4] As these products and related technological know-how become more mature and standardized, East Asian firms can enjoy diminishing unit design costs and economies in information, signaling, and transactions costs. Over time, these firms can also develop organizational routines to internalize these diminishing costs of upscaling.[5] Second, latecomer firms can develop new skills in technological knowledge, project execution, and production capabilities (Amsden and Hikino 1994). The role of transnational technopreneurs in this acquisition and development of new skills can be imperative (e.g., the case of Singapore's Venture Corp in chapter 4). Third, upscaling is necessarily dependent on rapid ramping up and increasing concentration of investment. The cases of Taiwan's Quanta and Hon Hai are again instructive in illustrating the importance of ramping up through substantial investment in production capacity. To Fuller et al. (2005, 96), "Taiwanese businessmen and engineers have spent so much time involved in manufacturing that their historically accumulated inclination, reinforced by continual successes, and their deep understanding of manufacturing lead them to continue to pursue this type of business."

While the development of the above mentioned second-mover advantages, particularly upscaling through state-led initiatives, is critical to the early success of domestic firms and industrial transformation in East Asian economies, it is necessary to point out that the effectiveness of these advantages in global competition tends to diminish over time, as this initial catching up process is completed and rapid achievement of scale economies can be imitated by new competitors, such as "late" latecomers (e.g., China, India, and Brazil). Moreover, once the technological regimes in these industries evolve into much greater complexity, the state can no longer dictate the kind of first-mover technologies and capabilities to be acquired, learned, and transferred to domestic firms in established industries.[6] State-led development of second-mover advantages becomes less useful in sustaining the competitive advantage of leading East Asian firms. In short, the story of catching up should *not* end with second-mover advantages, as we are commonly told in the developmental state literature. We need to ask another set of critical questions: What happens to these latecomer firms *after* they have achieved the initial second-mover advantages? What does it take for these East Asian firms to maintain or even develop further their firm-specific advantages such that they can emerge as dominant leaders transforming these markets and industries? How do East Asian firms overcome their strategic dilemma in order to make the risky transition from latecomer followers to industrial leaders?

These questions prompt us to move away from the static view of second-mover advantages in the existing literature to address the structural conditions of changing *state functions* and *industrial dynamics* in enabling the strategic coupling of East Asian firms with global production networks. Insofar as latecomer firms continue to engage in value creation in established industries, the concept of first movers is insufficient for understanding fully their evolutionary trajectories in global competition. This is because unless they develop disruptive products or original technologies to create entirely new markets or industries, East Asian firms can never be deemed first movers. Amsden and Chu (2003, 177) thus define such second movers as "the first firm from a latecomer country to sell a new 'mature' product." While they concede that both first movers from advanced industrialized economies and second movers from latecomer economies can succeed because they are the "first" in their respective home economies to make the three-pronged investment described in Chandler (1990), this conception of second movers tends to lock latecomers into a perpetual market position as followers of first movers, even when these first movers have gone into decline and obsolescence. As examined in the previous chapter, many studies of East Asian firms in the global electronics industry tend to follow this static view of latercomers and often conceive them as being locked into a particular dependent relationship with their OEM first-mover customers.[7] My empirical analysis has already shown how this dependent relationship can change over time through a coupling process of strategic partnership characterized by intense global competition among diverse sets of firms in different production networks.

In this chapter, I continue this argument for a more dynamic and evolutionary view of these latecomers from the three East Asian economies and analyze their incessant technological and organizational innovations that go beyond their initial second-mover advantages, such as upscaling.[8] As noted in chapter 2, the changing selection environment since the late 1980s has greatly facilitated or expedited the continuous development of their technological and organizational capabilities. In particular, through *specialization* in industrial products and niche markets, these latecomers firms have developed new firm-specific capabilities that fit into the description of neither first-mover (new industries) nor second-mover advantages (upscaling). These firm-specific capabilities are manifested in three critical dimensions: new product or process technologies, flexible production and product diversity, and organizational know-how and proprietary access to market information. This capability development at the firm level is also conditioned by a peculiar combination of new state roles and competitive industrial dynamics. As these new state roles are less interventionist in nature, their direct influence on the firms and industries to be analyzed later is harder to trace. The point here is not to reinstate the developmental state, but to identify these new state functions and their possible relevance to the respective firms in these capital-intensive industries.

First, latecomer East Asian firms can develop their own and more sophisticated technologies over time on the basis of their production capability and manufacturing excellence, even after they have already achieved scale economies and outcompeted first mover firms from advanced industrialized economies. As evident in the following analysis of heavy and high-tech industries, these new technologies are crucial in sustaining their market leadership in capital-intensive industries that have become more competitive over time and required greater firm-specific dynamic capabilities (e.g., continuous learning and upgrading of technologies). Reflecting on South Korea, Linsu Kim (2003, 107) argues that "smart followers often outperform pioneers in the long run . . . because smart partners can engage in more sophisticated technological activities and enjoy a greater degree of control and autonomy than otherwise." In addition, East Asian firms can create dynamic capability through the nonincremental creation of complementary and integrative knowledge built on the existing incremental or underutilized knowledge of first movers from the United States, Western Europe, and Japan. This creation typically involves process innovation in high-tech production in sectors such as semiconductors and TFT-LCD display panels (Hu 2012). These capability-building efforts also benefit from the home state's horizontal industrial policy that broadly enhances the innovative capacity of the domestic economy through public investment in human resources and research institutes. A stronger domestic regime for the protection of intellectual property rights (e.g., patenting services) also promotes firm-specific technological development. Financial incentives (e.g., tax benefits and expenditure rebates) for new product or technology development are relevant for promoting these firms to invest in risky frontier technologies.

Second, specialization in industrial market leadership enables these East Asian firms to develop greater economies of scope through flexible production and product diversification. While scale economies are important in their initial catching up with first movers, continual success in global production networks in these industries requires East Asian firms to engage in flexible specialization. In capital-intensive global industries, competing on the basis of lower per unit cost of each product or service is not as effective and sustainable as capturing higher value through product differentiation or service varieties. The competitive dynamics of these industries tend to favor firms that provide *both* scale and scope economies in order to avoid lock-in to particular products or services. As argued by Hobday et al. (2004), leading East Asian firms in these industries tend to adopt a portfolio of strategies tailored to different products, markets, and business cycles. The role of the state is particularly useful here. For example, supportive policies in favor of higher value creation at the firm level are implemented through market-promotion activities organized by various trade and investment facilitating agencies. Trade fairs and investment promotion trips can serve as policy tools for increasing and diversifying the international market reach of these domestic firms. While the postdevelopmental state can no longer directly subsidize these large firms through discretionary policy loans, its lead agency for industrial development can provide a common institutional platform for domestic and foreign firms in the same industry to share information, concerns, and knowledge during different business cycles.[9] This role of state agencies in facilitating collective action and risk mitigation is particularly significant in capital-intensive industries characterized by highly disruptive business cycles, such as shipbuilding (ten to fifteen years on average) and semiconductors (five to ten years on average).

Third, as East Asian firms deepen their coupling with different global production networks in these industries, they develop new organizational routines and innovations that strengthen their relationship with key customers and suppliers and enable them to exercise better control of market information and access. The competitive dynamics of these industries are manifested in the great diversity of industrial applications of capital goods. Ships in the marine industry can be intermediate goods to many different industries, ranging from passenger and commercial transport to extractive industries. Semiconductors have even wider industrial applications, from electronics and automobiles to aerospace and robotics. This unique condition of industrial dynamics increases substantially the costs of information asymmetry and market intelligence at the firm level. The state can play a helpful role in the firm-specific development of these capabilities. Apart from setting up market development agencies and research institutes, the state's role is also effective in the broader arena of facilitating international trade. The successful negotiation and implementation of bilateral and multilateral trade agreements are often useful to these East Asian firms as they need to import components and machinery from their foreign suppliers for the production of these capital goods for exports to their customers in different global industries. A more liberal and well-functioning trade regime can provide a favorable structural context for these latecomer firms to consolidate their strategic relationships with lead firms in different global industries.

Taken together, these firm-specific capabilities go well beyond economies of scale and cost efficiency to incorporate new technological and organizational innovations; they combine first-mover advantages in new technologies and know-how and second-mover advantages of scale economies. Since they choose to specialize in providing products or services to other firms in different global production networks rather than to final consumers, these East Asian firms tend not to develop strong firm-specific capability in branding and distribution, such as most first movers in advanced industrialized economies.[10] Through this specialization in industrial markets and niche products for different global industries, East Asian firms have grown from being scale followers of first movers to become specialized market leaders over time. The following two empirical sections will illustrate how this process of strategic coupling operates respectively in the marine engineering industry and the global semiconductor industry.

Big Is Beautiful in the Marine Industry

In contrast to light and consumer-oriented industries (e.g., personal computers and household electronics), scale economies are apparently much more important in major segments of the marine engineering industry, such as shipbuilding and rig production.[11] Being big is therefore generally deemed "beautiful" in this heavy industry that caters to demands from other specialized industrial users, such as maritime transportation services, petroleum exploration and production, and so on. The Gulf of Mexico oil spill in April 2010, the worst in the history of the global petroleum industry, reveals the intricate interfirm relationships in a marine global production network, bringing together some of the world's leading players in oil and gas exploration, offshore drilling, shipbuilding, and rig production.[12] The Deepwater Horizon, an offshore oil rig drilling on the Macondo well operated by BP (formerly British Petroleum), was built by South Korea's Hyundai Heavy Industries (HHI), the world's largest shipbuilder, for US$365 million, and it entered into service in 2001.[13] Transocean, the world's largest offshore drilling company incorporated in Switzerland, owned and operated the semisubmersible rig under a long-term contract with BP through to September 2013. It contracted its key supplier, Cameron International, for the blowout preventer that failed to work and to prevent the massive oil spill. After BP had tried several unsuccessful methods of capping the well, it called on three rigs made by two Singaporean companies—Keppel FELS and SembCorp Marine—that managed to seal the well and ended the spill. These two firms happened to be the world's two largest offshore oil rig producers and together accounted for 70 percent of the world's order for jack-up oil drilling platforms.[14]

Both shipbuilding and rig production are highly specialized industrial markets, and competitive success in these markets demands sustained investment in technological and organizational capabilities. As they approached the late 1970s, all three East Asian economies encountered a new challenge to their export-oriented industrialization drive—how to diversify into more capital-intensive and technology-driven industries beyond labor-intensive manufacturing, such as textiles, garments, plastics, and electronics assembly? Specialized segments of the marine industry, such as shipbuilding and rig production, were selected as one of the key heavy industries targeted for early industrialization. By the late 1980s, the competitive success of latecomer shipbuilders from South Korea had often been hailed as the positive outcome of state-led development to attain massive economies of scale in an industry characterized by mature technologies and high sunk costs. HHI was a poster boy of South Korea's developmental state and a premier example of its state-led industrialization well described in Amsden's (1989) *Asia's Next Giant*.[15] Without President Park Chung Hee's relentless drive toward developing heavy and chemical industries in his Fourth Five Year Plan (1977–1981), HHI would not have become the world's largest shipbuilder within one decade of building its first ship in March 1973. Singapore's Keppel Corp and SembCorp Industries, respective parent company of Keppel FELS and SembCorp Marine, were state-owned enterprises established in the 1960s to take over the dockyards left behind after the departure of the British during the 1959–1971 period. Both companies remain as government-linked companies with substantial ownership by the state investment vehicle Temasek Holdings in 2015.[16]

In the following two subsections, I analyze how world-class shipbuilders from South Korea and rig producers from Singapore go beyond their initial second-mover advantages in favor of developing new firm-specific capabilities through continuous technological and organizational innovations. These new capabilities contribute to their industrial market leadership that in turn underpins their successful strategic coupling with specific segments of the global production networks in the maritime transport and offshore oil industries. Despite the continual strength of earlier movers, such as Japan, and new entrants from China, my four case study firms—South Korea's Hyundai Heavy Industries and Samsung Heavy Industries, and Singapore's Keppel Corp and SembCorp Industries—remain as the top two producers respectively in shipbuilding and rig-building markets in the 2010s. Most important, their continual domination in these industrial markets during the past two decades is buttressed by their sustained investment in new production technologies, product diversity, strong control of supply chains, and well-developed relationships with major customers. In these ways, they have clearly moved on from their initial scale economies developed through state-led sectoral policy interventions in the 1970s and the 1980s.

South Korea's Quest for Global Leadership in Shipbuilding

In the global shipbuilding industry since the Second World War, Japan began to undermine the industrial leadership of European and American shipbuilders by constructing gigantic shipyards and capitalizing on much lower costs through imported raw materials in coal and iron ores (Bunker and Ciccantell 2007, chap. 3).[17] In 1950, Japan's shipbuilding industry produced 829,000 gross tons of new ships and accounted for 15.6 percent of world production. In 1965, Japan's output reached 5.4 million gross tons and its global market share increased rapidly to 43.9 percent. At its peak in 1975, Japanese shipbuilders produced 18 million gross tons or 50.1 percent of new ships. As illustrated in figure 5.1, Japan's market share in shipbuilding was about half of total world output from the mid-1960s through the mid-1980s. During this period, ship-

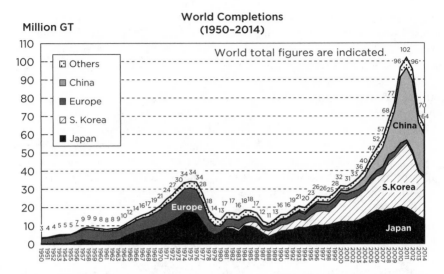

Figure 5.1. World completions of shipbuilding by country, 1950–2014 (in million GT).
Source: *Shipbuilding Statistics,* March 2015, and unpublished IHS (Formerly Lloyd's Register) Maritime World Shipbuilding Statistics data from the Shipbuilders' Association of Japan, http://www.sajn.or.jp/e, accessed June 30, 2015.

building was one of Japan's most important export industries. In the 2000s, Japan remained one of the world's three largest shipbuilding nations. But the global shipbuilding industry suffered from the two major oil crises in the early and the late 1970s, and did not recover until the early 1990s. Between 1974 and 1976, the annual shipbuilding orders worldwide dropped by 54.6 percent, from 28.4 million gross tons in 1974 to 12.9 million gross tons in 1976. Annual completion was also reduced from 33.9 million gross tons in 1976 to 18.2 million gross tons in 1978 and 13.1 million gross tons in 1980 (Amsden 1989, 270, table 11.2). In 1988, global shipbuilding output plummeted to a trough of 11 million gross tons.[18] This global crisis in the shipbuilding industry compelled Japanese shipbuilders to enter into a prolonged period of depression, as the industry's global competitiveness steadily declined vis-à-vis new entrants from South Korea in the late 1970s and, later, China in the late 1980s (see figure 5.1).

By the 2000s, the global shipbuilding industry had finally turned around because of substantial growth in the global economy and global trade in manufactured goods. These trends contributed to the emergence of cross-border production networks in many global industries. The rise of China as the world's factory also prompted high demand for bulk shipping and thus the construction of new ships by yards in South Korea, Japan, and China. In 2002, South Korea overtook Japan to become the world's largest shipbuilding economy, until China caught up in 2010 (see figure 5.1). In 2003, a new peak since the early 1970s, new ship orders placed with South Korean shipyards totaled 27.8

million gross tons and were valued at US$23.9 billion. New orders for Japanese shipyards amounted to 16.1 million gross tons valued at US$11.7 billion, whereas Chinese shipyards had orders for 11.5 million gross tons valued at US$8.1 billion (Bunker and Ciccantell 2007, 184–85). Since the mid-2000s, the world's three largest shipbuilders have all been from South Korea—Hyundai Heavy Industries, Daewoo Shipbuilding and Marine Engineering, and Samsung Heavy Industries.[19] In 2005, their combined orders accounted for 25 million gross tons or almost 30 percent of the world's total orders at 72 million gross tons. As of 2006, HHI and Daewoo Shipbuilding were ranked respectively as ninth and twenty-fourth largest among the top thirty chaebol in South Korea.[20] In table 5.1, the world's top five largest shipbuilders at the historical peak in 2011 were all from South Korea, and their combined output was 9.8 million gross tons or 25.3 percent of the world's total output of 38.8 million gross tons.[21] As of June 2012, South Korea's order book of 30.8 million CGT was dominated by higher-value products, such as container ships and LNG tankers, whereas shipbuilders in Japan and China tended to supply lower value bulk carriers. How did these chaebol emerge or remain as dominant industrial market leaders in shipbuilding during the 2000s? In the following analysis, I argue that their strategic coupling with global production networks is made possible through developing new firm-specific capabilities rather than relying on direct state interventions or second-mover advantages.

From building its first ship, a very large crude carrier, in March 1973, Hyundai Heavy Industries (HHI) had emerged to be the world's largest shipbuilder by the mid-1980s with cumulative production exceeding 10 million gross tons in 1984 (Amsden 1989, 272–73, table 11.3).[22] In 1984, HHI's size measured in production was more than double the second largest shipbuilder, Daewoo, and over 50 percent more than the combined production of the next three shipbuilders (Daewoo, Korea Shipbuilding and Engineering Corporation, and Samsung). This was the period when the global shipbuilding industry suffered from high excess capacity and cutthroat price competition. HHI was able to increase its market share because of two important and complementary factors: firm-specific capabilities and state-led policy interventions. First, the Hyundai group had accumulated significant experience in heavy industries by the early 1970s. During the Vietnam War in the 1960s, Hyundai's first international contracts came from US government projects in Southeast Asia: the Pattani-Narathiwat Highway in Thailand and dredging work in Vietnam (Woo 1991, 96).[23] By the early 1970s, Hyundai had accumulated substantial skills in project feasibility studies; project taskforce formation; access to foreign technical assistance, training, equipment purchase; and new plant design and construction. The operation of project start-ups in the construction business had also helped its new shipbuilding business (Amsden and Hikino 1994).[24] HHI could benefit from cross-subsidization within the Hyundai group of companies and develop significant forward and backward vertical integration in its shipbuilding operations. As noted by Amsden (1989, 273), HHI's

Table 5.1 World's top shipbuilding production and firms by country in 2011 and ship order by country as of end June 2012

Rank	Country	2011 production CGT¹ (million)	Share (percent)	2012 order (in percentage) Container ships	LNG tankers	Bulk carriers	2012 total order in GT (million)	Top ten shipbuilders Firm name	Country	2011 CGT¹ (,000)	2011 Share (percent)
1	China	14.7	37.9	15.6	1.2	49.6	71.9	Hyundai HI	S. Korea	2,774	7.1
2	S. Korea	13.1	33.8	36.5	16.3	9.5	62.8	Samsung HI	S. Korea	2,400	6.2
3	Japan	7.0	18.0	2.8	5.6	61.4	29.7	Daewoo	S. Korea	1,866	4.8
4	Philippines	0.6	1.5	—	—	—	3.9	Hyundai Samho	S. Korea	1,587	4.1
5	Italy	0.4	1.0	—	—	—	0.8	Hyundai Mipo	S. Korea	1,192	3.1
6	Germany	0.4	1.0	—	—	—	1.3	STX SB	S. Korea	987	2.5
7	Taiwan	0.3	0.8	—	—	—	1.9	Dalian SB	China	941	2.4
8	Vietnam	0.3	0.8	—	—	—	1.9	Sundong SB	S. Korea	788	2.0
9	Norway	0.2	0.5	—	—	—	0.2	Imabari SB	Japan	694	1.8
10	Turkey	0.2	0.5	—	—	—	0.5	Shanghai Waigaoqiao	China	583	1.5
	Others	1.6	4.1	—	—	—	11.0	Others	—	24.9	64.5
	Total	38.8	100.0	—	—	—	185.9	Total	—	38,800	100.0

¹CGT is the gross tonnage (GT) of the ship weighted to reflect its work content per GT. For example the weight for a container ship might be 1.0 and the weight for a big tanker 0.25.

Source: Using data from Clarksons Shipping Intelligence Network, http://www.clarksons.net, accessed on November 4, 2014.

guiding slogan in the 1980s was "our own ships, our own engines, our own designs." It developed basic in-house design capability and produced its own engines and core electrical equipment in order to ensure better control over its shipbuilding process and timely delivery of both core inputs and the final product.

Second, Park's developmental state was undoubtedly instrumental in directly steering the early growth of the South Korean shipbuilding industry.[25] Amsden (1989, 243) argues strongly that the springboard for further industrialization in the 1970s and the 1980s did not come from labor-intensive cotton spinning and weaving, but rather from "the government's more management-intensive, early import substitution projects." One such project was the shipbuilding industry that was targeted in the acutely competitive decade of the 1970s. She further notes that the state provided a multitude of capabilities and a protective cover to latecomers, particularly HHI, wishing to enter world trade. In 1973, Park was deliberately targeting the shipbuilding industry, one critical sector within the marine industry. The state nationalized the existing shipyards to form Korea Shipbuilding and Engineering Corporation in the early 1960s, imported advanced shipbuilding technology from Japan and Europe in the early 1970s, and promoted domestic production of shipbuilding machineries and ship parts in the mid-1970s (Sohn et al. 2009, 39–42). In the case of HHI, these state-led interventions included offering a temporary monopoly over steel structures to one of HHI's industrial units, creating demand for HHI ships by ordering South Korea's crude oil to be delivered by the shipping unit of the Hyundai group, guaranteeing HHI's own foreign loans, providing extensive subsidies for infrastructure, and offering extensive financial guarantees to help it win its first order. These interventions contributed to HHI's rapid building up of scale economies to compete against leading Japanese shipbuilders, such as Mitsubishi Heavy Industries, Sumitomo Heavy Industries, and Ishikawajima-Harima Heavy Industries.

The case of HHI is particularly interesting in that it is part of a family-owned chaebol, not a state-owned enterprise, such as Korea Shipbuilding and Engineering Corporation (KSEC),[26] which was a common practice among the developing economies kick-starting industrialization in the heavy marine industry. HHI therefore enjoyed the best of both worlds—the entrepreneurial flair of Chung Ju-yung,[27] the late founder of the Hyundai group, and immense financial and policy supports from the developmental state in South Korea. Combining both group-based competitive advantage and state-distorted comparative advantage (i.e., "getting the prices wrong"), HHI was able to outcompete its Japanese counterparts on the basis of scale economies and lower costs and emerge as the world leader in shipbuilding by the mid-1980s. During the next two decades and with much less direct state interventions, HHI continued to excel in shipbuilding and diversified into offshore engineering and heavy machinery and equipment engineering. After investing more than 40 billion won, HHI finally produced its first proprietary HiMSEN engine for its ships in 2002 (Sohn et al. 2009, 42). As indicated in table 5.1, Hyundai remains the world's largest shipbuilder group comprising HHI, Hyundai Samho, and Hyundai Mipo, with a combined 14 percent share of the global market in 2011.[28] The global success of HHI appears to lend support to the conventional wisdom of latecomer's catching up strategy through state-sponsored development of second-mover advantages in scale economies.[29] But this story of scale economies is challenged by two important exceptions: the rise of Samsung Heavy Industries (SHI) and the failure of the state-owned shipbuilding industry in Taiwan.

As a true latecomer, Samsung Heavy Industries (SHI) was rather late in joining the South Korean shipbuilding fraternity, but its eventual success is predicated on its strategic coupling with global production networks through industrial market specialization rather than merely scale economies or state interventions.[30] While established in 1974, SHI's first shipyard in Geoje was not completed until 1979. In Amsden's (1989, table 11.3) analysis, SHI's ship production started modestly at 13,858 gross tons in 1980, when Hyundai's production was already 518,565 gross tons. In 1983, SHI was finally consolidated after its merger with two other heavy industries firms within the Samsung group: Samsung Shipbuilding (established in 1977) and Daesung Heavy Industries (acquired in 1977). By the time Hyundai became the world's largest shipbuilder producing 1.3 million gross tons in 1984, SHI's output was still small at just 123,974 gross tons or about 10 percent of the global leader. SHI's takeoff started only in the early 1990s when it began to produce large oil and LNG tankers and completed the third dock of its shipyard in Geoje. As part of the post-1997 crisis "Big Deal" in South Korea, SHI had to dispose its ship engine business to Korea Heavy Industries. In 1998, SHI also sold its transport and heavy machinery businesses to Clark from the United States and Volvo from Sweden. This restructuring enabled SHI to focus on its shipbuilding business during the 2000s when it built some of the world's largest container ships and LNG tankers. In 2005, it became the world's third largest shipbuilder, after Hyundai and Daewoo, with 9 percent of the global market in shipbuilding. Its total revenue reached US$7.6 billion in 2007. Since then, SHI has become the market leader in the high-tech and high-value segment of the global shipbuilding industry, accounting for the *largest* share of drill ships, ultra-large container ships, and LNG-FPSO carriers. In 2011, its revenue increased further to US$11.9 billion and came close to Daewoo's US$12.4 billion. It was the world's largest producer of oil tankers and second largest in container ships in 2011.

Unlike Hyundai, SHI did not start with substantial economies of scale and was not a primary beneficiary of state support. Facing strong domestic incumbents (HHI and Daewoo) and international competitors (e.g., Mitsubishi), SHI had to engage with the process of industrial specialization and niche production in order to couple with lead firms in global production networks. This coupling process works particularly well in specialized industrial markets, such as petrochemicals (oil tankers) and shipping (container ships). But what are

SHI's underlying factors for successful strategic coupling in the 2000s? In general, the home base advantages of SHI and HHI are not too different since both shipbuilders could achieve second-mover advantages in scale economies through intra-chaebol subsidization, access to cheap steel, and, in the case of Hyundai, state-directed benefits and incentives. First, both of them belong to two of the largest chaebol groups that have core businesses in other industries, such as automobiles (Hyundai), construction (Hyundai), electronics (Samsung), and semiconductors (Hyundai and Samsung). They enjoy no substantial difference in their intragroup cross-subsidization. Second, both shipbuilders could tap into low-cost steel produced efficiently in South Korea. An interviewee from SHI notes that "the most basic job for a shipbuilder is to get steel and cut it into the right shape and put them together." As pointed out by Amsden (1989, 271, 293), the state-owned Pohang Iron and Steel Company (POSCO) was founded in 1968 to support South Korea's industrialization. By the early 1980s, it had already become one of the lowest cost steelmakers in the world and run neck to neck with Japan's integrated steel mills. As materials and components contributed to about 65 to 70 percent of total costs in shipbuilding, Hyundai's total costs were fairly similar to Japan's "Big Seven" shipbuilders in 1983. But one crucial difference existed between these two South Korean shipbuilders. Whereas SHI's foray into shipbuilding had become substantial only by the late 1980s, Hyundai had already benefited from more than a decade of directed support from the developmental state and emerged to be the global industrial leader. SHI's leapfrogging to match industry leaders, such as Hyundai and Daewoo, by the late 2000s could only be achieved through developing *new* firm-specific capabilities beyond scale economies already enjoyed by both incumbents in South Korea. This is where technological and organizational innovations are most crucial in enabling SHI to achieve higher-cost competitiveness and product differentiation in high-tech shipbuilding.

To catch up with industry leaders in Japan and South Korea, SHI has engaged in continuous technological and organizational innovations since the early 1990s. Its core competitiveness is underpinned by its firm-specific innovations in production methods and product diversity. These new innovations contribute to SHI's technological capabilities comprising both production and innovation capabilities. On its innovation in production methods, SHI has successfully pioneered the *sea-surface crane* production method that significantly reduces the time required to build a ship and increases production efficiency. In the past, European, Japanese, and even South Korean shipbuilders specialized in shipbuilding using dockyards on land. Each ship was made in these docks using blocks of steel plates that included all parts of the ship. A 100,000-ton ship, for example, could be formed by processing, assembling, and fitting of up to 90 blocks. The main disadvantage of this land-based production method was that the heavy crane moving those blocks to the dock for shipbuilding could only carry up to 500 tons, and thus each block must be less than 500 tons. With its sea-surface crane production method, SHI is able to build ships on sea surface for the first time. Each of its blocks is now moved to the dock via a giant offshore floating crane that can carry up to 3,000 tons. The successful deployment of these "megablocks" of up to 3,000 tons can substantially reduce the time required for the construction of a 100,000-ton oil tanker from three months to one and a half months, dramatically improving SHI's production throughput and efficiency. As my SHI's interviewee notes, "The competitiveness of the shipbuilding business comes in how you make the materials and the parts efficiently within the fixed area. In this, our core competitiveness lies in the sea-surface crane production method (as compared with production in the dockyards). Because we lack space we have a dock floating on water, which increases our capacity. In Japan, this is not possible because their docks are old fashioned."[31]

Another key competitive strength of SHI is its product differentiation. While Japanese shipbuilders tend to achieve high efficiency in building midsize ships through standardization of designs and production, SHI's organizational flexibility allows it to produce higher value-added ships of varying sizes, from gigantic oil tankers and container ships to passenger ships and offshore drill ships. For example, LNG carriers are generally known as the ultimate symbol of cutting-edge shipbuilding technology and require highly sophisticated design and production technologies (Sohn et al. 2009, 46). SHI's design teams can handle ships of different sizes and are ahead of its competitors. Its production facilities can also be flexibly rearranged to build ships of different sizes. As described by my interviewee, SHI "makes diverse sized ships. Because of this, the Japanese cannot be flexible in responding to the requests by ship owners. The bigger ships are mostly made in Korea. Our docks are designed to be able to produce big ships and other specialized ships like LNG ships or FPSO (combined ship with floating facilities for drilling) ships. Japan has already given up on this area. The cost is too much for them if they enter the market now." By the end of the 2000s, SHI had managed to corner the global market in oil tankers, LNG carriers, and ultra-large container ships. Of the 976 ships ordered between its first production in 1980 and end December 2011, SHI built 367 crude oil tankers, 362 container ships, and 95 LNG carriers.

Samsung's case illustrates that state-led sectoral industrial policy targeting specific shipbuilders is neither a necessary nor a sufficient condition for catching up to occur in late industrialization.[32] This exception to state-led development is further evident in Taiwan's failure to develop a strong shipbuilding industry *despite* the heavy involvement of its state-owned enterprises (SOEs) and its early technological lead over South Korea. As early as in 1969—well before Hyundai built its first ship in 1973, Taiwan had already produced a 100,000-ton oil tanker. Between 1969 and 1978, Taiwan's shipbuilders made nine such large oil tankers, including Burma Endeavor, a 450,000-ton oil tanker for the British merchant navy that was then the world's third largest (Sohn et al. 2009, 42). Taiwan's shipbuilding industry, however, did not progress further through developing new core technologies and innovations (Chou and Chang 2004). It also did not have the benefit of diversified business groups being "targeted" and "selected" as in South Korea. Instead, the developmental state in Taiwan took the shipbuilding business in its own hands and created a large SOE, China Shipbuilding Corp (CSBC), in July 1973 to produce "virtually all ships of more than a few thousand tons, while many small private shipyards produce fishing boats and yachts" (Wade 1990, 100). This shipyard was one of the state's four major import substitution and large lump projects of the 1970s. It was directly supported by disbursement from the state budget and access to foreign credit on terms considerably softer and cheaper than domestic credit (Wade 1990, 170). This active participation of the developmental state in the economy through its SOEs was not surprising in the context of its claim to be the legitimate ruler of China. K. T. Li, the influential minister of economic affairs during the 1960s and the early 1970s, first worked for the Central Shipbuilding Corporation in Shanghai after the Second World War and then for the Taiwan Shipbuilding Corporation in 1948, becoming its general manager in 1951 (Greene 2008, 123).[33] As the economic architect of Taiwan's developmental state, his enormous personal knowledge of this industry should have facilitated his choice of SOEs in this industry and made CSBC a successful public enterprise in the global shipbuilding industry.

While CSBC was and still is the largest in the domestic shipbuilding industry, Taiwan as a whole remained a small player in the global shipbuilding industry. Unlike Japan and South Korea, Taiwan's share of new ship orders in 1986 was a meager of only 0.7 percent. In table 5.1, CSBC was not among the top 20 shipbuilders in 2011. CSBC also suffered consistently from losses during the global slump between the mid-1970s and the late 1980s. In December 2008, it was privatized through public listing in the Taiwan Stock Exchange. This case illustrates that state ownership per se cannot guarantee the success or failure of the emergence of East Asian firms as global leaders in the heavy marine industry. The strong show of the developmental state's "visible hand" in the case of CSBC perhaps accounts more for its failure than for its nurturing and emergence.[34] State ownership also did not work in favor of Korea Shipbuilding and Engineering Corporation (acquired and renamed to Hanjin Heavy Industries in 1989). Today, both shipbuilders remain distant followers of the "Big Three" private sector giants from South Korea—Hyundai, Daewoo, and Samsung—whose combined revenues reached US$72.2 billion in 2011, the most recent peak in the global shipbuilding industry.[35] With hindsight, the targeting and picking of national champions could be quite readily performed by the developmental state enacting SOEs to take over the industrial vacuum left by private entrepreneurs.[36] But the nurturing and growing of these SOEs into world-class companies requires a particular combination of the state's role as a catalyst and the domestic firm's strategic coupling with global production networks that was not quite right in the case of Taiwan's shipbuilding industry.

The "Accidental" Champions from Singapore

Such a mix of supportive state efforts and firm-specific coupling is indeed evident in the case of two former SOEs in Singapore's marine industry—Keppel Corp and SembCorp Industries. These domestic firms have become the world's largest offshore rig builders for different global production networks emerging from the oil and gas boom of the 2000s. Singapore's case represents another variant of the developmental state in which the success of national firms requires both initial nurturing and subsequent "letting go," so that former SOEs can grow out of state-led development to become full-fledged competitors in the global economy. This evolutionary trajectory in attaining industrial market leadership in specialized oil and gas global production networks is best illustrated by the stories of Keppel Corp and SembCorp Industries.[37] Both cases illustrate the importance of indigenous innovation through sustained firm-specific efforts in developing new products and process technologies.

Keppel Corp's marine pedigree dates back to the construction of Singapore's first ship repair dry dock by Captain William Cloughtonat in Keppel Harbor in 1859.[38] After Singapore's independence from Britain in 1959 and becoming a nation-state in August 1965, the developmental state coordinated and developed the ship repair and shipbuilding industry as an integral part of its industrialization program. In 1963, the Economic Development Board, the state's elite pilot agency, entered into a joint venture with Japan's Ishikawajima-Harima Heavy Industries to incorporate Jurong Shipyard. In 1968, three domestic marine firms were established under the state's tutelage: Jurong Shipbuilders, Sembawang Shipyard, and Keppel Shipyard. These four companies would eventually become today's SembCorp Industries (first two and Jurong Shipyard) and Keppel Corp (renamed from Keppel Shipyard in 1986). In 1971, Keppel Shipyard entered into offshore rig production and acquired a 40 percent stake in Far Eastern Shipbuilding Industries (FELS), a company previously established in 1967 by US-origin Levingston Shipbuilding Company to extend its rig production to Asia. FELS was renamed to Keppel FELS in 1997, and Keppel Offshore and Marine (O&M) was established in 2002 to integrate all marine businesses within the Keppel Group. Meanwhile, SembCorp Industries was incorporated in October 1998 to bring together state-controlled Sembawang Corp and Singapore Technologies Industrial Corporation (STIC). After the merger, SembCorp Industries renamed Jurong Shipyard to SembCorp Marine in 2000.[39]

In retrospect, Singapore's domination in global offshore rig production is "accidental" in the sense that the state under the newly elected People's Action Party was forced by highly unusual circumstances in the 1960s to take over obsolete shipyards and docks left behind by the British. The initial founding of Singapore's ship repair, shipbuilding, and offshore rig production was undoubtedly a state-led development. This included the state taking control of four of the largest shipyards and shipbuilders that would eventually constitute Keppel O&M and SembCorp Marine. After Singapore had produced its first jack-up rig in 1969, it quickly became one of the world's largest builders five years later in 1974. By the mid-1970s, Singapore had already established itself as a major international ship repair center, partly facilitated by its geographical advantage and deep seaports. From total revenue of S$100 million in 1968, the marine industry grew to S$2 billion, and Singapore became the world's largest offshore rig builder in 1981.[40] In 1983, Singapore also became the world's largest ship repair center. Moreover, the state's ownership of key marine players was critical in helping them tide over a twenty-year gloom in the global offshore and marine industry since the mid-1980s. As shown in table 3.5, the state investment vehicle, Temasek Holdings, held 58.5 percent shareholding of Keppel Corp before divestments between 1989 and 1993. As of end 1999, it controlled 57.9 percent shareholding of SembCorp Industries. As of end 2014, Temasek Holdings remained as the controlling shareholder of both Keppel Corp and SembCorp Industries. In 1996, the Economic Development Board launched the Local Industry Upgrading Program (LIUP) in the marine industry and worked with several major shipyards to advance automation and develop new production processes. During the 2000s, the state also implemented a fairly liberal foreign labor policy to allow rig producers to stay cost competitive by hiring up to 70 percent of foreign workers to build their rigs in Singapore. The state also cofunded applied R&D centers established between these major rig producers and local universities.

After both Keppel Corp and SembCorp Industries had consolidated their respective marine businesses by the early 2000s, Singapore's offshore rig production took off dramatically. As shown in table 5.2, ship repair accounted for more than 50 percent of the S$3.9 billion revenue in Singapore's marine industry in 1998. Offshore rig production was relatively small at less than S$1 billion, and shipbuilding was even smaller. But by the mid-2000s, offshore rig production had gathered momentum when energy prices set record levels, and demand for offshore rigs by major oil and gas companies increased rapidly. While ship repair in Singapore grew steadily between 2005 and 2009, offshore production surged from S$3.2 billion in 2006 to peak at S$9.7 billion in 2013. Since 2008, offshore rig production has surpassed ship repair and shipbuilding to become the largest segment of Singapore's marine industry. Through Keppel and SembCorp, Singapore took up 70 to 80 percent of the global offshore jack-up rigs market between 2006 and 2015. In 2009, the marine industry achieved record revenue of S$16.8 billion (or US$13.7 billion) and contributed to 7.4 percent of Singapore's manufacturing output and 12.2 percent of total value added in manufacturing.[41] At their peaks in 2009, Keppel O&M and SembCorp Marine achieved respective record revenues of US$6.8 billion and US$4.7 billion.[42]

The emergence of Keppel Corp and SembCorp Industries as the world's largest offshore rig producers for the global oil and gas production networks

Table 5.2 Singapore's marine industry by activity, 1998–2013 (in S$billion)

Year	Revenue	Ship repair	Shipbuilding	Offshore production
1998	3.86	1.99	0.92	0.95
1999	3.12	2.16	0.44	0.52
2000	2.76	1.68	0.45	0.63
2001	4.03	2.56	0.54	0.93
2002	4.40	2.73	0.53	1.14
2003	3.79	2.29	0.72	0.78
2004	5.30	3.10	0.90	1.30
2005	7.43	3.79	1.26	2.38
2006	9.80	4.90	1.67	3.23
2007	13.05	6.26	1.83	4.96
2008	16.80	7.06	1.67	8.06
2009	16.83	6.73	0.84	9.26
2010	13.47	4.85	0.54	8.08
2011	13.32	5.20	0.67	7.46
2012	15.01	4.80	1.13	9.08
2013	15.30	4.74	0.84	9.72

Source: Association of Singapore Marine Industries, http://www.asmi.com, accessed on May 5, 2015.

in the 2000s reflects a combination of firm-specific technological and organizational innovations. For shipbuilders to succeed in rig production, a high degree of industrial market specialization is required in order to handle complex demands from major oil and gas lead firm customers before and during production. The first and foremost condition lies in the production sophistication of offshore rigs. In Cho and Porter's (1986, 545, table 17.1) analysis of the global marine industry, oil tankers have the lowest level of sophistication, and offshore rigs are the most sophisticated ships in modern merchant fleets, next only to navy warships. Building these sophisticated rigs to withstand harsh offshore operating environments is certainly much more than about getting the steel, cutting it into the right blocks, and putting them together, as the case in making large tankers and carriers. Keppel O&M understood well this demand for technological sophistication in its rig production for offshore oil and gas exploration and development.[43] Keppel's major technological upgrading did not occur until after 1997, when its acquired FELS and the proprietary rights to the Friede and Goldman MOD V and MOD VI jack-up models. It also established the Offshore Technology Development (OTD) unit to specialize in the design and engineering of rigs and related critical equipment. In the mid-2000s, the Deepwater Technology Group (DTG) was formed to specialize in semisubmersibles and floating structures. In 2007, the Keppel O&M Technology Centre was developed to engage in R&D to augment the design and engineering work of OTD and DTG.[44] In 2011, the majority of its record new orders of twenty-four jack-up rigs were for Keppel FELS' own proprietary designs, indicating its strong industrial leadership in rig design and technologies.

Technological solutions and continuous product innovations in offshore rig production, however, are not sufficient to guarantee the market success of rig producers. As noted by my SembCorp interviewee, "In the rig business, we own certain technology and licenses which competitors find it difficult to get into. In the area of design and licensing arrangement I think we have some protection. But then the protection only gives you certain number of years each. So we need to keep inventing ourselves to keep the leading edge." *Organizational innovations* are just as critical for these rig builders to weather different business cycles in the volatile offshore oil and gas market. First, organizational processes, such as strong relationships with customers and suppliers and project execution skills, are critical intangible advantages enjoyed by strong market leaders like Keppel. As described by my Keppel interviewee, "I would say the intellectual property [IP] that we have—how to do the whole thing, the design, the solution, and to understand customer needs, execute—gives us a niche over our competitors. IP in the sense that it's not tangible: people, system, and culture that we hope are more enduring. It's not so easy to duplicate." While scale economies can be useful in the shipbuilding industry, size alone cannot help shipbuilders overcome the highly volatile and customer-centric nature of the offshore rig business. The global gloom in the rig market between the mid-1980s and the late 1990s is instructive because Keppel and SembCorp consolidated their organizational capability and investing in more productive equipment while their competitors from South Korea made serious mistakes by diversifying and expanding into rig production. For example, Keppel merged its Keppel Shipyard with Hitachi Zosen in 1999 and incorporated the merged entity into Keppel O&M in 2002 to establish an integrated offshore and marine production powerhouse.

Second, Keppel and SembCorp continue to innovate in their organizational forms through the geographical expansion of their shipyards. Unlike the three leading South Korean shipbuilders that concentrate their production activity in gigantic domestic shipyards, both Singaporean rig builders understand fully the highly customer-centric nature of the rig business and therefore their global customers' strong preference for the localization of rig production near oil and gas extraction sites. Globalization of shipyards represents the explicit organizational strategy of coupling with the demand of lead firms in these global production networks. Keppel's strategy is to be "near market, near customer." It started its global footprint of yards as early as 1975, when it established a shipyard in the Philippines. Its globalization efforts were intensified in the 1990s, and Keppel's production capacity was established in Texas, Azerbaijan, Bulgaria, Norway, and the UAE. By the end of the 2000s, Keppel set up more yard facilities in Brazil, China, Indonesia, Kazakhstan, Qatar, the Netherlands, and Vietnam. Commenting on this localization strategy, my Keppel interviewee explains that "the reason to be there is because of the customers and the market. So it's not because of the lower cost there—it's very expensive there. We're there because the customer is there; near the market has clear advantages. We can operate within the host system. Offshore business has significant barriers to entry. A country often likes work to be done within its shore." To lower its entry cost, Keppel typically buys over unproductive assets and bankrupt yards, and reorganizes them to become part of the Keppel family of yards with the latest technological and organizational capabilities. By the late 2000s, it was operating the largest yards in Brazil, Texas, Rotterdam, and Azerbaijan.[45] This global footprint has given Keppel an enormous advantage over its competitors from South Korea (e.g., Samsung Heavy Industries). Even its "duopolistic" competitor from Singapore, SembCorp Marine, has established shipyards only in Brazil, India, Indonesia, and the United Kingdom. SembCorp's organizational strategy is to operate its eleven shipyards out of these four strategic hubs, and to customize its areas of expertise and market niches to specific clients in different regions.

To sum up this empirical section on the global marine industry, size does matter, and scale economies are useful to laying the initial competitive foundation of major shipbuilders from South Korea and offshore rig producers from Singapore. As the state's role in directing industrialization has diminished since the late 1980s, these state-led initiatives could upscale national champions only to the point that they begin to enjoy scale economies over their domestic and foreign competitors. The rise of Samsung Heavy Industries to be among the world's top three shipbuilders by the late 2000s, however, has less to do with scale economies directly supported by the developmental state in South Korea. More important is the competitive advantage derived from its engagement with strategic specialization in high value-added shipbuilding through its continuous and firm-specific technological and organizational innovations. The same evolutionary dynamic is also evident in the case of Singapore's Keppel O&M. While it owes its initial founding and continual shareholding to the developmental state in Singapore, Keppel's extraordinary growth and profitability since the mid-2000s are more predicated on the favorable demand dynamics in global production networks and its own firm-specific capabilities sustained through continuous technological and organizational innovations. As latecomers in the global marine industry, these shipbuilders and rig producers have not only gained second-mover advantage in scale economies, but also developed *new* firm-specific advantages that allow them to outcompete the original first movers in advanced industrialized economies and to couple with the demands of lead firm customers in different global production networks. In the next empirical section, I will examine if this coupling process of industrial market specialization can also be effective for East Asian firms to succeed in the global semiconductor industry where scale economies and technological innovations are both integral to competitive success.

More than "Tiger Chips": Specialization in Semiconductors

Unlike the marine industry where leading shipbuilders and rig producers from East Asia manufacture complete and integrated industrial products for their major customers in different industries, industrial concentration in electronics is relatively lower, and thus there is a plethora of opportunity for latecomers to specialize and couple with different global production networks. Metaphorically, value chains in global electronics are much longer than those in shipbuilding and rig production. By specializing in *niche markets or products* through technological excellence, strong organizational and production capability, and scale economies, some East Asian firms have emerged as successful market leaders in producing semiconductors that drive a wide range of electronics goods. The rise of East Asian economies in the semiconductor industry, arguably the most challenging segment of the electronics industry, has received significant attention in the developmental state literature.[46] The industry originated in the late 1950s from the early founders located in Silicon Valley in the United States, such as Shockley Laboratories and Fairchild Semiconductor. Between 1967 and 1973, the arrival of integrated device manufacturers (IDMs), such as Intel (manufacturing the world's first 1K DRAM integrated circuit in 1971), National Semiconductor, Motorola, and Advanced Micro Devices (AMD), meant that by the late 1970s, the United States had virtually dominated the entire semiconductor industry. As noted in Henderson (1989, 6, 32), American semiconductor firms produced forty-eight of the fifty-two major innovations in semiconductor technology between 1947 and 1981, such as the transistor (Shockley and others, 1947), the "planar" wafer fabrication process (Fairchild, 1958), the integrated circuit or IC (Fairchild and Texas Instrument, 1962–1963), and the microprocessor (Intel, 1971). These vertically integrated IDMs designed, manufactured, and marketed specialized semiconductor products, such as chipsets and memory devices, as core components for the production of modern electronics products. Some of them also integrated backward into semiconductor equipment manufacturing.[47] In 1980, US producers accounted for nearly 60 percent of the world market in semiconductor devices (Angel 1994, 31, 65).

From less than US$10 billion in 1980, the global sales of semiconductors grew massively to about US$50 billion in 1990 and US$151 billion in 1995 (Mathews and Cho 2000, figure 1.1, 32). During this period, Japan and some European countries, such as France, Germany, and the Netherlands, had emerged as the major challengers to American dominance in the industry. By the late 1980s, the US share had dropped to 37 percent, and Japanese firms had replaced American firms as the dominant market player with almost 50 percent of the semiconductor market.[48] In 1986, some 75 percent of world's DRAM products came from Japanese firms (Y. Kim 2011, 310). As argued by Angel (1994, 66), while Japan's state-sponsored cooperative research program during the late 1970s was instrumental in the catching up of Japanese firms in semiconductor process technology, "the subsequent competitive success of Japanese firms, however, had less to do with this much publicized form of government intervention than with the internal development efforts of individual firms and the superior manufacturing performance achieved by Japanese semiconductor producers throughout much of the 1980s."[49] Japan's technological and market leadership in the global semiconductor industry persisted through to the late 1990s. As noted in table 5.3, five Japanese firms—NEC (merged with Renesas in 2010), Toshiba, Hitachi, Fujitsu, and Mitsubishi—were among the top ten semiconductor firms in 1995. Market leader Intel's revenue of US$13.2 billion was only slightly more than the next two largest semiconductor firms from Japan: NEC (US$11.3 billion) and Toshiba (US$10.1 billion).

By the 2010s, the global semiconductor industry had expanded much further, and total market revenue had doubled from its first peak in 1995 to reach US$306.8 billion in 2011. While Intel has now surged ahead to become the unquestionable global industry leader with US$50.7 billion sales and 16.5 percent market share, the fortunes of most top Japanese semiconductor firms and other early pioneers (Motorola and Philips) have been seriously undermined by two groups of newcomers.[50] First, two latercomer semiconductor IDMs from South Korea—Samsung Electronics and Hynix Semiconductor (formerly Hyundai Electronics until its merger with LG Semiconductor in October 1999)—have become prominent producers in chipsets and memory devices. In 1995, Samsung was ranked sixth after Motorola, and Hynix (then Hyundai Electronics) did not yet make the top ten list. Today, both South Korean IDMs can compete effectively against leading IDMs from the US (Texas Instruments) and Japan (Toshiba).

Second, several "fabless" chip design firms became prominent in 2011. These are Qualcomm and Broadcom from the United States, which specialize in designing chipsets for mobile communications devices. Lacking manufacturing capacity, these fabless firms have entered into long-term contracts with semiconductor foundries in Taiwan and Singapore to produce their chipsets and other semiconductor devices. Table 5.4 lists the world's top 10 semiconductor foundries in 2011.[51] Founded respectively in 1980 and 1987 as spin-offs of the state-sponsored Industrial Technology Research Institute (ITRI), Taiwan's United Microelectronics Corporation (UMC) and TSMC have been market leaders in semiconductor foundries since the early 1990s. But their growth trajectory has been very different. In 1992, both market leaders had sales of slightly over US$250 million. By 1997, TSMC had sales almost double of UMC. In 2011, TSMC dominated the semiconductor foundry market and accounted for 48.8 percent of its US$29.8 billion market (almost 10 percent of the total sales of all semiconductor firms in table 5.3). Its US$14.5 billion revenue would place it next to only the top two semiconductor firms in table 5.3—Intel and Samsung. UMC's annual revenue of US$3.6 billion was only one quarter of TSMC's. But it was slightly more than GlobalFoundries, a new corporate en-

Table 5.3 World's top ten semiconductor firms by revenue in 1995–2011 (in US$billions)

Rank 2011	Rank 2010	Vendor	2011 sales	2010 sales	2010–2011 growth (%)	2011 market share (%)	2005 sales	2000 sales	1997 sales	1995 sales
1	1	Intel[1]	50.7	42.0	20.7	16.5	35.5	30.2	21.7	13.2
2	2	Samsung Electronics	27.4	27.0	1.0	8.9	17.2	8.9	5.9	8.3
3	3	Toshiba	11.8	12.4	−4.8	3.8	9.1	10.4	7.3	10.1
4	4	Texas Instruments[2]	11.8	11.8	−0.6	3.8	10.8	9.2	7.4	7.8
5	6	Renesas Electronics[3]	10.7	10.2	4.4	3.5	5.7	8.2	10.2	11.3
6	9	Qualcomm[4]	10.0	7.2	38.8	3.3	3.5	—	—	—
7	5	STMicroelectronics	9.6	10.3	−6.1	3.1	8.9	7.9	4.0	—
8	7	Hynix Semiconductor[5]	9.4	9.9	−5.0	3.1	5.6	5.1	3.3	4.1
9	8	Micron Technology	7.6	8.2	−7.1	2.5	4.8	6.3	—	2.6
10	10	Broadcom[6]	7.2	6.6	8.4	2.3	2.7	—	—	—
		Others	150.8	155.8	−3.2	49.1	—	—	—	—
15	11	Hitachi (Elpida)[7]	3.9	6.5	−40.2	1.2	—	5.7	6.3	9.1
—		Motorola	—	—	—	—	—	—	8.1	8.7
25	22	Fujitsu	2.7	3.1	−0.5	0.9	—	5.0	4.6	5.5
—		Mitsubishi	—	—	—	—	—	5.8	4.5	5.3
16	17	Philips (NXP)[8]	3.8	4.0	−4.7	1.2	5.6	6.3	4.4	3.9
		Total Market	306.8	301.5	1.8	100.0	237.1	220.5	147.2	151.0

[1] Infineon's wireless division was sold to Intel, effective in the first quarter of 2011, and thus is included in Intel's total revenue.

[2] Texas Instruments acquired National Semiconductor in September 2011. The estimated third and fourth quarters of National's 2011 revenue are attributed to Texas Instruments in 2011.

[3] Renesas Electronics' data before 2010 refer to NEC that merged with Renesas Technology in April 2010 to create Renesas Electronics (a merged entity comprising Mitsubishi and Hitachi Semiconductors in November 2002).

[4] Qualcomm's 2011 revenue includes three quarters of Atheros' revenue.

[5] Hynix was formed in October 1999 after a merger of Hyundai Electronics with LG Semiconductor. In March 2012, SK Telecom became its largest shareholder and renamed it to SK Hynix.

[6] Broadcom acquired Provigent in the second quarter of 2011.

[7] Elpida Memory was formed in 1999 through a merger of DRAM divisions of Hitachi and NEC. In 2003, it acquired Mitsubishi's DRAM division.

[8] Sold to private equity and renamed to NXP in 2006.

Sources: 1995 and 1997 data from Mathews and Cho (2000, 37, table 1.2); 2000–2011 data from Gartner Research (http://www.gartner.com, accessed on October 20, 2014) and IHS iSuppli Research (http://www.isuppli.com, accessed on October 27, 2014).

Table 5.4 World's top ten semiconductor foundries by revenue and market share in 1992–2011 (in US$millions)

2011 rank	2010 rank	Company	Economy of HQ	2011 Sales	Share (%)	2010 Sales	Share (%)	2007 Sales	Share (%)	1997 Sales	1996 Sales	1995 Sales	1992 Sales
1	1	TSMC	Taiwan	14,533	48.8	13,332	47.1	9,810	47.7	1,534	1,416	1,092	262
2	2	UMC	Taiwan	3,604	12.1	3,824	13.5	3,760	18.3	839	825	900	254
3	3	GlobalFoundries[1]	Abu Dhabi	3,580	12.0	3,520	12.4	1,460	7.1	410	360	285	—
4	4	SMIC	China	1,319	4.4	1,554	5.5	1,550	7.5	—	—	—	—
5	6	TowerJazz	Israel	613	2.1	509	1.8	—	—	—	—	—	—
6	8	IBM Microelectronics	USA	545	1.8	500	1.8	—	—	—	—	—	—
7	7	Vanguard	Taiwan	516	1.7	505	1.8	490	2.4	90	90	—	—
8	5	Dongbu HiTek	South Korea	483	1.6	512	1.8	510	2.5	—	—	—	—
9	10	Samsung[2]	South Korea	470	1.6	390	1.4	—	—	—	—	—	—
10	19	Powerchip Tech	Taiwan	431	1.4	149	0.5	—	—	—	—	—	—
		Top 10 for 2011		26,094	87.7	24,795	87.6	19,010	92.4				
		Others		3,660	12.3	3,510	12.4	1,563	7.6				
		Total		29,754	100.0	28,305	100.0	20,573	100.0				

[1] GlobalFoundries' revenues in 1995–1997 and 2007 refer to Chartered Semiconductor from Singapore that it acquired in September 2009.

[2] Samsung revenue does not include ASIC business from Apple.

Sources: 1992–1997 data from Mathews and Cho (2000, 38, table 1.3 and 49, table 1.8); 2007 data from Market Intelligence & Consulting Institute (2008); 2010–2011 data from Gartner, March 2012, http://www.gartner.com, accessed on October 20, 2014.

tity created and financed by Abu Dhabi to acquire AMD's former semiconductor manufacturing facilities and Singapore's Chartered Semiconductor in 2009.[52]

How did these semiconductor firms from South Korea, Taiwan, and to a limited extent, Singapore evolve from their earlier embeddedness in state-led initiatives of industrial catching up to develop subsequent firm-specific technological and organizational innovations that have contributed to their niche leadership in the global semiconductor industry? During the 1970s and the 1980s, the developmental state in all three East Asian economies targeted the semiconductor industry as a priority national initiative for high-tech development. But each of them pursued a different route to establishing such a capital-intensive industry. South Korea was the first to promote the industry through selecting the chaebol in the late 1960s and the early 1970s. Taiwan's foray into semiconductors started with state-funded research institutes in the mid-1970s. Singapore was the last to venture into semiconductors—only since the mid-1980s—and depended mostly on foreign firms. This initial significant difference in state-led approach to developing the semiconductor industry produced contrasting industrial outcomes into the 1990s and the 2000s, when state-led initiatives became less effective due to changing state roles (e.g., shift toward horizontal industrial policy) and new windows of opportunities in global production networks (e.g., the rise of fabless semiconductor firms).

Since the late 1990s, leading domestic semiconductor firms have coupled strategically with global lead firms that require the former's production technologies and scale economies to sustain their own market positions in the rapidly moving world of globalized electronics industry. To a large extent, this market position of East Asian semiconductor firms is underscored by their substantial in-house R&D activity and therefore their world-leading technologies. While state-funded R&D institutes were important to the early founding of these semiconductor firms in all three economies, their efficacy had significantly diminished by the late 1990s when these semiconductor firms had acquired world-class technologies and grown massively to become market leaders. In the case of Taiwan, Fuller (2005, 142) argues that "by 1994 the technology necessary to transfer IC designs to foundries had been completely developed. Many of the current managers of TSMC's fabs returned to Taiwan from the United States to work for TSMC at this time, as the promise of this model was fully realized." As shown in table 5.5, the patents granted by the United States Patent and Trademark Office (USPTO) to top semiconductor firms from Taiwan (UMC, TSMC), South Korea (Samsung and Hyundai), and Singapore (Chartered) grew rapidly between 1997 and 2001. By 2001, these semiconductor firms had obtained far greater number of patents than the state-funded research institutes in their home economies, such as Taiwan's ITRI and Electronics Research Service Organization (ERSO), and South Korea's Electronics and Telecommunications Research Institute (ETRI) and Korea Institute of

Table 5.5 USPTO patent statistics of leading semiconductor firms and research institutions from South Korea, Taiwan, and Singapore, 1997–2001

Name	1997	1998	1999	2000	2001	1997–2001
South Korea						
Samsung Elec.	584	1,305	1,545	1,441	1,450	6,325
Hyundai Elec.	154	212	242	294	533	1,435
LG Elec.	113	215	229	220	248	1,025
Daewoo Elec.	215	319	273	120	54	981
LG Semicond.	119	235	311	255	42	962
ETRI	58	120	130	124	72	504
KIST	29	44	41	35	35	184
Taiwan						
UMC	149	174	266	430	584	1,603
TSMC	130	218	290	385	529	1,552
ITRI	153	218	208	198	221	998
VISC	53	120	112	131	112	528
Winbond	24	59	115	115	126	439
Mosel-Vitelic	15	32	38	66	68	219
Singapore						
Chartered SM	30	39	44	79	135	327
China						
WSMC	0	0	6	61	37	104

Source: Adapted from Mathews (2007, 323, table 16.3).

Science and Technology (KIST). The following two subsections examine how this strategic coupling process of industrial market specialization promoted through continuous firm-specific technological and organizational innovations has enabled these leading East Asian firms to become major players in two segments of the global semiconductor industry—semiconductor foundries and IDMs.

The "Pure Play" of Chip Making in Taiwan and Singapore

In semiconductor manufacturing, specialized manufacturers, known as "foundries," and their preferred testing and assembly service providers had emerged from Taiwan and Singapore in the early 1990s, but their industrial leadership and global success were truly attained only in the 2000s. Specializing in semiconductor manufacturing, these leading foundries serve major chip design firms that do not have either in-house wafer fabrication facilities at all (i.e., are fabless) or sufficient production capacity to meet growing demand for their chipsets. The rise of semiconductor foundries in Taiwan and Singapore involves a unique and dynamic combination of initial state interventions and the subsequent coupling process of industry market specialization through continuous innovations. Prior to the mid-1990s, state-led initiatives in both Taiwan and Singapore laid important foundations for these leading foundries.[53] In Taiwan, the developmental state steered the industry during the 1970s and the 1980s mainly through technology transfer led by state-sponsored ERSO and ITRI and their subsequent spin-offs, rather than through direct state allocation of credits to the industry. As documented in table 5.6, these research institutes obtained the initial, and often obsolete, technologies in IC fabrication (7-micron LSI) from the US firm RCA in 1976 and 2-micron VLSI technologies from Philips a decade later. These technologies were transferred to UMC and TSMC at the time of their spin-offs in 1980 and 1987. As argued by Breznitz (2007, 98–99), the success of these foundries stems "not from massive investment of patient capital but from a distinctive institutional system of industrial innovation—a system built around public research institutions-led R&D science-and-technology (S&T) industrial policy, and a policy goal of attaining a defined position within the IT industry's global production network."

Although these initial state-facilitated endowments in both technology transfer and capital investment were foundational, the most significant growth

Table 5.6 International technology linkages of leading firms in Taiwan's semiconductor industry, 1976–2009

Year	Global lead firm	Taiwan firm/ institute	Technology
1976	RCA	ERSO pilot plant	IC fabrication (LSI)
1986	Philips	TSMC	VLSI IC fabrication
1989–91	Texas Instruments	TI-Acer	DRAMs
1994	Oki	Mosel-Vitelic	DRAM fabrication
1994	MEMC	TEM	Silicon wafers
1994	Hewlett-Packard	Winbond	RISC processor
1994	MIPS (Sun)	Macronix	RISC processor
1994	IBM, Motorola	NewPC consortium	PowerPC processor
1995	SEH	SEHT	Silicon wafers
1995	Kanematsu	TKEM (Nanya)	Silicon wafers
1995	Oki	Nanya Technology	DRAMs
1995	Mitsubishi	Powerchip	DRAMs
1995	Toshiba	Winbond	DRAMs
1997	Siemens	ProMOS	DRAMs
1998–2000	IBM	Nanya	DRAMs
2002	Infineon	Nanya and Inotera Memories	DRAMs
2005	Hynix	ProMOS	Strategic alliance in DRAMs
2006	Renesas Technology	Powerchip	DRAMs
2008	Micron	Nanya	Joint development of DRAMs
2009	Elpida Memory	ProMOS	Strategic partnership in DRAMs

Sources: 1976–1997 from Mathews and Cho (2000, 189, table 4.2); the rest from company websites and annual reports.

period for both TSMC and UMC indeed came from the semiconductor booms in the mid-1990s and the mid-2000s. In other words, their rise to global prominence occurred only at least ten to fifteen years *after* they had been spun off from ITRI, an indication of the stronger role of firm-specific coupling initiatives. During this period, their gradual disembedding from state agencies, such as ITRI, necessitated an evolutionary process of reembedding in new configurations of global production networks. This was when their firm-specific strategic initiatives and technological-organizational innovations to promote their market specialization became most significant for their continual and successful coupling with high growth customers, particularly fabless design houses, in the global semiconductor industry. In particular, two firm-specific innovative efforts were most critical to sustain their rapid growth beyond the initial state-led initiatives in the 1980s: continuous technological leadership and organizational specialization.

Apart from the initial technologies transferred from ITRI at the time of the spin-offs, these foundries have engaged in continuous technological leadership in order to go beyond second-mover advantage in scale economies. In its early days, TSMC took advantage of the decoupling of the design and fabrication stages of IC development. This technological innovation was made possible by the use of computer-aided design technology to codify knowledge of device characteristics in computer models. While complete computer modeling was possible by 1993–1994, TSMC had actually anticipated this trend and begun using the computer model as early as the late 1980s, thus creating a first-mover advantage (Fuller et al. 2005, 80–81). But TSMC took a tremendous risk with this move toward "pure play," as it was not clear if the digital interface between fabrication and design of IC devices would work in commercial production. By the early 2000s, continuous technological innovations at TSMC and UMC had paid off. Taiwan's leading foundries were well placed at the technological frontiers of wafer fabrication, alongside with leading IDMs from the United States and Japan. In 2000, TSMC exported approximately 60 percent of its foundry production and UMC exported 40 percent. For the first time in its history, TSMC made the transition to twelve-inch wafers through in-house process development rather than relying on poaching Taiwanese engineering talents in American IDMs or on technology transfer from its top global lead firm customers.

In organizational terms, TSMC's Morris Chang was an early pioneer of foundry manufacturing in the late 1980s by introducing an innovative way of organizing semiconductor production through which high-tech design houses, particularly in the United States, could specialize in IC chip design.[54] The arrival of this "pure play" foundry business model means that TSMC or UMC can meet the wafer fabrication needs based on designs supplied by these high-tech houses or fabless semiconductor firms.[55] The dominance of two leading fabless firms, Qualcomm and Broadcom, in the 2010s shows that this organizational separation of the design and fabrication of semiconductor chips has offered both fabless firms and their foundries a significant joint window of opportunity in the rapidly growing global production networks of mobile telecommunications devices. The enormous success of these fabless design houses, primarily from the United States and Taiwan, is illustrated by their massive growth between 2000 and 2011 in table 5.7. In such rapidly moving industries as mobile communications, leading fabless firms, such as Qualcomm since its inception in 1985 have eschewed the vertically integrated model of global production networks pursued by IDMs such as Intel and developed a horizontally organized global production network leveraging the core competencies of its foundry partners (e.g., TSMC) and downstream customers (e.g., handset makers). In 2000, Qualcomm and Broadcom had revenue of just over US$1 billion. In 2011, they became top ten world semi-

Table 5.7 World's top twenty-five fabless semiconductor firms in 2000–2003 and 2009 (in US$millions)

Ranking		Company name	Economy of HQ	Sales				
2009	2000			2009	2003	2002	2001	2000
1	3	Qualcomm	US	6,600	2,510	1,942	1,395	1,215
2	—	AMD[1]	US	5,300	—	—	—	—
3	4	Broadcom	US	4,200	1,595	1,083	962	1,096
4	13	MediaTek	Taiwan	3,500	1,170	854	447	411
5	7	Nvidia	US	3,100	1,835	1,915	1,275	699
6	21	Marvell	US	2,700	780	482	275	135
7	1	Xilinx	US	1,700	1,265	1,125	1,149	1,560
8	—	LSI	US	1,400	—	—	—	—
9	2	Altera	US	1,200	830	712	839	1,377
10	—	Avago	US/SG	870	—	—	—	—
11	22	Novatek	Taiwan	819	311	193	124	121
12	—	Himax	Taiwan	685	—	—	—	—
13	19	Realtek	Taiwan	615	300	265	214	174
14	—	Mstar	Taiwan	605	—	—	—	—
15	—	CSR	UK	600	—	—	—	—
16	14	QLogic	US	530	520	415	357	362
17	—	Atheros	US	530	—	—	—	—
18	8	PMC-Sierra	Canada	495	245	213	323	695
19	—	MegaChips	Japan	480	—	—	—	—
20	23	Silicon Lab	US	440	310	182	74	103
21	26	Zoran	US (Israel)	345	213	141	100	68
22	20	SMSC	US	280	202	145	128	163
23	17	Semtech	US	250	160	170	170	215
24	—	Richtek	Taiwan	244	69	—	—	—
25	—	Conexant	US	240	650	1,942	646	—

[1]AMD became fabless after spin-offs of its fabrication facilities to GlobalFoundries in 2009.

Sources: 2000–2003 data from Breznitz (2007, 121, table 3.3) and 2009 data from David Manners, "Top 25 fabless companies," January 19, 2010, ElectronicsWeekly.com, http://www.electronicsweekly .com, accessed on September 20, 2014.

conductor firms, with Qualcomm achieving US$10 billion sales for the first time and overtaking such IDMs in memory chips as Hynix and Micron (see table 5.3). As a spin-off from UMC in 1997, Taiwan's leading fabless firm, MediaTek, also experienced considerable growth from US$411 million sales in 2000 to US$3.5 billion in 2009. It has become Taiwan's most successful fabless semiconductor firm, and its close relationships with both TSMC and UMC are critical to satisfying its wafer fabrication needs. This organizational innovation is a consequence of vertical specialization through which neither foundries nor fabless firms serve as global lead firms. As high-tech firms specializing in the design or manufacturing of core components such as IC chips, these firms engage in a dynamic and yet differential process of strategic coupling—industrial market specialization.

Looking back, the continual firm-specific technological innovations and organizational change through specialization in foundry services described above have proved to be vital in the unprecedented growth of these foundries in the 2000s. The massive growth of TSMC since 1995 came about after ERSO and ITRI had withdrawn from their earlier active role as the leading actor steering the development of Taiwan's semiconductor industry. The listing of TSMC in the New York Stock Exchange in October 1997, three years after its IPO in Taiwan, has allowed it to tap into global capital markets to finance its continual and critically important capital investment in semiconductor fabrication capacity both in Taiwan and abroad. This investment has enabled it to meet the next major wave of demand from fabless firms designing chipsets for wireless mobile devices in the 2000s. To retain its production autonomy and to control its capacity growth through organic expansion, TSMC has carefully managed its organizational change since the early 2000s. These firm-specific efforts have further consolidated its leadership through industrial market specialization in the semiconductor foundry business. Instead of going into unwieldy ventures with its customers,[56] TSMC prefers to build up its own fabrication capacity to serve diverse demands from different customers. Describing how TSMC confronts this demand from its customers to develop joint ventures, my interviewee notes that "we really tried to tell them the best way is for TSMC to build up our own capacity. Then we can serve as a central kitchen. If he wants burger, I can make burger. If he wants *chao mien* [Chinese fried noodles], I will make it for you."[57] Given this "pure play" foundry model, TSMC has the organizational capability to serve more than ten customers and fabricate more than one hundred products in the same manufacturing facility.

Since the mid-1990s, TSMC's sustained organizational specialization in foundry services has coupled well with the enormous growth of fabless design houses, particularly in wireless and mobile communications devices and digital multimedia solutions. As the preferred foundry house for chipsets designed by Qualcomm, Nvidia, Apple, and MediaTek for mobile devices and computers, TSMC has attained high capacity utilization and thus gained enormously from its specialization in semiconductor manufacturing. UMC also gains much from its special supplier relationship with MediaTek and others. In short, their strategic coupling with leading chip design firms has sustained mutual benefits so that both parties can concentrate on their core competencies in order to compete against other semiconductor firms, such as IDMs. Through this coupling process, both leading fabless firms and foundries can attain much greater economies of scale and rapid time-to-market vis-à-vis their IDM competitors.

While some of these organizational innovations specific to TSMC can also be observed in the case of Singapore's state-funded Chartered Semiconductor Manufacturing (CSM), a well-developed domestic ecosystem in the electronics industry can make a critical difference. This ecosystem refers to both upstream equipment suppliers and testing and assembly services, and downstream fabless customers and their end users comprising global lead firms and their ODMs and EMS providers. Established in 1987 (the same year as TSMC) and with technology transfer from National Semiconductor (IDM) and fabless Sierra Semiconductor, CSM began as a division in the state-owned Singapore Technologies (ST) group.[58] As indicated in table 3.5, ST was 100 percent owned by the state investment vehicle Temasek Holdings until the end of 1999. By the late 1990s, as observed by Mathews and Cho (2000, 222; my emphasis) in *Tiger Technology*, "Singapore Technologies' activities encompassed IC design (through TriTech), wafer fabrication (through CSM) and test and assembly (through STATS)—all on a contract basis, without producing products of its own. The Singapore Technologies group is a *perfect example* of a technology leverage player, lifting itself into new phases of the industry through joint ventures, technology transfer agreements and by expanding its customer base."

The case of Singapore's CSM might appear to be a textbook case of state-led catching up in a highly capital-intensive industry—semiconductor foundry services. It was established at the time when the developmental state's industrial policy was switching toward promoting high-value added manufacturing industries such as semiconductors. It had the technological backing of industry leaders, such as Sierra Semiconductor and Toshiba,[59] and the full financial support of state-owned ST group and its controlling shareholder Temasek Holdings. By the late 1990s, CSM had been blessed with a vertically integrated foundry value chain comprised of its own design services (TriTech) and test and assembly (STATS), and Singapore's semiconductor industry had been quite firmly established. By the late 2000s, the output of Singapore's semiconductor industry was valued at US$26 billion.[60] CSM was seemingly well positioned to take on major competitors in foundry services, such as Taiwan's TSMC and UMC. Throughout the 2000s, it counted on Microsoft, Broadcom, and Qualcomm as its largest lead firm customers. But something is missing in this story because CSM has not performed well since the late 1990s.[61] It suffered from major losses between 1998 and 2008.[62] In comparison, TSMC was highly profitable almost every year between 1996 and 2011, with a profit margin of 25 to 48 percent in all years, except 2001 and 2002. Its profit margins between 2004 and 2011 were consistently above 32 percent. Similarly, UMC was quite profitable between 1995 and 2011. In September 2009, Temasek Holdings divested and sold its entire stake in CSM to Abu Dhabi-backed Global-Foundries that has since merged CSM with fabrication facilities spun off from loss-making AMD. GlobalFoundries paid US$1.8 billion for CSM and assumed its outstanding debts of US$2.2 billion.[63]

This comparative analysis of the performance of the world's top three foundry providers points to the relative importance of coupling processes through firm-specific initiatives vis-à-vis state ownership in such a capital-intensive industry. Continuous technological and organizational innovations since the 1990s have clearly enabled TSMC to exercise industrial leadership and market specialization in global production networks. On the other hand, Singapore's state-sponsored project in semiconductor foundry had come to an abrupt end by 2009 not because of the lack of state-led initiatives. Even at the beginning of the 2000s, CSM was backed by Temasek Holdings to invest aggressively in the latest technological platforms in semiconductor foundry. Nevertheless, the enormous size of capital investment required in building new fabs in the face of major losses between 1998 and 2008 had irked even one of the wealthiest state holding companies. By the late 2000s, Temasek Holdings had realized that Singapore's indigenous foundry was no longer affordable and viable. During the 2000s, CSM was plagued by its strategic-organizational *misfit* with its lead firm customers, such as Microsoft and Hewlett-Packard. As a second sourcing practice to ensure timely delivery and to reduce dependency risks, these customers typically engaged CSM and another leading foundry provider, such as TSMC or UMC. But the market power and technological advantage of TSMC compelled these customers to ask their second source supplier, i.e., CSM, to follow the manufacturing blueprints of TSMC. This alignment of solutions in both sources allowed lead firm customers to standardize their chip design processes and to increase their time-to-market. This organizational disadvantage occurred even when CSM's manufacturing solution for a particular semiconductor product was sometimes better and more advanced than TSMC.[64] In short, CSM found it hard to capitalize on its own technological solutions and innovative manufacturing processes; it remained as a reluctant follower of the foundry industry leader—TSMC.

More critically, CSM suffered from the weaker ecosystem in Singapore's domestic ICT industry, particularly the lack of a critical mass of fabless design firms and the decreasing presence of their downstream "consumers," such as ODMs and EMS providers. Singapore's semiconductor industry was, and still is, dominated by foreign IDMs, most of which did not engage third-party foundry services offered by CSM and others. As pointed out by my interviewee from CSM's testing and assembly firm, "I think the linkage to the foundry is an advantage and Taiwanese firms truly enjoy an advantage over us because of the cluster in Taiwan. They have the linkage to the foundry that happens to be the two largest in the world. The linkage feeds back to the proliferation of fabless design houses in Taiwan. So you have these cluster structures that feed one and another. That's important and that's an advantage—something we lack and we don't enjoy."[65] Unlike Singapore's CSM, both TSMC and UMC have benefited not only from Taiwan's prominent position in global ODMs and EMS providers, but also from a well developed *domestic* ecosystem of hundreds of fabless IC design firms and world-class testing and assembly firms. As early as in 1993, the IC design industry in Taiwan was only in its infancy with about 64 firms raking in modest turnover of approximately US$433 million. The industry grew tremendously in the next ten years. By 2001, the industry hosted some 180 design houses, with combined turnover of about US$3.7 billion (Fuller 2005, 145–46). As indicated in table 5.7, the world's top ten largest fabless design firms in 2002 were no longer exclusively from the United States. MediaTek and VIA from Taiwan became the fifth and sixth largest IC design firms in the world.[66] In 2012, Taiwan's semiconductor industry had 260 fabless firms, 11 wafer suppliers, 3 mask makers, 15 fabrications, and 37 packaging and testing service providers (Hwang and Choung 2014, 1248). This mutually reinforcing development of fabless design firms, foundry providers, testing and assembly services, and ODMs-EMS in Taiwan's semiconductor ecosystem has been acknowledged by Breznitz (2007, 126), who concludes that "the development of the IC design subsector thus enriches the Taiwanese IT industry with positive feedback, strengthening the Taiwanese position as midlevel supplier within the global IT product networks. Each part of the Taiwanese IT hardware industry—OEM-ODMs, pure play foundries, and IC design companies—strengthens and is in turn strengthened by the existence, outputs, and demands of the others." Facilitated institutionally by the state's horizontal industrial policy, these cluster economies are clearly both geographical and social in nature, and greatly enhance market responsiveness and production flexibility unmatched outside Taiwan.

Integrated Chipmakers from Taiwan and South Korea

Apart from foundries, a second and much larger segment of semiconductor manufacturing refers to integrated device manufacturers (IDMs) of chipsets and memory devices from Taiwan and South Korea. As introduced earlier in table 5.3, these IDMs have dominated the world's largest semiconductor firms. Intel's US$50.7 billion sales in 2011, for example, almost doubles the combined sales of all top ten foundries (US$26 billion in table 5.4). The previous subsection has shown that state-led initiatives during the 1980s in developing a vibrant domestic semiconductor foundry segment have been significantly more successful in Taiwan and South Korea than in Singapore. As of 2011, four semiconductor foundries from Taiwan were among the top ten, and they collectively accounted for over 64 percent of the US$30 billion foundry market in table 5.4. After a decade-long loss record, Singapore's only domestic foundry,

CSM, was sold in September 2009. Meanwhile, the more ambitious state-directed development of a strong domestic IDMs segment has confronted with the harsher reality of tougher barriers to entry and market competition. In this segment, only state agencies in Taiwan and South Korea were strong enough to nurture domestic IDMs. But as illustrated below, few IDMs from Taiwan have managed to break successfully into the most challenging segment of the semiconductor industry. Unlike their highly successful "cousins" specializing in foundry services (i.e., TSMC and UMC), most of these IDMs from Taiwan are lagging behind in terms of *new* technological and organizational innovations. Instead, these innovations have been continuously developed in two South Korean chaebol giants—Samsung and Hynix. In particular, Samsung has successfully integrated its IC chips and memory devices into a wide range of electronics products manufactured by its intrachaebol divisions and other electronics giants, such as Apple from the United States.[67] Once again, the role of state-led initiatives has been important mostly at the initial stage of achieving second-mover advantages by these IDMs. But once they have articulated into different global production networks, new and firm-specific technological and organizational innovations are necessary to stay ahead of their competitors and to sustain their continual growth and profitability.

Indeed, Taiwan's semiconductor IDMs started off on a solid ground laid and led by state-funded ITRI in the mid-1980s. But the segment did not take off in the same manner as the semiconductor foundries. Between 1983 and 1998, a steady number of IDM firms specializing in DRAM and flash memory chips were established in Taiwan (Mathews and Cho 2000, 174–77). From such early entrants as Mosel-Vitelic, Winbond (ERSO's "unofficial" spin-off taken over by the Walsin Lihwa group), and Macronix (a specialist maker of volatile memories) to family-owned Nanya Technology in the Formosa group (and Inotera Memories, its joint venture with Infineon) and independents, such as Powerchip Technology and Elite Semiconductor, these IDMs has leveraged technologies licensed from global lead firms, as indicated in table 5.6, and developed into significant producers of memory devices for different computing and telecommunications equipment and consumer electronics by the early 2000s.[68] These IDMs supplied specialized components for leading ODMs and EMS providers that in turn designed and assembled for global brand name lead firms in notebook computers and consumer electronics. In the first decade of their development, these IDMs successfully exploited the technologies licensed from leading memory chip producers from Japan, the United States, and Germany. By specializing in memory devices, these IDMs could improve on these technologies and develop cutting-edge memory products for a rapidly growing global market in the 2000s. As described by Mathews and Cho (2000, 179), "The major indicator of the growing sustainability of the Taiwan semiconductor industry has been the flourishing of private-sector developments in the 1990s. New firms such as Winbond, Macronix and Mosel-Vitelic have not had to go through an 'apprenticeship' in simple IC product development, since they were launched from the higher level of collective learning achieved by the Taiwan industry as a whole."

Intense industrial competition in the global market for memory devices occurred during the 2000s when the technologies of these devices became standardized fairly quickly, and product life cycles were compressed sharply. Many Taiwanese IDMs specializing in memory devices became victims of industrial lock-in and could not resist the inevitable trend toward declining prices and profitability. Their overemphasis on upscaling to lower production costs has not led to new technological or organizational innovations (Ernst 2013, 3; Chen 2014, 27–28). As noted by Fuller (2007, 212–13), most Taiwanese DRAM producers became captive suppliers to their foreign partners and had to pay licensing fees and assume most of the investment risks. In the early 2000s, several top Japanese memory IDMs exited the market.[69] Once Taiwan's cutting-edge leader in memory business with a market value of US$3 billion in 1997 and a sizeable number of patents granted between 1997 and 2001 (table 5.5), Mosel-Vitelic had to withdraw from the DRAM market in 2006 and shift its focus to solar cell and RFID businesses.[70] While it started off as Mosel in Silicon Valley, an R&D intensive design firm in semiconductors, the merged company Mosel-Vitelic relied on mature technologies transferred from Oki in their DRAM production during much of the late 1990s and the early 2000s. Its demise by the late 2000s was largely due to its lack of new technological and/or organizational innovations in a fast-moving industry. From being the first IDM in Taiwan to develop its own 0.12 submicron process technology and 512MB DRAM chips in the 1990s, Mosel-Vitelic became a market follower and exited the semiconductor industry altogether in 2009. By the late 2000s, all remaining IDMs in Taiwan had faced enormous competitive pressure from market leaders, such as Samsung and Hynix from South Korea, Toshiba and Renesas from Japan, and Micron Technology from the United States. These Taiwanese IDMs began to cave in to industrial giants that could afford continual decline in the prices of memory devices and the industry's trend toward greater integration between IDMs and their industrial end-users, such as equipment or set manufacturers.

In particular, the most significant competitors to Taiwan's memory IDMs came from two South Korean chaebol—Samsung Electronics and Hynix Semiconductor. The emergence of these two winners in the global market for memory devices by the 2000s indicates that second-mover advantages, such as scale economies, can be a potent competitive advantage in favor of these chaebol IDMs. Samsung Electronics did not venture into semiconductors until the mid-1970s. President Park's fourth Five-Year Plan of 1977–1981 set the pace of development of the electronics industry as one of South Korea's key sectors. In this historical context, the developmental state was imperative in the initial inducement of a chaebol such as Samsung to diversify into electronics.[71] On December 1, 1983, Samsung shocked South Korea, if not the world, with a good working version of a 64K DRAM based on design technology licensed from the US fledgling DRAM producer Micron and process technology from Japan's Sharp.[72] But state support was no longer crucial to their massive growth since the mid-1980s. Between 1983 and 1989, Samsung, LG, and Hyundai invested some US$4 billion in VSI semiconductors. Only US$350 million of this came from state-initiated low-interest credit under the terms of the Promulgation of Basic Long Term Plan for the Semiconductor Industry (1982–1986) announced in 1981. In fact, ETRI's national R&D consortium for 4MB DRAMs between 1986 and 1989 failed to induce cooperation and sharing of technologies among its participants, such as Samsung, Hyundai, and LG, despite spending $110 million over the three years. Instead, each of these chaebol went ahead to develop their own 4MB designs through in-house R&D efforts (Dedrick and Kraemer 1998, 124).

Into the 1990s, Samsung closed the technology gap with its major competitors from Japan and the United States (which had become much weaker). Table 5.8 shows that the number of Samsung's DRAM patents registered with the USPTO in the 1990–1994 period was close to NEC, Toshiba, and Hitachi, its three top Japanese competitors. By the mid-1990s, Samsung was able to transfer its 16MB synchronous DRAMs (SDRAMs) technology to Japan's Oki. According to Mathews and Cho (2000, 137), this represents the first known

Table 5.8 Number of USPTO patents in DRAM products by South Korean and Japanese firms, 1990–2009

Firm name	1990–1994	1995–1999	2000–2004	2005–2009	Total
South Korea					
Samsung	30	39	92	61	222
Hynix[1]	20	76	67	46	209
Gold Star	5	9	0	NA	14
LG Semicond.	0	28	6	NA	34
Hyundai Electronics	15	39	37	NA	91
Hynix	NA	NA	24	46	70
Japan					
Hitachi	32	70	142	51	295
NEC	49	89	69	11	218
Toshiba	38	80	73	18	209
Fujitsu	13	33	33	14	93
Renesas[2]	NA	NA	27	57	84
Elpida[3]	NA	NA	5	39	44

[1] Hynix was formed in October 1999 after a merger of Hyundai Electronics with LG Semiconductor. In March 2012, SK Telecom became its largest shareholder and renamed it to SK Hynix.

[2] Renesas Electronics is a merged entity comprising Mitsubishi Semiconductors and Hitachi Semiconductors (since November 2002), and NEC (since April 2010).

[3] Elpida Memory was formed in 1999 through a merger of DRAM divisions of Hitachi and NEC. In 2003, it acquired Mitsubishi's DRAM division.

Source: Adapted from Y. Kim (2011, 303, table 2).

case of South Korea–Japan technology transfer in semiconductors. In 2001, Samsung became the first company in the world to use 300-nanometer wafer (12-inch) technology (Keller and Pauly 2003, 157; Shin 2015, 16). Likewise, Hyundai's Hynix committed some US$400 million between April 1983 and 1988 to develop its memory chips products (Mathews and Cho 2000, 108–9; 130–33). It began with the 64K DRAM based on licensed designs from two Chinese-American start-ups in Silicon Valley—Vitelic and Mosel (these were latter merged to form Mosel-Vitelic based in Taiwan).[73] It came late, however, with its 256K DRAM and again with the 1MB chip. By the 1990s, Hyundai had experienced almost ten years of losses in semiconductors. Still, it soldiered on by hiring Min Wi-Sik to head its development team and eventually broke through to successful production with the 4MB DRAM in the early 1990s. The company finally started to make profit in its semiconductor business.

It is misguided, however, to attribute the competitive success of Samsung and Hynix in the 2010s exclusively to their earlier scale economies founded on state-induced investment drive. As argued by Y. Kim (2011, 309–10), "We could hardly say that Korean overtaking in the semiconductor industry happened by chance or owing to government assistance. Korean firms accumulated technological capability by their own initiative, and implemented better strategies which were appropriate for the environment, thereby gaining significantly higher performance." In the mid-1990s, leading Japanese IDMs had much larger fabrication capacity than these chaebol producers. Taiwanese IDMs, such as Winbond and Nanya Technology, belonged to major business groups that could comfortably finance their capacity expansion. Just like TSMC, continuous technological and organizational innovations were the more critical platforms through which Samsung and Hynix could outcompete IDMs from not just Japan and Taiwan, but also the United States and Western Europe. Unlike IDMs from Taiwan, Samsung has chosen a distinct developmental trajectory through path-breaking catching up in its semiconductor technologies and internationalization.[74] While state-led promotion efforts had laid important preconditions for Samsung, its strategic coupling through technology licensing and joint development agreements with respective global lead firms provided the initial knowledge base for its subsequent engagement with leapfrogging as a successful pathway to global industrial leadership.[75]

This dynamic process of strategic coupling was particularly critical during the early phase of its entry into specialized product categories, such as IC and memory devices for digital TVs and mobile phones. For example, Samsung achieved rapid catching up through various technology agreements in the semiconductor industry between 1983 and 1997 (Lim 1999, table 4.9). Cyhn (2002, chapter 3) observes that by the early 1990s, chaebol groups, such as Samsung and LG, had become much less dependent on state-sponsored research institutes for their technological innovation. Instead, they turned to in-house R&D labs, friendly global lead firms, and international industrial associations. As early as in 1991, Samsung already invested 9 percent of its total sales in R&D, comparable to leading Japanese competitors (Hobday 1995, 62). To Lee et al. (2005, 42), both Samsung and LG have gone beyond second-mover advantages through their successful combination of "technological regimes, the competitive advantages of the innovation outcomes in the market, the foreign and domestic knowledge base, the government policies and firm strategies." The success of Samsung in semiconductors was clear by the mid-1990s when it was ranked among the world's top ten semiconductor IDMs (table 5.3). Since the late 1990s, Samsung's heavy investments in R&D and production facilities have been strategic in order to achieve further economies of scale and pose formidable barriers to entry to latecomers and other competitors from Taiwan. As one leading IDM from Taiwan laments, "If you look at Samsung in the first ten years, they're losing money because they built a fab. But they learned how to do DRAMs. Once they have built another ten fabs, any new fab on top of that is only a fractional increment, instead of us having to jump two to three times with the new fabs. So any company that is smaller in scale will face this problem regardless of foundries or IDMs."[76] In the memory chip market, Samsung has not only emerged as the world leader as early as 1992, but also continued to sustain its technological leadership in the next many generations of DRAMs. During the 2000s, it has created a greater gap from its competitors in memory chips such as Micron Technology (United States) and Toshiba (Japan). Table 5.8 further shows that Samsung had more DRAM patents in the 2000–2004 period than all of its Japanese competitors, except Hitachi. In the 2005–2009 period, Samsung's sixty-one DRAM patents was the largest number among *all* South Korean and Japanese DRAM producers. Its critical success factors are related to timely investments, speedy ramping up of production scale, and process innovations.[77]

By the 2010s, the two South Korean chipmakers had grown rapidly and consolidated their market position as the world's top ten semiconductor IDMs. Both chaebol IDMs in memory chips have clearly outsized and outcompeted other memory chip IDMs from Taiwan. But Samsung's competitive advantage extends well beyond its scale economies, sophisticated applied design, and process yield. Apart from its enormous lead in semiconductor technologies through continuous investments in R&D activity, Samsung has also benefited from unique *organizational synergies* unavailable to Hynix and these IDMs from Taiwan. These synergies are embedded in Samsung's firm-specific business model of organizing its IDM business to supply both in-house own brand products, such as televisions and mobile phones, and third-party vendors, such as global lead firms in computers, telecommunications devices, and other consumer electronics. As will be discussed in the next chapter, Samsung Electronics had become a globally recognized brand name in consumer electronics products only in the mid-2000s. It has since expedited and increased substantially the functional and production integration of its semiconductor devices across its different product lines. Through this vertical integration of its key semiconductor components, such as IC chips and memory devices, Samsung has emerged to become a world leader in its own electronics products by rapidly adding new features, miniaturizing technology, and reducing costs.

In the late 2000s, Samsung Electronics was reorganized into two major business areas: (1) Set Business for consumer electronics products; and (2) Device Solutions for its core component businesses, such as memory, IC products and systems, and LED displays. By organizing its semiconductor products *within* Samsung Electronics (SEC), the group as a whole can benefit from speedy delivery of digital solutions and semiconductor devices unmatched by other independent systems integrators that have to depend on a vast network of major suppliers. As my SEC interviewee argues, "Some analysts and scholars advise us to split SEC into some specialized units and adopt a network management, following American models. But these people do not understand how firms are operating and how the market is moving. The market demands speed and customers demand solutions. It takes time for specialized firms to respond to these demands by establishing networks with other firms."[78] In short, SEC has developed its own global production network and derived significant first-mover advantage in speedy time-to-market from its intragroup organizational synergy. To this SEC interviewee, Samsung cannot become world leader in products after products within a decade if "we develop the products as units within specialized firms. But we aim to achieve this by utilizing the trend of convergence within the electronics industry. Our strength lies in providing convergent products more quickly than our competitors."

Conclusion

This chapter has analyzed in-depth the strategic coupling process of industrial market specialization engaged by leading East Asian firms in marine engineering and semiconductor manufacturing—two major and, yet, contrasting industries that have benefited from substantial state-led initiatives during the 1970s and the 1980s. During their initial founding, heavy investment from state-directed sources was necessary for domestic firms in these capital-intensive industries to develop second-mover advantages in scale economies in order to compete effectively against then incumbents from advanced industrialized economies. In semiconductors, the developmental state in South Korea and Taiwan was actively involved in soliciting technology transfer from first mover economies through their state-funded research institutes. In classic studies of the East Asian developmental state (Amsden 1989; Wade 1990; Evans 1995; Amsden and Chu 2003), the successful emergence of both industries has been largely attributed to the developmental state's institutional capacity and political expediency in cajoling private interests to take on these mammoth tasks of industrializing the nation. In the case of Singapore, the state took direct ownership of both the marine and the semiconductor industries in order to expedite Singapore's articulation into global production networks.

My detailed empirical case studies have shown that since the early 1990s, changing state roles and the intensification of global competition have led to a much more complex selection environment significantly different from the earlier decades. These dynamic contextual changes have necessitated national champions to engage in new firm-specific initiatives in order to go beyond second-mover advantages or to sustain their market leadership in highly specialized industries. In the marine industry, I have analyzed the critical importance of continuous technological and organizational innovations *after* these national champions have attained second-mover advantages in scale economies. In an era of declining state support since the late 1990s, these innovations have been most important in enabling further catching up and market dominance to take place. The rapid rise of Samsung Heavy Industries as the world's second largest shipbuilder in 2010 is a true testimony of these technological and organizational innovations. Even though SHI is embedded in the same domestic context as Hyundai Heavy Industries and Daewoo Shipbuilding, its catching up is credited to its new technological breakthrough in production methods and its organizational specialization in high-value shipbuilding. In Singapore, its two world-leading offshore rig builders, Keppel and SembCorp, have also developed since the mid-2000s unique engineering solutions and internationalization strategies in order to couple with the rapid growth trajectory of their key customers in the offshore oil and gas global production networks. While the state remains a significant shareholder in both rig builders and plays a supportive role in ensuring a favorable domestic labor market, the successful coupling of these rig builders with the global offshore oil and gas industry owes much to these technological and organizational innovations that capitalize on changing industrial organization in favor of specialized equipment suppliers, such as rig builders.

In semiconductors, long regarded as one of the most important sectors in the industrialization of many latecomer economies, the rise of East Asian firms as global market leaders did not really take place until the late 1990s. During the 1980s, the developmental state in all three economies steered domestic firms to enter into this high-tech industry through industrial specialization in either foundry production for third-party customers or manufacturing devices for end users in different global production networks. As evident in my empirical analysis, Taiwan's state-led initiatives have been more successful in developing the initial foundations of such semiconductor foundry providers as TSMC, UMC, and Vanguard, all of which were spin-offs from the state-sponsored research institute ITRI. But my empirical evidence has shown that these foundries owe their eventual success and global dominance less to these initial state efforts during the 1980s than to their successive technological and organizational innovations since the late 1990s. This lends support to Fuller's (2008, 252) view that "although the Taiwanese state originally created both TSMC and UMC, the continued competitiveness of its semiconductor fabrication has had little to do with government policy beyond preferential tax treatment." In particular, TSMC's enormous market power is premised on its tight coupling with major global fabless firms (e.g., Qualcomm and Broadcom), domestic fabless giants (e.g., MediaTek), and the home base advantage of cluster economies. The home state and its industrial agencies have been lagging behind major players, such as TSMC, in these competitive fields since the late 1990s. By the 2010s, the highly divergent growth trajectories and industrial prowess among these three former state spin-offs testify to the crucial role of strategic coupling with global production networks through continual industrial market specialization.

In the case of integrated device manufacturers, Taiwan's track-record has not been strong *despite* the state's strong support for the semiconductor industry. Almost all of the successful IDMs from Taiwan showcased in Mathews and Cho (2000, chapter 4) faced major crises by the end of the 2000s. These IDMs did not develop new technological or organizational breakthroughs to go beyond their initial market entry facilitated by state-led efforts. Instead, only South Korea's Samsung and Hynix could grow from strength to strength in the 2000s and emerge as top players in the global semiconductor industry. Their industrial leadership and market success have quashed Bello and Rosenfeld's (1990, 164) earlier view that South Korea's race against American and Japanese incumbents in high-tech semiconductors was a "strategic mistake." Samsung's success, in particular, hinges mostly on its relentless investment in new technologies and its unique organizational solution of specialization in core semiconductor products. By developing its own global production network and yet serving key customers in other global production networks, Samsung has benefited from enormous organizational synergies absent in its IDM competitors from Taiwan and South Korea. Taken together, these leading East Asian firms in the marine and semiconductor industries have illustrated how firm-specific initiatives can enable them to engage and sustain their industrial market specialization in capital-intensive industries—the second of my three component processes of strategic coupling. Their evolutionary trajectories are also different from those in the ODM and EMS segments analyzed in the previous chapter. What remains to be seen in the next chapter, though, is whether these East Asian economies can produce global lead firms in different manufacturing or service industries, and how their state-led initiatives might help in such a transformation in the strategic orientation of leading domestic firms.

Chapter 6

Emergence of East Asian Lead Firms

With the rise of East Asian firms as strategic partners and specialized leaders in different global production networks, the developmental state has evolved from its earlier husbandry or demiurge role, as succinctly argued in Evans's (1995) *Embedded Autonomy*, to become a catalyst of domestic industrial development providing broader institutional and functional policy support. As these leading East Asian firms are more articulated into the global economy during the past two decades, we begin to witness a further and much more torturous process of industrial transformation—*some* national firms have strategically reoriented their competitive positioning from being partners and niche leaders *in* global production networks to becoming lead firms orchestrating their *own* global production networks in a wide range of manufacturing and service industries. In other words, these East Asian firms have emerged to be first movers or global lead firms in their respective industries. This emergence represents the third and most difficult kind of strategic coupling with global production networks. As "dragon multinationals" (Mathews 2002), they have truly caught up with their global competitors from advanced industrialized economies.

By the early 2010s, this transformation of some East Asian firms from their earlier role as low-cost suppliers, then beholden to captive value chain governance by their major customers, and domestic service providers to global brand-name manufacturers and global service providers has become a highly significant developmental phenomenon.[1] It heralds the completion of the late-comer catching-up and industrialization of their home economies that was painstakingly kick-started in the 1950s and the 1960s through state-led initiatives. As I have argued in earlier chapters, the accomplishment of this ultimate industrial transformation through the ascendance of global lead firms from East Asian economies cannot be comprehended without a fuller understanding of different component processes of strategic coupling. In short, the rise of East Asian lead firms in the global economy serves as a crucial indicator of the successful development of their home economies. State-led initiatives alone, however, cannot make this transformation work because it requires the concomitant determination and efforts on the part of these domestic lead firms. After all, states—developmental or otherwise—do not directly compete against each other in the economic realm, but business firms and their strategic partners in different global production networks do.[2] Krugman (1994, 31) famously argues that "when we say that a corporation is uncompetitive, we mean that its market position is unsustainable—that unless it improves its performance, it will cease to exist. Countries, on the other hand, do not go out of business. They may be happy or unhappy with their economic performance, but they have no well-defined bottom line." The competitive success of East Asian lead firms in different global industries thus provides the prima facie evidence for why different coupling processes matter in understanding economic development in an era of global competition.

In this final empirical chapter, I examine how some East Asian lead firms have indeed evolved into first movers in global industries through manufacturing brand names and organizing excellence in service provision. In order to elucidate this evolutionary transformation through strategic coupling with global production networks, I will first elaborate in the next section on the conceptualization of network-level strategic reorientation through firm-specific initiatives, such as brand building, design and product development, and service excellence. In particular, the need for market knowledge and product definition becomes paramount in this evolutionary process of becoming a global lead firm. The section also revisits the critical role of home base advantages in enhancing the global competitiveness of these East Asian lead firms. As illustrated in figure 3.2, the effective coupling of these lead firms is contingent on the availability of such external economies as strong interfirm networks and industrial clusters. This is where dynamic changes in industrial organization and the more sophisticated form of state support, as two structural conditions of strategic coupling, can make a difference in augmenting the geographical endowment of these East Asian economies. Similar to the case of industrial market specialization in the previous chapter, the emergence of transnational communities is relatively less significant in facilitating this coupling process. The next three substantive sections provide several in-depth case studies of global lead firms from these East Asian economies in order to shed light on leading brand name manufacturers in electronics (e.g., Acer, Samsung, and LG) and automobiles (e.g., Hyundai), and leading global service providers in air transport (e.g., Singapore Airlines).

Strategic Reorientation in Global Competition

In the global production networks perspective foregrounded in chapter 1, I have argued that the contemporary dynamics of global competition have allowed global lead firms occupying a primary role in their global production networks to create, transform, and capture more value from the processes associated with the market success of their products or services. In the three industrial sectors exemplified in chapters 4 and 5, leading East Asian firms have emerged as strategic partners or specialized leaders in different production networks governed by global lead firms. In these industries, such as computers, semiconductors, maritime transport, and offshore extraction, East Asian firms supply the crucial manufactured products for global lead firms to thrive in final markets. Because of their world-class technological leverage and organizational innovations, these East Asian firms are not subject to the captive form of value chain governance that often occurs in developing country firms coupled with global lead firms in labor-intensive industries, such as apparels, footwear, and agro-food. Nevertheless, these East Asian firms are *not* yet global lead firms because of one critical missing link—market control and definition. They do not or cannot exercise market control through defining final products or end user markets. In other words, they have to work with their industrial customers, that is, global lead firms in different industries, that are first movers in developing and, sometimes, dominating in their final markets often located in advanced industrialized economies.

This final market-oriented perspective on different firm roles in global industries is important because it helps us differentiate the technological and industrial achievements of East Asian firms from their eventual market definition as global lead firms. Not surprisingly, this evolutionary transformation from strategic partners to lead firms defining their own products and markets and coordinating their own global production networks is highly arduous because of substantial investment required in R&D in design and product/service development, branding and marketing, and distribution activity. More crucially in some industries (e.g., electronics), these latecomers may face huge switching costs when their existing brand name customers decide to terminate their orders or partnership with these East Asian firms, reducing substantially their access to new technologies and global markets.[3] In the electronics industry up to the mid-1990s, for example, few East Asian firms were expected to accomplish this transformational shift from their network position as an OEM supplier or an ODM partner to a globally recognized lead firm engaging in original brand manufacturing (OBM).[4] Concluding his *Innovation in East Asia*, Hobday (1995, 203) remains skeptical of such a final transformation: "To continue their success, much will depend on whether East Asian firms can overcome their latecomer disadvantages in design, capital goods, R&D and marketing. The strategy of larger companies is to invest heavily in R&D and in brand awareness campaigns. However, the results of these strategies are still unfolding and so far the results are mixed."

In this chapter, I argue that the successful emergence of global lead firms from the three East Asian economies requires both network-level strategic reorientation—facilitated by favorable industry-level dynamics—and extra-firm home-based advantages. The postdevelopmental state can play a useful role in enhancing these home-based advantages through an appropriate combination of functional policies (e.g., national marketing and branding promotion) and institutional support (e.g., investment in design and product development institutes). This section attempts to conceptualize the importance of this meso-level strategic reorientation toward defining and controlling the final market through brand building, and home-based advantages, such as interfirm networks, production systems, and industrial clusters. One of the most critical transformations necessary for East Asian firms to become global lead firms is their *repositioning in global production networks* in order to take advantage of organizational synergies emanating from the accumulation, diffusion, and integration of firm-specific knowledge and capabilities.

Most leading East Asian firms tend to belong to different business groups.[5] The initial state-led development in these East Asian economies has led to significant market power of these groups as dominant players in the domestic economy, and this initial state role differs among the three economies. The role of business groups in home economies can make a significant difference to the rise of East Asian lead firms in the global economy. In all three East Asian economies, there exist powerful business groups that are mostly family-owned and managed.[6] Their interaction with the domestic developmental state also contributes to divergent strategic choices in their evolutionary transformation.[7] To W. W. Chu (2009, 1064), "most leading firms had chosen different business strategies early in their formative years in Korea and Taiwan, partly due to different government policies and general environments. Lacking support from a national champion strategy, most of Taiwan's leading firms did not pursue the branding strategy in their early formative years. The South Korean government promoted national champions all along and had a mechanism in place to lessen risks for chaebol pursuing an own-brand strategy." In her view, South Korea has been able to produce global lead firms competing at the technological frontier and enjoying global brand name recognition. But Taiwan's largest information and communications technology (ICT) firms have only developed second-tier status in the global market, albeit playing a significant role as strategic partners and specialized leaders.

While the initial protective efforts and sectoral industrial policy of the developmental state can be effective in promoting the rapid growth of these large business groups in different East Asian economies, these initial state-directed efforts are less useful for understanding the contrasting phenomenon that only *some* business groups from even the same home economy have emerged as global lead firms in the 2010s. For example, among the top thirty chaebol groups in South Korea just before the 1997–1998 Asian financial crisis, only three have really evolved into global lead firms—Samsung, LG, and Hyundai. The same applies to Taiwan's top thirty business groups: only Acer, Asustek (ASUS), and to a lesser extent, BenQ are better-known OBM firms in computers and consumer electronics. In Singapore, several government-linked companies, such as Singapore Airlines, SingTel, CapitaLand, and DBS, are global or regional lead firms in the respective air transport, telecommunications, real estate, and banking sectors.[8] If the state-led promotion of national champions was as critical as W. W. Chu (2009) argues, we would expect more South Korean chaebol to become global lead firms and more government-linked companies from Singapore to emerge as global brand manufacturers or global service providers.

Instead, we witness both firm-specific and industry-level dynamics at work that contribute to these cross-national differences in developmental trajectories. While some leading firms from South Korea and Taiwan have been transformed into global lead firms in the electronics industry, only South Korea's Hyundai has succeeded as a global brand manufacturer in the automobile industry. However, virtually none of South Korea's chaebol or Taiwan's business groups has succeeded as a leading global service provider. And yet several Singaporean firms have performed well as regional or global lead firms in various service industries (e.g., transport, banking, telecommunications, real estate, and agribusiness). Even in the electronics industry, Samsung and LG are global lead firms only in consumer electronics, but they are less successful than Taiwan's Acer and ASUS in the personal computer segment of the global electronics industry. The role of state-led development can only account for the initial strategic choice of *some* chosen national firms to venture into these industries. A fuller analysis of their evolutionary trajectories needs to be grounded in more nuanced firm- and industry-specific competitive dynamics in global production networks. As argued by Whittaker et al. (2010, 451), "The differences between Korea and Taiwan, then, reflect differences in strategy, developed in a co-evolutionary manner with a set of deverticalizing customers [in global value chains], and not just different starting points in industrial structure."

Moving away from a statecentric account of global lead firms from these East Asian economies, a resource-based view of business groups offers a complementary analysis of the differential capacity of business groups in capitalizing on their intragroup knowledge and capabilities.[9] In short, business groups can substitute for the developmental state by providing the necessary resources for investment in technological or business innovation and market development. A global lead firm is more likely to evolve from a business group that can harness its intragroup resources to invest in unique branding, product definition, and market development. This capacity varies across different firms and/or business groups even within the same home economy, thereby contributing to divergent strategic choice made by different national firms in their transformation into global brand-name manufacturers or global service providers.

In particular, this coupling with global production networks vis-à-vis a strategic reorientation from cost-based competition to market capture through brand and product development is often contingent on three interrelated processes. First, many business groups in South Korea and Taiwan were major beneficiaries of the developmental state's earlier industrial targeting and therefore developed a tendency to depend on export subsidies and fiscal incentives in their investment decisions. During the heyday of the 1970s and the 1980s, they tended to enter into multiple industries in order to maximize their access to state benefits under a developmentalist industrialization regime. This tendency toward multiplying industrial presence persisted even after the developmental state had become less directive and interventionist in the 1990s and beyond. Guillén (2010, 749) points to "the continued growth of business groups even when the government starts worrying about their increasing power and leverage. The capability to combine resources for industry entry will remain inimitable as long as low-high foreign trade and investment flows persist, encouraging those who possess the capability to enter multiple industries so as fully to utilize it." In short, these business groups were locked into state-directed incentives and protected domestic markets. They found it neither profitable nor strategic to specialize and invest in international marketing and distribution in order to reach out to end users outside their home economy. Only those business groups that could break out of this incessant dependence on state subsidies and protective policies have successfully reorganized and developed sufficient intragroup resources to engage in OBM and to evolve into global lead firms coordinating their own global production networks.

Second, developing into a global lead firm entails substantial financial investment and organizational efforts in brand building and market definition. Unlocking dependence on state incentives represents only an initial step in the disembedding of leading East Asian firms from the postdevelopmental state described in chapter 3. New dynamic capabilities must be sought and accumulated within the group in order to support this investment. Developing first mover advantages through brand building can be daunting in emerging economies because of the lack of product information and consumer awareness in these markets. But the process is even more formidable in advanced industrialized economies if the newcomer firms are from emerging economies such as the three East Asian economies. Their liability of foreignness is much greater in these highly competitive markets.[10] To overcome this major barrier to foreign market success, the domestic market of East Asian lead firms can serve as a critical site for learning and gaining market knowledge in two ways: building group-based brands and local "test bed" marketing. East Asian firms belonging to business groups are more likely to achieve substantial economies of group-based brand building than their standalone domestic or foreign competitors. In South Korea, for example, global lead firms emerging from business groups have successfully harnessed their group-based identity built through brand development over several decades. To H. Kim (2010, 163), "By building group brands such as Samsung and LG, *chaebol* were able to economize on the time and the costs of developing individual brands. For instance, at the start of a new business, being able to use a reputable group brand signaled images of reliability, quality, and credibility to prospective customers, suppliers, and other business partners. Given a shortage of reliable firm-specific and product-specific information, the ability to develop and share group brands was crucial to gaining customer and supplier support during the rapid growth of the *chaebol*."

Moreover, the domestic market can be usefully deployed as a "test bed" to fashion out new products and services that help these East Asian firms accumulate their initial market knowledge before they launch their successful products or services in global markets. This opportunity for local testing of the market hinges on several favorable industry-level dynamics and functional state policies. Local firms must accumulate sufficient technological and managerial competencies as they move quickly through each product cycle in the domestic market. Domestic market segmentation, sometimes an outcome of state policies (e.g., nontrade barriers and regulation), is also useful because it tends to deter foreign competitors from launching their latest and state-of-the-art products or services in these East Asian economies. Furthermore, the close personal or organizational relationship between OBM firms and local distributors in East Asian economies gives these firms some breathing space to experiment with their own brand products or services. In the mobile handset industry, for example, the two global lead firms from South Korea, Samsung and LG, have benefited from using their home market as a "test bed" for path-creating technologies and capabilities (Lee and Lim 2001, 472; Jho 2007). Whang and Hobday (2011, 1366–67) argue that these national firms engage in "frequent product launch, short product lead times, and an ever changing customer segmentation. These local market dynamics, characterized by a diversity of products and frequent product turnover does not fit well with the MNC globalization strategies of the period, which tended to rely on supplying the global market with a small number of relatively standardized products." By working closely with domestic mobile service operators and state regulators (e.g., the Ministry of Information and Communications), these chaebol lead firms have managed to capture the highly segmented domestic market and to learn much from their domestic experience in market development before launching into the global market.

Third, a national firm can evolve into a global lead firm only if it has globalized at least some of its operations in various value-chain activities, such as R&D, production, and marketing, distribution, and after-sales service. For East Asian firms, this globalization process is organizationally demanding because it requires tight integration of its subsidiaries and suppliers across borders and swift responsiveness in different foreign markets.[11] These organizational demands are particularly difficult for their home state to support in terms of sectoral industrial policy and financial incentives, since much tacit knowledge within the globalizing firm is required to put to work this challenging organizational nexus of global integration and local responsiveness. The territorial boundedness of their home state's institutional capacity and political legitimacy also imposes a serious constraint on the nature and level of state support for the globalization of East Asian firms. In short, this process of global market development goes well beyond domestic production for exports, as was the case in the earlier phase of state-led industrialization, or the more recent relocation of production to lower-cost economies, such as China and Southeast Asia. It brings to the forefront head-on competition with the very global lead firms to which these East Asian firms had previously served as OEM suppliers or subcontractors.

While capital investment (e.g., state-facilitated access to credits) and functional policies (e.g., free trade agreements on goods and services) can be useful in promoting this globalization effort, leading East Asian firms need to tap into their intrafirm or intragroup organizational resources in order to sustain their existing competitive advantages, such as scale economies and new technologies/know-how, and to acquire new market knowledge. The recognition and implementation of this search for new market and product knowledge cannot be forced on by the home state, however powerful and efficacious it might be in a bureaucratic or policy sense. Rather, this strategic reorientation and repositioning in global production networks has to emanate from *within* the firm itself through entrepreneurial vision, harnessing intragroup resources, and perseverance in different product and market cycles in the highly competitive global market. It requires the continuous technological and organizational innovations similar to those described in the previous two chapters. More important, it entails a mindset shift in these East Asian firms from engaging with the coupling process of being value chain partners of global lead firms to participating in a new and most difficult coupling process of developing and integrating their own global production networks. In the next three empirical sections, I will analyze these evolutionary transformations in both manufacturing and service industries since the 1990s, drawing on some successful cases of East Asian lead firms. Taken together, my comparative analysis of these global lead firms in different industries aims to illustrate the importance of firm-specific initiatives and network-level dynamics in our understanding of the ultimate challenge to East Asian industrialization.

Manufacturing Global Brands in Electronics

Since the 2000s, several East Asian firms have managed to emerge as *global lead firms* in the electronics industry by focusing strategically on using branding and product development as the key organizational platform to capture more value in *their* own global production networks and to compete against other first movers in the global economy. In this section, I consider two contrasting examples of global lead firms in computers and consumer electronics—Taiwan's Acer Inc. and South Korea's Samsung Electronics (and

LG Electronics). While leading domestic firms from Taiwan and South Korea have firmly established their positions in global electronics, only a few of them have really succeeded in transforming from OEM and ODM into OBM (Hobday 1995; 1998). By venturing into OBM, these two East Asian firms are competing head-on with the likes of Hewlett-Packard and Dell in the personal computer industry, and Apple, Sony, and Philips in consumer electronics. In their early years of corporate development up to the mid-1990s, however, these East Asian firms engaged with the strategic coupling process of being value chain partners of global lead firms in the computer and electronics industry. Over time, they have harnessed significant intragroup resources to engage in OBM and to compete as first movers. By comparing these two examples, we can appreciate better the differential role of the home state and the critical importance of firm-specific initiatives in such a transformation of their strategic coupling with global production networks.

The case of Acer from Taiwan is a telling example of how an OEM supplier to global lead firms in the personal computer industry can evolve over time to become a global lead firm within two decades. Acer's case is particularly significant for two reasons. First, it is one of a handful of well-known brand names from Taiwan and perhaps the only global lead firm from Taiwan in the global electronics industry.[12] This rarity in successful global lead firms from Taiwan is unusual because its electronics firms have a substantial presence in the entire value chain of the global personal computer industry, such as semiconductors (e.g., TSMC and UMC), display panels (e.g., AU Optronics and Chi Mei Optoelectronics), power systems (e.g., Delta), components and peripherals (e.g., Winbond and Yageo), ODM (e.g., Quanta, Compal, and Inventec) and EMS (e.g., Hon Hai and Pegatron), and distribution (e.g., Synnex). In other words, despite these strong industrial linkages in the home economy, the successful evolution of Acer into a global lead firm is not easily replicable by other computer firms from Taiwan. Home endowment in the form of industrial linkages and production networks is a necessary, but insufficient, condition for the emergence of global lead firms from Taiwan in this highly competitive global industry.

Second, the industrial policy of Taiwan's developmental state was less oriented toward promoting the computer industry in general. Between the late 1970s and the early 1990s, Taiwan's industrial policy targeted more explicitly the capital-intensive and high-tech segments of the ICT industry, such as semiconductors and TFT-LCD displays. As I have argued in chapter 5, even the success of this sectoral industrial policy should be viewed in the context of firm-specific technological and organizational innovations. In the equipment segment, Taiwan's ODM and EMS providers did not benefit much from state-led initiatives. Instead, they strategically coupled with different global lead firms in order to compete in the global market. Through their strategic partnership arrangements, these ODM and EMS providers became top producers in their respective market segments. However, none of these ODM and EMS providers can be considered as a global lead firm. Likewise, Acer did not rely on the state's sectoral industrial policy to evolve into a global lead firm.[13] In short, the state's industrial policy was seemingly more effective in specialized intermediate markets, such as semiconductors and panel displays, than in final consumer markets, such as brand name personal computers. This points to the immense difficulty for any latecomer economy to produce global lead firms in the computer industry. In the case of Taiwan, extensive domestic industrial linkages and favorable industrial policy could only compensate for some of the latecomer disadvantages. Such an evolutionary transformation requires Herculean efforts on the part of the latecomer itself and points squarely to strategic reorientation as a coupling process to break out of the existing path dependency.

In Acer's case, this strategic breakout has taken three rounds of major corporate reorganization: 1976–1986, 1987–2000, and 2001 to now. By 2011, Acer had become a multibrand group in the global computer industry and ranked fourth in total personal computer (PC) shipments and second in total notebook shipments.[14] Its revenue grew rapidly from US$4.3 billion in 2002 to US$15.8 billion in 2006. In 2011, its revenue remained at US$15.5 billion. Founded by Stan Shih in 1976, Acer was originally known as Sertek in the domestic market. It was subsequently renamed to Multitech to engage in the manufacturing of personal computers for OEM customers. During much of the 1980s, Multitech was one of the approved IBM-compatible PC manufacturers in Taiwan. Given its technological and market dependency on IBM, Acer's supplier relationship with IBM was mostly captive in nature. It was subject to a high degree of monitoring and control by its major customers and had little control over product specifications and design blueprints in computer manufacturing. Acer's switching costs were also very high due to the market dominance of IBM in the computer industry during the 1980s. In 1984, Continental Systems Inc. was incorporated in the United States to provide computer peripherals as an added service to the brand name clients of Multitech.

Through participation in this initial subordinated supplier relationship with global lead firms, such as IBM and, later, Dell, Stan Shih learnt the important lesson of having one's own brand name in order to exercise market control and product definition and to capture greater value from the upstream design and R&D and downstream activities (e.g., marketing and distribution) of the personal computer industry. In 1987, Shih decided to start Acer as a brand name manufacturer, after commissioning Ogilvy & Mather to come up with branding suggestions, and incorporated Multitech into the newly named Acer Inc. This strategic repositioning of Acer as a future global lead firm was unprecedented among its peers and competitors in Taiwan's computer industry. To institutionalize this drive toward brand development and marketing, Shih also founded Taiwan's Brand International Promotion Association to promote internationally the branding of Taiwan-made products.

This transition to OBM heralded the second major phase of corporate growth in Acer's history (1987–2000). At the same time, Continental Systems Inc. was renamed to Acer Peripherals (and later Acer Communications & Multimedia in 2001). During the 1990s, Acer faced significant challenges in the low-margin OEM supplier business, and the strong New Taiwan dollar also cut into its profitability. It was still producing computers under OEM arrangements for AT&T, Unysis, and Siemens, but it broke out of the captive supplier relationship with IBM and others. Shih launched several rounds of aggressive organizational transformations, leading to backward integration into R&D activities and forward integration into marketing and distribution (Mathews 2002, 135–38). This firm-specific organizational change represented the most crucial step in Acer's evolution into a global lead firm coordinating its own global production network. Shih called this new organizational structure "client-server" architecture through which its different operating units worked together through organizational interdependence and agreed rules of behavior. In 1996, Acer Display Technology was incorporated to produce large-sized TFT-LCD panel displays for both computer and consumer electronics.

By now, Acer had a fully integrated production system comprised of brand name (Acer), peripherals, panel displays, and other critical components, such as transformers (Darfon), storage devices (Daxon), and wireless LAN chips (Airoha). By listing nine of Acer's business units on the stock exchanges in Taiwan, Singapore, Mexico City, and New York as of the end of 1999, Shih was able to leverage new financial resources in these listed firms to pursue his continuous brand building exercise at Acer Inc. These successful listings also enabled Acer to be independent of the home state's industrial policy and financial support. Shih's strategy of brand building finally paid off when Acer became one of the world's top ten PC vendors by the late 1990s. As noted in Dedrick and Kraemer (1998, 148), "By the 1990s, the surviving PC makers [in Taiwan] had returned to OEM production, except for Acer, which was able to develop successfully its own brand name internationally." Mathews (2002, 55–56) even declared that by the early 2000s, "Acer is the world's largest and most successful Chinese high-technology company" and "a 'Dragon Multinational' par excellence."

But not all was well within the Acer group. As Acer's brand name business grew substantially during the 1990s, it faced tremendous pressure from its OEM customers whose own brand PCs were increasingly threatened by Acer-brand computers by the late 1990s. As pointed out succinctly by my Acer interviewee, "So by that time, we restructured with a lot of challenges from the [OEM] manufacturing side. Although our brand business was not too strong, gradually we built up our competitiveness in notebooks. And the notebook business continuously grew at 50 to 60 percent annually. So we faced more confrontations from the manufacturing side. They're saying: 'Well, some large OEM customers don't like to have business with Acer because at Acer you have your brand business. If we support you, it's like we support our competitor in the market.'" Acer was at a major crossroad. Stan Shih had to make an unprecedented strategic choice of either pursuing even more aggressively its brand building and transforming Acer into a global lead firm or, like many of its domestic peers, retreating into a strategic coupling role as an OEM or ODM partner to its global lead firm customers. He opted for the former in order to exercise market control of its own brand name business, and that began a new era of Acer's emergence as a global lead firm in the 2000s and beyond.

In 2001, Acer underwent a third and most significant round of corporate reorganization that led to the founding of four independent companies: Acer, BenQ, AU Optronics, and Wistron. By spinning off its computer manufacturing and peripherals into separate businesses, Acer Inc. was transformed from an integrated manufacturer of computers and related peripherals into a global lead firm with a globally recognized computer brand and strong capability in product development and market definition. Some 90 percent of the resources within the Acer group went into the newly formed spin-off companies, with only about 300 employees staying on with Acer Inc., the global lead firm controlling the Acer brand and its portfolio of products. The domestic marketing team at Acer Sertek, the original company established in 1976, also joined Acer's sales and marketing division. Acer Communications & Multimedia (formerly Acer Peripherals) was reorganized into BenQ, a brand name manufacturer of lifestyle devices. This reorganization of the Acer group was necessary because previously Acer Peripherals was marketing computer peripherals with Acer's brand name that in turn led to the dilution of Acer's brand reputation in personal computers.[15]

My Acer interviewee complains about this brand confusion between Acer Inc. and Acer Peripherals that occurred at the beginning of the 2000s: "At that time, Acer Peripherals was using the Acer brand selling all the peripherals. But they're also one of the public listed companies, and we had different interests in the brand's market position. How to manage the brand was something critical to us. And they're using the brand name or phrase in different ways for the peripherals. So at the end, we asked that only Acer Inc. could use in the Acer brand, and they changed the name into BenQ." From Acer Peripherals' perspective, brand business was critical in its diversification into lifestyle products under its own BenQ brand name. My interviewee from BenQ notes that "I think brand business is very important for us to have the room and freedom to introduce our innovation. From my perception and experience with OEM business, we normally have a lot of limitation from those OEM customers who discourage us from certain kind of innovation. They don't like this one. They just want to pick up this area. So we have strong limitation in this OEM business in terms of innovation." The separation of Acer Inc. and Acer Peripherals (now BenQ) into two independent brand businesses was instrumental in enabling Acer and BenQ to develop into strong brands in personal computers and lifestyle products.

Moreover, Acer Display was merged with Unipac, a former subsidiary of semiconductor foundry UMC, in September 2001 to become AU Optronics, a dedicated producer of TFT-LCD panel displays.[16] Acer's computer manufacturing operations were grouped into Wistron, an independent ODM producer of personal computers, which serves as a strategic partner of global lead firms, such as Dell and Lenovo (see table 4.3). Through this vertical *dis*integration of the Acer group into separate and specialized manufacturers, Acer Inc. was able to focus on its global brand building and market expansion in the 2000s. It could now source its own brand products from any suppliers in Taiwan and elsewhere, giving it much more flexibility in product innovation and cost competitiveness. By 2004, Acer's combined brand value with BenQ exceeded US$1 billion for the first time in its corporate history. It marked the accomplishment of Shih's vision for Acer to be the leading computer brand name from Taiwan. By 2007, Acer became the world's third largest PC vendor after Hewlett-Packard and Dell. After acquiring Gateway in October 2007 and Packard Bell in March 2008, Acer became a multibrand global lead firm in the personal computer industry and was poised to overtake Hewlett-Packard as the world's largest notebook brand name firm. In 2011, Acer's brand value reached US$1.9 billion.[17]

Meanwhile, Acer's former affiliates were no longer subject to intra-Acer organizational constraints and could now compete freely as strategic partners (e.g., Wistron and BenQ) of and specialized industrial producers (e.g., AU Optronics) for any global lead firm. Because of their organizational independence from Acer and access to new customers and capital, these Acer spin-offs have grown rapidly since 2001. Wistron was listed in the Taiwan Stock Exchange in 2003 and became a top ODM provider with revenue of US$20.8 billion in 2013.[18] In table 4.3, Wistron was the world's third largest ODM manufacturer in the notebook computer market, shipping more than 27 million units in 2010. In this market segment, Acer's global shipment of 33.5 million units in 2010 was second only to Hewlett-Packard (40.3 million units). Interestingly, Acer did not give all of its notebook orders to Wistron. It was only Wistron's second largest brand name customer. Instead, Acer gave more than 50 percent of its notebook orders to Compal, the world's second largest notebook ODM, and became its largest client in 2010. This multiple-vendor allocation of Acer's notebook orders is particularly telling because it illustrates the success of Wistron as an ODM producer for both Acer and its major competitors, such as Dell and Lenovo.[19] Since its separation from Acer, BenQ was struggling in its global branding strategy. After its reorganization in 2007, BenQ's manufacturing of lifestyle devices was brought into Qisda, which was formerly Quanta Display and acquired by AUO in 2006. Both Qisda and AUO were incorporated into the BenQ group of more than fifteen companies in seven business segments. In 2012, BenQ group's combined revenue reached US$20 billion.

In the personal computer industry, the evolutionary transformation of Acer Inc. from one of the earliest OEM suppliers in Taiwan into a global lead firm with its unique brand name and channel business model for distribution has occurred primarily through network-level strategic reorientation and firm-specific reorganizational efforts in relation to the new coupling process. The role of the home state in supporting such a corporate transformation—a crucial step for the emergence of global lead firms from Taiwan—is rather limited. While the state does recognize the need and significance of this transformation in the strategic orientation of leading ICT firms from Taiwan, it does not have the necessary market expertise or financial resources to nurture directly such "national brands," as it had done earlier in promoting national champions in semiconductors during the 1980s. The new international trade environment under the World Trade Organization (WTO) regime has also made it much harder for the state to subsidize directly such marketing and brand development efforts by leading ICT firms from Taiwan. For example, the Industrial Development Bureau (IDB) of the Ministry of Economic Affairs has found it challenging to take on this direct promotion of marketing and branding efforts by emerging lead firms from Taiwan and preferred to leave them in the hands of private firms. As observed by my IDB interviewee,

> It's very difficult for us to promote. Marketing and branding are the strategies of private companies. And how should the government push this part is a bit tricky, and we are thinking about that. When private companies do marketing and branding, what role can the government play to assist them? This is the major part that we have to communicate with private companies in the future. I think the government policy now is how to provide a sound environment for business. And how to push the companies to develop their brand names is very difficult. You have to put in a lot of finance, but this is a route you have to go. Private companies may need government assistance in some areas, and it may involve capital, loan, or tax break/exemption. But all of these cannot violate WTO regulations and you have to think carefully. I think offering low interest loans is easier.[20]

As a functional support, the Knowledge Services Division of the IDB is involved in the promotion of Taiwan's leading brands to the public through organizing annual surveys of Taiwan International Brand Value with Business Next magazine and the brand consultancy Interbrand. This annual ranking is also intended to raise the awareness of Taiwanese firms about the critical importance of developing brand names as the core competitive tool in global competition.

The case of Acer Inc. is indeed an exception to W. W. Chu's (2009) observation that most leading ICT firms from Taiwan did not pursue own brand development as a pathway to becoming global lead firms in their early formative years.[21] But more important, my analysis shows that such a strategic choice by Acer to go into brand business since 1987 has little direct relationship with the state's sectoral industrial policy. Stan Shih's decision was made at a time when Taiwan's developmental state was putting almost all of its resources earmarked for the electronics industry into developing the semiconductor segment of the industry. His OBM strategy was more guided by his own experience as a captive OEM supplier to IBM and Dell and his ambition of developing Acer into a global lead firm with its own brand name and global production network. Acer's rise as a global lead firm is also fraught with challenges and difficulties, particularly its conflict of interests with OEM customers and intragroup organizational dissonance during the 1990s. It did not emerge fully as a global lead firm exercising strong market control until the completion of its 2001 corporate reorganization. In the realm of product innovation and market definition—both key characteristics of a global lead firm, there is clearly much less scope for sectoral policy interventions from the state. While W. W. Chu (2009) argues that the South Korean state's long-term industrial policy has led to global lead firms, such as Samsung Electronics and LG Electronics, my comparative analysis of two such global lead firms from South Korea below points further to the relatively modest effect of sectoral industrial policy in nurturing the emergence of such global lead firms.

As leading brand name producers in mobile handsets and digital televisions by the 2010s, Samsung and LG are curiously the *only* two chaebol from South Korea to emerge as global lead firms in the electronics industry.[22] In Interbrand's *Best Global Brands 2014*, Samsung was ranked seventh after six globally recognized American brand name firms (Apple, Google, Coca-Cola, IBM, Microsoft, and GE), but was ahead of Toyota (eighth), McDonald's (ninth) and Mercedes-Benz (tenth). Its brand value rose 15 percent from the previous year to reach US$45.5 billion.[23] In comparison, Taiwan's global lead firms in the electronics industry are much smaller in size and product diversity: Acer (computers), ASUS (computers), and HTC (mobile handsets). Their combined brand value in 2011 was only US$7.1 billion. Samsung's emergence as a global lead firm in consumer electronics, particularly mobile handsets, can be traced to three interrelated firm-specific initiatives—its relatively recent global branding efforts, its home-based configuration of production networks, and its exploitation of intrachaebol group synergy.

First, the evolutionary transformation of Samsung into a global lead firm is a recent phenomenon, and it occurs well after the developmental state has receded from its husbandry role in the domestic economy since the early 1990s. By all accounts, Samsung did not really emerge as a global lead firm, with its unique OBM and market-leading consumer electronics products, until at least the early 2000s. To S. J. Chang (2008, 65), Samsung was still "a completely generic brand until the mid-1990s." Its journey to OBM has not been straightforward and has indeed taken over three decades.[24] In its early years of corporate development during the 1980s and up to the mid-1990s, Samsung engaged with the coupling process of serving as a value chain supplier to global lead firms in the computer and electronics industry (Hobday 1995; 1998). Similar to its Taiwanese counterparts, Samsung was viewed as a captive manufacturer of low-end finished electronics products prior to the 1997–1998

Asian financial crisis (L. Kim 1997). Samsung's global branding efforts started seriously in the mid-1990s and were supported through intragroup resources rather than state-directed industrial policy (S. J. Chang 2008, 72–74; 83). After Samsung's Frankfurt Conference held on June 7, 1993, Chairman Kun-hee Lee began to realize the significance of branding to the group's long-term development. He started the "new management movement" to emphasize quality over quantity and to pursue innovation and quality management. In 1995, the then CEO of Samsung Electronics, Kwang-ho Kim, set aside an internal marketing fund of US$400 million to improve its branding in ten emerging markets. In 2000, it spent US$508 million on advertising to increase its brand value. Since 1994, its advertising expenditure has consistently exceeded 2 percent of Samsung's total sales. Overseas subsidiaries have also been mandated to spend at least 3.5 percent of their sales on advertisement in order to prevent them from increasing profits through reduction in marketing efforts.

Since the late 1990s, Samsung has refocused its business by investing heavily in corporate branding and R&D and managed to develop into a globally recognized brand name as a key organizational platform to compete in the global economy. In June 2003, Samsung launched the second phase of its "new management movement" and switched its role model from Japanese *keiretsu* to Jack Welch's management initiatives at General Electric. This initiative has led to mind-set change in its employees and subsequently business restructuring to enable it to be a globally recognized leader in innovation (S. J. Chang 2008, 84–85). By venturing into OBM, Samsung is competing head-on with the likes of Sony and Philips in consumer electronics. Focusing on its own branding in consumer electronics, Samsung has been able to achieve global market leadership in mobile handsets and home appliances. According to its vice chairman and CEO Jong-Yong Yun (2005, 72), Samsung's brand value doubled from US$5.2 billion in 2001 to US$10.8 billion in 2004. By 2000, Interbrand ranked Samsung as forty-third in the world, and it moved to twentieth in 2006 and seventh in 2014. In comparison, Sony was eighteenth in 2000, and dropped to twenty-sixth in 2006 and fifty-second in 2014.

Second, while Samsung and LG have actively pursued a strategy of OBM with their own distinctive technological strength and marketing capability, their success in mobile handsets and televisions since the 2000s has been intimately linked to their peculiar configuration of global production networks.[25] Both lead firms have been reluctant to internationalize their R&D and manufacturing activity and have preferred to keep a large portion of their manufacturing activity in South Korea, particularly within the Seoul Metropolitan Area. The home region benefits from the enormous innovative capability, employment generation, and industrial linkages of both chaebol.[26] In particular, Samsung has pursued a home-based and export-oriented production system that offers several key competitive advantages, such as faster time-to-market and better control of production cost and technological know-how. This organizational strategy of home-based production is particularly feasible in the mobile handset business. Samsung started to produce mobile handsets for the domestic market in the early 1990s and expanded into exports only by the mid-1990s. Unlike other products in Samsung's consumer electronics division, a strategy of brand image has been actively pursued. An interviewee from Samsung's mobile handset division claims that "the core of cellular phone business in Samsung is quality rather than quantity. Samsung has made a strategy of developing brand image at the mid- and high-end rather than focusing just on market share."[27]

Moreover, most of Samsung's products in mobile handsets do not require localization to cater to changing local tastes and preferences of global consumers. They can be distributed worldwide through air cargo services. Samsung thus prefers to integrate the design, R&D, and manufacturing of its mobile handsets within its domestic production network. As described by another interviewee from Samsung Electronics' global strategy division, "The change in our strategy is similar to that in the US military strategy. The US military has changed it global strategy from 'frontal deployment' to 'speedy deployment' by relying on its air attacking capability. Now we have much better logistics and information flows, and our products are easy to ship."[28] In globalizing its production networks, Samsung has taken an incremental approach in order to retain its home-based production system and competitive advantage. But in host countries with significant trade barriers or policy preferences for local production, Samsung has established its own manufacturing facilities. During the early 1990s, it ventured into emerging markets, such as Southeast Asia, the Commonwealth of Independent States (former Soviet republics), Central and South America, the Middle East, and Africa. By the late 1990s, Samsung had identified "six core and seven priority countries": the United States, China, Russia, Britain, Thailand, and India as core countries, and Germany, France, Italy, Brazil, Indonesia, Mexico, and Iran as priority countries. In the 2000s, it established design centers in Italy and host regions in order to understand better customer desires.

Third, Samsung's intrachaebol organization of production enables faster decision and better supply chain management that allows for high-quality materials and functionality of its key products at lower price over time. This intragroup synergy in R&D capability, information and material flows, and joint branding has given its mobile handset division a much stronger competitive position vis-à-vis major global mobile handset producers, such as Apple, Nokia, and Motorola. In global marketing, Samsung's mobile handsets can also benefit from cross-marketing through the group's more than sixty sales offices worldwide. As described by an interviewee from Samsung's global marketing division, "This is a great competitiveness of Samsung that is better than other global companies. The sales organizations between Nokia and Samsung are different. Samsung's business is diverse. There are cases that we have sold our products through others within the Samsung group."[29] His view is echoed by an interviewee from Samsung Corporation, the chaebol's general trading company: "Our trading is more likely business-to-business. There are things that bear the Samsung logo, as well as ones that have their own. Anything that bears the Samsung brand, we are particularly careful. We do the brand marketing. We also assist in overall business management."[30]

In product design, R&D, and production, Samsung's mobile handsets gain from the group's market leading technological solutions in LCD technologies and semiconductors. Its long experience in designing consumer goods can also be useful in the design of mobile handsets. The interviewee from Samsung's mobile handset division points to these advantages not available to its competitors such as Motorola and Nokia:

> The way of development in cellular phone is mobile multimedia. The industry trend of audio, video, LCD, and semiconductors, and the synergy we are having makes a great match. Motorola has only telecommunications. We have an advantage in multimedia. . . . Samsung has focused on making the world's best products. The reason that Samsung releases products faster than others is that Samsung has a market of advanced demand and an ability to integrate quickly multimedia functions into its products. Nokia and Motorola are better in fundamental technology. But Samsung makes cellular phones smaller with many more functions.[31]

Samsung relies on its product design and multimedia functionality as the core branding in mobile handsets. To speed up its product life cycles, Samsung's mobile handset division sources key components, such as processing chips, from its semiconductors division and batteries and display from its affiliate, Samsung SDI. Up to the mid-2000s, Samsung had to rely on Qualcomm Inc., the platform leader in chip design for mobile devices, to supply the digital multimedia broadcasting chips for its mobile handsets. But as noted in chapter 5, Samsung's Device Solutions division has since the late 2000s become Apple's top supplier of IC chips for mobile and media solutions and memory devices in its iPhones. Samsung's mobile handsets are able to tap into this intrachaebol supply of crucial chipsets and semiconductor devices. In addition, as the world's largest supplier of lithium ion batteries to mobile handsets and one of the largest in plasma display panels, Samsung SDI provides technological and marketing synergy to Samsung's mobile handsets. An interviewee from Samsung SDI thus notes that "all of these technologies are utilized for mobile technology. These are important in the aspect of sales and marketing as well. Samsung SDI is the world's top supplier of components for products of mobile display."[32]

It is clear that few national firms in the electronics industry can grow from being low-cost captive suppliers to OEM customers to becoming global brand name firms coordinating their own global production networks. While the sectoral industrial policy of their home developmental states mattered in the earlier period of their growth, Taiwan's Acer and South Korea's Samsung Electronics have resisted dependency on these state subsidies and protective policies, and reorganized their corporate resources to invest massively in new capabilities in design and product development, branding and marketing, and global distribution since the mid-1990s. Both global lead firms have also pursued drastically different forms of corporate reorganization to achieve their ascendance to global market leadership. In the early 2000s, Acer Inc. adopted vertical disintegration in order to focus on its brand business in the global personal computer industry and to leverage significant interfirm networks and resources within Taiwan's flourishing ICT industry. In contrast, Samsung has engaged with a peculiar coupling process of vertical integration and home-based production organization in order to attain greater intrachaebol synergy, and has succeeded as a leading global brand name producer in the mobile handsets and televisions segments of the consumer electronics industry. In both cases, firm-specific initiatives in favor of strategic repositioning in global production networks and dynamic organizational processes are much more significant than state-led initiatives in accounting for their evolutionary transformation into global lead firms.

Manufacturing Global Lead Firms in Automobiles

The above comparison of Acer and Samsung points to the changing importance of firm-specific dynamics and evolutionary organizational processes vis-à-vis state-led initiatives in the global electronics industry. However, industry- and network-level dynamics are crucial too because of the differential barriers to entry and prospects for upgrading and repositioning in production networks in different global industries. Because of its highly globalized and fragmented nature and its rapid shifts in product and process technologies, the electronics industry offers significantly more windows of opportunities for latecomer firms to catch up and to transform into first movers when a new disruptive shift in products or technologies occurs (e.g., the importance of mobile devices to Samsung's prominence in the 2010s). In the automobile industry, however, such rapid shifts in product cycles, technologies, and diversity in markets are less common. Instead, scale economies, supplier networks, and home markets are critical preconditions for competitive success. Reflecting on the South Korean context, K. H. Lee (2013, 63–64) thus argues that "[a]s far as the car sector is concerned, an oligopolistic structure, assembler-supplier relations, and local assembler-multinationals relations are the most significant factors determining the context in which cars are built and automobile capital accumulates. However, as emphasized, the effects of industrial policy are diverse as a result of the different conditions obtaining in different countries." The organizational dynamics of the automobile industry is also very different from electronics. As OEM firms, all automobile assemblers are de facto lead firms in their respective production networks, whether these networks are global in operations or merely domestic in market orientation. In this capital and technologically intensive industry dominated by first movers in advanced industrialized economies since the first half of the twentieth century, it is particularly hard for East Asian firms to catch up. If the state-led promotion of national champions as global lead firms in the electronics industry has proven to be quite so challenging for policymakers in these East Asian economies, it would be even more difficult in automobiles. Among the three East Asian economies, South Korea's Hyundai serves as the *only* example of the successful emergence of a truly global lead firm. As will be analyzed below, this competitive success is highly contingent on the globalization of its branding and manufacturing.

In his 1946 book *The Conception of the Corporation*, Peter Drucker reckoned the automobile industry as "the industry of industries" because of its strong linkages across multiple industrial sectors.[33] All large industrial nation-states and their latecomer industrializers want a share of this pillar manufacturing industry. By its very nature, the automobile industry today encompasses nationally based assemblers and their different tiers of global, regional, and local suppliers. These assemblers or automakers are often viewed as lead firms with their own brand names and geographically extensive production networks. One of the most significant factors for success in the automobile industry is the existence of a sufficiently large domestic market so that a national firm can catch up through import substitution administered by a protective home state and its sectoral industrial policy. Historically, the catching up of Japanese automakers with their American and European first movers by the late 1970s and the early 1980s is one of the most spectacular examples of such state-led success in latecomer industrialization. In *The Machines That Changed the World*, Womack et al. (1990) have shown the meteoric rise of these Japanese automakers as the most powerful challengers to national champions in the United States, Germany, the United Kingdom, France, and Italy.

Among the three East Asian economies, only South Korea has the domestic market potential and strong business groups to support such own brand automakers.[34] In fact, South Korea is the only successful example of catching up in the automobile industry among *all* new industrialized economies in the world (Malerba and Nelson 2011). In this section, I analyze the emergence of Hyundai Motor Company (HMC) as a global lead firm in automobiles. Complementing my earlier analysis of Acer and Samsung, I show how the initial state-led industrialization in South Korea's automobiles has over time given way to firm-specific organizational innovations and meso-level strategic repositioning in global production networks. In the case of Hyundai, it did not become a truly global lead firm with distinctive global brand recognition and market penetration until the 2000s. Its resurgence in the post-1997 crisis period owes more to its group-based capacity in developing new product innovations and in restructuring its newly acquired affiliates, such as Kia Motors, than to the postdevelopmental state that failed to complete its Big Deal restructuring of the automobile industry in South Korea (S. J. Chang 2003, 207; 2006b, 62; K. H. Lee 2013, 80–81). Before I analyze Hyundai's group-based capacity in recent decades, it is necessary to revisit briefly the role of the developmental state in laying the early foundation of South Korea's automobile industry.

South Korea's initial foray into the automobile industry was situated in the context of renewed South Korea–Japan economic ties between 1965 and 1982. During this period, Japan provided much of the capital (loans and grants), technology (licenses), and management know-how (technical assistance) in support of Park Chung Hee's drive toward promoting heavy and chemical industries. In fact, Park enacted the automobile industry protection law as early as in 1962, as part of its first Five Year Economic Development Plan (1962–1966) (Amsden 1989, 81; Wade, 1990, 309–12). As an integral part of its import substitution strategy, the first automobile assembly plant was established as a state-owned enterprise in 1962 in cooperation with Nissan, and it was subsequently transferred to a private firm with a new technology agreement with Toyota. Between 1965 and 1969, three more private firms were permitted to enter into the industry.[35] Based on technological licenses and agreements with Ford, Hyundai began its automobile venture as a completely knocked-down (CKD) assembler for Ford's Cortina passenger car in 1967. In 1974, Park promulgated the Long Range Automobile Industry Promotion Plan to encourage domestic automakers to develop integrated automobile manufacturing facilities and thereby to nurture a national car industry for global exports. Three producers were picked as "winners"—Hyundai, Kia, and GM Korea (later Saehan and then Daewoo). By 1980, this strategy had delivered some results in production and exports. South Korea's automobile production rose from less than 20,000 in 1970 to 120,000 in 1980 (Ravenhill 2003, 109).

This early success of Park's state-led promotion of the automobile industry, however, masks some important state-firm dynamics that began to evolve in favor of the chaebol, such as Hyundai. The developmental state's capacity in steering the automobile industry between the 1960s and the early 1990s has been generally overestimated. As discussed in detail in Ravenhill (2003) and K. H. Lee (2013), the Ministry of Trade and Industry and Economic Planning Board faced immense difficulties in rationalizing different chaebol's involvement in the nascent automobile industry. The state bureaucracy's weak coherence in reining in competing private sector interests led by the chaebol was particularly evident in its industrial planning and policy for the automobile industry. In addition, the state's role in technological development in the automobile industry was certainly not as prominent as in the semiconductor industry. The state served in a supportive role through policy loans and export monitoring, but did not engage directly in acquiring and developing relevant technologies to be transferred to the chaebol. As argued by Ravenhill (2003, 127), "The state left the task of technology acquisition and development in the hands of the car companies." As a consequence, the three chaebol automakers had substantially different strategy for technology acquisition. Kia and Daewoo were heavily dependent respectively on Mazda and General Motors for their technologies and manufacturing capabilities. By the late 1980s, K. H. Lee (2013, 79) observes that South Korea's industrial policy in the automobile industry "became more politicised, fragmented and uncoordinated than those of previous periods. As shown earlier, lack of strategic policy perspective on industrial promotion coupled with implementation of deregulation policies in the sector contributed to exposing the peculiar pattern of competition between local assemblers and uncoordinated changes of relational structure between local assemblers, suppliers and multinationals in the sector."

Taking a lead firm approach to strategic coupling with global production networks, Hyundai deliberately pursued a self-reliance strategy and avoided dependence on any single foreign partner in order to maintain its managerial autonomy and, eventually, to achieve technical autonomy through its in-house R&D. It also established its own sales network in the United States in order to exercise greater control over its marketing and distribution in then the world's largest market. As well documented in L. Kim (1998), this torturous process of deliberate capability building at a high performance level through internal crisis construction has taken Hyundai almost two decades between the mid-1970s and the mid-1990s, but it is the key pillar underscoring Hyundai's subsequent successful transformation into a global lead firm in the automobile industry.[36] Between 1974 and 1976, Hyundai entered into some eighteen technology transfers from Japan (engine block design, transmissions, and rear axles), England (factory construction, layout, and internal combustion engines), and Italy (car designs). In 1975, Hyundai finally introduced its first own brand model, the Pony (Amsden 1989, 175).[37] But this first mass produced own brand model did not succeed in foreign markets, particularly the United States, due to its failure to meet all safety requirements. It was not until the second model, Excel, launched in 1985 that Hyundai had finally succeeded in the exports market. Its Excel became the best-selling import model in the United States in 1987. Before 1985, Hyundai rejected alliances with Volkswagen, Renault, and Alfa Romeo after its unhappy alliance with Ford, because each of them wanted participation in management. Instead, Hyundai chose to partner with Mitsubishi after the latter had acquired a 10 percent stake in Hyundai in 1981. Mitsubishi's role was limited to technical assistance in engines and transmissions. Hyundai did not give up management control or its strategy for acquiring technology in unpackaged form from multiple sources and integrating them into its own production. In the period up to 1985, Hyundai licensed fifty-four foreign technologies from eight different countries. When no foreign supplier was willing to provide state-of-the-art engines, it developed its own (Ravenhill 2003, 127–28). By 1988, Hyundai had become the undisputed domestic leader, producing some 650,000 units of

South Korea's total national production of 1.1 million units. At that time, its production volume was just about half as many as Fiat and Renault (Wade 1990, 311).

While Hyundai's Excel gave it the early taste of success as a leading domestic automaker, its internal design, technological, and manufacturing capabilities were still fairly weak by the early 1990s. Excel's engines and transmissions were still completely made by Mitsubishi in Japan and imported to Hyundai's assembly plant in Ulsan. By the early 1990s, Hart-Landsberg (1993, 155) noted the decline of Hyundai's automobile sales in the United States from its peak of 264,282 in 1988 to 137,448 in 1990, and concluded that "Hyundai Motors is still using the same basic engine that Mitsubishi Motors defined for it some years ago. Hyundai is now trying to design its own engine but officials admit that even if successfully produced, it will be only as good as one that Mitsubishi introduced in Japan several years ago." Similarly in their *Dragons in Distress*, Bello and Rosenfeld (1990) offer the same bleak assessment of South Korea's automobiles and identify several major constraints on their ambition in the 1990s, such as rising protectionism in Western Europe and the United States; declining profit margin at lower-end models and thus the necessity for upgrading; the urgent need for greater technological innovation and more cost-effective production; weak domestic suppliers measured in cost, quality, and efficiency; and the need for greater domestic demand. They conclude that "despite its initial success, Hyundai and the other Korean vehicle manufacturers face immense challenges in the fierce battle for the international automobile market that is expected to unfold in the 1990s" (136). The early 1990s also saw Samsung's entry into the domestic industry characterized by overcapacity, excess competition, lack of economies of scales, and high exit costs among existing producers. By 1996, South Korea's automobile industry had produced some 2.9 millions units and was responsible for 5 percent of its GDP and 6 percent of exports (Ravenhill 2003, 109; 112). Overtaking France and the United Kingdom, South Korea became the fourth largest producer in the world on the eve of the 1997 Asian financial crisis. By the mid-1990s, Hyundai and Daewoo, each producing about 1 million units, were still outside the list of the world's top ten automobile manufacturers.

Completely unanticipated by the evolving developmental state, the 1997 Asian financial crisis provided the necessary disciplining force to shake up the unwieldy domestic automobile industry to the extent that only Hyundai could emerge as a sole survivor in this new international selection environment. Due to low profitability and overleveraged capacity investment through foreign debts, both Daewoo and Kia went bankrupt. During the postcrisis restructuring General Motors acquired Daewoo and Renault bought Samsung Motors.[38] Acquiring Kia in 1998, Hyundai has since remained as the only nationally owned automaker and grown substantially to become the world's eighth largest automobile producer in 2008, and fourth largest in 2010 and thereafter (just after Toyota, General Motors, and Volkswagen). From a modest production volume of respectively 899,000 units and 365,000 units in 1998, Hyundai and Kia's combined output reached 5.8 million units in 2010 and 7.2 million units in 2013.[39] Hyundai also rebounded quickly from the 1997 crisis. Hyundai (with Kia) sold 853,000 cars in the United States in 2000, compared to 333,000 cars in 1999 (L. Kim 2003, 95–96). In 2012, Hyundai and Kia respectively sold 703,007 and 557,599 vehicles in the United States and 850,000 and 577,386 vehicles in China, the world's two largest markets.

Hyundai's success as a global lead firm since the early 2000s can be largely attributed to several firm-specific initiatives in technological innovation, quality improvement, and localization of production.[40] Building on its past experience in assimilating foreign technologies, Hyundai has taken a major risk of licensing technologies from multiple sources and integrating them into a workable mass production system as rapidly as possible throughout the production process (L. Kim 2003, 95–96). In fact, even in 2000, Hyundai's R&D expenditure remained low, at less than one-third of Toyota (Ravenhill 2003, 130). After more than three decades of automobile manufacturing, Hyundai was able to develop for the first time its own V6 Delta engine only in 1998 and its passenger diesel engine in 2000. To develop new generation models, Hyundai has aggressively invested in R&D to accumulate design and innovation capabilities. It has established major R&D centers in South Korea (1996), Japan (1997), the United States (2002), and Germany (2003). In 2006, Hyundai independently developed its world-class V6 diesel S engine. Its Tau engine was selected as Ward's Auto 10 Best Engines in the United States between 2009 and 2011, heralding the technological maturity of Hyundai in automobile engineering.[41]

Apart from technological innovation, Hyundai has strategically reorganized its global production networks to leverage its key subsidiaries and first-tiered suppliers through deepening interfirm relations and tacit forms of network governance.[42] In global marketing, Hyundai has leveraged its affiliate, Kia Motors, to pursue a two-brand strategy. Hyundai has moved away from being a regional producer of low price and average quality vehicles to become a major global lead firm producing high-quality automobiles. To shed its cheap-car image, Hyundai has passed the production and marketing of lower-cost vehicles to its affiliate, Kia Motors. In the US market, Hyundai aggressively pursues brand building through quality improvement and assurance and yet maintaining price competitiveness. As an interviewee from HMC explains,

> The most important factor was the remarkable improvement in quality and the price competitiveness. Quality wise, our products are equal to those of the Japanese, and in some ways more advanced, whereas the prices are 10 to 15 percent lower. I think our customers are choosing our products because the quality and performance compared to prices are high. Brand quality might not be as high as the Japanese cars, and so we have worked on improving the quality to overcome this. For example, we provided ten-year best warranty in the United States,

and I think this was the factor of the success in the American market. Our sales in Europe are also increasing.[43]

From its automobile design to its smallest components, Hyundai works closely with its key suppliers to ensure high quality control.[44] It also provides thorough quality management guidance to its partners and suppliers.

In order to serve better its global markets through organizational localization, Hyundai has become one of the few major chaebol to globalize its production networks. It has leveraged the Hyundai group's global network to develop its market outreach through six thousand dealers and thirty-two overseas sales and production subsidiaries. Starting with its earliest plants established in Turkey (1997) and India (1998), Hyundai has built production facilities in China (2004), the United States (2005), Brazil (2007), Czech Republic (2009), Russia (2010), and Brazil (2012). This globalization of production is necessary to overcome trade barriers and protective measures, particularly in BRIC countries (Brazil, Russia, India, and China), and to mitigate risks associated with exchange rate fluctuations. Localized production can also help reduce transportation costs and induce better consumer loyalties. My HMC interviewee argues that "the automobile industry is different from electronics, especially the mobile handset industry, because our products are very bulky. It is advantageous to produce locally due to the high transportation cost for the big volume. On top of this, because it is a durable good, customers have a tendency to prefer the ones produced domestically. Made in USA in the United States and Made in Europe in Europe are more preferred, and I think this is related to nationalism." From about 17 percent of overseas production in 2005, Hyundai managed to increase its foreign production to 67 percent by 2011.

Hyundai's coupling process of localizing its global production networks is generally well supported by its key suppliers in South Korea. This strong and trusting relationship with its suppliers represents Hyundai's most significant home-based advantage. While its intrachaebol relationship might have benefited from earlier state policy interventions (e.g., lax ownership regulation), Hyundai's continual organizational transformation through coupling its key domestic suppliers with its evolving global production networks goes far beyond any form of direct state planning and policy for the automobile industry. When asked about the role of the South Korean state in Hyundai's globalization, my interviewee from Hyundai Mobis, a top supplier to Hyundai and Kia since 2000, responds emphatically that "there wasn't any. As you know, Korea has been liberalized after the financial crisis [in 1997]. If you only focus on the automobile industry, there wasn't any intervention from the government. The automobile industry had to look out into the world from the start because it couldn't survive just on the domestic market."[45] To him, the postdevelopmental state's diplomatic work and functional trade policies (e.g., trade facilitation and free trade agreements), under the auspices of the Ministry of Foreign Affairs since 1998 (until 2013), could smooth Hyundai's entry into foreign markets. But there is little scope for direct state intervention through sectoral industrial policy, as the automobile industry has become highly globalized in production capacity and market organization. Firm- and industry-specific dynamics are the most critical conditions shaping the success of individual automakers.

The rise of Hyundai as a global lead firm and the only indigenous automaker from the three East Asian economies is instructive. While it benefited from the initial state preferences and target-specific industrial policy in the 1970s and the 1980s, its successful weathering of the 1997–1998 Asian financial crisis and its resurgence in the 2000s should be viewed in the context of its strategic reorientation toward becoming the lead firm controlling its expanding global production network. By reducing its dependence on domestic production for exports, Hyundai (and Kia) has undergone a truly game-changing transformation in its corporate development and strategic coupling. From producing pickup trucks for American troops in the Vietnam War, Hyundai has emerged to become a global brand in automobiles. The above analysis shows that the most significant phase of Hyundai's evolutionary transformation occurred at the time when the South Korean state could no longer dictate the direction and growth of the automobile industry. Instead, Hyundai's coupling process of developing its own global production networks provided the favorable organizational platform for its competitive success and transformation. At last, Hyundai has become a global lead firm in its own league in the "wheels of change."[46]

Organizing Service Excellence in Civil Aviation

The foregoing analysis of the strenuous emergence of several global lead firms in electronics and automobiles from Taiwan and South Korea offers a particularly revealing contrast to the relative lack of service providers that have been able to lead the regional or global market. Despite their industrial prowess and active industrial policy, Taiwan and South Korea are much better known for producing internationally competitive manufactured goods than for offering superior consumer or producer services for the regional and the global economy.[47] The city-state of Singapore, on the contrary, has managed to develop a highly competitive service sector. In 2013, service-producing industries contributed to 66.2 percent of its GDP of US$283 billion.[48] Some of its leading domestic service providers have also emerged to become world-class service lead firms. This divergent industrial outcome among the three East Asian economies is partly attributed to their initial difference in state-led industrialization. Since the mid-1960s, Singapore's openness to global lead firms and their direct investments in electronics, machineries, petrochemicals, and biomedical industries has led to fewer entrepreneurial opportunities for the likes of Acer, Samsung, and Hyundai to grow out of its small domestic market.

Rather, Singapore's tiny domestic market and an active interventionist state have proven to be productive for the emergence of regional and global service providers. Mostly "born global" at their inception, these Singapore-origin service providers have developed strong regional or global market positions in different service industries, such as transport and logistics (Singapore Airlines, NOL, and PSA), telecommunications (Singapore Telecom), real estate (CapitaLand, Far East, and City Development), banking (DBS, UOB, and OCBC), utilities (SembCorp Industries), and agribusiness (Olam and Wilmar).

Elucidating further the coupling process of network positioning as a global lead firm, this final section analyzes how a domestic service firm from Singapore—Singapore Airlines—has grown into a leading global service provider for final consumers in the civil aviation industry. Best known perhaps for its corporate branding, "A Great Way to Fly," Singapore Airlines epitomizes the global success of a national firm from Singapore through its impeccable service standards and organizational excellence. In the civil aviation and telecom sectors worldwide, the state continues to play a significant role as a regulator of service provision and competitive rights. In the global market for these services, competition is limited to countries that are open to market liberalization and deregulation of formerly state-controlled providers of these services. Examining the experience of the United States and the European Union, Cowhey and Richards (2006, 301) argue that while both aviation and telecom sectors have become more open to international competition, their globalization is embedded in different institutional and regulatory regimes. Whereas the telecom industry is more squarely embedded in a multilateral trade regime associated with the World Trade Organization, the aviation market persists as a separate domain governed by rigid bilateral reciprocity pacts negotiated between different nation-states on behalf of their "national" airlines.

In all three East Asian economies, state policy and domestic politics can make a significant difference to the competitiveness of their *national airlines* (see firm-level details in table 6.1). In Taiwan, its national carrier, China Airlines, was founded in 1959, privatized in 1992, and listed on the Taiwan Stock Exchange in 1993.[49] But the influence of the state through its China Aviation Development Foundation, the airline's majority shareholder, remained strong even by the 2000s. Hampered by its military-style top management, the airline was often accused of nurturing an atmosphere of cronyism, nepotism, and lack of accountability, and serving as a Petri dish for inbred officialdom.[50] While it was a major player in the air cargo sector supporting Taiwan's burgeoning regional production networks, China Airlines was unable to compete effectively in passenger transport against the privately held passenger airline EVA Airways, which was much more nimble in operational efficiency and entrepreneurial in pushing for new destinations. Founded in 1989 as part of the Evergreen group, the leading transport business group in Taiwan, EVA rapidly emerged as a leading domestic passenger airline in the 2000s, with fifty-eight aircrafts in service, operating revenue of US$3.6 billion, and net income

Table 6.1 Leading airlines from Taiwan, South Korea, and Singapore

Airline name (year of founding)	2014 revenue (US$b)	2014 net income (US$m)	Market capitalization in May 2015 (US$b)	Number of profitable years	Number of aircrafts in 2014/15	Majority ownership in 2014
Taiwan						
China Airlines (1959)	4.9	−24.4	2.5	3 (2005–14)	81	State
EVA Airways (1989)	4.3	−42.5	2.7	6 (2004–14)	68	Evergreen group
South Korea						
Korean Air (1962)	10.9	−439	3.0	11 (1993–2014)	148	Hanjin group
Asiana Airlines (1988)	5.3	56.8	1.3	8 (2000–14)	84	Kumho group
Singapore						
Singapore Airlines (1972)	11.8	278.3	10.3	All (1984–2014)	106	State

Sources: Company reports in OSIRIS database (osiris.bvdinfo.com, accessed on May 11, 2015), *Bloomberg Businessweek* (http://investing.businessweek.com, accessed on May 11, 2015), and airlines websites.

of US$412 million in 2010.[51] With sixty-eight aircrafts, China Airlines had operating revenue of US$5.1 billion and net income of US$364 million in 2010. But in 2014, both airlines suffered losses. As lamented by my interviewee from China Airlines, "Government officials in China Airlines are afraid of the legislators and politicians. In private companies, they might have more private resources to ask the legislators to challenge our concessions. So we cannot take advantage as a national carrier. Also because of several accidents, we're held back by the government as a kind of punishment. We are not supposed to try any new destination within one or two years of these accidents. EVA got to do things and push: 'I want this and that.' We just stand still there." The political fragmentation of the state in Taiwan, as described in chapter 2, has certainly not helped China Airlines expand its presence in the international market. It remains primarily as a national airline oriented toward the domestic market.

Similar to Taiwan, the developmental state in South Korea did not provide favorable conditions for its national carriers until the 2010s. Korean Air, the de facto national airline, was founded in 1962 and sold to the Hanjin chaebol in 1969. In 2010, it had operating revenue of US$10.5 billion, and net income of US$510 million, but it suffered significant loss in 2014 (see table 6.1).[52] With a fleet of 148 aircraft in August 2014, it is ranked among the world's top twenty airlines in terms of passenger loads. While its air cargo business is highly competitive because of strong demand from major chaebol, such as Samsung and LG Electronics, Korean Air's international passenger service is limited by the lack of open sky agreements concluded between South Korea and other countries, an indication of the state's unwillingness and/or inability in steering and facilitating the growth of service industries. As of the mid-2000s, only the United States had an open sky agreement with South Korea. As pointed out by an interviewee from Korean Air, "If an open sky policy is not agreed on, it is very difficult for us to increase the number of flights. We can only send as many airplanes to the other country as it sends to Korea. Therefore, cargo service was the only part we could enlarge. Even compared to Cathay Pacific [Hong Kong-based], which is mainly dealing with cargos, the proportion of cargo services in Korean Air is quite high. We had no choice but to diversify our products due to the poor business environment of the industry."

This lack of direct state support in negotiating for new sky rights and market opening exacerbates the existing constraint imposed by the continual state regulation of domestic airlines such as Korean Air. In the 1970s and the 1980s, the developmental state was highly protective of the domestic airline industry. But this strict state regulation continued through to the 2000s and made it difficult for Korean Air to expand its international routes and destinations. According to another interviewee from Korean Air, "The Korean government then played an important role to protect us from overseas airline companies, as we were not strong enough and had little experience. However, now we are much more experienced and possess the know-how to handle other competitors. What we want from the government is liberalization of the air service industry." Even though the state funded the new Incheon International Airport, opened in March 2001, as a form of functional policy support for Seoul's ambition to become an air hub of East Asia,[53] this infrastructural investment did not target the two domestic carriers for policy support. The limited scope for expanding international rights has been the most challenging disadvantage to Korean Air and Asiana Airlines. Like Taiwan's China Airlines, Korean Air also faces competitive pressure from Asiana Airlines, its significantly smaller domestic competitor established by the Kumho chaebol in 1988 and with eighty-four aircrafts in March 2014.

Compared to these domestic carriers from Taiwan and South Korea, the emergence of Singapore Airlines as a leading global service provider in the civil aviation industry is indeed quite unique in its combination of state ownership and professional management. It is a case of state interventions that have worked in a globally competitive industry. While its history can be traced back to its founding as Malayan Airways in 1947, Singapore Airlines' contemporary operation commenced only in 1972 as a fully state-owned enterprise of the Singapore government. As of March 2015, Singapore Airlines remained as a government-linked company, with 56 percent majority shareholding controlled by Temasek Holdings. Contrary to the inward-looking policies of Taiwan and South Korea in the aviation industry, Singapore's developmental state has consistently supported Singapore Airlines, the only national flag carrier, for over four decades through pro–open sky polices that have positioned Singapore as an important hub for aviation in the Asia Pacific region. As the controlling shareholder of Singapore Airlines, the state not only negotiates bilateral rights on its behalf, but also provides substantial complementary infrastructure and services to augment the home advantage of the airline. Singapore's Changi Airport, managed by the Civil Aviation Authority of Singapore, is the world's most awarded "Best Airport."

More important, the state's involvement in Singapore Airlines extends further to cover its occasionally turbulent labor relations. When the pilots of Singapore Airlines took industrial action through a work slowdown over salary and benefit matters in 1980, Prime Minister Lee Kuan Yew intervened personally to resolve the dispute and got the airline back into full operational efficiency. To Lee, Singapore Airlines operated an essential service, and any industrial action would cause irreparable damage to the country's international reputation and its major economic sectors, such as air transport, tourism, and financial services. The Singapore Airlines Pilots' Association, the only union not incorporated under the state-sanctioned National Trade Union Congress, was then deregistered in February 1981, and its officials were charged for initiating illegal industrial action. A new pilots' association was registered under the Trade Union Act as the Airline Pilots Association—Singapore (Alpa-S) in May 1981.[54] Since then, Singapore Airlines has been free of any disruptive industrial action, even though Alpa-S has been continuously involved in disputes with management.

In November 2003, a potential industrial action against the airline could have occurred after a secret vote among members of Alpa-S had led to the sacking of their leaders. Some 55 percent of member pilots were unhappy about their leaders' acceptance of a 16.5 percent pay cut in July 2003, when Singapore Airlines subsequently earned a net profit of US$178 million in the July-September quarter. The deal was a part of the airline's aggressive cost cutting measures in response to a challenging year of severe downturn due to a global slump in passenger travel and the deadly SARS epidemic in Asia. In response Lee Kuan Yew threatened to "break heads" if necessary and called on the airline's management to arrive at an amicable solution with the pilots. But he made clear publicly that no strike or industrial action would be tolerated. Responding to a letter from Alpa-S's new president Mok Hin Choon in February 2004, Lee was reconciliatory and stated that "I do not consider SIA management or Alpa-S to be blameless. I have passed the list (of Alpa-S's grievances) to the management who will address these issues with you. It is for management and unions to work through such issues and thereafter put them behind and move forward."[55] He also explained that the airline's S$900 million net income in 2003 was needed to justify its S$11 billion of working capital, with a weighted average cost of capital at about 8 percent. As the airline remained profitable throughout the entire post-2003 period (see table 6.1), this potential industrial action was averted through further negotiated agreements between management and Alpa-S. The personal involvement of Lee in resolving Singapore Airlines' labor disputes in 1980 and 2004 is clearly unique to Singapore's developmental state and its working relationship with state-linked national champions. But it ensured the uninterrupted service of the national carrier and its continuous profitability since 1984.[56]

Attributing the emergence of Singapore Airlines (SIA) as a global service provider exclusively to the state's demiurge role and favorable open sky policies, and the direct intervention of the country's top statesmen, however, will do serious injustice to the airline's professional management and its firm-specific strategic and organizational capability-building over a period of forty years. As reflected by the CEO of its majority owner, the state's Temasek Holdings, "From day one, SIA knew it had to innovate and compete internationally, or fold—after all, there was not much domestic air traffic opportunity for an island which is all of 30 miles at its widest span; just a little further than a marathon run! SIA never had to ask Temasek, much less the Government, whether it should buy Boeing or Airbus planes, or whether it should add or withdraw capacity from particular routes—SIA made its own commercial decisions as an airline company."[57] Through the strong vision and competence of its managerial team, Singapore Airlines has emerged as a globally recognized lead firm in the civil aviation industry and enjoyed a strong brand premium and substantial market share in the 2010s.

Coming from a small city-state economy, its size of 106 passenger aircrafts and market capitalization of US$10.3 billion in May 2015 were far larger than many national airlines from advanced industrialized economies.[58] Even the largest among the four airlines from Taiwan and South Korea, Korean Air, had a market capitalization of only US$3 billion in May 2015 (see table 6.1). In December 2010, the International Air Transport Association ranked Singapore Airlines second largest in the world, measured by market capitalization, after Air China (US$20 billion). With US$14 billion in market capitalization then, Singapore Airlines was ahead of Cathay Pacific (Hong Kong), Delta (USA), and Lufthansa (Germany).[59] The size of its home market therefore does not seem to limit Singapore Airlines' continual growth and transformation to become a global service provider in the aviation industry. It has turned the home-based disadvantage of a small market into its competitive driver by going global and coupling with global production networks right at the start. In 2014, Singapore Airlines had revenue of US$11.8 billion and net income of US$278 million. Its revenue and profitability throughout the 2000s put it significantly ahead of all four airlines from Taiwan and South Korea. As indicated in table 6.1, it is the only airline among these five airlines to be profitable every year since 1984.

Apart from leveraging the strong support of the home state, Singapore Airlines has successfully pursued a unique strategy of strong branding and superior service excellence as its core competitive advantages. Since 1972, its

"Singapore Girl" branding has offered a highly visible international icon of Asian hospitality, grace, and service for its customers worldwide. Its fleet of the most up-to-date and advanced aircraft has set high industrial standards in international passenger travel, winning Singapore Airlines many "Best Airline" awards since the 1990s. Its continual commitment to operational efficiency and cost containment has also allowed it to weather several major slumps in the international travel industry during the 1990s and the 2000s. Its two subsidiaries, SIA Cargo and SIA Engineering, are leading suppliers of cargo services and aircraft maintenance services in the global production networks of the air transport industry. By spinning off SIA Engineering as a separate company listed on the Singapore Exchange, Singapore Airlines can gain access to its wide range of technical expertise and extensive capabilities in aircraft maintenance services, and yet allow SIA Engineering to leverage its expertise to serve new customers and to achieve greater economies of scale. In 2014, SIA Engineering had revenue of US$882 million and net income of US$199 million.[60]

Overall, the above comparative analysis of national airlines from the three East Asian economies points to the critical role of product definition and service excellence as the underlying condition for an airline to become a leading global service provider. The husbandry or demiurge role of the home state can be a double-edged sword. In the case of Taiwan and South Korea, national airlines have not been well supported by favorable industrial policy to the same extent as their high-tech ICT siblings. Since the 1990s, the transformation of state roles and domestic politics in these economies has also left these national carriers to find their own niche in this highly regulated global industry. As the only domestic full service airline, Singapore Airlines benefits enormously from stable state ownership and intergovernmental negotiation of open sky rights. Unlike China Airlines from Taiwan, the case of Singapore Airlines shows that home state involvement can positively impact its evolution from a regional airline to one of the most respected global service providers in the civil aviation industry. But like its counterparts from South Korea, Singapore Airlines has taken enormous firm-specific initiatives to produce and sustain such a transformation into a global lead firm from a small city-state.

Conclusion

The emergence of global lead firms from East Asian economies marks the completion of its state-led industrialization that began earnestly in the 1960s. In the midst of the state's transformation from a husbandry or a demiurge role, as defined in Evans (1995), to a more catalyst and regulatory function since the 1990s, some leading national firms have grown and developed rapidly to become global brand manufacturers and global service providers in their respective industries. For all national firms from developing economies, this strategic (re)positioning as global lead firms is the most difficult of my three component processes of strategic coupling with global production networks. It is also the most demanding industrial growth dynamic for successful policy interventions by the state. This chapter has given detailed accounts of *how* this coupling process has been successfully engaged by several such global lead firms from Taiwan (Acer), South Korea (Samsung, LG, and Hyundai), and Singapore (Singapore Airlines). Three concluding remarks are necessary here to highlight this coupling process entailed in my empirical analysis. First, while these case study firms are clearly prominent global lead firms in their respective industries, their emergence is not commonly replicated among other domestic national champions pursuing the coupling process of either strategic partnership or industrial market specialization. This high road of becoming a global lead firm clearly requires more than state-led initiatives and, later, functional policies and supportive institutions. In the cases of Acer and Samsung/LG, firm-specific efforts in reorganizing production networks and developing product and market definition through branding have translated the entrepreneurial visions of their founders into a reality of competitive successes. While state initiatives in the earlier historical period have ushered in strong home base advantages, these firm-specific efforts are the necessary condition to create such world-class lead firms (Mathews 2002; S. J. Chang 2008).

Second, even if we give analytical significance to the earlier husbandry or demiurge role of the state, my comparative case studies show that the efficacy and outcome of this role in nurturing or creating global lead firms can vary considerably among the three East Asian economies. In Taiwan and South Korea, the state's influence in the globalization of their lead firms in the 2000s was no longer as critical and strong as it had been in the 1980s. As these national champions have gained greater access to global finance and in-house R&D capabilities, global lead firms such as Acer, Samsung, LG, and Hyundai can pursue with a higher degree of freedom their competitive strategy in the global economy. In both functional and organizational terms, they are strategically coupled much more with other firms embedded in their own global production networks than with the home state's policy regimes and political bureaucracy. Moreover, the case of Singapore Airlines illustrates that state ownership continues to be a political preference in such a regulated industry. Taiwan's China Airlines also lingers on as a state-owned enterprise even after its privatization and public offering in the early 1990s. The peculiarity in Singapore Airlines' case does not rest on its enduring state ownership but rather on its coupling process in the global civil aviation industry. In short, Singapore Airlines has thrived *despite* its majority state ownership.

Third, industry-level dynamics matter much in limiting the extent and efficacy of state involvement and point to the need for more sophisticated forms of state-firm relations and functional industrial policy. In global manufacturing industries, such as electronics and automobiles, domestic firms in all three economies are fairly mature and well developed. Extensive industrial linkages have also been formed within domestic business groups in Taiwan and South Korea. Their technological, organizational, and financial competencies are far greater than the state bureaucracy that has to navigate in a much more politicized domestic environment. In service industries, such as civil aviation, telecommunications, and banking, national regulations are the major barriers to the market entry of foreign firms and the development of competitive markets. In these more regulated sectors, the husbandry or demiurge role of the home state might make a difference. The positive effect of such state involvement on the emergence of domestic firms as regional or global lead firms, however, is contingent on other coupling processes beyond the control of the state. Coming from a very small urban economy, Singapore firms are often "born global" in their strategic orientation and coupling with global production networks far earlier than their counterparts from Taiwan and South Korea. As these East Asian economies have become much more developed and industrialized, and their national champions have emerged as major players in the global economy, the politics of industrial policy and institutional spaces for state choice are necessarily constrained by the growing disembedding of domestic firms from the state bureaucracy in favor of strategic coupling with global production networks. The next and concluding chapter will examine such an evolutionary trajectory in the international political economy of development.

Chapter 7

Beyond the Developmental State

A New Global Political Economy of Industrial Transformation

For more than three decades since Chalmers Johnson's (1982) *MITI and the Japanese Economic Miracle,* a group of pioneering scholars of East Asian development has advanced a comparative political economy perspective that places its analytical power and institutional efficacy squarely on the developmental state as performing the "governor" (Wade 1990) or "husbandry" and "midwifery" (Evans 1995) role in driving export-oriented industrialization.[1] Economic development in a particular East Asian economy is deemed to have occurred through the catching up of its latecomer firms with first movers or global lead firms in advanced industrialized economies. This catching up process took place not because of the right mix of market-based economic incentives, but rather through state-led efforts that provided organized help and intentionally got prices wrong. Situated in historically peculiar geopolitical and institutional conditions, the developmental state had to make politically tough decisions in order to experiment with this highly selective and interventionist form of industrial development through financial inducement and, sometimes, market-distorting coercions and picking national champions under a peculiar set of bureaucratic rationality and sectoral- or firm-specific industrial policy. Taken together, this powerful political economy perspective points to the indispensable role of the developmental state in governing the industrial transformation of such East Asian economies as South Korea, Taiwan, and Singapore since the late 1950s and the 1960s.

In this book, I have argued for a revised and *international* political economy perspective that focuses on national-global articulations in understanding the industrial transformation and, more broadly, the economic development of these East Asian economies. Through this integrative form of comparative national-global analysis, my perspective incorporates not just the domestic state in its changing political dynamics and developmental roles, but also its "object of desire"—the capitalist firm—and the latter's strategic coupling with global production networks (GPN), defined as a new economic structure for organizing the global economy.[2] This evolving state-firm-GPN assemblage is critical for understanding East Asian development in an era of global competition, because no matter how cohesive and powerful, the developmental state or its defining elite bureaucracy does not perform the actual catching up process. It is rather the national firm, chosen or otherwise, that acts on these state-led directives and incentives to industrialize the nation. Insofar as the capitalist system is in place, the developmental state alone cannot produce industrialization without the cooperation of capitalist firms. Economic development is always contingent on this state-firm nexus that has been well analyzed in the existing developmental state literature.

Once this process of late industrialization gets going, two interrelated evolutionary dynamics begin to work in tandem; over time, they tend to undermine the embedded autonomy of the developmental state and to provide national firms with new sources of knowledge and learning, capital accumulation, and capability building. As analyzed in-depth in this book, the first process refers to the disembedding of national firms from the home state through greater firm-specific initiatives and access to resources outside the domestic state's control. Changing domestic politics toward democratization and liberalization also contribute to the greater fragmentation of the developmental state and its elite bureaucracy. As these national firms become more successful in the global export market, they are increasingly embedded in a complex interfirm organization of global industries, known as global production networks and global value chains (GVC).[3] In this book, I have developed a midrange concept, *strategic coupling*, to specify this second, and relatively underestimated, process of reembedding East Asian firms in global production networks for understanding industrial transformation. This meso-level process of strategic coupling is premised on and accomplished through three component processes, defined as strategic partnership, industrial market specialization, and (re)positioning as global lead firms. These coupling processes have collectively enabled leading East Asian firms to articulate into different global industries and to grow and prosper in today's world economy. In doing so, East Asian firms have embodied the evolutionary shift in the central dynamics of economic development, away from state-directed initiatives and toward firm-specific technological and organizational innovations in the context of accelerated global competition. Industrial transformation is now predicated on the dynamic integration of evolving home-based advantages—a contingent outcome of state interventions—with new learning and opportunities arising from domestic firms' deeper articulation into the global economy.[4]

Organized in three sections, this concluding chapter aims to draw some important theoretical implications and policy lessons from my comparative study and to examine further the changing international political economy of development. The next section offers a reconceptualization of strategic coupling as a dynamic mechanism of industrial transformation in the global economy. Taking a mechanism approach developed in the broader social sciences, I propose a mechanism theory of strategic coupling in order to consolidate the key findings identified in my core empirical chapters. This consolidation allows for a clearer appreciation of the book's potential contribution as a theoretically grounded empirical analysis of the new development opportunities emerging from national-global articulations in different industries. The second section reconsiders the shifting contextual factors influencing state involvement in late industrialization and argues for a comparative institutional approach that incorporates a broader range of state and nonstate institutions. In the final section, I propose a new political economy of development to reflect on the current state-firm relationships in the three East Asian economies and to point to new state roles in terms of the more calibrated industrial policy and niche approach to promoting economic development in an interdependent world economy.

Strategic Coupling as a Dynamic Mechanism of Industrial Transformation

As noted briefly in chapter 1, I have argued that we can theorize strategic coupling (process) and firm-specific initiatives (action) as constitutive of a *mechanism* of industrial transformation. This conceptual integration of the action-process-mechanism terminology can also demonstrate our epistemological evolution in theorizing late industrialization in an interdependent global economy—from the developmental state thesis in the late 1980s to a more causal and dynamic perspective characterized by midrange concepts, such as strategic coupling and global production networks. This reconceptualization of strategic coupling as a dynamic mechanism, however, requires greater conceptual clarity on action, process, and mechanism that I have intentionally kept only to this concluding section. Here, I draw explicitly on the social mechanisms literature in analytical sociology, political science, and the philosophy of social science.[5] In this mechanism approach, action is one of the core principles because, as argued forcefully by Hedström and Swedberg (1998b, 24), "it is actors and not variables who do the acting. A mechanism-based explanation is not built upon mere associations between variables but always refers directly to causes and consequences of individual action oriented to the behavior of others." Grounded in James Coleman's (1986; 1990) well-known schema of sociological explanation, they suggest that specifying a mechanism requires articulating the purposive action of actors, through which a variable produces a change in another variable. This microlevel mechanism is known as an individual action-formation mechanism. But when social actors interact with each other and individual actions are transformed into a collective outcome—intended or unintended, a micro- to macrolevel transition is deemed to have taken place, and the resultant mechanism is known as a transformational mechanism.[6]

How then does my book's analysis of strategic coupling as a process fit into this causal conception of social action and mechanisms? I believe a strong case can now be made for defining mechanism as a *particular* kind of process that enables a specific cause to produce its eventual outcome in broadly similar contexts. While my reading of the social mechanisms literature seems to support this conception of a mechanism as a specific process connecting cause and outcome, it is important to note that the literature does not have a singular and generally agreed definition of mechanism.[7] But as Hedström and Swedberg (1996, 299; original italics) have wisely advised sometime ago, "it is not so much the definition *per se* that is important, as the type and style of theorizing it encourages." To Zürn and Checkel (2005, 1049), mechanisms are "intermediate processes" that "connect things; they link specified initial conditions and a specific outcome."[8] In their *Dynamics of Contention*, McAdam et al. (2001) treat causal mechanisms and processes as almost synonymous in their analysis of dynamic interactions in different historical episodes of social movements and political struggles. In fact, they seem to view processes as comprising mechanisms such that "social processes, in our view, consist of sequences and combinations of causal mechanisms" (12–13, 84; emphasis omitted). And yet, they explicitly acknowledge the arbitrary nature of this distinction: "Mechanisms and processes form a continuum. It is arbitrary, for example, whether we call brokerage a mechanism, a family of mechanisms, or a process" (27).

If a causal mechanism is a particular or concrete process constitutive of the working of a cause on its effect, I argue that this particularity is premised on the specificity of action and outcome. In general, a process such as strategic coupling is just a generic process connecting two or more sets of actors and their preexisting relations. It will only be a concrete mechanism if we can specify its particularity—what is this process *for* and how does it make a *difference* to the specific outcome(s)? This specification requires the articulation of action or initiatives taken by actors, such as firms and states, with their collective outcome (e.g., industrial transformation). After all, a mechanism will not be efficacious unless actors do what they intend to do. This intentionality is where strategy originates. But when these actors do take initiatives that can be specified through empirical analysis and abstraction, a process—as a general set of events leading to an outcome—will be turned into a (particular) mechanism for explaining such an outcome. Without this specification of particularity in action and outcome, we cannot determine a priori if a set of events is necessarily a mechanism. For example, globalization is often seen as a macroprocess involving different mechanisms, such as the formation of cross-border production networks and transnational migration. But put into a particular analytical context, it might be viewed—though rather contentiously—as a transformational mechanism for explaining the rescaling and reconfiguration of state power in an interdependent world economy.

Based on the abstraction method grounded in critical realism,[9] I have developed the concept "strategic coupling" as a dynamic mechanism of industrial transformation in the three East Asian economies. Indeed, strategic coupling can be viewed as a general process applicable to many different phenomena, for example, regional development, industrial change, social formation, political coalitions, and so on. When applied in a necessary relation to a *particular* case and/or outcome (i.e., East Asian economic development), this process becomes a transformational mechanism, which is constituted by its component mechanisms or, in Gambetta's (1998) terminology, its "concatenations." This process-to-mechanism transformation needs to be grounded in empirical specifications. Moreover, firm-specific actions and initiatives are the constitutive elements of this dynamic mechanism that is attentive to temporality and historical emergence. Developmental outcomes, such as industrial transformation, occur through particular actions of firms and states that enable these firms to connect with global production networks and to compete in the global economy. As a dynamic mechanism, strategic coupling embodies both firm-specific actions and meso-level dynamics (e.g., emergence of production networks and increasing degree of network ties). Firm initiatives are efficacious because they establish connections between the global economy and the domestic economy; these network connections in turn allow firms to access markets, information, resources, and technology, among other things. These initiatives are strategic because firms choose certain courses of action but not others, all with an eye on particular economic and other objectives. In other words, particularity arises from strategic firm initiatives that create specific types of ties with lead firms in different global production networks. Even firms from the same industry and/or home economy may therefore engage with *different* mechanisms to couple with lead firms in global production networks.

In what follows, I revisit this particularity of coupling mechanisms and their concomitant firm-specific initiatives entailed in my detailed empirical chapters in order to substantiate this mechanism theory of industrial transformation. As a midrange concept, strategic coupling connects opportunities in the global economy (as embodied in global production networks) to development outcomes in national economies (i.e., the rise of domestic firms in different industries). Through their initiatives, firms actively engage with specific coupling mechanisms in order to compete in the global economy. What they do (e.g., technological and organizational innovations) are firm-specific initiatives, but they are not the same as the meso-level mechanisms (e.g., industrial market specialization) through which these firms couple successfully with global production networks. At the broadest level, this book has analyzed comparatively how three East Asian economies had resolved their development dilemmas by the late 1980s and, subsequently, developed world leadership in electronics, semiconductors, shipbuilding, and some service industries by the 2000s and beyond. It is important to note that this continuous industrial transformation toward technological and service excellence does not refer to the initial launch of industrialization in the 1960s through state-led efforts to overcome the Gerschenkronian collective dilemmas, defined as the need for large-scale new investments to create intersectoral and interindustry linkages and to upgrade the productivity of any new or infant industrial sector.[10] Rather, this transformation was underpinned by *new* developments in the context of evolving state-firm relations and new opportunities to benefit from economic globalization.

In this book, these new developments refer to the dynamic mechanism of strategic coupling with global production networks and firm-specific technological and organizational innovations. In table 7.1, I have summarized the three component mechanisms of strategic coupling and their underlying competitive dynamics and favorable structural conditions. My empirical analysis has shown that each of these mechanisms is driven by different sets of competitive dynamics and facilitated by a range of favorable structural conditions applicable to different industries. Instead of state-imposed discipline on private capital, as argued by Amsden (1989), Waldner (1999), and others, my empirical analysis in the previous three chapters points to the diminishing effectiveness of direct state discipline or interventions in a world of complex global production networks where the true discipline for domestic firms and national champions comes from intense interfirm competition for spatial, organizational, and market fixes identified in table 7.1. These competitive dynamics have reduced the scale and scope of the state's developmental roles in transforming the national economy. They call into action firm-specific initiatives for completing the process of industrial transformation first induced by the developmental state.

This interpretation of coupling dynamics in the global economy is best illustrated by revisiting the Apple-Samsung-Hon Hai case first introduced in chapter 1. For Samsung to be a core supplier of semiconductor chips to Apple's iPhone, it had to develop extremely strong and dominant market leadership in such a specialized intermediate industry as semiconductors. But this is not an industry that can be easily developed in any latecomer economy. The Gerschenkronian "big spurt" is certainly necessary to overcome the initial obstacles of high costs and technological sophistication. Even in the United States, the development of its semiconductor and, more broadly, computer industry owes much to the federal state and its continuous military procurement.[11] While its initial foray into semiconductors was clearly induced by state-led initiatives and sectoral policy directives in South Korea, Samsung's emergence as one of the world's leading producers of semiconductors since the 2000s owes less to the state's disciplining action than to its firm-specific technological and organizational innovations. In the case of Taiwan's Hon Hai, its emergence as the world's largest electronics manufacturing services (EMS)

Table 7.1 Strategic coupling with global production networks and trajectories of economic development in East Asia

	Component mechanisms of strategic coupling		
	Strategic partnership	Industrial market specialization	(Re)positioning as global lead firms
GPN dynamics			
• spatial fix	Capability to cost efficiency	Initial public subsidies and state investment	Globalization and industrial clusters
• organizational fix	International outsourcing of manufacturing and design	Emergence of specialized suppliers and platform leaders	Business groups and intragroup synergy
• market fix	Faster time to market	New product and process technologies	Brand development, integrated production, and service excellence
Favorable structural conditions			
• transnational communities	Managerial competence and intermediaries through reverse "brain drain" and technological returnees	Technopreneurs limited to specific cases; no industrywide effects	Transnational links, business intelligence and market knowledge
• industrial organization	Rise of strategic partners and global localization of lead firms	Market leadership and strong links with industrial end users	Rise of national champions and new lead firms
• state policies and institutions	Upgrading of labor, technology, and infrastructure, and trade and investment facilitation	Sectoral industrial policies and picking winners, and state institutes for innovations	Functional policies through fiscal and financial incentives
East Asian examples			
• leading national firms	Quanta, Compal, and Hon Hai Precision (Taiwan) and Venture (Singapore)	Hyundai and Samsung (South Korea), Keppel, SembCorp, and CSM (Singapore), TSMC/UMC (Taiwan)	Acer (Taiwan), Samsung/LG and Hyundai (South Korea), Singapore Airlines (Singapore)
• relevant industrial sectors	Computers and consumer electronics	Shipbuilding and offshore equipment, and semiconductors	Electronics, automobiles, and transport services

provider and the dedicated assembler of Apple's iPhones has virtually nothing to do with state-inducement in its formative years, except that the state's sectoral industrial policy would have promoted the broader industrial ecosystem and cluster advantages in Taiwan's thriving electronics industry. The intensive growth and innovation led by both Samsung and Hon Hai have provided much impetus to a dynamic form of industrial transformation in South Korea and Taiwan. But this phenomenal success of both latecomer firms would not have happened without their strategic coupling with different global lead firms (e.g., Apple Inc. and others) prompted by their firm-specific initiatives. As I have examined in detail in chapters 4 to 6, this story and its necessary mechanisms have also occurred in a much wider range of sectors and industries in South Korea, Taiwan, and Singapore.

To consolidate my key findings in these empirical chapters, table 7.2 specifies the particularities of the relevant coupling mechanisms for each case study firm that have in turn underpinned industrial transformation in their domestic economies since the 2000s: strategic partnership, industrial market specialization, and (re)positioning as global lead firms. Collectively, these mechanisms constitute what Gambetta (1998, 104) calls "concatenations of mechanisms" or what McAdam et al. (2001, 8) term "component mechanisms" of strategic coupling. In personal computers and consumer electronics, *strategic partnership* with global lead firms represents a common coupling mechanism for East Asian firms to emerge as the world's leading providers of original design manufacturing (ODM) and EMS. Their particular pathway to successful strategic partnership with global lead firms is premised on a combination of vertical specialization and systems integration in different interfirm networks, and of diversification of customers, knowledge diffusion, and international production. Through these specific mechanisms engaged by respective firms, several strategic partners (e.g., Taiwan's Compal and Hon Hai) have graduated from their earlier relationships as captive suppliers governed by the superior technological know-how, industrial standards, and market access controlled by their global lead firm customers. From this unequal relationship of supplying to the original equipment manufacturing (OEM) lead firms, they learned the crucial importance of developing firm-specific design, technologies, and production capabilities. Other East Asian firms (e.g., Taiwan's Quanta and Singapore's Venture Corp) were born directly as ODM or EMS providers through entrepreneurial innovations and sustained investment in technological and production capabilities. In all of these cases, their successful coupling with global lead firms in different production networks, such as Apple, Dell, Hewlett-Packard, Toshiba, and so on, has been made in the context of intense competitive pressures confronting these lead firms to lower production cost and to increase organizational flexibility and time to market. The manufacturing excellence and organizational capabilities of these East Asian strategic partners have allowed their global lead firm customers to

Table 7.2 Mechanisms of strategic coupling and firm-specific initiatives in industrial transformation

East Asian firms	Coupling mechanisms in global production networks	Firm-specific initiatives
	Strategic partnership	
Quanta and Compal (Taiwan)	Vertical specialization; systems integration; customer diversification and leverage	Provision of original design manufacturing services; codevelopment of notebook products; technological upgrading and capability enhancement
Hon Hai Precision (Taiwan)	Vertical specialization; systems integration; international acquisitions	Provision of electronics manufacturing services; capability in turnkey solutions; rapid upscaling of production; close partnership with Apple Inc.
Venture (Singapore)	Vertical specialization; systems integration; brain circulation and international knowledge diffusion	Provision of electronics manufacturing services; highly selective partnership with key customers; "seamless transition" from design to manufacturing to fulfillment
	Industrial market specialization	
Hyundai Heavy Industries (South Korea)	Catching up and leapfrogging; market segmentation by industrial customers	Accumulation of industrial experience; sustained investment through cross-subsidization and intrachaebol integration; rapid upscaling of production
Samsung Heavy Industries (South Korea)	Catching up and leapfrogging; product differentiation	Sustained investment through cross-subsidization; new process technologies and flexible production
Keppel Corp (Singapore)	Catching up and leapfrogging; product customization	New product technologies and diversity; global presence of shipyards;
SembCorp Industries (Singapore)	Catching up and leapfrogging; product customization	Regional shipyard hubs; strong state ownership and support

TSMC (and UMC) (Taiwan)	Pathbreaking catching-up and leapfrogging; vertical specialization and organizational fitting; brain circulation and international knowledge diffusion	Rapid up-scaling of foundry production; new process technologies and organizational knowhow and autonomy in "pure play"; capitalization on market power and broader ecosystem
Chartered Semicond (Singapore)	Catching up and leapfrogging; vertical integration	Rapid upscaling of foundry production; strong state ownership and support
Samsung Electronics (and Hynix) (South Korea)	Pathbreaking catching up and leapfrogging; vertical integration with end users	Sustained investment through intrachaebol cross-subsidization; rapid upscaling of production; new product and process technologies

(Re)positioning as global lead firms

Acer Inc (Taiwan)	Strategic reorientation towards market definition; international knowledge diffusion; vertical disintegration	From OEM to OBM; continuous reorganization of production networks; brand development and spin-offs
Samsung Electronics (South Korea)	Strategic reorientation towards market definition; global integration and network coordination; international knowledge diffusion	From OEM to OBM; achieving first-mover advantage; sustained investment in R&D and international distribution
Hyundai Motor (South Korea)	Market control and definition; global integration and network coordination	OBM; achieving first-mover advantage; sustained investment in R&D and international distribution
Singapore Airlines	Market control and definition; global integration and network coordination	Brand development and service excellence; achieving first-mover advantage; strong state ownership and support

manage better competitive pressures and provided a solid and more equal raison d'être for their coupling relationships.

This coupling mechanism of strategic partnership between East Asian firms and global lead firms is also facilitated by important structural conditions, some of which are products of more sophisticated sectoral and functional industrial policy of the state. First, the transnational communities of technopreneurs have played a vital role in enhancing the technological and managerial competence of these East Asian firms and in intermediating their strategic coupling with global lead firms. Instead of offering direct subsidies to chosen winners, the state in all three economies was active in promoting overseas returnees through various national policies for human resource development and knowledge innovation. The effect of this functional industrial policy is most pronounced in the case of Taiwan where a significant number of strategic partners of global lead firms were established by these overseas returnees. Second, the state has developed supportive industrial and trade policies to promote this coupling mechanism through which domestic firms emerge as strategic partners of global lead firms. While often aiming at the information and communications technology (ICT) sector, these policies are mostly functional in nature since they are primarily concerned with the upgrading of labor, technology, and infrastructure and the facilitation of trade and investment in intermediate and final goods.

In more capital-intensive industries, such as shipbuilding and marine engineering and semiconductors, strategic partnership is not an effective coupling mechanism because East Asian firms in these industries manufacture intermediate goods for other lead firm end users who produce final goods or services in different global industries. Instead of highly tacit interfirm production organization in strategic partnership, technological and product specificities are the more critical considerations in this mechanism of interfirm coupling relationship. *Industrial market specialization* becomes the more effective mechanism for a number of East Asian firms to couple with their major customers (see table 7.2). In particular, this mechanism is buttressed by the catching up and leapfrogging of these East Asian specialists that enables their coupling with lead firm customers worldwide. In the shipbuilding and marine engineering industry, this coupling mechanism is also associated with the market segmentation or production differentiation and customization in different interfirm networks. In semiconductors, industrial market specialization is characterized by vertical specialization and organizational fitting with end customers (e.g., TSMC) or vertical integration with end users (e.g., Samsung Electronics).

In both industries, massive investment and scale economies were necessary firm-specific initiatives to achieve second-mover advantages for latecomer firms well analyzed in the existing developmental state literature. But my empirical analysis in chapter 5 has shown that the Gerschenkronian "big push" in these capital-intensive industries in all three East Asian economies did not go beyond second-mover advantages, such as production upscaling and lower costs. As summarized in table 7.1, the initial state-directed development of these two capital-intensive industries through public subsidies and state investment was able to provide only the temporary spatial fix to the competitive dynamics in global production networks that led to a geographical shift toward these East Asian economies as major producers in these two industries. To sustain their competitive dynamism through organizational and market fixes beyond attaining second-mover advantages, emerging East Asian firms have focused on developing *new* advantages embodied in technological and organizational innovations. Through firm-specific initiatives described in table 7.2, East Asian industrial leaders, such as South Korea's Samsung Heavy Industries, Singapore's Keppel Corp, and Taiwan's TSMC, have developed new product and process technologies to manufacture market-leading ships and chips. Through the coupling mechanism of specializing in the manufacturing of intermediate goods for industrial markets in different global production networks, these firms have dominated a particular market segment or platform in different global industries, such as marine transportation, offshore oil exploration, and ICT.

Unlike in strategic partnership, the role of transnational communities has been relatively weaker in facilitating the engagement of industrial market specialization by East Asian firms. With few exceptions in the semiconductor industry (e.g., Taiwan's TSMC), transnational communities did not play a strong role in the technological and organizational innovations of East Asian firms, particularly those in the shipbuilding and marine sector. More important structural conditions for their successful coupling with industrial end users are the changing industrial organization and the shift of state policies toward functional support for innovations and market development. In terms of industrial organization, the decoupling of design from the manufacturing of semiconductors represents one of the most favorable industry-level conditions for the emergence of "pure play" chipmakers from Taiwan. In their close collaboration with leading fabless semiconductor firms (e.g., Qualcomm, Broadcom, and Nvidia), these Taiwanese foundries play an instrumental role in the rapid growth and market domination of their industrial customers. Operating through vertical specialization and organizational fitting (TSMC and UMC in table 7.2), this reciprocal coupling mechanism works both ways, since their highly successful fabless global customers give even more orders to the specialist foundries. This unique coupling mechanism in semiconductor global production networks is particularly prevalent in Taiwan's semiconductor industry. In South Korea, integrated device manufacturers (IDMs), such as Samsung and Hynix, have dominated the global market in memory chips and beaten different industry cycles through continuous investment in R&D and intrachaebol synergies through vertical integration with end users (table 7.2). These contrasting examples even in the same industry show the critical role of different coupling mechanisms in the divergent growth trajectories of East

Asian firms. Similar to their counterparts from the shipbuilding and marine engineering industry, the strategic coupling of East Asian semiconductor firms with global production networks is premised on firm-level initiatives that have led to significant technological and organizational innovations. Meanwhile, the role of state policies was and remains important in these capital-intensive industries. Though the state can no longer pick winners in the 2010s and beyond, its functional policies of developing R&D infrastructure and state-funded institutes remain useful in facilitating the continual interest of these specialized East Asian industrial leaders in innovating new products or processes for global markets.

Of the three coupling mechanisms, *(re)positioning as global lead firms* epitomizes the most enduring challenge to East Asian firms and industrial transformation. My empirical analysis has shown that the kinds of learning and risks associated with developing global brand names, a necessary precondition for the strategic reorientation toward market definition described in table 7.2, are much greater than the other two coupling mechanisms. Indeed, only a small number of East Asian firms have engaged successfully with market control and product definition—the key mechanism for a global lead firm to create and manage its own products and markets and to coordinate its own global production network. In chapter 6, I have focused on four such global lead firms from East Asia in the ICT (Acer and Samsung), automobile (Hyundai), and civil aviation (Singapore Airlines) industries. My case studies show significant industry-level effects on the operation of this coupling mechanism in global competition. In the ICT industry, both Acer and Samsung have experienced changing coupling mechanisms over time—from captive suppliers beholden to OEM customers to becoming strategic partners and eventually global lead firms with their own brand names. In this evolutionary process, they have learned the crucial lessons of market control and product definition from their global lead firm customers. Translating this learning from participation in global production networks into the strategic practice of brand name development and market domination requires sustained firm-specific investment in design and product development, branding and marketing, and distribution activity. In the automobile and civil aviation industries, a small number of East Asian firms started as lead firms defining their own products and/or markets. Since their initial founding respectively in 1967 and 1972, Hyundai and Singapore Airlines have already internalized self-reliance and brand development as their pathway to become global lead firms in their respective industries. They have engaged with global integration and network coordination as their coupling mechanism to emerge as global lead firms in their respective industries. Similar to the ICT cases, these two lead firms have invested substantially in their organizational, financial, and technological/service competencies.

This arduous coupling mechanism of (re)positioning as global lead firms, however, is limited only to a small number of leading domestic firms from the three East Asian economies. As noted in tables 7.1 and 7.2, this limit to the emergence of global lead firms is shaped by both competitive dynamics in global production networks and structural conditions favorable to strategic coupling. First, successful coupling in this mechanism requires East Asian lead firms to overcome all three fixes in competitive dynamics. The globalization of Samsung and Hyundai's production networks has allowed them to extend their geographical reach in different markets and territories. Both chaebol groups have also benefited from their intragroup synergy in terms of branding, production, and marketing. This organizational fix is also applicable to Acer, which can tap into its vertically disintegrated industrial group and yet maintain its own organizational flexibility. Finally, all four East Asian firms have achieved a market fix through their firm-specific initiatives in brand development and production/service integration. These unique advantages have allowed them to penetrate the most competitive markets in North America and Western Europe.

Second, the (re)positioning of these global lead firms from East Asia has occurred in the context of favorable structural conditions. The role of transnational communities is again relatively more conducive to the ICT lead firms. But their role in the automobile and airline industries is not as pronounced. Similarly, there is a great deal of difference in the state's promotional policies in all three economies. In the ICT industry, the positive support of the state's sectoral industrial policy in favor of technology transfers through state-sanctioned R&D institutes was quite important in the early development of Acer and Samsung. But this sectoral support became less efficacious after both firms had begun their repositioning as global lead firms in the 2000s. Since then, functional policies, such as national brand and marketing promotion and trade and investment facilitation, are more relevant to the emergence of these global lead firms. In the automobile and civil aviation industries, state support or even direct ownership was necessary at the initial launch of both industries. But again, there are different pathways to their eventual development. In automobiles, the contrasting success of Hyundai (and Kia) vis-à-vis other automakers from South Korea and Taiwan points to the useful, but not deterministic, role of state policies in support of the industry, particularly in its formative years during the 1970s. Firm-specific initiatives have played the more crucial role in successful strategic coupling. In the civil aviation industry, strong state support, particularly in the form of negotiating for open sky agreements, is vital to the international market reach of these national airlines from East Asia. But state ownership per se does not necessarily produce successful strategic coupling in the industry, as the contrasting examples of China Airlines (Taiwan) and Singapore Airlines have illustrated. In all four cases in table 7.2, the state's favorable support through functional policies in promoting trade, investment, and R&D infrastructure provides the most useful condition for the (re)positioning of East Asian firms as global lead firms in their respective industries.

Taken as a whole, this book has shown the usefulness of an international political economy perspective on late industrialization that incorporates the state, capitalist firms, and their global production networks. As state-firm relations evolve over time in favor of the disembedding of domestic firms from state inducement for resolving the Gerschenkronian collective dilemmas, a dynamic process of industrial transformation occurs through the above strategic coupling of domestic firms with production networks in diverse global industries. This shift from state-firm relations to interfirm global assemblages represents one of the most significant transformative changes in the current trajectories of East Asian development. This international political economy perspective on East Asian development points to three potential contributions of this book. First, it has broadened the comparative political economy analysis of late industrialization to *both* the state and its national firms in global production networks. Taking an evolutionary approach to theorizing this transformation, I have shown how changing state-firm relations in these economies during the past two decades have affected both differently—the state in its effort to industrialize the nation and the firm in its effort to thrive. Any analysis focusing solely on either the state or national firms is likely to be inadequate in capturing this dynamic process of political-economic change because of the inherent assumption of passive state or firm responses. While some scholars have already pointed to this need for a more evolutionary and contextualized analysis of the developmental state, this book has provided the empirical basis for such an understanding of state-firm relations in more dynamic terms, particularly in relation to different configurations of global production networks and their coupling mechanisms for East Asian firms. In short, I have shown how both states and firms matter in late industrialization, even though their relative strength and importance changes over time. These changes require careful documentation and analysis.

Second, my global production networks approach has offered an integrative analytical framework that incorporates evolutionary dynamics within global industries and between domestic actors (e.g., states and firms) in different national economies. Adding to the original developmental state literature, this mechanism-based approach views economic development no longer just as a matter of domestic political choices and state-led initiatives, for it must be firmly grounded in the broader global dynamics of industrial competition mediated through global lead firms and their complex production networks. Bringing together the enormous developmental state literature and the parallel and fast-growing work on global production networks and global value chains, this book has combined the more local/national focus of the former with the top-down approach characterizing most work in the latter. This integrative framing allows for a more systematic analysis of industrial transformation on the basis of the mechanisms, interactions, and outcomes of both domestic political, policy, and institutional conditions in their changing historical contexts, and firm-specific initiatives in strategic coupling.

Third, my comparative analysis of three East Asian economies illustrates robustly that the same initial state-led industrialization can lead to divergent evolutionary outcomes due to substantial differences in the political and institutional bases of the developmental state. In South Korea, the much greater concentration of chaebol power today has dramatically reduced the policy space for the democratized state. In Taiwan, domestic party politics and leading high-tech business groups have become more, not less, divergent in their strategic orientation toward economic development. In both cases, changing political dynamics lead to the reconfiguration of the developmental state in favor of a less interventionist state in a postdevelopmental era. Unlike South Korea and Taiwan, the developmental state in Singapore has uniquely benefited from political continuity and institutional legitimacy to prolong its demiurge role in major industries and sectors. Favorable domestic politics and one-party domination have allowed the People's Action Party (PAP)–led state to remain developmental in a world of global competition. This substantial variation in the state's political basis has in turn conditioned how national firms from the three East Asian economies have taken contrasting pathways to benefit from their strategic coupling with global production networks. In short, this dynamic mechanism of strategic coupling works out differently in contrasting national political economies due to differential preexisting structural conditions and firm-specific initiatives.

Beyond the Developmental State

Having consolidated the key findings and possible contributions of this work, I can now address the broader political economy view that late industrialization is not a natural process driven by market forces, but a deliberate and contested outcome of interaction among different agents in contemporary capitalism, such as states, nonstate institutions, and firms. As argued by Albert Hirschman (1958, 8) in *The Strategy of Economic Development*, the "lateness" in this catching-up process of developing economies "is bound to make their development into a less spontaneous and more deliberate process than was the case in the countries where the process first occurred. . . . Once economic progress in the pioneer countries is a visible reality, the strength of the desire to imitate, to follow suit, to catch up obviously becomes an important determinant of what will happen among the nonpioneers."[12] This renewed political economy approach to economic development focuses our attention more explicitly on the key growth coalition in the *state-firm nexus* and the need to understand their evolutionary relations and divergent strategic goals over time. Here politics refers to the balances of power, ideas, ideologies, and interests of leaders, elites, and coalitions in the development process, and the formal and informal institutions through which they work. To Leftwich (2008, 5), developmental states "can not be had to order, but are the product of the interaction between internal and external political processes in the context of their historical legacies." The importance of understanding the evolutionary dynamics of state-society relations is thus predicated on shedding light on the conditions and possibilities of developing and/or sustaining positive developmental outcomes in the context of structural constraints and global opportunities.

This section offers further insights into this comparative institutional approach to the political economy of development and discusses the contemporary political dynamics that influence the changing roles of both states and nonstate institutions in industrial transformation. To begin, my approach conceives the state as one set of institutions rather than the only unitary force that drives development. As argued by Haggard (1990, 4) in *Pathways from the Periphery,* " 'The state' is not only an actor but a set of institutions that exhibit continuity over time; a field of play that provides differential incentives for groups to organize. Because of variations in institutional structure, political elites differ in their organizational capabilities and the instruments they have at their disposal for their goals. Institutional variation is critical for understanding why some states are capable of pursuing the policies they do. It is at the intersection between choice and institutional constraints that political explanations of economic growth must be constructed." The extent to which these institutions are themselves transformed in the course of economic development can be as important as the process of late industrialization itself. This calls for a more dynamic perspective that appreciates the coevolution of political institutions under the aegis of the developmental state and the multifaceted processes of economic development.

The State in Economic Development Redux?

The successful industrial transformation of the three East Asian economies has led to much analytical attention being placed on the developmental state and far less on the unique historical and geographical circumstances of its emergence in the first place.[13] In this statist dictum, a strong state oriented toward developmental initiatives is deemed applicable to almost any latecomer economies, and development is simply a matter of making the state and/or its bureaucracy strong, "just like" South Korea, Taiwan, or Singapore.[14] Concluding his *Embedded Autonomy,* Evans (1995, 244) cautions us that "the East Asian amalgam depends on specific historical circumstances. The concept of embedded autonomy is a useful analytical guide-post, not an engineering formula that can be applied, with a few easy adjustments, to states in other regions and historical periods in the same way that the formula for a suspension bridge can be applied regardless of where a river or chasm is located." In other words, the embedded autonomy in his East Asian case, South Korea, is predicated on unique historical and geographical conditions, without which the analytical effectiveness of his Weberian concept may be jeopardized.

The common origin of these three states rests with their unique, but different, mix of postwar decolonization and Cold War geopolitics. The colonial origins of South Korea and Taiwan in Japan's prior state-directed industrialization were critical to the underdevelopment of a strong domestic capitalist class, without which the dictatorial state could not wield sufficient power in charting new directions for economic development. The emergence of a strong state needs further impetus and external support that can be traced back to the US-led Cold War. The Korean War necessitated a strong state in South Korea. Park Chung Hee's regime was strongly supported by generous financial aid from and unfettered market access to the United States. In Taiwan, Chiang Kai-shek's continual ambition of "recovering the mainland" meant that economic development in Taiwan was never on his top agenda, and the result being that Taiwan's developmental state emerged only in the late 1970s (Wu 2005; Greene 2008; Mattlin 2011). In Singapore, the establishment of the People's Action Party in 1954 and the PAP-led self-government in 1959 was a historically specific response to the political vacuum created by the departure of the British colonial administration. But the ultimate determinant of Lee Kuan Yew's relentless drive toward economic development was the existential threat from left and communal politics that prevailed in the early to the mid-1960s, which led to Singapore's separation from the federation of Malaysia on August 9, 1965. Faced with dire political, economic, and social uncertainties, state-led industrialization was the only viable option for the newly inaugurated Republic of Singapore.

The historical similarities in the origin of these three developmental states, however, end with the common influences of decolonization and geopolitics. Indeed, each of them was shaped *differently* by these influences. Similar to Japan described in Johnson (1982; 1995), the role of nationalism and independence was particularly strong in the origin of these developmental states. Once formed, the three developmental states have pursued drastically different pathways to industrial transformation. As indicated in table 7.3, South Korea inherited strong links to Japan and its state-sponsored industrial system, particularly the domination by the large business conglomerates—the chaebol. When Park took power in 1961, his immediate instinct was to cajole the chaebol to turn his vision for a strong and industrialized South Korea into a reality (Amsden 1989). This political choice has since made a permanent imprint on the industrial organization of the South Korean economy. Today, South Korea continues to be heavily dominated by these large chaebol groups, as is evident in my case studies of Samsung and Hyundai in chapters 5 and 6. In Taiwan, Chiang's émigré regime had to navigate carefully domestic ethnic and political divisions that have subsequently become much more visible and confrontational since the late 1990s. Between the 1950s and the 1970s, Chiang's Kuomintang (KMT) state took control of most industries through state-owned enterprises (Wade 1990). After the state had become truly developmental by the late 1970s, these state-owned enterprises were privatized

Table 7.3 Strategies and histories of state developmentalism in comparative perspective

Strategies	South Korea	Taiwan	Singapore	Ireland	Israel
Accumulation strategy	National champion and export firms	Global region based on indigenous firms	Global region based on foreign firms	Global region based on foreign firms	Global region based on indigenous firms
Selectivity of state support of firms	High	Low	High with direct state ownership	Low	Low
Reliance on FDI	Low	Medium	High	High	Low
Integration of indigenous firms in global networks	Low	High	Medium	High	High
The development project (1950–1973)	Chaebol links to Japan; state-sponsored industrial system	State developmentalism at arm's length from bourgeoisie; ethnic and political divisions	FDI; keep wage costs low through repression and subsidies for social reproduction	FDI; tax incentives the central instrument	Rapid growth through close state-business-union ties
Liberalization (1973–1990)	Upgrading through learning; increased power of chaebol	Upgrading through "institutional thickness"	Upgrading by autonomous state	Liberalization and crisis; political space alongside the FDI agenda	Liberalization and crisis; political space for new state agenda
The globalization project (1990–)	Liberalization and crisis	Network institutions around transnational technical communities and FDI	Attempts to build "institutional thickness" around FDI	Network institutions around FDI	Network institutions around transnational technical communities

Source: Compiled from O'Riain (2004, tables 10.1 and 10.3).

in the 1980s and the 1990s to pave the way for new industrial formation and the eventual growth of Taiwan's high-tech business groups described in chapter 3. This heavy state ownership of the domestic economy in the initial phase of Taiwan's industrialization did not really occur during Park's regime in South Korea. Rather, it took place in Singapore under the PAP state since the late 1960s that has continued as a major stakeholder in the domestic corporate sector. The difference between Taiwan and Singapore in this initial state ownership of the domestic economy, though, is that Singapore's developmental state has been able to nurture its former state-owned enterprises into world-class competitors in manufacturing and service industries, such as Keppel, SembCorp, and Singapore Airlines analyzed in chapters 5 and 6.

An even more pronounced difference among the three developmental states is their receptiveness to direct integration with the global economy—the main focus of this book. In this regard, only Singapore's PAP state has been consistently open to foreign direct investment (FDI) by transnational corporations for over four decades. Faced with exceptional historical difficulties associated with its geographical reality as a small and open urban economy, the PAP state not only took control of domestic industries through direct ownership, but also induced transnational capital to kick-start its manufacturing industries for exports. Its elite pilot agency, the Economic Development Board, has been chartered since its establishment in 1961 to focus on attracting foreign investment in order to create jobs and to upgrade domestic industries. Singapore's developmental state was, and still is, both "demiurge" and "husbandry" in Evans's (1995) typology of state roles. Singapore's internationalism of the developmental state entering into a cooperative alliance with foreign capital in its state-led industrialization therefore differs substantially from the reliance on national champions in South Korea and the promotion of indigenous firms in Taiwan. Indeed, South Korea's reliance on technonationalism was so dominant under Park's regime that legal and bureaucratic mechanisms were evoked to regulate the interaction of the domestic economy with foreign capital (Mardon 1990; B. K. Kim 2003). Shaped by different geographical endowments, this divergence in their initial articulation into the global economy has produced a considerable difference in the presence of foreign firms in all three economies. Transnational corporations and their FDI activity are clearly much more dominant and important in Singapore's city-state, characterized by its deep integration into the global economy. In this sense, the PAP state's embedded autonomy is always more multifarious than its counterparts from South Korea and Taiwan in their historical context.

This dimension of internationalism brings us to the final point about the origin of the three developmental states in a world economy at the relative early and expansionary phase of economic globalization. When these three economies began their industrialization in the 1960s, the first movers in advanced industrialized economies were much more amenable to lending capital, technology, and expertise to support East Asian industrialization. In

Ha-Joon Chang's (2002; 2003) terminology, these first movers had not yet "kicked away" the ladder of economic development, and the three East Asian economies were still given different windows of opportunity to climb the ladder. It was a world of immense developmental opportunities for the articulation, albeit via different modalities and mechanisms, of the three economies into globalizing industries. For all its institutional capacity and bureaucratic rationality, the developmental state was riding on this historically specific rising tide; the efficacy of its industrial policy was premised on the global shift of economic activity toward East Asia. Without the relocation of the labor-intensive production of American and European electronics firms to the three economies, it would hardly have been possible to imagine the accumulation of production experience, managerial and technological know-how, and export practices by domestic firms that subsequently allowed them to upgrade from captive OEM subcontractors to market leaders within a timespan of two to three decades. In the semiconductor industry, the developmental state's direct involvement in capital investment and technology transfer in the late 1970s and the 1980s would not be successful if global competition between American, European, and Japanese semiconductor firms had been less intense and cutthroat. As shown in chapter 5, the rise of "Tiger chips" has much to do with the willingness of these first movers to transfer their lesser technologies, initially via East Asian state-sponsored research institutes, to the chosen national champions in South Korea, Taiwan, and even Singapore.[15]

In retrospect, these peculiar historical-geographical circumstances are much harder to be replicated today. State formations elsewhere are now much less prompted by the exigencies of decolonization and Cold War geopolitics. The postwar open internationalism that prevailed between the 1950s and the 1980s has been replaced by intensified economic and other rivalries among the world's leading superpowers, such as the United States and China.[16] Different regional groupings, such as the Organisation for Economic Cooperation and Development, the European Union, Association of South East Asian Nations, and BRICs (Brazil, Russia, India, and China), have developed more formal and informal rules that pose constraints on individual member states. International organizations, such as the World Trade Organization (WTO) and the International Monetary Fund (IMF), are vested with more regulatory authority over key policy instruments that used to be most critical in the initial push for industrialization in the three East Asian economies. Newcomers are much less likely to succeed in deploying the same set of sectoral industrial policy and blunt financial instruments, such as trade-distorting countervailing measures and direct subsidies of chosen national champions. Last but not least, the rise of new "global rulers" through the privatization of regulation has made it even harder for newcomers to harmonize their domestic institutional structures to align with global standard-setters (Büthe and Mattli 2011; Ponte et al. 2011). In this highly transformed global context, the earlier analytical focus on state capacity and bureaucratic coherence may not be able to hold as much analytical traction in our future understanding of industrial transformation in "late" latecomer economies or, in Amsden's (2001) terms, "the rest" of the world's many developing economies.

What then remains of the state's role in economic development, and how can we revive it in a globalized world economy? The historical-geographical contexts of East Asian industrialization described above point squarely to the observation that the developmental state might be a necessary, but certainly not sufficient, condition for economic development to take place.[17] My empirical evidence in this book has made clear that the Gerschenkronian "big push" under the aegis of state-led initiatives can only account for the *beginning* of a protracted and transformative process of East Asian industrialization. When private capitalists were resistant to deploying their limited assets for productive investments in the face of tremendous risks, the developmental state had to step in to serve as a risk-bearing institution and to spread these risks across multiple capitalists.[18] There is no guarantee, however, that continual state intervention is necessarily effective in economic development for at least two reasons.

First, while it is true that all three economies were characterized by a strong developmental state at the time of their late industrialization, it might be too much of a leap of faith then to assert that state bureaucrats knew exactly how to balance Gerschenkron's economic backwardness against the obstacles to economic progress.[19] As I have argued in chapter 2, state coherence and bureaucratic rationality were more an assumption than a reality in East Asia. The developmental state's embedded autonomy could no longer be sustained by the late 1980s. The initial success in state-directed industrialization generated much greater popular demand for market liberalization and political change. The domestic politics of development were reframed in ways less in favor of the developmental state and its transformed bureaucracy. While South Korea's Park Chung Hee was personally able to supervise his economic planners and chaebol leaders, Taiwan's Chiang Kai-shek and his son were confronted with a far more fragmented state bureaucracy and vested private interests.[20] After Park's assassination in 1979, South Korea's strong developmental state began to dismantle in favor of growing chaebol power. Even in Singapore, Lee Kuan Yew and his economic lieutenants had to appease foreign investors right at the beginning in order to industrialize the city-state quickly. After two decades of FDI-led industrialization, its state bureaucracy could scarcely be characterized as autonomous from demands and pressures from domestic private interests and global firms. In short, the inducement role of the developmental state has often been overstretched to explain the entire treacherous process of East Asian industrialization. Economic planners and state bureaucrats did not know in advance which sectors or technologies would really work for their backward economies in the 1950s and the 1960s. They carefully steered industrialization by learning through trials and errors and experimenting with different policy mixes. There was no magic bullet, as we know it today, in their drive toward economic development.

Second, the state's role in inducing large-scale industrialization changes over time and should therefore be viewed in dynamic and evolutionary terms. As the initial state-induced industrialization took place in the three East Asian economies, private sector actors began to accumulate dynamic capabilities through processes of coordinative management and interfirm learning, and to access new sources of financial resources in global financial markets. The same set of sectoral industrial policy for kick-starting an industry became ineffective as soon as these private firms were ready to take on a leadership role in the next phase of industrialization. This dynamic context of policymaking was already well anticipated by Hirschman (1958, 124): "If our analysis is correct, then an economic policy designed to encourage industrialization ought to be one thing after new domestic industry has come into being and quite another before the infant has been born." As East Asian firms have emerged to become a master of their own future, their relationship with domestic banks, particularly state-controlled ones, necessarily evolve into a more complicated form than the usual dependency of the former on the latter.

Nonstate Institutions

If the developmental state cannot be conceived of as the sole institutional actor in late industrialization, a more comprehensive and dynamic approach requires us to incorporate a wider range of nonstate institutions in analyzing the politics and mechanisms of economic development. This broader institutional approach to the political economy of late industrialization is mindful of not just the state as a set of institutions beyond individual political elites, but also other nonstate institutions, such as firms and their production networks, business coalitions, industry associations, public-private consultative groups, labor organizations, nongovernmental and civic society organizations, and so on. In this book, I have focused primarily on evolutionary state-firm relations and industrial transformation in the three East Asian economies, and their dynamic articulation into diverse global production networks. I have therefore paid much less attention to other nonstate institutions.[21] Still I believe broadening our analysis of late industrialization to include nonstate institutions can serve to transcend the market-state dichotomy in much of the existing literature on economic development. In retrospect, the developmental state approach is itself a reaction to, and critique of, the then dominant neoclassical market explanation of East Asian development. In this "market enhancing" explanation, state policy is conceived as facilitating or complementing private-sector coordination and thus the promarket mechanism as the determinant of efficient allocation of scarce resources.[22] My analysis in this book has shown that neither the market nor the state can serve as the adequate analytical device through which East Asian industrialization can be understood. Clearly, different configurations of state-market relations in East Asia are possible within the so-called "varieties of capitalism" framework in comparative political economy studies.[23] But whatever this capitalist variety in the three East Asian economies might be, the state-market dichotomy is not particularly helpful in analyzing their evolutionary development because of the missing or underestimated roles of nonstate institutions.

More specifically, domestic nonstate interest groups have critical roles to play in overcoming the Gerschenkronian collective dilemmas during late industrialization. My empirical analysis has identified broadly three such roles that can be summarized briefly here. First, nonstate interest groups are necessary to make the state's embedded autonomy work by providing the vital consultation and advice for the state to pursue favorable economic policies. Of course, the extent of such state embeddedness in society changes over time and varies among the three East Asian economies. The need for such public-private consultation increases substantially if the state is confronted with greater institutional fragmentation and multiple policy arrangements due to increasing domestic political pressures and/or international regulation. In Taiwan, recent studies have shown that since the 2000s, the state's economic bureaucracy has not been able to keep up with the rapid development and globalization of the private sector.[24] This applies particularly to those domestic firms that have coupled successfully with global production networks. As argued by Haggard and Zheng (2013, 436), "delegation to key policy bodies played a significant role in signaling government intent and making policy signals credible. However, these institutions reflected different constellations of political interests at different points of time, with clear implications for policy." Shifting to a more "followership" role described by Wade (1990, 28–29), the state's economic planning and coordinating agencies have increasingly relied on sector-specific consultative groups for the latest industry information and policy recommendations. These groups often comprise representatives from industry association, R&D labs and organizations, and universities.[25] In Singapore, such public-private consultation is less visible in light of the continual institutional cohesion of the developmental state and its elite bureaucracy (e.g., the Ministry of Trade and Industry and its Economic Development Board). But for important policy shifts in relation to human resources (e.g., foreign labor and productivity drive), these state agencies do regularly consult business associations, such as the Singapore Chamber of Commerce and Industry, the Singapore Business Federation, and the Singapore National Employers Federation.

Second, nonstate institutions are often an important organizational platform for collective action at the industry and sectoral levels. Through group representation, industry associations can put significant pressures on state bureaucrats for more favorable industrial policy and financial and other incentives. While this role as a pressure group has become more visible in the postdemocratization era since the late 1980s, it had taken place in South Korea even during Park Chung Hee's era. In the 1970s, the Federation of Korean Industries (FKI) represented some of the largest and most powerful chaebol and had a systematic influence on Park's economic policies in favor of heavy and chemical industries. By the late 1980s, the FKI was able to influence the state's financial policy, such as blocking state efforts to liberalize interest rates and to reduce policy loans (Zhang 2002, 424). In Taiwan, the democratization of electoral politics in the late 1980s led to the KMT chasing for new voters and constituents in the face of new political challenge from the Democratic Progressive Party (DPP). The establishment of the Industrial Consultative Commission in March 1985 opened the door for the private sector to influence policy making directly (Wu 2005). A variety of private sector groups, including industry associations, began to pressure previously insulated technocratic bureaucracy by funding and supporting their own elected politicians (Haggard and Zheng 2013, 452). The same phenomenon has also occurred in South Korea since the 1990s, when industry groups made substantial contributions to all major political parties during elections in order to win political favors and policy shifts from the new government.[26]

Apart from making collective representation to the state, these nonstate institutions have also been active in building interfirm alliances and hastening the processes of enhancing organizational capabilities and learning among their constituents in order to compete in the global economy. This sectoral role has been particularly strong in the ICT industry where technological shifts are frequent and disruptive. In Taiwan, high-tech firms have shown interest in such sector-based collective action for facilitating interfirm cooperation and coordination and for promoting the coupling of local firms with global lead firms. Noble's (1998) exceptional study has pointed to the vital importance of these industrial consortia in standard setting and provision in promoting Taiwan's emerging computer industry up to the 1990s. My case study of Acer in chapter 6 has also shown the strong desire for collective action by its founder Stan Shih when he established Taiwan's Brand International Promotion Association as an institutional platform to promote the international branding of Taiwan-made products. Other industry associations in computers (e.g., Taipei Computer Association) and semiconductors (e.g., Taiwan Semiconductor Industry Association) have engaged in R&D consortia, joint development, and information-sharing and joint marketing among their member firms. In Singapore, these sector-based associations are established to cater to industry-specific issues and needs among their member firms, e.g., the Singapore Manufacturing Federation, the Association of Electronic Industries in Singapore, the Singapore Semiconductor Industry Association, and the Association of Aerospace Industries (Singapore). As one of the oldest industry associations, the Association of Singapore Marine Industries has played a strong role in promoting the marine sector since its founding as a nonprofit trade association in 1968. It provides a common platform for all members in the sector to address their common issues with labor, safety, training, industry promotion, and capability building, and to communicate with relevant state agencies these core concerns of member firms.

Third, nonstate institutions, such as labor unions and social welfare groups, can put some significant constraints on the developmental state's autonomy in governing the market and in directing the growth trajectories of national firms. The experience of all three East Asian economies has shown how labor movements could alter the structural conditions for state-led economic planning and firm development.[27] But their effects on industrial transformation vary significantly in relation to their roles and capabilities. South Korea's labor unions are known for their strong organizational capability and militant approaches to negotiations with the state and the chaebol. The escalation of labor disputes in the late 1980s, for example, compelled the developmental state to relax labor-related laws and the chaebol to offer better working terms and conditions. In Taiwan, such escalation did not occur because the KMT had strong control of labor unions, and most workers were organized at the firm level. After democratization in the late 1980s, labor unions in Taiwan went into decline due to rapid loss of membership and the increasing isolation of the Labour Party (formerly the left wing of the DPP). In Singapore, the Trade Union Act of 1966 and the PAP-controlled National Trade Union Congress have kept labor disputes at bay for five decades. When an industrial action became eminent, the strong corporatist state would not hesitate to step in, as illustrated in the case of Singapore Airlines and the Airline Pilots Association—Singapore in chapter 6.

In addition, social welfare spending and other benefits demanded by different social interest groups have limited the state's financial resources and complicated the state's efforts to steer economic development through sectoral industrial policy and generous financial incentives. By the 1990s, it was clear that all three East Asian states had been compelled to increase their social and welfare spending in order to satisfy competing demands from different fragments of society. This led to decreasing budgetary allocation to industrial development at the time when private firms became less dependent on the state for policy loans and financial support and was able to cut the umbilical cord that had previously nurtured them. Stronger pressures from social and welfare groups have subsequently reduced state autonomy in developmentalist planning and coordination that in turn provides a conducive structural condition for domestic firms to seek new sources of capital and technologies through their strategic coupling with global lead firms in different production networks.

These shifting roles of nonstate institutions in relation to domestic political change and state transformation illustrate the importance of a comparative institutional approach that goes beyond the developmental state in analyzing late industrialization. Only by incorporating a greater range of capitalist institutions can we really grapple with the dynamic and complex reality of industrial transformation in latecomer economies. In this vein, Pempel's (1999) idea of a "developmental regime" is helpful because it allows for actors and relations far more than just the state or the market. In my study, these actors refer primarily to the developmental state and its bureaucracy, private sector firms and different domestic business groups, and global lead firms and their production networks.[28] But they ought to include other nonstate institutions, such as business or industry associations, public-private consultative groups, and civil society organizations. A developmental regime in the global economy can also incorporate multiple relations and causal mechanisms, such as the domestic state's embedded autonomy in society and the strategic coupling of domestic firms with global production networks. The examination of multiple actors and their evolutionary relations has the merit of better mapping this complex reality in the context of changing domestic political dynamics and the evolving global economy. In the final section below, I examine the key lessons of this study for rethinking new economic policies in an international political economy of development.

Toward a New Political Economy of Development

When East Asian economies were feverishly catching up through state-led industrialization in the 1960s and the 1970s, their only benchmark was the first movers in advanced industrialized economies. In the context of today's intensified global competition, a developmental state's relentless pursuit of sectoral industrial policy to catch up with first movers can fall into the danger of missing a rapidly moving target.[29] Catching up with the "wrong" or obsolescent first movers may turn out to be a temporary gratification, and indeed "falling behind" the "real" movers can become the reality. This was clearly evident in chapter 5's analysis of the rapid decline of Taiwan's integrated device manufacturers in the semiconductor industry during the 2000s and beyond. Because of drastic and rapid market shifts in response to changing technological regimes, new product innovations, and consumer preferences, industrial transformation through such state-induced second mover advantages as scale economies does not necessarily generate sustained growth, *even after* such transformation has taken place. There is also no guarantee that the state's planning agencies and policy implementation bureaus possess the requisite competence to help domestic firms anticipate and respond effectively to these rapid shifts and unknowable changes in the global economy. As evident in the global electronics and marine industries in chapters 4 and 5, this dynamic scenario poses a much more serious challenge to the practice of conventional industrial policy in the global economy today, as compared to over four decades ago when the three East Asian economies were catching up.

Whether in East Asia or in the United States or the United Kingdom, it is clear that industrial policy—particularly in its functional or horizontal variant—matters in economic development. But its relevance and effectiveness depends very much on the policy details and political contexts.[30] Empirical evidence in this book has shown that "picking the winners" by the state, as a form of sector-specific intervention, can no longer be useful because successful industrial transformation is increasingly dependent on the strategic coupling of domestic firms with global production networks. In a world economy dominated by cross-border production networks, this national-global articulation has become the necessary mechanism for development to be kick-started and sustained over time in most economies. While it is now much harder for almost any national economy to develop fully vertically integrated industries that are internationally competitive, there remains significant room for a new kind of industrial policy promoting domestic firms to tap into the developmental opportunities inherent in most global industries. But there are sectoral specificities to these network-level opportunities. There is no doubt, for example, that in technological and organizational terms, strategic coupling in automobiles can be much more challenging than in apparel or agro-food. Interestingly, there is also substantial intrasectoral differentiation. In the ICT industry analyzed in chapters 4 and 5, articulating into global production networks in consumer electronics is relatively more actionable in functional policy terms than it would be in advanced semiconductors or high-end electronics equipment (e.g., medical devices or computing servers). Developing industrial policy oriented toward promoting a specialized niche in a particular sector or an intrasectoral segment can make good sense for economic development.[31]

Before I go into the specificities of this GPN-oriented industrial policy, however, it is necessary to caution that strategic coupling is a selective mechanism incorporating only the more productive and capable domestic firms and non-firm institutions. My empirical analysis in chapters 4 through 6 has also pointed to different coupling mechanisms engaged by East Asian firms, and these mechanisms are likely to be subject to change over time. It is unrealistic for policymakers to expect such national-global coupling to be always inclusive; it is even more dangerous for them to rely exclusively on a particular coupling mechanism as the only pathway to industrial upgrading and positive development outcomes. As argued by Coe and Hess (2011, 134), "although the articulation of regions in global production networks can produce significant economic gains on an aggregate level, in many cases it also causes intraregional disarticulations, for instance, through uneven resource allocation and the breakup of existing cultural, social and economic networks and systems." There is therefore a critical role for state and nonstate institutions and diverse groups of social actors to engage in joint decision and collective action in order to mitigate the negative consequences of such strategic coupling and to consider a more balanced and inclusive form of development. In emerging economies, this role calls for the policy consideration of both strategic coupling with global production networks and the domestic market-oriented form of industrial development. More specifically, UNCTAD's (2013) *World Investment Report 2013* contains a comprehensive policy framework for economic development in a world economy organized through the extensive presence of global production networks.[32] I summarize below key considerations in such a policy framework:

1. Moving from national industries to specialized niches within global production networks;
2. Recognizing the need for detailed knowledge and analysis of development prospects in different global production networks;
3. Promoting new domestic capacity and/or foreign investment in value-adding segments of global production networks and developing a global supply base through a combination of local and foreign firms;
4. Coordinating and matching capabilities and capacities of domestic firms with global lead firms;
5. Facilitating trade and investment in production inputs and intermediate goods and services;
6. Leveraging global production networks for international market access and the development of domestic firms;
7. Providing basic prerequisites for economic activity: skills, infrastructure, logistics, tax regimes, intellectual property rights, and so on.

This recognition of new developmental challenges and policy considerations has at least three significant implications for rethinking industrial policy in latecomer industrialization: its intended recipients, policy foci, and politics of choice. First, the question of the *recipients* of state-led initiatives becomes much more complicated in this national-global articulation. When the three East Asian economies entered into the new international division of labor, there was no question who should be the beneficiaries of state-led industrialization—domestic firms and national champions, such as Taiwan's TSMC and South Korea's Samsung and Hyundai described in chapters 5 and 6. But as today's national firms are less domestic in their outlook and activity because of their strategic coupling with global production networks, it is questionable if they should be the only beneficiaries of a renewed form of industrial policy. Analyzing South Korea's globalization since the 1990s, Pirie (2008, 31–32) thus argues that "as firms denationalise an increasing array of their activities—a process the state must encourage if nominally domestically based firms are to remain competitive—it becomes increasingly difficult to justify an economic strategy that is exclusively based upon domestically based firms." This greater domestic coupling with global production networks also entails a more extensive presence of foreign firms in the national economy.

Instead of highly selective sectoral industrial policy promoting specific firms through investment coordination, policy loans and credit rationing, or trade and investment protectionism, a more catalyst-oriented industrial policy promoting industry-level growth dynamics, such as cooperative industrial ecosystem and interfirm and interindustry linkages, is likely to be more effective. This kind of industrial policy can support local firms to leverage new sources of technologies and market access in global production networks; it can also facilitate the location or further upgrading of value-adding activity by existing or new foreign firms in the national economy. All in all, this new kind of industrial policy can potentially bridge the sectoral-functional divide by developing production systems-level synergies that are cross-national and multi-industrial in nature. As argued by H. J. Chang et al. (2013, 20), "When we assess the industrial policy of a particular country, we need to look at things like its ability to generate new technologies, make structural shifts, and compete in the world market, and not just what is going on in the targeted industries." This industrial policy should be about promoting capabilities, externalities, linkages, and shifts across industries, with the aim of upgrading the structure of the entire national economy.

In the global electronics industry discussed in chapter 4, the developmental state in Singapore and, to a lesser extent, Taiwan was much more open to supporting and facilitating the strategic coupling of its domestic firms through functional industrial policy that promoted inward investment, technology transfer, and capability building. But more important, it also identified important export and investment opportunities abroad in order to ensure the sustained participation of its domestic firms in these global industries. In contrast, the state in South Korea relied on domestic production, market protection, and indigenous technological development that in turn isolated its domestic firms from much of the dynamism of these networks, such as new technologies, fast and responsive suppliers, and sophisticated end users (Dedrick and Kraemer 1998, 24). The future of industrial policy in fast-moving global industries therefore demands a much more outward-looking mentality among policymakers. The logic of industrial policy in a globalized world economy necessitates the comprehensive mapping of these networks and their differential points of entry for latecomer economies. As argued by Breznitz (2007, 208), this globalization of production makes it much more necessary for emerging economies "to map what kind of capabilities, business models, and relationships with the global production networks their industry will have. By deciding how and where to locate the main R&D conducting agents, nurturing particular relationships with leading MNCs both inside and outside their borders, and influencing the role of foreign financiers and financial markets, emerging economies can partly shape the development path of their rapid innovation industries." The top-down and command-economy-type of industrial policy of the earlier era is simply too rigid and slow to cope with the enormous challenges and opportunities in a global economy coordinated by these sophisticated interfirm production networks (Ernst 2009, 48).

Second, this call for a more calibrated approach to bridging the sectoral-functional divide in industrial policy brings us to the possibilities of *focusing* on niche policies that nudge strategic coupling with global production net-

works. As industrial production becomes ever more fragmented and globalized, state planners and their advisors in newcomer economies will find it even
harder to identify exactly the products and technologies that should be developed in their domestic industries. This increasing complexity in devising appropriate industrial policy to promote late industrialization tends to reduce
the value of state inducement for resolving the Gerschenkronian collective dilemmas. The obstacles to economic development are less about large capital
outlays and scale of investment than about developing specialized niches
within different global industries. Reflecting on the failure of Taiwan's industrial policy in developing a domestic automobile industry, Cunningham et al.
(2005, 131) argue that "the policy prescriptions of a 'little-niche' world are very
different than a 'big-push' world. Rather than pursue grandiose industrial
policy, government agencies could provide market advice (e.g., sponsoring
trade fairs, facilitating relations with buyers, etc.) and work to develop and dis-
seminate new technologies and production techniques within and between
sectors." They note that Taiwan's competitiveness in the automobile industry
rests with OEM production, aftermarket part makers, and auto suppliers rather
than full-scale domestic assemblers such as South Korea's Hyundai and Kia
examined in chapter 6.

In most global industries characterized by vertical specialization and modularization (e.g., transport equipment, ICT, agro-food, and so on), a niche approach to industrial policy is likely to yield stronger coupling of domestic
firms with global production networks than a Gerschenkronian big spurt approach to state-led industrialization. Indeed, this nudging approach may not
produce grandiose industrial complexes of the size and scale that match South
Korea's chaebol shipyards and automobile plants or Taiwan's Hsinchu Science-
Based Industrial Park. But it does offer a more realistic pathway to achieving
capitalist development in the Global South. One such niche approach is about
developing favorable policies, such as start-up supports and financial and social incentives for returnees, to engage more systematically with transnational
communities of technopreneurs and managerial actors. As examined earlier
in my empirical chapters, these communities of what Saxenian (2006) calls
"the new Argonauts" are particularly conducive to the strategic partnership
mechanism of coupling with global lead firms. National policymakers should
make a conscious effort to identify such transnational actors who have established themselves abroad in different global industries. The technological,
managerial, or entrepreneurial instincts of these new Argonauts are likely to
be different from those embedded in the "home" economy. Because of their
international perspectives and experience, these transnational actors are more
likely to identify and take advantage of the opportunities arising from vertical specialization in global production. Tapping into their knowledge and network repertoires can allow economic planners and policymakers to develop a
more thorough understanding of the GPN relevance of their existing national
capabilities and positions in value-chain segments.

In more practical terms, engaging these transnational communities can enable a more direct participation in global industries through new enterprise formation and the capability development of domestic firms. Such a niche approach of tapping into social capital for industrial transformation, however, needs not be possible only in high-tech industries. In more traditional industries, such as agro-food processing and consumer goods manufacturing, the key intermediaries in global production networks are quite different. Engaging with transnational communities who hold important positions in these intermediaries (e.g., international trading companies and sourcing and supply chain firms) is equally critical to the successful "plugging" of domestic firms into respective market or industrial segments. This practice of building strong bonds with transnational communities from the same national economy can be helpful to the upgrading of skills and knowledge, ranging from industrial to services and managerial skills that might be lacking among domestic firms and institutional actors. Complementing the more horizontal policies of education, training, technical and infrastructural support to firms, it goes a long way in enhancing the capability of domestic firms in coupling with other domestic or foreign firms in order to enter into specialized niches within global industries.

Third, the *politics* of industrial and sectoral choice is much more confounded by the growing uncertainties inherent in today's capitalist global economy. When the three East Asian economies began their industrial transformation in the 1960s and the 1970s, highly selective sectoral industrial policy promoting labor-intensive industries and heavy and chemical industries was relatively straightforward.[33] Described by Wade (2014b, 793) as the Mark I version, the developmental state erected trade and nontrade barriers to protect specific domestic infants and/or incumbent monopolies. To Wong (2011, 17), the developmental state was merely engaging in mitigating risks through "upgrading and technological 'catch-up,' compelling firms and industry to move into sectors they otherwise would have eschewed if left on their own." As these industries become much more mature today, value creation and capture tends to be much greater in new innovation-based industries in both manufacturing and service sectors. In these dynamic new industries (e.g., nanotechnology, biomedical, green-tech, and digital media), catching up is not just a matter of Gerschenkronian capital investment led by state-controlled financial institutions and elite industrial development agencies. The sheer complexity and wide ranging set of actors with specialized knowledge and expertise and interests and priorities in these industries makes it rather unruly for bureaucratic targeting through even well-coordinated industrial policy. Some of these new industries also involve serious social and environmental concerns that far exceed the technocratic politics internal to the state or its restricted set of elite actors. To Evans (2014), resolving these concerns entails a new kind of state embeddedness in society and demands the dense sets of interactive ties to connect the state's apparatus administratively and politically to civil society.

In biotechnology, for example, Wong (2011, 14) finds that the myriad of uncertainties inherent in developing such a new industry "involves gambling on a more distant process of innovation, in which the results are intrinsically uncertain, rather than on a particular product, application, or firm. Bets are now being made on the uncertain potentialities of innovation instead of on proven winners. The state has not retreated into obscurity, but rather, decision makers have been forced to bet differently. The political economy of state leadership in science-based industries such as biotech has evolved beyond the postwar developmental state." Even in the ICT industry examined in my empirical chapters, the challenge to industrial upgrading has shifted from a fast-follower strategy toward a strategy of balancing firm-industry level upgrading and national-global integration. To Ernst (2010, 316), the challenge for industrial policymakers and corporate planners is significant and continuous—"the right balance is a moving target, it is context specific and requires permanent adjustments to changes in markets and technology." In such a challenging world of extraordinary uncertainties, industrial policy is but one political approach to industrial transformation and economic development. As argued recently by Evans (2014), the practice of a new kind of industrial policy for promoting capability expansion in the national economy signals the transition from a highly selective developmental state to a capability-enhancing state that pursues collective goals defined by a broad cross-section of civil society, rather than responds to the subjectively defined, immediate, and particularistic demands of industrial elites.

What then are the possibilities for a new political economy of development in this complex global economy? The possibility for a continual role of the state in economic development is predicated less on its transformative role than on its repositioning as a transformed institution of contemporary capitalism. Experience from earlier statist transformations in advanced industrialized economies points to several arenas of engagement for this transformed institution.[34] As well explained in Kwon (2004) and Haggard and Kaufman (2008), the need for social policy may come to trump industrial policy, as the state becomes less a harbinger and more a catalyst of the capitalist system. Levy et al. (2006, 134) therefore argue that "the road to a more market-centered political economy is paved with new state interventions. Specifically, getting the state out of industrial policy may require getting the state into social and labor market policy." This repositioning of the state toward social provisions in East Asian economies is likely to be much more pronounced in the near future. It is important, however, to note that this transformation in state role is not about searching for a "state-free" option for statist political economies; it is rather a question of *how* (not whether) to increase state spending. The fundamental uncertainties in the global economy require national responses to globalization or external processes that may take the form of a redeployment of the state in ways akin to the Schumpeterian form of institutional creative destruction.

As the developmental state enters into Wade's (2014b, 794) Mark II form, becomes more adaptive to global challenges, and delegates more of its steering role in industrial development to domestic firms and their international partners, its role should evolve with the strengthening of these domestic and foreign firms in industrial transformation. This coevolution of state policy agendas with the strategic coupling of domestic firms with global production networks has led to what Whittaker et al. (2010, 439) call "policy stretch," as the state has to adapt to a new reality of global complexity and simultaneous challenges at home. Evans (2010, 37–38; original italics) also cautions against a "cookie cutter" approach to (re)constructing capability-enhancing developmental states in the twenty-first century and argues that "only a flexible, creative process of exploration and experimentation that pays careful attention to local institutional starting points will succeed. . . . My argument is that a successful 21st century developmental state will have to have all the capacities of the 20th century version and *others in addition*." Looking forward, I believe this adaptive postdevelopmental state should focus on creating broad-based capabilities in new technologies, product and process innovations, and market development rather than on choosing specific winning firms, industries, or sectors. The state can be more effective as an adaptive institution whose primary economic role must coevolve with private sector capitalists. As argued by Khan and Blankenburg (2009, 338), successful industrial policy must be compatible with domestic political economies that enable the state to create incentives and compulsions in critical areas. In the post-2008 crisis world, Wade (2010) has recognized this need for a "renewed" developmental state that hinges on an even balance between the state and business groups, inculcates a public service mindset among state officials, ensures delivery of patronage resources separately from the economic bureaucracy, and provides an industrial extension service, with tight limits on its officials' discretionary control of resources. To him, a large part of this renewed developmental state "should be of the incremental, nudging, followership kind rather than picking the winners kind" (Wade 2010, 156).[35]

In the final analysis, the archetypical East Asian developmental state of the 1960s and the 1970s might well have occupied just a peculiar historical and geographical interregnum. Its near extinction or, at least, reconfiguration in today's globalized world economy does not exempt the capitalist state from its broader guardian role in economy and society. Yet this evolving state formation throws into sharp relief a new mode of economic development based on the strategic coupling of national firms with global production networks. Elucidating this evolutionary shift of the state-firm role in industrialization and its transformational mechanism in a world of global production networks has been the primary goal of this book. I hope future research into the international political economy of late development can take some cues from this work and avoid the debilitating market-state dichotomy so prevalent in our existing understanding of East Asian development.

Appendix

Research Methodology

The primary empirical evidence presented in this book originates from a major transnational research project in which personal interviews with top executives of leading East Asian firms were conducted in South Korea, Taiwan, Singapore, and Hong Kong. Between June 2004 and 2008, my research team conducted more than one hundred personal interviews with CEOs, managing directors, presidents, and other senior executives from a total of seventy-two leading East Asian firms: thirteen in South Korea, twenty-three in Taiwan, sixteen in Singapore, and twenty in Hong Kong. These firms were selected on the basis of their operating revenue or turnover as given in the OSIRIS database published by Bureau van Dijk Electronic Publishing, a comprehensive database with detailed financial information on publicly listed companies worldwide. We selected the top fifty firms from each of the four economies and approached them for personal interviews with their top executives. Among the seventy-two leading East Asian firms interviewed, sixteen were in the top ten and twenty-nine were in the top twenty, ranked by operating revenue in their respective home economies. In UNCTAD's *World Investment Report* database, four of them were ranked among the top fifteen and another fifteen among the top one hundred transnational corporations (TNCs) from developing economies.

Appendix table 1 documents the positions of sixty-nine interviewees among the fifty-two leading firms from South Korea, Taiwan, and Singapore. Some twenty-seven were chairmen/CEOs/presidents or managing directors, whereas another thirty-one were executive directors, general managers, or (senior/executive) vice presidents. In some cases (e.g., Samsung Electronics), personal interviews with several top executives were conducted. In all interviews lasting between one to two hours, we took an open-ended approach and used only brief interview aides. Extensive background information from all available public sources was consulted to form the basis of highly customized qualitative

Appendix Table 1 List of East Asian firms interviewed and the positions of interviewees

	Name of company	Category A	Category B	Category C	Total
	South Korea				
1	Daewoo International	1			1
2	Hyundai Engineering & Construction	1	2		3
3	Hyundai Mobis	1	1		2
4	Hyundai Motor Company	1			1
5	Korean Airlines		4		4
6	LG Chemical		1	1	2
7	LG Electronics			1	1
8	Samsung Corp		1		1
9	Samsung Electronics		4	1	5
10	Samsung Heavy Industries		1		1
11	Samsung SDI		1		1
12	SK Corporation		1	2	3
13	SK Telecom			1	1
	Subtotal	4	16	6	26
	Taiwan				
1	Acer Inc.	1			1
2	Arima Group	1			1
3	AU Optronics	1			1
4	BenQ	1		1	2
5	Cathay Financial Holdings	1			1
6	China Airlines		1		1
7	Compal Electronics			1	1
8	Delta Electronics	1			1
9	Macronix International	1			1
10	Mosel-Vitelic Inc.	1			1
11	Nan Ya Plastics		1		1
12	Nanya Technology		1		1
13	ProMOS Technologies	1			1
14	Quanta Computer		1		1
15	Siliconware Precision			1	1
16	Synnex Technology	1	1	1	3
17	Taiwan Cellular		1		1
18	Taiwan Semiconductor Mfg Co			1	1
19	Teco Electric		1		1
20	VIA Technologies		1		1
21	Winbond Electronics		1		1
22	Yageo Corp	1	1		2
23	Yang Ming Marine		1		1
	Subtotal	11	11	5	27

Appendix Table 1B List of East Asian firms interviewed and the positions of interviewees

| | Name of company | Number of interviewees | | | |
		Category A	Category B	Category C	Total
	Singapore				
1	Capitaland Limited		1		1
2	Chartered Semiconductor (CSM)		1		
3	Hong Leong Asia Ltd	1			1
4	Keppel Corp	1			1
5	MMI Holdings	1			1
6	Natsteel		1		1
7	OLAM	1			1
8	SembCorp Industries	1			1
9	Singapore Petroleum	1			1
10	Singapore Press Holdings (SPH)	1			1
11	Singapore Technologies Engineering (ST Engg)	1			1
12	Singapore Telecommunications (SingTel)		1		1
13	STATS ChipPAC	1			1
14	TT International	1			1
15	Venture Corp	1			1
16	WBL	1			1
	Subtotal	12	4		16
	Total	27	31	11	69

Category A: chairman/CEO/president/managing director
Category B: COO/(Sr) vice president/general manager
Category C: senior manager
Source: Author's fieldwork.

questions during each interview. All except one interview were taped and transcribed. Almost all interviews in Hong Kong, Taiwan, and Singapore were in English. Apart from these corporate interviews, we also conducted another sixteen personal interviews with top government officials, such as directors general and directors, in various state ministries and nonstate institutions that are directly involved in economic planning and industrial development. These institutions are detailed in Appendix table 2. Collectively, almost eighty-five qualitative transcripts have been obtained and transcribed, and this massive amount of primary data form the main empirical basis of this book.

During our fieldtrips in these East Asian economies, we collected a significant amount of quantitative and qualitative data and material on general economic development, industrial policies, business environments, and political change in these economies. This secondary dataset is highly useful in contextualizing my empirical analysis.

Appendix Table 2 List of East Asian state and nonstate institutions interviewed and the positions of interviewees

Institution	President or director general	Director	Manager or specialist
South Korea			
1 Export-Import Bank		1	
2 Korea Automotive Research Institute	1		
3 Korea International Trade Association		1	
4 Ministry of Commerce, Industry and Energy		1	
Taiwan			
1 Ministry of Economic Affairs—Department of Industrial Technology		2	1
2 Ministry of Economic Affairs—Department of Investment Services			2
3 Ministry of Economic Affairs—Industry Development Bureau		1	1
4 Ministry of Economic Affairs—Bureau of Foreign Trade	1		1
5 Taiwan Confederation of Trade Unions	1		
6 Taiwan External Trade Development Council	1		
Singapore			
1 International Enterprise Singapore	1		
Total	**5**	**6**	**5**

Source: Author's fieldwork.

Notes

1. East Asian Development in the New Global Economy

1. "Apple Reinvents the Phone with iPhone," January 9, 2007, Apple's press release, http://www.apple.com/pr/library/2007/01/09Apple-Reinvents-the-Phone-with-iPhone.html, accessed on November 7, 2014.

2. Dan Graziano, "IDC: Samsung Passes Apple to Become No.1 in Smartphones," May 1, 2012, http://www.bgr.com/2012/05/01/apple-samsung-idc-market-share, accessed on November 7, 2014.

3. Apple's iPhone data are from Sam Costello, "How Many iPhones Have Been Sold Worldwide," March 9, 2015, http://ipod.about.com/od/glossary/f/how-many-iphones-sold.htm, accessed on May 14, 2015. Samsung data are from "Gartner Says Smartphone Sales Surpassed One Billion Units in 2014," March 3, 2015, Gartner press release, http://www.gartner.com/newsroom/id/2996817, accessed on June 23, 2015.

4. A 2010 World Bank report on the post-2008 world economy, for instance, claims that global value chains "have become the world economy's backbone and central nervous system" (Cattaneo et al. 2010a, 7). Analysts in many international organizations now recognize global value chains and global production networks as the new long-term structural feature of the global economy. See, for example, OECD 2011, 2013; Elms and Low 2013; OECD-WTO-UNCTAD 2013; and UNCTAD 2013.

5. Quoted in Charles Duhigg and Keith Bradsher, "How the U.S. Lost Out on iPhone Work," *New York Times*, January 21, 2012. See also Pisano and Shih 2009; 2012.

6. Charles Duhigg and David Barboza, "In China, Human Costs Are Built into an iPad," *New York Times*, January 25, 2012. See also Lorraine Luk, "Foxconn Struggles to Meet New iPhone Demand," *Wall Street Journal Digits*, September 17, 2014.

7. Company-specific data are from Bloomberg Businessweek online database, http://investing.businessweek.com, accessed on April 10, 2015.

8. Through its market-leading production of high-value crucial processor and memory chips, for example, Samsung accounted for an astonishing 47 percent of the US$169.40 value-added in the manufacturing of each iPhone 4 (OECD 2011, 40). At US$80.10, Samsung's value-added to each iPhone 4 far exceeded Apple's own inputs from the United States, valued at US$24.60.

9. See chap. 2 for a critical discussion of this literature, and Woo-Cumings 1999a; K. S. Chang et al. 2012; and Haggard 2015 for further reappraisal.

10. The state is defined in this book as a set of contested institutional structures and social practices that possess specific power and authority to effect changes and to achieve specific policy goals.

11. I give a brief reprise of this diverse literature in chap. 2. Note that the developmental state literature is quite diverse. Recent critiques of the conventional wisdom are O'Riain's (2004) "developmental network state," Breznitz's (2007) "neo developmental state" of choice, and Pirie's (2008) "neoliberal developmental state." Hundt (2009) offers a study of changing state-capital relations in the form of a "developmental alliance" over time, whereas Wong (2011) challenges the state's capacity in steering industrialization under the condition of uncertainty.

12. Recent works are not unanimous about the changing role and capacity of the developmental state in guiding innovative high-tech industries. Breznitz (2007) believes in the "neo-developmental state" of choice, whereas Wong (2011) argues that the decentralization of functional expertise within the state has seriously weakened state leadership. The increasing complexity and uncertainties associated with globalized high-tech industries also mean that state bureaucrats are simply unable to cope with the challenge.

13. Compared with Taiwan Semiconductor Manufacturing Company (TSMC), a world-class semiconductor wafer fabrication foundry much celebrated in the developmental state literature, Hon Hai Precision is a quiet achiever. In fact, neither Hon Hai Precision nor its subsidiary Foxconn Technology are mentioned in the best-known works published on the developmental state in Taiwan (e.g., Wade 1990) or on the success of Taiwan's ICT industry in the global economy (e.g., Hobday 1995; Dedrick and Kraemer 1998; Mathews and Cho 2000; Breznitz 2007). Hon Hai's success is relatively recent and is discussed in chaps. 4 and 5.

14. Samsung was one of the few chaebol groups whose founders had accumulated wealth under Japanese colonial rule (Woo 1991, 66; Amsden 1989, 235–38). By the 1950s, founder Byung-Chull Lee had already owned a small rice mill, some real estate, and a trading concern. In 1969, the Electronics Industry Promotion Law was enacted to stimulate domestic investments, and Samsung began its electronics production in a joint venture with NEC and Sanyo of Japan (Hobday 2000, 136; Mathews and Cho 2000, 106). The fourth Five-Year Plan of 1977–1981 further specified the electronics industry as a key sector. In this context, the developmental state was imperative in inducing Samsung and Hyundai to diversify into electronics. Chapters 3 and 5–6 give a detailed empirical discussion of the contemporary industrial prowess of these South Korean chaebol groups.

15. I note two relatively recent and parallel schools in international political economy: the global value chain approach (Gereffi 1994; Gereffi et al. 2005) and the global production networks perspectives (Dicken et al. 2001; Henderson et al. 2002; Coe et al. 2004; Yeung and Coe 2015). See Parrilli et al. 2013; and Neilson et al. 2015 for an integration of these two strands of the literature and Coe and Yeung 2015 for an integrated theory of these cross-border production networks.

16. South Korea and Taiwan are uncontroversial choices; most of the original works on the developmental state focused on these two economies. Singapore seldom features in the literature, in part because it is much smaller: to Wade (1990, 34), Singapore is so minuscule in population and national income that it is really a "gnat," not a "tiger." This substantial difference in size makes the comparative analysis of the evolution of state-firm relations in these three economies very interesting. As I show in later chapters, the Singapore state is not only developmental in the conventional sense, but unlike South Korea and Taiwan, its continuity and efficacy also remain strong in the 2000s.

17. We might theorize strategic coupling (process) and firm-specific initiatives (action) as constitutive of a *mechanism* of industrial transformation. Such a theorization speaks well to the social mechanism literature in analytical sociology (Hedström and Swedberg 1998a; Hedström and Wittrock 2009; Demeulenaere 2011; Manzo 2014), political science (Elster 1989; Tilly 2001; Checkel 2006; Gerring 2008; 2010; Falleti and Lynch 2009; Sil and Katzenstein 2010), and the philosophy of social science (Stinchcombe 1991; Bunge 1997; 2004; Reiss 2007). However, I leave the task of conceptually integrating the initiative-process-mechanism terminology to chap. 7. By holding back this conceptual language of mechanisms in the earlier chapters, I aim to focus on my core argument of strategic coupling and on bringing greater clarity to the empirical analysis.

18. This book is not primarily an in-depth political study of state evolution. The changing nature of the developmental state is an important, but not ultimate, part of my analysis.

Rather, my central purpose is to develop a new concept (strategic coupling) and to elucidate its core components (meso-level processes) in the globalizing context of economic transformations in three East Asian economies since the 1990s. I thank an anonymous reader at Cornell University Press and Peter Katzenstein for this insightful comment.

19. Similarly Dedrick and Kraemer (1998, v–vi) argue that neither the market nor the plan/developmental state perspective can fully explain the transformation of East Asian industrialization: "We discovered that the plan versus market, or country versus company, dichotomy was useful in focusing the analysis but provided insufficient explanation for the differences observed. We identified a new force . . . the emergence of a 'global production network' that operated more or less independently of company or country boundaries and was based on a changing international division of labor."

20. I have chosen not to pursue a chronological narrative of the developmental state. Such historical-analytical strategy can be found in the classic works to be examined in the next chapter.

21. The management literature (e.g., Mathews 2002; De Meyer et al. 2005; Yeung 2007b) tends to emphasize firm-specific corporate strategies and competitive advantages, thereby ignoring the wider historical and institutional contexts from which these East Asian firms have emerged. Management researchers also pay insufficient attention to how the performance of an individual Asian firm can be linked to its participation in global production networks.

22. Concluding his *State-Directed Development*, Atul Kohli (2004, 377–78) offers a clear rationale for these state interventions in their historical context: "Private investors in late-late-developing countries need organized help, help that effective states are most able to provide to overcome such obstacles as capital scarcity, technological backwardness, rigidities in labor markets, and to confront the overwhelming power of foreign corporations and of competitive producers elsewhere. . . . As I review this evidence, the general position I come to is that the global economy offers both opportunities and constraints to developing countries and that much depends on how well state authorities are situated to maneuver."

23. In Rodrik's (1995) economic analysis of East Asian state interventions, this "organized help" is deemed critical to removing what he termed "coordination failures" in economies where the latent return to investment was already high due to availability of initial conditions, such as high levels of educational attainment relative to income and relatively equal distribution of income and wealth that insulated political leadership from social pressures.

24. In comparison, South Korea had a far smaller public enterprise sector. The percentage share of state-owned enterprises in gross fixed capital formation under the Park Chung Hee regime (1961–1979) dropped from 31.2 percent in 1963 to 22.8 percent in 1980 (Wade 1990, 177, table 6.2).

25. For an early analysis of state finance in the East Asian economic success, see Skully and Viksnins 1986. This critical, but often underestimated, point is well recognized in two early works on South Korea's industrialization (Cole and Park 1983; Woo 1991).

26. See also Wade's (1990, 175–82) discussion of the role of public enterprises in Taiwan's industrialization between the 1950s and the 1970s.

27. For a brief history on the role of British capital in preindustrial Singapore up to 1959, see Rodan 1989; and Huff 1994.

28. Examples of these foreign banks were HSBC, Standard Chartered, and Citibank. Major local ethnic Chinese banks were United Overseas Banks, Overseas Chinese Banking Corporation, and Overseas Union Bank (acquired by United Overseas Banks in 2001). See Hamilton-Hart 2002 for further details on Singapore's banking sector before and after 1965.

29. See studies of Singapore's public housing program in Tremewan 1994; Chua 1997; and Sung 2006. The state was active through the Housing and Development Board (HDB) in the provision of public housing and in "correcting" distortions in the housing market, which has assisted the reproduction of (cheap) labor for deployment by export-oriented production (Castells et al. 1990; Tremewan 1994). The HDB has the statutory rights to use capital from the national saving scheme, the Central Provident Fund, for constructing heavily subsidized public housing. At its peak in 1990, almost 87 percent of Singapore's resident population was living in

public housing. The ratio declined only slightly to 82 percent in 2014. Data from the HDB website, www.hdb.gov.sg, accessed on April 10, 2015.

30. As we shall see in the subsequent chapters, the much greater access to financial resources among national firms in these three East Asian economies since the late 1980s has led to the gradual decline in the state's capacity to implement its industrial policy through credit allocation. One may thus argue that the availability of policy loans and other financial incentives was instrumental in the developmental state's success only in the earlier period of industrialization.

31. For detailed accounts of these elite bureaucracies, see Chibber 2002; and Lim 2010 on South Korea; Wade 1990; Wu 2005; and Greene 2008 on Taiwan; and Low et al. 1993; Schein 1996; and Chan 2002; 2011 on Singapore's Economic Development Board.

32. Its predecessor was the Council for United States Aid (CUSA) established in 1948 to plan the use of US aid funds. Wade (1990, 199) notes that "because U.S. aid constituted a large part of the economy's investment, CUSA was in effect a central planning agency." After a mission to South Korea's Economic Planning Board in 1977, the state decided to increase the power of its planning agency and renamed the EPC to the CEPD. See Haggard and Zheng 2013 for a reassessment of this institutional evolution during the 1950s–1970s period.

33. It is useful to note that the PAP was then a very young political party established by Lee Kuan Yew and his close political allies only on November 21, 1954. After a turbulent period of political struggles against the socialist Left and the British colonial administration, Lee's PAP won the general election in May 1959 and was ushered in as the dominant ruling party in modern Singapore, a position it has held ever since (Rodan 1989, 56–62; Rodan and Jayasuriya 2009, 27–28).

34. One of the best examples is the chaebol in South Korea. The growth and development of the chaebol is often seen as the direct policy outcome of the developmental state in South Korea, particularly during its early phase of heavy industrialization in the 1970s under President Park Chung Hee. See examples of Hyundai Heavy Industries and POSCO in Amsden 1989. Writing in the late 1980s, Woo (1991, 15) reflects that "Daewoo did not even appear until the late 1960s. The others [Hyundai and Samsung] did not grow into anything big until the 1970s; thus, the conglomerates are a very recent phenomenon."

35. White and Wade (1988, 12; my emphasis) also point out in their introductory chapter to *Developmental States in East Asia* that "what none of the chapters on Taiwan and South Korea say much about is the basis of state power, the way it is organised, or the micro principles with which officials make allocation decisions. *Still less* do they talk about the *organisational arrangements* that coordinate activities within business firms, and those that link them to government. These are exceedingly important questions."

36. To Jayasuriya (2005, 386), this statist view of East Asian development "now shows all the hallmarks of a degenerating research programme that is no longer capable of setting out an interesting or relevant agenda." Similarly, O'Riain (2004, 27) argues for understanding the constitutive role of globalization in state-led development because "under the globalization project, transnational firms, networks and flows of money, information, and resources have deeply penetrated the most successful localities and nations—the global is no longer a context for developmental strategies but rather a constitutive element of them."

37. The importance of large firms, particularly transnational corporations, in the global economy is best examined in Peter Dicken's (2015) *Global Shift*.

38. For an analysis of transnational corporations as interorganizational networks, see Gulati 2007. As Dunning and Lundan (2008, 490) point out, "Such systems enable firms to structure and locate each part of their value chains more closely in line with the existing comparative resource and institution advantages of countries (for example, in Asia and Latin America), while also allowing for the dynamic reconfiguration of these assets, depending on the role assigned to the affiliates, and their degree of integration with local firms."

39. Some examples are Hatch and Yamamura 1996; Borrus et al. 2000; and Hatch 2010.

40. In his more recent work, Evans (2008, 293) provides an example of such strategic coupling with labor activism in the newly industrialized economies and argues that "production networks created by transnational corporations offer another case in which global power

structures and local oppression are intimately connected, generating global-local activist networks in response."

41. Some classic works informing this study are Nelson and Winter 1982; and Teece 2009. Their ideas are incorporated into my conceptual discussion in chaps. 2–3.

42. See the Appendix for details on my research methodology and original empirical materials. Apart from deploying a wide range of secondary materials, my primary data are based on personal interviews with sixty-nine top executives in more than fifty leading firms and with sixteen senior government officials in eleven state institutions in South Korea, Taiwan, and Singapore conducted between 2004 and 2008. Most of these fifty firms belonged to the top thirty firms in these economies, and almost half of my interviewees were CEOs or chairmen. This comprehensive dataset underpins most of my detailed case studies in the empirical chapters.

43. Reflecting on this "market versus state debate" in understanding East Asian development, Hobday (2001, 25) is quite right in arguing that "because of the dominance of this debate, there are few studies which derive 'bottom-up' policy conclusions from firm-level studies. The activities and strategies of firms in engaging with international production networks cannot be properly accounted for within theories of the developmental state, as latecomer firm behaviour tends to be treated (usually implicitly) as an automatic response to policy and economic circumstances, rather than as a shaping influence in its own right."

2. Transformation of State-Firm Relations in the 1980s and the 1990s

1. In a critique of the "declinists," Thurbon (2011, 7) argues for defining the developmental state in terms of its "relentless pursuit of common *ends*—specifically the goal of catching and keeping-up with advanced industrialised countries for nation-building (and nation-sustaining) purposes." While this *ends* definition is necessary, it is not sufficient because what distinguishes a true developmental state from a wannabe is the state's capacity to *achieve* such ends through dirigste means. This is why much debate in the literature has focused on the institutional capacity of the developmental state. Missing this critical ends-means linkage in defining a developmental state will simply lead to "an inevitable conceptual slippage whereby any evidence of policies that seek to leverage maximum benefits from foreign investments or support industrial innovation is taken as proof that the developmental state remains a relevant concept and model for emulation" (Pirie 2013, 147).

2. Interestingly, this idea of embedded autonomy was anticipated in the earlier work of Cumings (1987) and White and Wade (1988). Cumings (1987, 71) deploys the term *bureaucratic-authoritarian industrializing regimes* to describe the strong states that had emerged in Taiwan and South Korea by the mid-1960s. To him, these states were "ubiquitous in economy and society: penetrating, comprehensive, highly articulated, and relatively autonomous of particular groups and classes." In a similar vein, White and Wade (1988, 10; emphasis added) use this notion of autonomy to describe the state in both Taiwan and South Korea: "Both governments have been centrally concerned to prevent emerging groups from acquiring autonomy from the state, to prevent independent channels of interest aggregation from forming. The strategy has been to create groups whenever the leadership sensed needs or demands for groups in the population, in order to be able to control them. The result is that in both countries the central state managers have had *unusual autonomy* (in a capitalist context) to define national goals, and unusual powers to get those goals accomplished, without having to enter into the bargaining and shifting alliances such as has characterised the policy process even in the more authoritarian regimes of Latin America."

3. Kohli (2009, 406) calls this "difficult ISI" initiated by developmental states committed to creating modern but sovereign political economies to help mobilize domestic resources, limit foreign capital, and build indigenous technology and industry. This contrasts sharply with the pursuit of "easy ISI" in Latin America where "Latin American rulers often meant enhancing national incomes so that a narrow ruling class could rapidly join the lifestyles of Europeans and Americans, with whom they identified." As evident briefly in chap. 1, the nationalization of industries in the early phase of development in Taiwan during the 1950s falls somewhere between these "difficult ISI" and "easy ISI."

4. In his later reflections, Johnson (1999, 42–43) admitted that his model exhibiting four main attributes of Japan's developmental state was added at the persistent request of his chief editor at Stanford University Press. Well-known follow-ups of this initial model can be found in Haggard 1990; Wade 1990; Evans 1995; Weiss 1998; Woo-Cummings 1999; and Chibber 2002. In his work on state types and industrialization, Kohli (2004, 10n14) substitutes the developmental state with his own concept, the "cohesive-capitalist" state. In this book, I have retained the use of "the developmental state" term primarily because it is a widely accepted concept, albeit often abused, caricatured, and misunderstood, in the study of industrial transformation of the three East Asian economies. I will return to the question of bureaucratic coherence in the next section of this chapter, which casts doubt on the validity of the "cohesive-capitalist" state.

5. Johnson's (1982) original model of four elements is folded into Wade's (1990) points 3 and 5.

6. This phenomenon was first described by Johnson (1995, chap. 7) in his detailed historical analysis of Japan's practice of "descent from heaven," or *amakudari*.

7. This comment requires further elaboration, as theory development was not the explicit goal of Johnson (1982) and Amsden (1989), the two earliest proponents of the developmental state. Their work was primarily empirical in the sense that they respectively used historical evidence in Japan and South Korea to counter the then prominent neoclassical and dependency explanations of economic growth and rapid industrialization in developing economies. It was not until Evans (1995) in *Embedded Autonomy* that an explicit theory of the developmental state was articulated in order to explain *why* such state-led interventions in industrial transformation could be possible and effective. This theoretical articulation of the developmental state has been very influential in the subsequent understanding of the developmental state's efficacy in steering industrial change and private investments through its "midwifery" and "husbandry" roles. See Fine 2013 (20) and Haggard 2015 for recent critical reassessments of this developmental state paradigm as "buzz" and "fuzz."

8. In his recent work, Evan (2014) has attempted to reconceptualize the developmental state as a "capability-enhancing" state. This rethinking emerges from his critical assessment of evolution in state roles since the 1980s.

9. These original studies are associated with founding proponents such as Johnson 1982; White 1988; Amsden 1989; Haggard 1990; Wade 1990; and Evans 1995.

10. Some contemporary examples are Lim 2010; Thurbon 2011; and S. Y. Kim 2012 on South Korea; Hu 2012 on Taiwan; and Pereira 2008 on Singapore. But even in Thurbon's (2011) study of South Korea, she has shown that the chaebol were unwilling to follow the state's "requests" to invest in service robotics that had been designated as a strategic industry in 2003.

11. As lamented by Jayasuriya (2005, 383; my emphasis), "developmental state theorists, because they understand 'policy capacity' as a set of *fixed* institutional endowments or attributes, are unable to grasp how these capacities change in response to broader changes in the constellation of social and economic interests." His view of stateness as transformation and building rather than as an ensemble of institutions per se is broadly similar to the earlier theoretical views on the state as a constellation of networks (Mitchell 1991) and strategic relations (Jessop 1990). This relational view also supports Chibber's (2002, 956) critique that the apportionment of power among state institutions, i.e., intrastate relations and interagency power configuration, is a crucial dimension for understanding the developmental state.

12. For examples of this institutional continuity, see Weiss 2003a; Kalinowski 2008; Thurbon 2011; and Evans 2014 on South Korea; and Haggard and Zheng 2013 on Taiwan.

13. These classics are White 1988; Amsden 1989; Rodan 1989; Bello and Rosenfeld 1990; Haggard 1990; Wade 1990; Woo 1991; Hart-Landsberg 1993; and Kohli 2004. Wade (1988; 1990), for example, published his well-known work after four months of fieldwork in Taiwan in 1983 (Wade 1988, 60) and another two months in Taiwan in 1988 (Wade 1990, 50–51). The narratives in Amsden's (1989) seminal work on South Korea, while spanning the early postwar period to the mid-1980s, focus mostly on the 1960s and the 1970s.

14. These examples are Cumings 1987; Amsden 1989; Woo 1991; Hart-Landsberg 1993; Kohli 2004; and Pirie 2008. To Cumings (1987, 71), Japan's colonial influence on the emer-

gence of the bureaucratic developmental state in South Korea and Taiwan was very signifi-cant. Kohli (2004, 51n77) also argues that the cooperation between the Japanese colonial state and some Korean capitalists meant that "Korean capitalism as a 'system' was being cre-ated under Japanese tutelage."

15. This term was coined by David Scott (1999, 7) with reference to neoclassical and de-pendency explanations in development studies during the 1970s.

16. As argued by Sil and Katzenstein (2010, 420–21) in the context of world politics, "there is little agreement on what constitutes a causal mechanism" beyond its positioning in explain-ing how some set of initial conditions (e.g., state-led initiatives) in one or more contexts gener-ates some set of outcomes or variations: "Many interesting mechanisms operate across time and space, but we need to leave open the possibility of singular phenomena having ef-fects in the same manner that recurrent phenomena can. Neither generality and constancy, nor specificity and complexity need to be intrinsic attributes of a mechanism" (see also Falleti and Lunch 2009).

17. Up to the late 1990s, TSMC and UMC were given only a short discussion in two key books on innovation in the ICT industry in East Asia (Hobday 1995, 106–7; Dedrick and Krae-mer 1998, 168). Their presence in the analysis of the global semiconductor industry was only apparent in the 2000s, e.g., Mathews and Cho 2000; and Breznitz 2007.

18. See examples of in-depth studies of these global production networks and global value chains in Gereffi et al. 2005; Cattaneo et al. 2010b; Sturgeon and Kawagami 2011; Lüt-hje et al. 2013; Ferrarini and Hummels 2014; and Coe and Yeung 2015.

19. My empirical material is based on primary interviews with relevant state officials and institutions in all three East Asian economies and secondary sources in the existing literature. See the Appendix for more details on my interviews and interviewees.

20. While Wade (1990) was interested in the developmental state's efficacy of using eco-nomic policy to govern and lead the market (e.g., his seven policies on 27), his analysis of Taiwan focused particularly on industry-specific policy through trade and investment man-agement, more broadly known as vertical or sectoral industrial policy. He defined the out-comes of this state governing the market as state followship versus state leadership of the market (cf. a typology of four state roles in Evans 1995). In evaluating the efficacy of indus-trial policy, however, Wade (1990, 32–33) was acutely aware of the intractable problem of counterfactuality (see also Pack and Saggi 2006; H. J. Chang et al. 2013).

21. For example, even into the 1990s, Wade (2003, xl) acknowledges "the state in Taiwan continuing to act more as a developmental state than as an Anglo-American liberal market state. The state in Taiwan continues to exercise foresight about the future evolution of the economy and acts to pave the way; it takes a view about what industries are important for the economy's future growth, and has the legitimacy and the instruments to help shape the econ-omy in line with this view" (see a recent reprise in K. S. Chang et al. 2012). But as I will show shortly, this political legitimacy and efficacy of policy instruments was undermined by signifi-cant domestic and international changes during the 1990s.

22. For a comparative study of the effects of democratization on financial reforms in South Korea and Taiwan in the late 1990s and the 2000s, see Lim 2009.

23. See a special issue of *Asian Survey* in 2007 on the developmental state ten years after the crisis (Dittmer 2007).

24. See Lee's (2007) detailed study of the making of *minjung* as political movements in the 1970s and the 1980s. For more in-depth analysis of South Korea's pathway to democ-ratization, see also Saxer 2002; S. Kim 2003; and Diamond and Shin 2014.

25. L. Kim (2000, 337) observes that "while promoting liberalization publicly, govern-ment technocrats behind the scene have tried to maintain their orchestrating role even dur-ing the 1980s and 1990s. Their self-interest in preserving their bureaucratic power and the inertia to continue the existing practice has inhibited the dynamic growth of private initia-tives. As a result, many government developmental programs were inappropriately applied or were many steps behind the private sector." Similarly, Chung (2007, 89) argues that "the five-year economic development plans in the decades of the 1980s and 1990s could be character-ized more as indicative than as directive."

26. For a detail discussion of the KMT state and politics between 1949 and 1987, see Tien 1989. For helpful discussion of post-1988 politics in Taiwan, see Gold 2000; Tan 2000; Lee 2010; Cabestan and deLisle 2014; and Diamond and Shin 2014.

27. However weak opposition voices were, the 1980s marked the new beginning of opposition politics in Singapore. In a landmark event, the PAP lost to the Worker's Party in a by-election for the Anson constituency held on October 31, 1981. This was the first time since Singapore's independence that a PAP candidate lost an election for a seat in Parliament.

28. Space constraint does not allow me to go into detail about the various political instruments and tactics used by Lee Kuan Yew and his PAP to secure such an unlikely string of wins in all general elections. Among these, the most controversial was Lee's introduction of the Group Representation Constituencies (GRCs) in 1988 through the amendment of the Parliamentary Elections Act. See Mauzy and Milne 2002 and Chong 2007 for a critical analysis of the PAP and its domination in Singapore's domestic politics.

29. After taking over from Goh Chok Tong, Prime Minister Lee Hsien Loong took the PAP to victory again with 66.6 percent of all votes and 82 out of 84 seats in Parliament in the May 2006 general election. In the September 2015 general election, Lee led the PAP to win 69.86 percent of all votes and 83 out of 89 seats in Parliament. He is the elder son of Lee Kuan Yew and served as deputy prime minister in Goh Chok Tong's cabinet between 1990 and 2004.

30. Much of the developmental state literature does not give due attention and credit to the role of East Asia in Cold War geopolitics between 1950 and 1980 and, in particular, the United States as the "ultimate guarantor" of state intervention in East Asia. A few exceptions are Woo 1991, chap. 3; Hart-Landsberg 1993, chap. 7; Doner et al. 2005; Greene 2008, chap. 3; Pirie 2008, chap. 4; and Gray 2011. But the most influential studies of the developmental state, such as Johnson 1982; Amsden 1989; Haggard 1990; Wade 1990; and Evans 1995 are rather muted when it comes to the complex relationships between geopolitical imperatives and state capacity, particularly during the export-industrialization drive in the 1960s through to the 1980s. This depoliticized view in the developmental literature has led Cuming (1999) to suggest the developmental state as "a web without a spider" (see also Pempel 1999, 146–47).

31. For a reprise of how industrialized states maneuver under the WTO regime, see Weiss 2005; and Cimoli et al. 2009b.

32. For more details on these reforms under Kim Young-Sam, see Gills 1996; Chang et al. 1998; Crotty and Lee 2007; Kalinowski and Cho 2009; and Lim 2009.

33. This view is found in E. M. Kim 1997; Minns 2001; Zhang 2002; Pirie 2008; and Lim 2009.

34. Interview with the MOCIE. See the Appendix for details on my interviews and interviewees. In 2008, the MOCIE was merged with elements of the Ministry of Information and Communication, the Ministry of Science and Technology, and the MOFE to form the Ministry of Knowledge Economy (MOKE).

35. This change was reversed in 2013 by the newly elected president Park Geun-He, daughter of former strong man Park Chung Hee, who attempted to take industrial policy more seriously.

36. Fields (1995, 27) also notices this less aggressive nature of the KMT state in Taiwan and its effects on its bureaucratic coherence: "As the economic limitations of this conservative policy have become more apparent and the political and social roots of the state's strength have declined, conflicts over appropriate policy both within the state and between the state and the business groups have undercut the internal coherence and autonomy of the state and its capacity and will to curtail the growth of the business groups."

37. Other examples of the weakening of state bureaucrats' coherence and autonomy from private sector interests in the post-Park era are found in S. J. Chang's (2003, 62) analysis: resistance of state directives by Daewoo's chairman Kim who blatantly demanded secured state funds to save Daewoo Shipbuilding from bankruptcy in 1988; Hyundai's Ju-yung Chung's running for the presidency in 1992; several chaebol chairmen's public acknowledgment of illicit contributions of political funds to presidents Chun and Roh in 1994; and Samsung's chairman Lee publicly denouncing the South Korean government as being third rate in 1995.

38. The MOIC did not last long. In February 2008, the newly elected president Lee Myung-bak abolished the MOIC and dispersed its officials and functions to newly created institutions

such as the Korea Communications Commission (KCC) and the Ministry of Knowledge Economy (MOKE). Rather than a single quasi-pilot agency, South Korea has witnessed the creation of multiple quasi-pilot agencies since the mid 1990s (Lim 2010, 198; S. Y. Kim 2012, 153–55).

39. See in particular Ngo 2005; Wu 2005; and Greene 2008.

40. Concluding his chapter on the economic bureaucracy in Taiwan, Wade (1990, 227) points to hostility and disagreements between the Ministry of Economic Affairs and the Ministry of Communications in relation to the use of public procurement of telecommunications as a strategic industrial policy tool to induce US companies to transfer advanced semiconductor technology to Taiwanese firms during the early 1980s.

41. This observation comes from my interviews with senior bureaucrats from three sections of the Ministry of Economic Affairs: the Department of Industrial Technology, Industry Development Bureau, and the Department of Investment Services.

42. The Department of Investment Services has a long heritage. It was formerly the Industrial Development and Investment Center established in 1959.

43. More sector-specific consultative bodies were created to bring together officials and representatives from related agencies, universities, national labs and research organizations, and industry associations. These bodies offered sector-specific information and policy recommendation for the various ministries in charge of economic development.

44. Both men had outstanding civil service credentials serving in Singapore's elite Administrative Service. Philip Yeo was permanent secretary in the Ministry of Defence (1979–1985) before becoming chairman of EDB in 1986. Tan Chin Nam served in the Ministry of Defence under Yeo's charge between 1977 and 1982. After his EDB stint, Tan served as chief executive of the Singapore Tourism Board (1994–1997), and permanent secretary of the Ministry of Labour (1997–2002) and the Ministry of Information, Communications and the Arts (2002–2007).

45. Current prime minister Lee Hsien Loong was minister for trade and industry (minister of state, 1984–1985 and acting minister, 1986, and minister, 1987–1992) who chaired the Economic Committee in 1985 to recommend new directions and policies for the Singapore economy.

46. Of the fifteen alumni listed on the EDB Society website, four served as ministers in various cabinets: S. Dhanabalan (1980–1993), Yeo Cheow Tong (1985–2006), Lim Swee Say (1999–present), and Lee Yi Shyan (2006–present), http://www.edb.gov.sg, accessed on November 16, 2014.

47. In the financial sector, Hamilton-Hart (2002) notes that the political leadership is entwined with leading members of the financial community. Several former and current ministers and top civil servants have links with three local banks in various capacities as former chairmen and directors. See also Yeung 2002; 2011 for an analysis of the interlocking directorship of cabinet ministers in Singapore's two sovereign wealth funds—Government Investment Corporation of Singapore and Temasek Holdings. Singapore's central bank, the Monetary Authority of Singapore (MAS), can hardly be seen as independent of the state. The president of Singapore appoints its senior management. The deputy prime minister and concurrently minister of finance, a former managing director of MAS, chairs its nine-member Board of Directors that includes three other ministers and one permanent secretary from the Ministry of Finance (http://www.mas.gov.sg, accessed on November 20, 2014).

48. Apart from the problem of counterfactuality (Pack and Saggi 2006), H. J. Chang et al. (2013) further argue that many important industrial policy measures cannot by definition be captured through quantifiable indicators. In the context of South Korea's "Big Push" in the 1970s under Park Chung Hee's developmental state, such measures included: (1) coordination of complementary investments; (2) coordination of competing investments; (3) policies to ensure scale economies, e.g., licensing conditional on production scale, emphasis on the infant industries starting to export from early on, state-mediated mergers and acquisitions; (4) regulation on technology imports; and (5) regulation on foreign direct investment.

49. These industry-specific policies were particularly important to Wade (1990, 28) because "it is in the histories of specific industries that one can most clearly see the government in action." But he went on to qualify this assertion by stating that the mere existence of these policies does not necessarily mean the state governing or leading the market, because

"they might merely put the government's seal of approval on some private sector projects by way of mild assistance for something that private firms would have done anyway in response to price signals alone." He described these passive sectoral policies as "hand-waving" or "window-dressing." Where sectoral industrial policy really made a difference and became "market leading," the state would take initiatives to encourage particular products or technologies and put public resources or influence behind these initiatives.

50. In reality, even functional industrial policy involves some degree of targeting. Karl Aiginger, a key author of the European Commission's industrial policy, argues that "the effects of broad horizontal policies can vary significantly from industry to industry, that competitiveness needs specific policy mixes for specific sectors, and that some sectors may require complementary measures that are not necessary or relevant in other sectors" (quoted in Aiginger and Sieber 2006, 579). H. J. Chang et al. (2013, 8) thus sum up that "given all this, we have to admit that we cannot 'not target' and should try to attain the best possible degree of targeting, which may differ across industries and countries." To Evans (2014), this practice of horizontal industrial policy remains critical to redefining the developmental state as capability enhancing or capability expanding. In this sense, even the archetypical neoliberal market state of the United States has been seen as a "hidden" developmental state through its national security-driven science and technology policies (see Block 2008; Block and Keller 2011; Mazzucato 2013; Wade 2014a; and Weiss 2014; cf. Fine 2013; Pirie 2013).

51. For example, under the Roh Moo Hyun administration (2003–2007), South Korea's spending on welfare increased substantially, from 17 percent of the state budget to 27 percent (Suh and Kwon 2014, 686). For studies of social welfare and economic policy in the three East Asian economies, see Kwon 2004; Wong 2004; and Diamond and Shin 2014. Haggard and Kaufman (2008) provide an excellent overall analysis of economic development and welfare provisions.

52. To Chen (2014), this shift from sectoral to functional industrial policy in Taiwan is most evident in the state's nurturing of high-tech industries and promoting the development of SMEs, as encapsulated in the abolition of the Statue for the Encouragement of Investment (sectoral industrial policy) and the enactment of the Statue for Upgrading Industries (functional industrial policy) in 1990. In Singapore, this industrial upgrading was particularly important in the electronics industry (Wong 1995; Perry and Tan 1998; McKendrick et al. 2000; Yeung 2007a), the petrochemical industry (Wang and Yeung 2000), and the biomedical industry (Tsui-Auch 2004; Pereira 2008; Wong 2011).

53. Chen (2014) argues that trade policy played a limited role in Taiwan's shift toward horizontal industrial policy in the 1990s. Although the Taiwan Relations Act of 1979 stressed the continued US commitment to Taiwan's security, Taipei suffered numerous diplomatic setbacks, including the expulsion of Taiwan from the United Nations. Due to complicated international legitimacy and diplomatic relations, Taiwan was able to join the World Trade Organization only in January 2002 and its first free trade agreement (FTA) was signed with Panama in 2004. These political conundrums led to immense difficulties for state agencies to establish trade and investment contacts with other countries. This issue on Taiwan's external trade relations is based on my interviews with senior officials from the Department of Industrial Technology, the Board of Foreign Trade, the Department of Investment Services of the Ministry of Economic Affairs, and Taiwan External Trade Development Council.

54. Singapore's case of the developmental state entering into a cooperative alliance with foreign capital contrasts sharply with South Korea's reliance on technonationalism through which legal and bureaucratic mechanisms were evoked to regulate the interaction of the domestic economy with foreign capital (see Mardon 1990).

55. In his analysis of the historical construction of this ideology of pragmatism in Singapore's political authoritarianism, Tan (2012, 69) argues that "the combination of ideological and pragmatic manoeuvring over the decades has resulted in the historic dominance of government by the PAP in partnership with global capital whose interests have been advanced without much reservation."

56. For a recent review of this enormous literature on innovation capability building and learning in latecomer firms, see Bell and Figueiredo 2012.

57. This dynamic perspective has been well developed in evolutionary theories of economic change, industrialization, and business competition, such as Gerschenkron 1962; Nelson and Winter 1982; Chandler 2000; Nelson 2005; and Teece 2009. For empirical studies of specific East Asia economies, see L. Kim 1997; Amsden 2001; and S. J. Chang 2003 on South Korea; Mathews 2002 and Amsden and Chu 2003 on Taiwan; and Amsden and Tschang 2003 and Yeung 2007a on Singapore.

58. For example, Amsden (2001, 2; original italics) argues that "the rise of 'the rest' was one of the phenomenal changes in the last half of the twentieth century. For the first time in history, backward countries industrialized *without proprietary innovations.* They caught up in industries requiring large amounts of technological capabilities without initially having advanced technological capabilities of their own. Late industrialization was a case of *pure learning,* meaning a total initial dependence on other countries' commercialized technology to establish modern industries. This dependence lent catching up its distinctive norms." But such a learning perspective tends to focus narrowly on resource endowments, such as technological capabilities. Whittaker et al. (2010, 444ff.) thus critique the dependency on learning through licensing and reverse engineering in Amsden's (1989) work by arguing that the rapid pace of technological change makes such borrowed technologies obsolete quickly (see also Breznitz 2007; Wong 2011).

59. Chapter 4 will detail the historical development and globalization of the electronics industry in these three economies.

60. By the late 1990s, even Samsung Electronics derived about two-thirds of its sales from OEM contracts with global lead firms, such as Tandy, Unisys, HP, Apple, IBM, Dell, and Tektronix (Guillén 2010, 755). Explaining how LG could catch up rapidly in the mobile phone business since its first entry in the late 1990s, my interviewee notes that "we actually have a fair amount of know-how about production which was accumulated through ODM and OEM experiences. If a new product is developed, it will not take us a long time to manufacture it in volume" (interview with LG Electronics).

61. Mathews and Cho (2000) and Hung and Tang (2008) have analyzed different technology acquisition modes by South Korean and Taiwanese electronic firms between 1985 and 2004. In South Korea, the seven largest chaebol accounted for around 60 percent of South Korea's total payments for royalties and fees by the end of the 1990s (Guillén 2010, 755). Other studies of technological innovation in East Asia also found the decreasing reliance of East Asian firms on advanced industrialized countries for technologies and the increasing regionalization of knowledge flows within East Asia (e.g., Hu 2009). Chapters 4–5 will detail the technological dynamics of leading East Asian firms in the computer electronics and semiconductors industries.

62. Chapter 5 will detail the competitive dynamics of these three East Asian firms in the global semiconductor industry.

63. Interview with TSMC.

64. TFT-LCD refers to the thin film transistor-liquid crystal display industries. See Mathews 2006 and Hu 2012 for two detailed analyses of the newcomer strategy and process innovation among South Korean and Taiwanese firms entering the market during industrial downturns in the mid-1990s.

65. Interview with AU Optronics. See also Chuang 2008.

66. The best known work is Saxenian's (2006) study of Taiwanese returnees shuttling between Silicon Valley and Hsinchu Science-Based Industrial Park (see also Haggard and Zheng 2013).

67. For example, Samsung employed Dr. Yim-sung Lee who held a Ph.D. from Stanford and had worked for Sharp, General Electric, and IBM. Dr. Lee brought with him four others who had worked for American semiconductor firms. Dr. Sang-joon Lee was previously in charge of semiconductor manufacturing process development at Control Data and Honeywell. Dr. Il-bok Lee developed 64K DRAMs at Intel and National Semiconductor. Dr. Jong-gil Lee was an expert in improving the production yields at Intersil and Synertek. Dr. Yong-eui Park was a memory chip designer at Western Digital and Intel.

68. In 1991 another competing chaebol, Hyundai, hired Dr. Min Wi-Sik, who had worked for Intel in the previous six years, to lead its 4MB DRAM development work. Dr. Min came

with substantial and wide experience in the semiconductor industry and managed to bring a 4MB DRAM to market in time to profit from the upswing cycle of the industry (Mathews and Cho 2000, 108).

69. Interviews with Samsung Electronics. With a Ph.D. from Stanford University, Dr. Kwon became the vice chairman of Samsung Electronics in 2011 and its CEO in 2012.

70. Chyi et al. (2012) shows positive domestic and international knowledge spillovers among a panel of ninety-two high-tech firms located in the Hsinchu Science-Based Industrial Park between 2000 and 2004.

71. The success of returnees in driving high-tech industries in South Korea and Taiwan during the 1990s, however, did not lead to a substantial increase in new students going abroad. In fact, Keller and Pauly (2003, 150, 153) observe a decline of US universities in training semiconductor Ph.D. students from Taiwan and South Korea since the mid-1990s. The number of Taiwanese receiving semiconductor-related Ph.D.s from US universities decreased from a high of 296 in 1995 to 173 in 1998. The same decline occurred to South Koreans receiving semiconductor-related Ph.D.s from US universities, from a high of 185 in 1994 to 116 in 1998. This trend can be partly explained by the greater domestic demand for engineers and technical staff in these economies since the mid-1990s that in turn reduces the incentives for overseas studies.

72. Interview with Macronix.

73. Lu first joined the state-funded Electronics Research Service Organization (ERSO), established in 1974 as a part of ITRI, as a deputy director general in the late 1980s and was responsible for the grand submicron project initiated by the Ministry of Economic Affairs. This project successfully developed Taiwan's first eight-inch, high-density DRAM/SRAM manufacturing technology and was subsequently spun off from ERSO in 1994 to form Vanguard International Semiconductor Corporation, with Lu as its first president.

74. Interview with AU Optronics and BenQ.

75. The fact that Singapore has many fewer such technologist returnees is telling about its small population size and the dominance of foreign firms in its ICT industry.

76. Wong (2011, chap. 2) shows the limited role of public funding in developing the biotech industry in the three East Asian economies.

77. For data from 1965 to 1998, see L. Kim 2003 (99, table 4.1); 2003–2008 data are from Ministry of Education, Science and Technology (http://english.mest.go.kr, accessed on November 20, 2014).

78. This information is based on Smith 2000 (73, table 2.12) and the 2012 GDP National Statistics, Directorate-General of Budget, Accounting, and Statistics, Executive Yuan (DG-BAS), available at http://eng.stat.gov.tw, accessed on May 15, 2014.

79. See Chu 2007 (166) and Fuller 2007 (213–14) for an analysis of the declining role of ITRI in steering the integrated circuits industry since the late 1990s. At the time of Vanguard's spin-off in 1994, large private firms launched major attacks on the perceived waste of public funds in such state-sponsored projects, and the Legislative Yuan decided to halve ITRI's annual budget. This limitation of ITRI-related labs also occurred in lower-technology sectors such as machine tools in the 1980s and the 1990s. In Chen's (2009, 531) study, local machine tools firms complained about the technological incompetence of ITRI's Mechanical Industrial Research Laboratories that introduced leading technologies with little application or commercialization value. These domestic firms relied on informal linkages with local customers, international trade shows, and foreign deals for their knowledge acquisition and learning opportunities.

80. See chap. 5 for a full empirical analysis of these spin-offs and global competitive dynamics in the semiconductor industry.

81. Interview with senior officials from the Department of Industrial Technology, the Ministry of Economic Affairs.

82. Fuller (2005, 152), for example, suggests that by the late 1990s, the unwillingness of such large semiconductor firms as the TSMC and UMC to participate in the state-sponsored R&D consortium (e.g., ASTRO) was the direct contributor to its inability to secure large state funding and its eventual termination. Since the implementation of the Science and Technology Basic Law in 1999, the role of state-sponsored research institutes has also been limited to strengthening the marketing and technological capability of small- and medium-sized enter-

prises, rather than as the technology-creating agent or the main provider of R&D services and technology channeling (Hu and Mathews 2009).

83. Wu and Mathews's (2012, 537) recent study of the emergent solar photovoltaic industry in South Korea and Taiwan shows that the development of new generation solar photovoltaic technologies in both economies has been dominated or initiated by the private sector since 1996. State-sponsored institutes are either late in Taiwan (joining only in the early 2000s) or in gradual retreat in South Korea (after the entry of Samsung and LG in 2002).

84. Interview with TSMC.

85. Interview with TSMC. A similar experience is shared by my interviewee from AU Optronics. Reflecting on the development of the TFT-LCD industry since the mid-1990s, he notes that "actually the government tried to support this industry by setting up the research project inside the government organization such as ITRI. But actually these people didn't turn out good products. They just became good talents for us to access. . . . We didn't invite any help from the government for that. But when we set up the deal with Japanese companies to transfer the technology, the whole industry became very self-reliant and autonomous." He believes that state support in human resource development and global branding of Taiwan's products is useful. But "in technology and development, we don't need the government's support." By May 2003, AU Optronics had 1,026 patents granted, another 1,398 patents pending, and more than two thousand R&D personnel.

86. After the 1997–1998 financial crisis, nearly all of these twenty-four merchant banks went bankrupt and were permanently closed (Hahm 2003, 87–88, 99). The state nationalized many bankrupt financial institutions by absorbing their bad debts to the tune of some US$140 billion (Crotty and Lee 2007, 84).

87. See Liu and Yang 2008 (825–26) for an analysis of these changes in the 1980s. While not exhaustive, major examples of initial public offering (IPOs) are Acer and Delta in 1988; Compal in 1992; SPIL and Yageo in 1993; TSMC in 1994; Macronix, MVI, Synnex, and Winbond in 1995; BenQ in 1996; Arima in 1998; Quanta Computer and VIA in 1999; and Nanya Technology in 2000 (interviews with all firms, company annual reports, and Taiwan Stock Exchange online database, http://www.twse.com.tw, accessed on October 26, 2014).

88. In his speech at the Singapore Economic Policy Forum 2010, Ravi Menon, permanent secretary of the Ministry of Trade and Industry, notes that Singapore's industrial policy during its first three decades of industrialization was "not simply a case of 'picking winners.' . . . Besides a focus on overcoming market failures, a distinguishing feature of Singapore's industrial policy is its strict adherence to market principles. The Government has never subsidised the running costs of firms. There are no protective barriers. There are no bailouts. The market, not Government, decides whether a company is viable. Many firms have gone under; many others have relocated from Singapore to more cost-competitive locations" (Quoted in *Straits Times*, October 25, 2010, A25).

89. For example, several former and current ministers and top civil servants have links with three local banks in various capacities as former chairmen and directors, e.g., former deputy prime minister and now president Tony Tan with Overseas Chinese Banking Corporation, former cabinet minister S. Dhanabalan with the state-controlled Development Bank of Singapore, and former EDB chairman Philip Yeo with United Overseas Bank. See also Yeung 2011 for an analysis of the interlocking directorship of cabinet ministers in Singapore's two sovereign wealth funds—Government Investment Corporation of Singapore and Temasek Holdings.

90. The president of Singapore appoints its senior management. The deputy prime minister and concurrently minister of finance, a former managing director of MAS, chairs its ten-member Board of Directors, which includes three other ministers and one permanent secretary from the Ministry of Finance. Information from the website of the Monetary Authority of Singapore, http://www.mas.gov.sg, accessed on May 15, 2015.

3. Strategic Coupling

1. My approach to conceptualization draws on John Gerring's (1999; 2012) important methodological work on concept formation and causal relationships as multiple pathways of

analyzing causation. Following his work on case study, my central purpose is to use detailed empirical material in the next three chapters to elucidate the concept's constitutive components, rather than to focus on its causal effects on economic development. Gerring (2004, 348) argues that "case studies enjoy a comparative advantage" in the identification of causal relationships through process-tracing and pattern-matching (see also Sayer 2000; Yeung 2003). But I differ from his view that it is sufficient for social science "to prove a causal relationship without having a clear supposition about the causal mechanisms at work" (Gerring 2010, 1506). I believe that the unpacking of these causal relationships along with an explanation about how a particular analytical concept works should be a necessary step in any causal analysis. I will return to this important epistemological issue of causal mechanisms in the concluding chap. 7.

2. This concept of strategic coupling with global production networks was first developed in Coe et al. (2004) and further elaborated in Yeung (2007a; 2009a; 2014). The concept has since been central to understanding industrial transformation and regional development in a number of recent conceptual discussions (Coe and Hess 2011; Mackinnon 2012; Coe and Yeung 2015; Yeung 2015).

3. For an integrated theory of these cross-border production networks in their own right, see Coe and Yeung's (2015) *Global Production Networks*.

4. See also Teece et al. 1997; Yeung 2002 and 2009b; Wong 2011; and Yeung and Coe 2015.

5. See also Scott 1988; Harrison 1994; Peck and Yeung 2003; Coe and Yeung 2015; and Dicken 2015.

6. There is a very large body of literature explaining this changing organization of the global economy in relation to global production networks or global value chains. Some of the most influential works are found in economic sociology (Gereffi 1994; 2014; Bair 2009), international political economy (Henderson et al. 2002; Gereffi et al. 2005; Neilson et al. 2014; 2015), economic geography (Dicken et al. 2001; Sturgeon 2002; Coe et al. 2004; 2008; Yeung 2009a; 2015; Yeung and Coe 2015), development studies (Ernst and Kim 2002; Humphrey and Schmitz 2002; Pietrobelli and Rabellotti 2011), and international economics (Feenstra 1998; Antràs and Helpman 2004; Antràs and Chor 2013; Milberg and Winkler 2013). See Coe and Yeung 2015 for a critical review and comprehensive reassessment of this literature.

7. See recent studies in Saxenian 2006; Zhou 2008; and Lüthje et al. 2013.

8. The previous professional experience of these transnational elite entrepreneurs in global lead firms is highly important to this strategic coupling process. Two classic examples from Taiwan are Macronix's founder Miin Wu who worked in Siliconix and Intel and was a founding member of VLSI Technology, and TSMC's founder Morris Chang who worked for Texas Instruments as its head of global semiconductor operations and, later on, became president of General Instruments. See also Liu et al.'s (2005) comparative study of the two entrepreneurial founders of TSMC and UMC.

9. See Coe and Yeung 2015 for an in-depth analysis of these competitive dynamics and their impact on lead firm strategies and the changing configurations of global production networks.

10. In arguably the most influential paper on global value chains, Gereffi et al. (2005) explain how these chains are governed by lead firm buyers or producers through modular, relational, or captive interfirm relationships. Each governance type is dependent on the role of the complexity and codifiability of interfirm transactions and supplier capabilities. My argument for strong interfirm partnership in global production networks is broadly similar to their characterization of modular and relational chain governance.

11. On the importance of systems integration to firm-specific capability building, see Hobday et al. 2005 and further elaboration in chap. 4.

12. A full analysis of the different fates of these state-initiated semiconductor firms will be offered in chap. 5.

13. See Haggard and Zheng 2013 (456ff.) for a case study of Taiwan's functional industrial policy for developing the Hsinchu Science-based Industrial Park.

14. As noted by an interviewee from MMI Holdings, a leading supplier of precise base plates for Seagate's hard disk drives, the EDB made a conscientious effort in the 1980s to establish the hard disk drive industry and to nurture promising local enterprises by coupling

them with global lead firms, such as Seagate and Toshiba. For a full history of Seagate's evolution with Singapore's hard disk drive industry, see McKendrick et al. 2000.

15. For an earlier excellent and yet underappreciated study of such collective action in industrial policy in East Asia, see Noble 1998.

16. Interview with the Department of Industrial Technology, the Ministry of Economic Affairs.

17. Interview with the Industrial Development Bureau, the Ministry of Economic Affairs.

18. In Gereffi et al.'s (2005) typology, this form of governance relationship in global value chains is considered as "captive" in nature because OEM customers have full control of their captive subcontractors.

19. This coupling process of strategic partnership is similar to Gereffi et al.'s (2005) modular or relational conception of governing global value chains.

20. This empirical proxy, however indicative, remains unsatisfactory because it does not differentiate the ownership and control of firms producing such goods in each of these economies. A country with a large presence of foreign firms, such as China and Mexico, may well have a significantly lower share of global trade in IMG by their domestic firms. Such entrepôts as Hong Kong and Singapore are also more likely to enjoy a greater share in the global IMG trade because of their transshipment functions in global production. In short, we need to probe in depth into firm-specific activities in order to understand fully such network embeddedness.

21. It should be noted that domestic manufacturing firms from all three East Asian economies have made substantial investment in production facilities in China, particularly in the electronics and machinery industries. They were regularly ranked among the top ten foreign investors in China between the 1980s and 2014 (see official statistics on foreign direct investment in http://www.fdi.gov.cn, accessed on October 20, 2014). A significant portion of China's trade in IMG can therefore be attributed to these East Asian firms.

22. For more detailed accounts of these changes in business groups, see Chang 2006a; Chung and Mahmood 2010; and H. Kim 2010.

23. Chang et al.'s (2006) comparative study of business groups in South Korea and Taiwan between 1991 and 1999 shows that affiliates of these groups tended to be more innovative during the period of weak domestic institutional structures due to changing state roles.

24. This greater domination by the chaebol has led Hundt (2014, 509–11) to characterize state-chaebol relations in the 2000s as a "degraded" form of developmentalism in which "the Korean elites adopt a strategic perspective on economic development, and use market-based instruments strategically in areas such as industrial policy and foreign investment. Moreover, the state's structural relationship with, and dependency on, the chaebol creates strong incentives to correct periodic corporate profligacy and dysfunction. State elites have adopted elements of neo-liberalism, and their commitment to strategic economic management remains intact, even if the state's capacity to discipline the chaebol has weakened."

25. As evident in Smith's (2000, chap. 4) detailed analysis, this shift in South Korea's industrial policy toward functional policies in support of industrial upgrading and sustaining losers started as early as in the 1980s. See also my analysis of changing state roles in chap. 2.

26. Interview with Daewoo International Corporation. See the Appendix for details on my interviews and interviewees.

27. This emergence of Samsung, LG, and Hyundai Motor as global lead firms will be analyzed in detail in chap. 6.

28. Chapter 5 will examine empirically the industrial leadership of both Hyundai Heavy Industries in shipbuilding and Hynix in semiconductors.

29. This increase in the share of foreign capital in publicly held stocks in South Korea was clearly dramatic, from a manageable 15 percent in 1997 to 22 percent in 1999 and 37 percent in 2001. Foreign shareholding of the top ten chaebol groups rose further to 54 percent by early 2005. Even Samsung Electronics, the leading chaebol, was 53 percent majority owned by foreign investors by the end of 2004 (interview with Samsung Electronics). Another leading chaebol construction firm, Hyundai Engineering and Construction, was also no longer controlled by the founding Chung family, but instead by several large bank creditors such as Korea Exchange Bank, Korea Industrial Bank, Woori Bank, and Kookmin Bank. Smaller shareholders

held only 34 percent of the total shares (interview with Hyundai Engineering and Construction). In 2011, Hyundai Motor Company successfully acquired the majority shareholding block of Hyundai Engineering and Construction from its bank creditors.

30. While the state nationalized many bankrupt financial institutions after the 1997 Asian financial crisis by absorbing their bad debts to the tune of some US$140 billion, many of these institutions were subsequently sold to mostly American private equity firms—48.6 percent of Korea First Bank to Newbridge Capital in 1999 and 50.5 percent of Korea Exchange Bank to Lone Star Funds in October 2003 at a knockdown price of US$1.2 billion (Crotty and Lee 2007, 84–85; Kim and Lee 2007, 114–16; Hamilton-Hart 2008, 60). Newbridge Capital subsequently sold Korea First Bank to Standard Chartered Bank in April 2005 for US$3.4 billion or almost seven times its purchase price. The bank was renamed SC Jeil Eun Haeng (SC First Bank). Meanwhile, Lone Star Funds sold Korea Exchange Bank to Kookmin Bank in March 2006 for US$5.2 billion, or over four times its purchase price.

31. Interview with LG Electronics.

32. Interviews with Hyundai Engineering and Construction, Hyundai Mobis, Hyundai Motor Company, and LG Chemical.

33. Interview with the Industrial Development Bureau, the Ministry of Economic Affairs.

34. In Wade's (1990, 28–29) conception of state roles, this would be considered as "big followership" since the state continues to offer functional policies and indirect assistance that extend the margin of firm-specific investments.

35. The sensitive nature of this quotation precludes me from identifying the name of the company.

36. As noted by an IDB interviewee, "In Taiwan's government, only the IDB is doing the 'guiding the industries' task. Other state agencies are more on the regulatory side. So when we promote industries, we will involve other departments and even local government regulations. We have to communicate and negotiate and mediate . . . that's the challenge" (interview with the Industrial Development Bureau, the Ministry of Economic Affairs).

37. Ibid.

38. This observation is based on interviews with three agencies in the Ministry of Economic Affairs: the Board of Foreign Trade, the Department of Industrial Technology, and the Industrial Development Bureau.

39. While the development state initiated these SOEs in lieu of the weak indigenous industrial capitalists during the 1960s and the early 1970s (Rodan 1989; Yeung 2011), the state and its financial holding firm, Temasek Holdings, did not engage in sectoral industrial targeting and discretionary subsidies to promote these SOEs. As Temasek's CEO, Ho Ching, noted at the Asia Business Leader's Award Dinner at the Banqueting House in London on October 27, 2014, "From the start [in 1974], the Government took a hands-off approach to Temasek. Subsidies were most definitely out of the question. Neither Temasek nor the Government would be there to bail them out. With the accountability came the responsibility to make their own decisions." (http://www.temasek.com.sg/mediacentre, accessed on November 1, 2014).

40. See my earlier detailed analysis in Yeung 2002; 2011.

41. See also an analysis of the internationalization of these GLCs in Yeung 2000; 2011; and Chong 2007 (961–69).

42. Interview with Keppel Corporation.

43. Some of these leading firms were established in the late 1980s or the early 1990s, particularly those in the ICT and trading sectors. While having a much longer history, the five firms in the banking and real estate sectors have grown massively to become the major regional players in the East and Southeast Asian region.

44. Similarly in their state-centric approach to latecomer upgrading policies in Taiwan, Amsden and Chu (2003) are quite right in crediting the developmental state for its role in stepping into the technological vacuum during the early decades of industrialization and for its "midwifery" role (Evans 1995) in promoting new growth poles and industrial clusters. But in their enthusiastic support of this continual state-led development, they have invariably overlooked the growing significance of translocal forces and processes that have begun to shape East Asian development since the late 1990s.

4. Strategic Partnership in Global Electronics

1. The classic works in the developmental state literature that examine specifically the electronics industry are Bello and Rosenfeld 1990; Evans 1995; Amsden and Chu 2003; O'Riain 2004; Breznitz 2007; and Greene 2008.

2. My choice of electronics as the industrial case study in this chapter does not mean that other sectors (e.g., services) and industries (e.g., textiles and garments and chemicals) are not important in the articulation of these East Asian economies into different global production networks. Nevertheless, the success of East Asian firms in these diverse sectors and industries is not as broad-based and consistent as in the electronics industry. The complex and yet highly competitive nature of the global electronics industry has also made it a particularly relevant case for examining the dynamics of industrial transformation in these three "Tiger" economies.

3. The case of semiconductors will be discussed in detail in chapters 5 (TSMC, Samsung, and others) and 6 (Samsung and LG).

4. In *The Rise of "The Rest,"* Amsden (2001) examines the changing composition of manufacturing value-added of 'the rest' (i.e., the Global South) vis-à-vis the North Atlantic and Japan between 1980 and 1995 and concludes that "Sectors in 'the rest' that exhibit dynamic comparative advantage are electrical and nonelectrical machinery and transportation equipment. These are among the most challenging sectors to develop because competing in them depends on scale, skills, brand name recognition, and reputation. These sectors were also heavily targeted by the developmental state" (262; emphasis omitted).

5. For a comprehensive analysis of such industrial history and its emergence in the three economies, see Hobday (1995), Dedrick and Kraemer (1998), Mathews and Cho (2000), Ernst (2009), and Lüthje et al. (2013).

6. For some excellent studies of this earlier process of internationalization in the electronics industry, see Fröbel et al. 1980; Henderson 1989; and Dedrick and Kraemer 1998.

7. As early as the late 1960s, Park's authoritarian state targeted electronics as a critical sector since his Promulgation of Law for Electronics Industry Promotion (1969–1976) and the Electronics Industry Promotion Law of 1973. The state provided financial backing and favorable state procurement contracts, and facilitated cooperative information-sharing infrastructure and institutions in order to increase industry production. See Kang 1989 (85–109); and O'Riain 2004 (195). The Fourth Five Year Plan (1977–1981) offered foreign loans of US$221.6 million and established the Electronics and Telecommunications Research Institute (ETRI) with a US$60 million fund (Hobday 1995, 52–53).

8. Domestic electronics firms from all three economies have also performed very well in the global economy. South Korea's Samsung Electronics can now rival Sony and Apple, whereas Taiwan's Hon Hai Precision and TSMC can compete against virtually any leading electronics and semiconductor manufacturers. They have become globally dominant players in the equipment and hardware segment of the digital era.

9. I borrow the term *degraded* from Hundt's (2014) work on South Korea.

10. At the beginning, the state took charge of technological development in the electronics industry by directly funding public research institutes, such as the Industrial Technology Research Institute (ITRI) and its Electronics Research Service Organization (ERSO), which acquired the right kind of technologies and transferred them to industry through such spin-offs as UMC (1980), TSMC (1987), Winbond (1987), and Vanguard (1994). As described by Breznitz (2005, 195), "the public research institutions do most of the research and development (R&D) up to the level of a working prototype, and then they diffuse the results to industry, which concentrates on final development and integrated design. The specificity of this division of labor, in contrast with that found in other countries, stems from the deep level of intervention the state has in the technological capabilities of the industry." See also Tso 2004 (304–5); and Bae 2011 (258–59).

11. Reflecting on Taiwan's electronics industry by the early 2000s, Fuller (2005, 150–51) observes that "Taiwanese electronics firms have also been exposed to new opportunities that influence their strategies and their interaction with the Taiwanese government. Firms have grown in size and capabilities. With this growth, they have felt less inclined to follow the state's lead or even to choose cooperation with the state over other possibilities, such as collaboration with foreign firms."

12. Between 1986 and the mid-2000s, for example, the state put substantial investment in education and seven large-scale science projects. Since the launch of the Hsinchu Science-based Industrial Park in 1979, two additional science parks were developed in south and central Taiwan after 1996 (Chu 2007, 163; Haggard and Zheng 2013).

13. For early work on Singapore's electronics industry, see Rodan 1989; Wong 1995; and Chia 1997.

14. For the globalization of the electronics industry, see Henderson 1989; Hobday 1995; Dedrick and Kraemer 1998; and Dicken 2015.

15. In their analysis of Taiwan's upgrading policies in the electronics industry, Amsden and Chu (2003, 174) also argue that "many national second movers in the 'new' mature high-tech industries of the 1990s owed their existence to the decision by first movers in advanced economies to lower their manufacturing costs by means of foreign subcontracting rather than foreign direct investment. This made it easier in latecomer countries for nationally owned firms to evolve. The international subcontracting decision, however, may conceivably have been only a fashion of the times."

16. In Gereffi et al.'s (2005) conceptualization of governance in global value chains, this shift is critical because it represents a major "upgrading" from captive governance to modular or relational governance structures through which latecomer firms (e.g., from East Asia) are able to improve their position in these evolving chains and to capture more value from their articulation into these chains. Instead of playing a subservient role to global lead firms in the captive mode of governance, these latecomer firms can now cooperate with lead firms as key production partners.

17. See Henderson 1986 and 1989 for these early production networks.

18. For an excellent chronology of these foreign investments in the three East Asian economies, see Mathews and Cho 2000 (appendix 2, 333–47). Henderson (1989, table 3.2, 46–47 and chap. 4) also contains very useful information on the international division of labor among twelve leading US semiconductor firms in Western Europe and East and Southeast Asia.

19. For example, to take advantage of President Park Chung Hee's Promulgation of Law for Electronics Industry Promotion (1969–1976) in South Korea, National Semiconductor from the United States entered into a joint venture with Goldstar Electronics (the predecessor of LG Electronics) to manufacture transistors in 1969. In the same year, Samsung made its first foray into electronics through its joint ventures with Japan's Sanyo and NEC (Mathews and Cho 2000, 106). These joint ventures laid the early foundation of these two chaebol giants in today's global electronics industry.

20. In South Korea, for example, joint venture or wholly owned foreign firms accounted for some 80 percent of total electronics exports in 1968. As late as 1977, some 60 percent of these exports remained handled by foreign firms (Woo 1991, 145). Hobday (1995, 51) thus declares that as of 1980, "South Korea had no substantial position in the electronics industry."

21. In South Korea, for example, several large electronics chaebol were highly active in producing consumer goods for OEM customers. Between 1981 and 1983, for example, Samsung received significant technology transfers from Toshiba (microwave ovens), Philips (color TV), JVC (videocassette recorders), and Sony (VCR) (Hobday 1995, 86). By 1992, videocassette recorders and microwave ovens had become Samsung's main exports, and it had taken a 20 percent share of the microwave ovens market in the United States.

22. See Bae 2011 for an analysis of the initial and differential coupling of South Korean and Taiwanese computer firms with these changing global production networks during the 1980s.

23. Indeed, Wade (1990, 106) has already recognized this phenomenon in his *Governing the Market* and noted that Taiwan "has also benefited from the movement of engineers and researchers back and forth between Taipei and California's Silicon Valley, where Chinese Americans are well represented among the design and computer firms. Some Taiwan firms are now beginning to make cheap, good-quality, though slow-performing, wire-bonding machines. They will soon be challenging Japanese and U.S. makers of other kinds of semiconductor equipment as well."

24. See Yeung and Coe 2015 (35–36) for a development of the concept "cost-capability ratio" in understanding the competitive dynamics of global production networks.

25. Interview with Venture Corp. See the Appendix for details on my interviews and interviewees.

26. As described vividly by Dedrick and Kraemer (1998, 13) in their *Asia's Computer Challenge*, sales of all computer systems grew rapidly from US$55 billion in 1985 to US$157 billion in 1996, and the share of PCs in these total sales more than doubled from 29 percent to over 69 percent between 1985 and 1995.

27. For early studies of this phenomenon, see Hobday 2001; Sturgeon 2002; and Berger and Lester 2005.

28. Based on a Bear Stearns survey of leading brand name electronics firms in the United States at the turn of 2000, Sturgeon (2002, 461–62) points out that 85 percent of these firms would further increase their production outsourcing to the tune of 73 percent of total production needs on average. Some 40 percent of these firms would ultimately outsource their entire final product manufacturing to independent electronics manufacturers.

29. In semiconductors—the industrial segment receiving the most developmental efforts of the home state in all three East Asian economies, leading domestic semiconductor firms have developed reciprocal relationships with global lead firms that require the former's production technologies and scale economies to sustain their own market positions in the rapidly moving world of globalized electronics industry (see a full analysis in chap. 5).

30. Major East Asian firms have also been leveraging on their direct presence in the United States and Western Europe for technological innovation and market development. For some relevant studies, see Poon et al. 2006; and Hsu et al. 2008.

31. See Kawakami 2009 (111–15) for a detailed description of this ODM workflow process in the notebook computers segment of Taiwan's electronics industry.

32. Unless otherwise specified, this case study is based on my interviews with Quanta Computer and other leading ODM firms from Taiwan, such as Compal, Wistron, and Arima. See the Appendix for details on my interviews and interviewees.

33. At their peak in 1989, OEM suppliers in Taiwan produced 69,275,980 calculators (Amsden and Chu 2003, table 2.4). Amsden and Chu (2003, 28; original italics) therefore argue that "in terms of sheer *number* (as distinct from value) of units manufactured, calculators towered over Taiwan's early principal electronic products."

34. Compal became the world's second largest notebook ODM firm by the mid-2000s (see table 4.3).

35. By the late 1990s, Compal was much larger in revenue than Kinpo Electric, its parent company.

36. As of 2012, six to seven of Quanta's vice presidents were formerly with Compal.

37. See Dedrick and Kraemer 1998 (50–53) for a history of IBM's first PC and its role in standard setting and new firm formation (e.g., Microsoft and Intel) in the early 1980s.

38. While the American firm RCA developed the first flat panel display in 1968, it was Japan's NEC and Sharp that respectively produced the first large panels in 1990 and pioneered the mass production of an 8.4-inch display for notebook computers in 1992 (Hu 2012, 541).

39. As shown in Amsden and Chu (2003, table 2.7), the factory unit value of a notebook computer was US$1,090 in 1999, almost three times of the value of a desktop PC (US$369).

40. The quotation is taken from the June 14, 1999 online issue. http://www.businessweek .com/1999/99_24/b3633055.htm, accessed on 10 September 2014.

41. See a similar observation in Kawakami 2009 (121–22).

42. In 1998, Apple was Quanta's first customer to transfer its product configuration-to-order system to the ODM (Kawakami 2009, 117). Quanta cooperated with Apple and brought in consultants and logistics companies to help set up this configuration system. While it took several months to put the system in place, this pioneering initiative had given Quanta an initial competitive lead over other ODM firms in Taiwan that began to follow in 1999.

43. See Yang and Hsia 2007 for a study of this direct shipment model by Taiwan's ODM firms.

44. In 2006, Quanta Display was merged into AU Optronics, led by BenQ.

45. In contrast, the earlier experience of South Korea in the computer industry was rather disastrous, as their techno-nationalist sentiments drove their developmental states into countering/competing rather than partnering with global lead firms (mostly from the United States). As argued by Fuller (2005, 147), "The Taiwanese accepted the Wintel standard and succeeded by being close followers of the lead firms while avoiding the costly and ultimately unsuccessful bets on alternative standards. Thus, dependence on the branded PC firms may actually have proven to be beneficial, with Taiwanese firms undergoing technologi-

cal upgrading and industrial expansion that the technonationalist Koreans can only look at with envy" (see also Fuller 2007, 214).

46. As argued by Breznitz (2007, 113–14), "The existence in Taiwan of local world-leading OEM-ODM companies also propelled the growth of the semiconductor industry in a particular trajectory. The existence of ODMs has given the Taiwanese IC design industry a competitive advantage and a unique opportunity structure focusing on second-generation innovation. The OEM-ODMs, in turn, have been strengthened by the success of the local IC design industry." This mutually beneficial role of ODM and semiconductor firms in Taiwan is best illustrated in relation to their evolving technological capabilities in the 2000s. In 2005, two leading ODM firms, Inventec and Compal, were ranked among Taiwan's top ten most innovative business groups (Mahmood and Zheng 2009, table A1). Wistron (Acer) and Quanta were also included in the top thirty.

47. As noted by Hobday (2001, 17), this trend toward contract manufacturing was started earnestly only in the mid-1990s and led by global lead firms from the United States (e.g., IBM, Hewlett-Packard, Intel, Fairchild, Texas Instruments, Dell Computers, and Cisco Systems), Europe (e.g., Ericsson, Philips, and ICL) and Japan (e.g., Toshiba and Hitachi) that outsourced their production to large EMS providers. For a detailed analysis of the rise of leading American EMS providers, see Sturgeon 2002.

48. Despite repeated attempts during the entire period of this research, I was unable to secure an interview with Hon Hai, a company well known for its secrecy and avoidance of publicity. The *Wall Street Journal* carried a report on Hon Hai's founder, Terry Gou, on August 11, 2007, entitled "The Forbidden City of Terry Gou." The reporter, Jason Dean, was the first from Western media to conduct an interview with Gou since 2002, and the interview was granted after more than five years of requests by the WSJ. The spate of worker suicides between 2009 and 2012 made Hon Hai even more wary of the media and academic researchers. The following case study is thus based on secondary materials (e.g., the WSJ article in 2007), company reports, and its corporate websites.

49. This size difference may explain why Hon Hai was not really featured in Amsden and Chu's (2003) study of the industrial upgrading of leading Taiwanese firms. None of the classic studies of the developmental state in Taiwan published prior to 2005 has analyzed its meteoric rise as Taiwan's largest industrial firm and the relevance of state policies in this rise.

50. Tam Harbert, "Hon Hai Plans on Becoming LCD Powerhouse," July 6, 2010, EDN. www .edn.com, accessed on September 18, 2014.

51. "Apple Reinvents the Phone with iPhone," January 9, 2007. Apple's press release, http://www.apple.com/pr/library/2007/01/09Apple-Reinvents-the-Phone-with-iPhone.html, accessed on November 1, 2014.

52. "Apple Announces iPhone 6 & iPhone 6 Plus," September 9, 2014. Apple's press release, http://www.apple.com/pr/library/2014/09/09Apple-Announces-iPhone-6-iPhone-6-Plus -The-Biggest-Advancements-in-iPhone-History.html, accessed on November 1, 2014.

53. "Apple Reports Fourth Quarter Results," October 20, 2014. Apple's press release, http://www.apple.com/pr/library/2014/10/20Apple-Reports-Fourth-Quarter-Results.html, accessed on November 1, 2014.

54. For detailed studies of such value chain distribution of profits, see OECD 2011. In the case of Hon Hai, while its profit margins decreased sharply from 17 percent in 1997 to 6 percent in 2007 and 3 percent in 2011, the decrease in its return on shareholders funds was less drastic, from 35 percent in 1997 to 29 percent in 2007 and 17.7 percent in 2011. In comparison, Apple's profit margins increased dramatically from −15 percent in 1997 to 20 percent in 2007 and 32 percent in 2011 and its return on shareholders funds grew from −87 percent in 1997 to 34 percent in 2007 and 45 percent in 2011 (all data from OSRIS online database, accessed on September 12, 2014). As shown in table 4.4, Hon Hai was the most profitable among all top ten EMS providers throughout the 2000s.

55. Unless otherwise specified, this case study is based on my interview with Venture Corp, company documents and reports, and secondary materials.

56. In 1970, Hewlett-Packard relocated the labor-intensive assembly of its core memory chips to a small operation in Singapore that began in a rented factory in Redhill with sixty-two employees, mostly young women. Sales office was added in 1975, and by 1977, Hewlett-

Packard Singapore had moved into its own factory with staff strength of fifteen hundred (Mathews and Cho 2000, 211).

57. Due to intense competition in the late 1990s, North America-based EMS providers began to grow by actively acquiring production capacity in East Asia. The period between 2000 and 2001 witnessed a number of these acquisitions of other smaller domestic EMS providers from Singapore, such as JIT Holding (acquired by Flextronics), Natsteel Electronics (acquired by Solectron), and Omni Industries (acquired by Celestica). Venture Corp's performance in this highly competitive industry during the 2000s should be viewed in relation to its continual growth and profitability in the midst of these acquisitions and mergers among loss-making EMS providers (e.g., Flextronics acquired Solectron in October 2007).

58. As of end 2011, these senior executives in Venture Corp were former employees of Hewlett-Packard: Tan Choon Huat (non-executive director), Soo Eng Hiong (non-executive director), Wong Chin Tong (chief marketing officer), Han Jok Kwang (chief information officer), Thian Nie Khian (chief technology officer), Amos Leong (SVP & GM for components), Lim Swee Kwang (SVP & GM for retail solutions and industrial products), Lee Ghai Keen (SVP & GM for R&D labs), and Tay Wui Kian (SVP for alliance management).

59. "HP Turns Supplier for New Venture Printer," August 24, 2002. VIPColor's press release, http://www.vipcolor.com, accessed on September 13, 2014.

60. In February 2007, Venture hired Tay Wui Kian as its senior vice president in charge of relationship and business management of several strategic customers. Having spent the previous twenty-three years with Hewlett-Packard, Tay was particularly familiar with its product engineering and design and management of supply chains, operations, and production. In Hewlett-Packard, he served as director of operations and R&D and played an instrumental role in setting up its Asia-Pacific Design Center in Singapore.

5. Industrial Specialization and Market Leadership in Marine Engineering and Semiconductors

1. These two conceptual terms describing state roles are from Evans's (1995) *Embedded Autonomy.*

2. The term "race to the swift" was the title of Woo's (1991) in-depth examination of South Korea's rush to industrialization.

3. Some key references are Amsden 1989 and 2001; Hobday 1995; Mathews and Cho 2000; and Amsden and Chu 2003; and K. Lee 2013. More recent reinterpretations from an industry studies perspective are Malerba and Nelson 2012; and Nübler 2014.

4. For a more recent example, see Wong's (2011, chap. 1) argument about second-mover advantage in the biotech industry. It should be noted, however, that such foreign borrowing is not particularly unique to the three East Asian economies. In his comparative analysis of the emergence of managerial capitalism in the United States, United Kingdom, Germany, and Japan, Chandler (1984, 503) concludes that "the Japanese . . . . have successfully moved into the international markets by using technological and organizational techniques very similar to those of the Americans and Europeans, indeed often borrowed directly from them—but using them more effectively and efficiently than the first comers."

5. As argued by Nelson and Winter (1982, 119; original italics), "a firm with an established routine possesses resources on which it can draw very helpfully in the difficult task of attempting to apply that routine on a large scale. Because the creation of productive organizations is *not* a matter of implementing fully explicit blueprints by purchasing homogeneous inputs on anonymous markets, a firm that is already successful in a given activity is a particularly good candidate for being successful with new capacity of the same sort."

6. See the case of the electronics industry in Ernst 2009.

7. This dependent relationship is characterized by Gereffi et al. (2005) as "captive" governance by lead firms in different global value chains.

8. For the nuts and bolts of different strategies of technological innovations in latecomer economies, see Forbes and Wield 2002. Malerba and Nelson (2011, 1647–48) offer an indigenous learning perspective on catching up. In this view, catching up is not about replicating

practices of first movers; it is rather about adapting these practices to local or national conditions, norms, and values that involves considerable risk taking and requires a lot of trial and error for such learning to be effective. See also Bell and Figueiredo 2012 for a dynamic view of latecomer firms' learning mechanisms and catching up.

9. Y. Chu (2009, 291–92) has noted this state role of articulating visions and promoting strong collaboration among industry players in South Korea during the 2000s, particularly in the telecommunications sector. See also S. Y. Kim 2012.

10. In the next chapter, I will consider this emergence of East Asian firms as global brand name lead firms through my third component process of strategic coupling with global production networks.

11. Other less capital-intensive segments of the marine industry are ship repair and conversion and marine-supporting industries, such as manufacturing or servicing marine equipment and components (e.g., diesel engines and turbochargers). Marine-related services include ship design and consultancy, electronics communication and navigation, marine inspection, and surveying.

12. The incident led to the death of eleven men and injury of seventeen others on the rig platform, and an estimated oil spill of about 5 million barrels costing BP at least US$40 billion in liabilities. Harry R. Webber, "BP Sues Rig Owner for $40B," *Pittsburgh Post-Gazette*, April 21, 2011. http://www.post-gazette.com, accessed on 15 September 2014.

13. "Deepwater Horizon Sinks Offshore Louisiana," *RIGZONE Industry News, Stories, Analysis and Editorial*, 22 April 2010. http://www.rigzone.com, accessed on September 15, 2014.

14. Kor Kian Beng, "Shipyards Set Example for Productivity," *Straits Times*, August 30, 2010. http://www.pmo.gov.sg, accessed on 15 September 2014.

15. In fact, Amsden (1989, 260–90) devotes the entire chap. 11 to the case study of HHI.

16. The role of their three rigs in BP's successful well-sealing operation was so critical that even the prime minister of Singapore highlighted them with rare visual illustrations in his 2010 National Day Rally Speech attended by thousands from all walks of life and broadcasted live to all four free-to-air channels. See http://www.pmo.gov.sg, accessed on September 15, 2014.

17. For a brief history of the global shipbuilding industry up to 1980, see Cho and Porter 1986 (550–58).

18. See Martin Stopford's (2004) *Shipbuilding World Overview 2004* for an overview of the recovery of world's shipbuilding by the early 2000s (Clarksons Shipping Intelligence Network. http://www.clarksons.net, accessed on October 27, 2014).

19. Unless otherwise specified in references, the following discussion of South Korea's shipbuilders is based on an interview with Samsung Heavy Industries. See the Appendix for details on my interviews and interviewees.

20. As discussed in chap. 3, the dissolution of the Daewoo Group in 2000 in response to its bankruptcy after the 1997–1998 Asian financial crisis has led to an independent Daewoo Shipbuilding and Marine Engineering funded by new investors. This lack of intragroup support has reduced its competitiveness vis-à-vis Samsung Heavy Industries that caught up with Daewoo's revenue in 2010.

21. 2011 data from Clarksons Shipping Intelligence Network. http://www.clarksons.net, accessed on September 20, 2014.

22. From a high rate of 82.4 percent dependence on ship imports in 1972, South Korea managed to reduce the rate of import dependence to 36.9 percent within four years in 1976 (Woo 1991, 137). By the mid-1980s, South Korea became the second largest producer of new ships only after Japan. In 1986, its new ship orders reached 18.9 percent of world total, compared to Japan's 37.1 percent (Amsden 1989, table 11.1).

23. See Glassman and Choi 2014 for a recent analysis of the rise of Hyundai in the US military–industrial complex during the Vietnam War.

24. As pointed out by Amsden (1989, 269), Hyundai organized its shipbuilding business first as a department within Hyundai Construction Company, until the establishment of Hyundai Shipbuilding and Heavy Industries Company in 1973 and its renaming to HHI in 1978.

25. Interestingly, this drive for shipbuilding represented merely a revival of an "industry" South Koreans used to know very well. In *Race to the Swift*, Woo (1991, 136) reminds us explic-

itly that "Koreans were skilled shipbuilders from time immemorial, a fate thrust upon them by geography, and they passed on shipmaking know-how to Japan. They were the first in the world to construct fleets of ships cast in metal, deployed at the end of the sixteenth century to push back Hideyoshi's invading armies."

26. Founded by Japan's Mitsubishi in 1937, KSEC was nationalized in 1945 and eventually sold to a shipping magnate in 1968. Between 1945 and 1968, KSEC was South Korea's largest shipyard (Amsden 1989, 275, 290). In 1987, KSEC went bankrupt. It was renamed to Hanjin Heavy Industries and Construction in May 1989 and incorporated into the Hanjin Group in July 1990 (http://www.hanjinsc.com/eng, accessed on September 18, 2014).

27. See Steers 1999 for a detailed study of Chung Ju-yung and his Hyundai group of companies.

28. From http://english.hhi.co.kr, accessed on September 18, 2014.

29. From its entry into shipbuilding in the early 1970s, size and scale have seemingly been the fundamental competitive advantage of HHI. When it built its first shipyard on an empty stretch of beach in Ulsan in March 1972, Hyundai began with what would become the world's largest shipyard.

30. This case is based on an interview with Samsung Heavy Industries and secondary materials. SHI's corporate website is also quite informative. http://shi.samsung.co.kr/Eng, accessed on September 20, 2014.

31. Other shipbuilders in South Korea and Japan have since benchmarked SHI's sea-surface crane production method, but few have achieved success. In the case of Japan, many of its shipbuilders have been locked into an earlier generation of shipbuilding technologies based on land production methods. Their huge investment in these land-based cranes has also increased their sunk costs and made it harder for them to switch to SHI's sea-surface crane production method.

32. Despite the question of allocation efficiency, many advanced industrialized economies in Western Europe continued to protect their shipbuilders at the time when Japan and South Korea were catching up in the mid-1970s and through to the late 1980s. The state in West Germany, for example, gave up to 20 percent of the ship price as a direct subsidy to its shipbuilders in order to encourage them to produce high value-added vessels such as containerships and LNG carriers. Between 1979 and 1980, the German state spent 480 million deutschemarks in subsidies (Cho and Porter 1986, 547). Up to the mid-1980s, the state in other European economies, such as the United Kingdom, Sweden, Italy, Spain, France, and the Netherlands, continued to provide direct and indirect supports to their domestic shipbuilders through direct ownership of shipyards, provision of building subsidies, and favorable tax systems permitting special depreciation.

33. In May 1946, the Taiwan Machinery and Shipbuilding Company (TMSC) was formed as a state-owned firm comprising of three former Japanese shipbuilding companies nationalized by the Takeover Commission set up under the Taiwan provincial government on October 25, 1945 (Wu 2005, 41). In April 1948, TMSC was split into two SOEs: Taiwan Machinery Corporation and Taiwan Shipbuilding Corporation (TSBC). In January 1978, TSBC was merged into China Shipbuilding Corp (CSBC). http://www.csbcnet.com.tw, accessed on September 20, 2014.

34. Tien's (1989, 136) critical view is that "the majority of Taiwan's public corporations are wasteful and inefficient. Overstaffing in conjunction with a political spoils system is the heart of the problem."

35. In 2010, the operating revenues of Hanjin Heavy Industries and CSBC were respectively US$2.5 billion and US$891 million (http://www.hanjinsc.com/eng and http://www.csbcnet.com.tw, accessed on September 20, 2014). They were far smaller than HHI (US$33.3 billion), Samsung (US$11.7 billion), and Daewoo (US$11.6 billion).

36. In *Governing the Market*, Wade (1990, 28) calls this strategy "big leadership" when the scale of state initiatives is large enough to make a real difference to investment and production patterns in an industry.

37. Singapore has a third state-controlled engineering group that is involved in the marine industry—ST Marine. As a subsidiary of the Singapore Technologies Engineering (ST Engg) group, ST Marine is engaged in military and commercial shipbuilding and repair. At

US$715 million sales in 2011, its size and scale are much smaller than Keppel and SembCorp. ST Marine's role within the ST Engg group is significantly lesser than ST Aerospace. Overall, ST Marine is a specialized niche supplier of shipbuilding, conversion, and repair service to naval and commercial customers (Interview with ST Engg).

38. The following discussion is based on my interviews with Keppel Corp, Keppel Offshore and Marine, SembCorp Industries, Singapore Petroleum Corporation, ST Engg, and secondary sources, such as corporate websites: http://www.kepcorp.com and http://www.sembcorp .com, and the Association of Singapore Marine Industries: http://www.asmi.com, accessed on October 20, 2014.

39. Earlier on, Jurong Shipyard was merged with Jurong Shipbuilders in 1976 and listed on the Stock Exchange of Singapore in 1987. It acquired Sembawang Shipyard in 1997.

40. The exchange rates of Singapore dollars hover between S$1 to US$0.57 in September 2000 to S$1 to US$0.78 in September 2014, http://www.xe.com, accessed on November 10, 2014.

41. Singapore's GDP data are obtained from http://www.singstat.gov.sg, accessed on October 20, 2014.

42. In 2011, Keppel Corp's offshore business contributed to US$4.7 billion of its total group revenue of US$8.2 billion. Its net order book stood at US$7.7 billion, with deliveries extending to 2015. Between 2002 and 2011, Keppel O&M's net profit grew over 600 percent from US$147 million to US$934 million and accounted for over 50 percent of Keppel Corp's net profit. At SembCorp Industries, its marine division also raked in US$3.2 billion or 43 percent of the group's total revenue of US$7.4 billion and over 50 percent of net profit in 2011.

43. Through its stakes in FESL in 1971, Keppel was involved in building its first jack-up rig and other semisubmersible and drillship units in the 1970s. The parent company of FESL, the Levingston Shipbuilding Company, was the only American rig builder at the forefront of the offshore oil boom in the 1950s and through to the early 1970s. It developed and built many of the early designs.

44. Since launching its "industry workhorse," the KFELS B Class rigs, in 2000, Keppel has sold more than thirty units worldwide. It has also developed much more sophisticated and technologically challenging models for premium customers operating in the extreme and harsh offshore environment of North Sea (KFELS A and N Class) and the deepwater of Brazil, Gulf of Mexico, and West Africa (DSS Series).

45. Of its various organizational efforts to localize its twenty yards, Keppel's presence in Brazil deserves special mentioning. Realizing the enormous potential of offshore oil production in Brazil and its domestic political context in favor of local production, Keppel established its BrasFELS yard in Brazil as early as in 2000. Its local presence has won the support and rig deals from Petrobras, the Brazilian state-owned oil company. With its strong relationship developed with Petrobas over the years, Keppel has since benefited from many new orders for rigs and production platforms from Petrobras and its drilling contractors (*Keppel O&M Annual Report 2011*, 12, http://www.keppelom.com, accessed on November 27, 2014).

46. Mathews and Cho's (2000) *Tiger Technology* remains the best and most comprehensive study of the semiconductor industry in the three East Asian economies examined in this book. Other book-length studies that include some discussion of leading East Asian firms in the semiconductor industry are Henderson 1989; Evans 1995; Hobday 1995; Dedrick and Kraemer 1998; Amsden and Chu 2003; and Breznitz 2007. The earlier classics on the developmental state, such as Amsden 1989; Rodan 1989; Haggard 1990; Wade 1990; and Woo 1991, have far less to say about the semiconductor industry in the three economies, partly a reflection of the still relatively early stage of the industry's development in these economies at the time of their studies.

47. Interview with a leading American semiconductor equipment manufacturer.

48. Leading European firms, such as Siemens (Germany), STMicroelectronics (France), and Philips (The Netherlands), were also serious competitors to American and Japanese semiconductor firms.

49. In the computer industry, Dedrick and Kraemer (1998, 105–6) also find that "MITI had become a victim of its own success in helping create Japan's manufacturing and export

powerhouse and was casting about for a new role. There was no longer a need for outright protection or subsidies for most industries. . . . Also, Japanese corporations had gained confidence in their own capabilities and were less willing to seek or follow MITI's guidance. The Ministry's role was therefore being reduced to the restructuring of declining industries and promoting imports to ease trade tensions—not a very appealing prospect for the oft-proclaimed architects of the Japanese miracle."

50. Motorola, for example, used to produce its PowerPC chip that was integrated into millions of Ford's automobiles microcontrollers (Dedrick and Kraemer 1998, 6).

51. In the calculation of total sales in the global semiconductor industry (e.g., table 5.3), outputs of semiconductor foundries are typically attributed to their customers, such as "fabless" firms (e.g., Qualcomm and Broadcom) or IDMs (e.g., Toshiba and Texas Instruments).

52. In March 2012, Abu Dhabi's state-owned Advanced Technology Investment Company acquired 100 percent ownership control from AMD (McGrath 2012).

53. See Mathews and Cho 2000 (chaps. 4 and 5) for fascinating details on these initiatives in Taiwan and Singapore up to the mid-1990s. For specific studies of Taiwan's IC industry, see Tso 2004; Ouyang 2006; and Fuller 2007.

54. As a transnational technopreneur, Morris Chang was invited by Taiwan's then premier Yu to head ITRI in 1985. He previously worked in General Instruments as its president and Texas Instruments as its head of global semiconductor operations. When TSMC was established in June 1986 as a spin-off of ITRI in collaboration with Philips, Chang became its first chairman and remains so in the 2010s. TSMC's organizational innovation in the "pure play" foundry model is thus often attributed to Chang's foresight into the future of the semiconductor industry. It should be noted, though, the pure-play foundry concept did not originate from Chang or TSMC, but from Orbit Semiconductor, a small semiconductor fabrication company established by Gary Kennedy in California in January 1985 to manufacture charge coupled devices (CCD) and CMOS devices for defense, aerospace, and industrial customers. This information is obtained from my interviewee from Macronix, Orbit Semiconductor's website (http://www.orbit-semi.com, accessed on September 25, 2014), and an article entitled "Charge Coupled Device Processing Offered by Orbit," *Defense Electronics*, June 1, 1987 (http://business.highbeam.com, accessed on September 25, 2014).

55. UMC was the first spin-off from ERSO in 1980 and expanded into logic and memory chips throughout the 1980s. According to Mathews and Cho (2000, 177), its strategic switch to become a pure-play foundry did not occur until the mid-1990s, partly in response to Intel's increasing legal action against microprocessor IDMs from Taiwan.

56. As the success of TSMC's "pure play" model had become visible by the mid-1990s, TSMC faced much greater interest from major customers to secure dedicated TSMC fabrication capacity. In 1996, several of its fabless customers, Altera, ISSI, and ADI, persuaded TSMC to enter into a US$1.3 billion joint venture to establish Wafer Tech in the United States in order to serve them exclusively. In this deal, these fabless partners could sell unused capacity in Wafer Tech to other fabless IC firms (Mathews and Cho 2000, 178–79). By the late 1990s, TSMC had realized that the joint venture did not make good organizational sense because it created conflicts with its other fabless customers, and it had sufficient in-house technology and capacity to serve these three customers. In a US$494 million deal in December 2000, TSMC acquired Wafer Tech and incorporated it into TSMC's suite of fabrication facilities located in Hsinchu and Taichung in Taiwan.

57. Interview with TSMC.

58. Interview with a former senior executive of CSM.

59. Sierra Semiconductor was renamed to PMC-Sierra in 1997 and remained as a top twenty fabless semiconductor firm throughout the 2000s (see table 5.7).

60. Katrina Nicholas and Andrea Tan, "Temasek's Chartered Semi Sale Speeds Up Chip Industry Exit," September 7, 2009, Bloomberg. http://www.bloomberg.com, accessed on September 27, 2014.

61. ST's fabless design house, TriTech, also went bankrupt after it had lost a major legal tussle in 2001.

62. All financial data are from OSIRIS database. osiris.bvdinfo.com, accessed on September 26, 2014.

63. Jeran Wittenstein and Katrina Nicholas, "Abu Dhabi to Buy Chartered for S\$2.5 Billion, Challenging UMC," September 7, 2009, Bloomberg. http://www.bloomberg.com, accessed on September 27, 2014.

64. Interview with a former senior executive of CSM.

65. Interview with STATS ChipPAC. In the downstream segment, Singapore's and Taiwan's Siliconware Precision Industries Corporation (SPIL) have rode on the industry's strong growth to become the world's two largest semiconductor testing and assembly solutions providers.

66. VIA's fortune has changed dramatically since 2003 (Interview with VIA). After the legal tussles with Intel between October 2001 and April 2003, VIA's chipsets business declined substantially, and it had to pay royalties to Intel that in turn affected its profitability. In 2009, it dropped out of the list of the world's top twenty-five fabless semiconductor firms.

67. It is useful to refer to chap. 1's opening vignette that Samsung contributes to some 47 percent of the US\$169.4 value-added in the manufacturing of each iPhone 4.

68. This section on Taiwan's IDMs is based on my interviews with Mosel-Vitelic, Winbond, Macronix, Nanya Technology, and ProMOS Technologies.

69. As shown in table 5.3, Elpida Memory was formed in 1999 through a merger of DRAM divisions of Hitachi and NEC. In 2003, it acquired Mitsubishi's DRAM division. In 2002, Mitsubishi Semiconductor merged its IC chip division with Hitachi Semiconductor to become Renesas Technology. In 2010, Renesas Technology merged with NEC to become Renesas Electronics. Between 1999 and 2011, only Toshiba and Fujitsu had remained intact, but their annual sales had stagnated or declined.

70. Interview with Mosel-Vitelic.

71. See full details in L. Kim 1997 (149–70) and Mathews and Cho 2000 (115–29).

72. In January 2011, Samsung's 64K DRAM was selected as one of the four national economic treasures by *Joongang Ilbo*, one of South Korea's most influential newspapers (Y. Kim 2011, 297, 310). The other three national economic treasures were Hyundai's Pony (its first own brand model in 1975), Kyungbu Highway (first segment opened in 1968), and POSCO (South Korea's first integrated still mill in 1968).

73. Mosel and Vitelic were merged in 1991 to become Mosel-Vitelic based in Taiwan. By 2009, Mosel-Vitelic was driven out of DRAM business completely. Only its former affiliate, ProMOS, was still producing DRAMs and stayed on as a small-scale IDM in memory chips.

74. For more specific studies of Samsung's catching up in semiconductors, see Lee et al. 2005; Lee and Slater 2007; Bae 2011; Y. Kim 2011; Hwang and Choung 2014; and Shin 2015.

75. As argued by Dedrick and Kraemer (1998, 122), "Surprisingly, the government was slow to get on board in supporting the DRAM Industry. Instead it was Samsung that instigated the move into DRAMs, followed by Hyundai and LG."

76. Interview with Macronix.

77. Interview with Samsung Electronics.

78. Ibid.

6. Emergence of East Asian Lead Firms

1. It is necessary to note here that this transformation in firm positioning in global production networks is not well developed in the literature on global value chain governance (e.g., Gereffi et al. 2005; Bair 2009; Ponte and Sturgeon 2014). This literature tends to focus on interfirm relationships *within* a particular type of already existed governance structures (e.g., captive, relational, or modular) and provides little analytical opportunity for a supplier firm to evolve eventually into a global lead firm under favorable conditions of strategic coupling.

2. In his highly influential *The Competitive Advantage of Nations*, Michael Porter's (1990) argument for national competitiveness tends to fall into this trap of equating firm-level industrial competition with competition between national economies. As pointed out shrewdly by Paul Krugman (1994, 30, 39), this idea is wrong because "it is simply not the case that the world's leading nations are to any important degree in economic competition with each other, or that any of their major economic problems can be attributed to failures to compete on

world markets." The obsession with national competitiveness is seductive because "many prefer a doctrine that offers the gain of apparent sophistication without the pain of hard thinking. The rhetoric of competitiveness has become so widespread."

3. This issue of branding in the governance of value chains is particularly significant because, as argued by Humphrey and Schmitz (2002), it allows lead firms to define and enforce product and process parameters. See Pike's (2015) work on branding and value creation/capture.

4. Few studies of East Asian development have focused on this process of national firms evolving to become OBMs and global lead firms. See exceptions in Mathews 2002; and W. W. Chu 2009.

5. For general work on business groups in the global economy, see Khanna and Yafeh 2007; and Colpan et al. 2010. Specifically, Schneider (2010) explains how different business groups are related to the policy and political overtures of the state.

6. For more on East Asian business groups, see Whitley 1992; Fields 1995; Yeung 2004; S. J. Chang 2006a; and chapters in Colpan et al. 2010; and Witt and Redding 2013.

7. There is a very substantial literature on national innovation systems that examines the cross-national variations in firm-specific differences in technological and innovation capacities (e.g., Lundvall 1992; Nelson 1993; 2005; L. Kim 1997; Kim and Nelson 2000a). With very few exceptions (e.g., Ernst and Kim 2002; Pietrobelli and Rabellotti 2011), this literature does not take into account the developmental opportunities for these national firms through their strategic coupling with global production networks. See a more detailed critique in Coe and Yeung 2015.

8. It is useful to note here again that the small size of the Singapore economy, relative to South Korea and Taiwan, makes it even harder for its national firms to develop into global lead firms, particularly in the manufacturing sector. I have therefore included some Singaporean firms that have emerged as major lead firms within Asia.

9. See earlier studies of East Asian firms from such a resource-based perspective in Mathews 2002; Mahmood and Mitchell 2004; S. J. Chang et al. 2006; and H. Kim 2010.

10. For an explanation of this concept of "liability of foreignness," see Zaheer 1995.

11. Two highly influential early works on the severe challenges faced by globalizing firms from the United States and Western Europe are Prahalad and Doz's (1987) *The Multinational Mission* and Bartlett and Ghoshal's (1989) *Managing Across Borders.*

12. Other well-known brand names from Taiwan in the global electronics industry are HTC (mobile handsets) and ASUS (computers). Compared to Acer, these are relatively specialized and newer lead firms. ASUSTeK Computer, for example, was established by Jonney Shih in 1990. Jonney Shih used to work for Acer and managed its PC business. Most of ASUSTeK's senior executives were also former employees of Acer Inc. See also W. W. Chu 2009.

13. In *Governing the Market,* Wade (1990, 106–7) devoted two pages to the case of Acer as Taiwan's leading computer firm. The role of the state in facilitating Acer's initial entry into the computer global production networks during the 1980s was to fund joint development of new products between private firms (e.g., Acer or Mitac) and public R&D institutes (i.e., ITRI's Electronics Research Service Organization) and to use ERSO's research projects and technology transfer to strengthen the hand of these firms in warding off IBM lawsuits. It is useful to note that Acer during this period was locked into a more captive form of value chain governance led by IBM, then the global market leader in personal computers.

14. The following case analysis of Acer is based on my interviews with Acer and two of its former spin-offs, BenQ and AU Optronics, and secondary materials, including its corporate website: http://www.acer-group.com, accessed on October 15, 2014. See the Appendix for details on my interviews and interviewees. For a fascinating case analysis of Acer from 1976 to 2000, see Mathews 2002 (55–92, 135–57).

15. Mathews (2002, 154–55) documents a case of such branding conflict in the parallel development of CD-ROM products by Acer Peripherals Inc. (API) and the Information Products Group (IPB) within Acer Inc. in 1997–1998. Both developers of their CD-ROM products wanted to deploy the Acer brand, but only one group, API, was finally allowed to do so. IPB had to market its CD-ROM products under the brand "AOpen," and the group was eventually spun off in 1998.

16. AU Optronics subsequently went on to become one of the world's largest producers of TFT-LCD display panels in the 2010s, generating revenue of US$14 billion in 2013 and a market-leading share of 16.7 percent in large-sized panels. http://www.auo.com, accessed on December 5, 2014.

17. Data from Interbrand. http://www.interbrand.com, accessed on October 16, 2014. In comparison, Hewlett-Packard's brand value in 2011 was US$26 billion (dropped to US$23.8 billion in 2014), no doubt a reflection of its longstanding reputation as one of the world's largest and leading technology groups with a diverse portfolio of cutting-edge products and services.

18. Data from Wistron's corporate website: http://www.wistron.com, accessed on October 15, 2014.

19. China's Lenovo has retained the branding of IBM ThinkPad notebooks since acquiring IBM's PC division in 2005.

20. Interview with the Industrial Development Bureau, Ministry of Economic Affairs.

21. Other exceptions in the electronics industry are HTC (mobile handsets) and ASUS (computers).

22. Due to limited space, I will focus my analysis on Samsung's emergence as a global lead firm in the consumer electronics industry. As a market leader in digital televisions and mobile handsets, LG Electronics is significantly smaller than Samsung Electronics and does not enjoy global leadership in core components such as semiconductors.

23. Data from Interbrand. http://www.interbrand.com, accessed on November 16, 2014. To put Samsung's achievement in perspective, Sony, once the formidable Japanese giant in consumer electronics and Samsung's ultimate benchmark for catching up (S. J. Chang 2008), had a brand value of only US$8.1 billion in 2014. Similarly, the brand value of Philips, the Dutch giant in consumer electronics, was US$10.3 billion in 2014. They were ranked respectively fifty-second and forty-second in the *Best Global Brand 2014.*

24. See Samsung's humble origin in the early 1950s as a firm specializing in trade and the manufacturing of daily necessities in chap. 1's endnote 14.

25. The following analysis of Samsung and LG is based on interviews with Samsung Electronics and LG Electronics, and their various affiliated companies.

26. For recent studies of these localized linkages in South Korea, see Lee 2009; and Lee et al. 2014.

27. Interview with the mobile handset division, Samsung Electronics.

28. Interview with the global strategy division, Samsung Electronics.

29. Interview with the global marketing division, Samsung Electronics.

30. Interview with Samsung Corporation.

31. Interview with the mobile handset division, Samsung Electronics.

32. Interview with Samsung SDI.

33. This quotation and reference are taken from Dicken's (2015, 478) *Global Shift*, which provides an excellent discussion of the global automobile industry.

34. The developmental state in Taiwan did attempt to nurture an indigenous automobile industry as early as 1961. But its small domestic market and highly politicized industrial policy led to the failure of its first attempt in the 1960s and the subsequent Automobile Industry Development Plan of 1984 (Wade 1990, 101–3; 214–15). For more detailed studies of Taiwan's unsuccessful case of developing automobile assemblers, see Arnold 1989; and Cunningham et al. 2005. Established in 1953 as Taiwan's first automobile firm, Yulon produced from a joint venture with Nissan the first Taiwan-assembled passenger car in 1960 (Wade 1990, 92). In 2014, Yulon remains as a local assembler for OEM global automakers in Taiwan—Yulon Motor as a producer for Nissan and General Motors and China Motor for Mitsubishi (http://www.yulongroup.com.tw, accessed on October 17, 2014). In 2013, each of them assembled about 110,000–120,000 cars for these Japanese lead firms that were sold in Taiwan's domestic market. Both Yulong Motor and China Motor also invested in joint ventures established by their Japanese lead firms in China and the Philippines.

35. More details on these firms and industrial policy can be found in Ravenhill 2003, 116–22; and K. H. Lee 2013, 69–70.

36. L. Kim (1998) shows how this organizational learning in Hyundai Motor took place in a circular sequence involving four activities: internal preparation through developing human resources, the acquisition of external knowledge, assimilation and integration of acquired knowledge, and subsequent improvement in order to create a higher knowledge base for the preparatory phase of the next cycle of learning.

37. As noted in chap. 5, one of South Korea's most influential newspapers, *Joongang Ilbo*, selected Hyundai's Pony, Samsung's 64K DRAM, Kyungbu Highway, and POSCO as the four national economic treasures in January 2011.

38. A smaller automaker, SsangYong, was bought by Daewoo in 1997 and absorbed into GM Daewoo in 2000. It was sold to China's SAIC in 2004. In 2011, India's Mahindra & Mahindra bought it from SAIC (http://www.smotor.com, accessed on October 17, 2014).

39. Data from production statistics collected by the International Organization of Motor Vehicle Manufacturers (http://oica.net, accessed on October 17, 2014).

40. The following analysis is based on interviews with Hyundai Motor Company, Hyundai Mobis, Korea Automotive Research Institute, secondary materials, and corporate websites of HMC (http://worldwide.hyundai.com, accessed on October 17, 2014) and Hyundai Mobis (http://www.mobis.co.kr, accessed on October 17, 2014). For a detailed study of Hyundai Motor Company, see Lansbury et al. 2007.

41. Data from Ward's Auto (http://wardsauto.com, accessed on October 17, 2014).

42. In the global value chains literature, this interfirm relationship is known as "relational governance" through which a global lead firm works tacitly with its subsidiaries and suppliers to achieve collective action through mutual dependency and higher levels of asset specificity (Gereffi et al. 2005, 84).

43. Interview with Hyundai Motor Company.

44. A recent study by Kwon (2012, 22) notes that Hyundai and Kia have developed very long term relationships with their suppliers. In 2011, 207 of their 290 suppliers had more than twenty years of business relations with either Hyundai or Kia. Only eleven firms had less than ten years of supplier relations. Many of these suppliers have followed Hyundai to establish their parts production facilities abroad.

45. Interview with Hyundai Mobis.

46. This phrase is taken from Dicken (2015, 477) who uses it to describe the global automobile industry.

47. Few studies of the developmental state in Taiwan and South Korea have examined the domestic and international competitiveness of their service industries. The only exception is Amsden and Chu (2003), which examines the role of business groups in *domestic* services, such as banking, retailing, and transport. But their study has not analyzed the regional and global significance of these service sector business groups.

48. Data are from the website of the Department of Statistics, Singapore: www.singstat.gov.sg, accessed on October 23, 2014.

49. This analysis is based on my interview with China Airlines. Corporate data are from http://investing.businessweek.com, accessed on October 18, 2014.

50. One example was Christine Tsung who joined China Airlines as its president and CEO in July 2000 and was appointed as the first female minister of economic affairs in January 2002 (http://news.bbc.co.uk/2/hi/asia-pacific/1780153.stm, accessed on October 23, 2014). Due to her lack of experience in public office and brutal politics in Taiwan under the Democratic Progressive Party regime, Tsung resigned after only several months in office.

51. Data from EVA's website: http://www.evaair.com, accessed on October 18, 2014.

52. This analysis is based on interviews with several senior executives from Korean Air. All corporate data in this section are from Bloomberg Businessweek (http://investing.businessweek.com, accessed on October 18, 2014).

53. In its Airport Service Quality (ASQ) Awards—the industry's most prestigious accolades—the Airports Council International consecutively named the Incheon International Airport as the Best Airport in the Asia Pacific Region between 2005 and 2014 (http://www.airport.kr, accessed on May 11, 2015).

54. See website of Alpa-S. http://www.alpas.org, accessed on October 18, 2014.

55. Quote taken from "SM Urges New Alpa-S Council to Work with SIA," *Today*, February 24, 2005, 6; http://newspapers.nl.sg/Digitised/Article/today20040224-1.2.13.1.aspx, accessed on October 18, 2014.

56. Data on Singapore Airlines in the OSIRIS database are dated back only to 1984 (osiris.bvdinfo.com, accessed on May 11, 2015). Singapore Airlines was profitable before then.

57. Ho Ching's speech at the Asia Business Leader's Award Dinner at the Banqueting House in London on October 27, 2014 (http://www.temasek.com.sg/mediacentre, accessed on November 1, 2014).

58. These figures do not include other affiliates of Singapore Airlines. The cargo division of Singapore Airlines, SIA Cargo, is a separate entity established in 2001. Singapore Airlines also owns SilkAir, a regional airline based in Singapore, and has stakes in Tiger Airways and Scoot, both regional budget airlines.

59. Giovanni Bisignani, IATA's director general and CEO, "Global Media Day, Geneva," December 14, 2010. http://www.iata.org, accessed on October 18, 2014.

60. Its "local" competitor—ST Aerospace, the subsidiary of Singapore Technologies Engineering—is also a government-linked company and the world's largest aircraft maintenance, repair, and overhaul (MRO) service provider.

7. Beyond the Developmental State

1. The classic studies of the developmental state are found in White 1988; Amsden 1989; 2001; Rodan 1989; Haggard 1990; Wade 1990; Woo 1991; Evans 1995; Woo-Cumings 1999a; Kohli 2004; and Wu 2005. More recent and critical studies are available in Kang 2002; O'Riain 2004; Boyd and Ngo 2005a; Breznitz 2007; Greene 2008; Pirie 2008; and Wong 2011. See Leibfried et al. 2013 for a recent collection on state transformations.

2. See O'Riain 2004, Breznitz 2007, and Fine et al. 2013 for some examples of a complementary approach from the developmental state perspective that argues for a more evolutionary and contextually grounded analysis of the state.

3. The social science literature on these global value chains and global production networks is dated back to Gereffi and Korzeniewicz's (1994) *Commodity Chains and Global Capitalism*. The two influential articles by Henderson et al. (2002) and Gereffi et al. (2005) represent the most significant development of this perspective in the field of international political economy. See the 2014 special issue of *Review of International Political Economy* (Neilson et al. 2014; 2015) and Coe and Yeung's (2015) *Global Production Networks* for recent reprises of this fast-growing literature.

4. This structural shift in the mechanics of economic development supports Cimoli et al.'s (2009b, 23) view that "the dynamics of industrialization rest upon major structural transformations which entail a changing importance of different branches of economic activity as generators of both technological and organizational innovations."

5. The key references in this vast literature are found in note 17 in chap. 1.

6. In McAdam et al. (2001, 25–26), these two mechanisms are respectively known as cognitive and relational mechanisms.

7. Gerring (2008, 163, 178; 2010) identifies at least nine distinct meanings of this "ambient concept" and "ubiquitous term." But he prefers only the above "process" meaning as the minimal (core) definition that is consistent with all contemporary usages and practices within the social sciences. Others have also identified many different understandings of mechanisms in the social sciences (Gross 2009, 360–62; Hedström and Ylikoski 2010, table 1, 51; Bengtsson and Hertting 2014). As well noted in Sil and Katzenstein (2010, 420), "there is little agreement on what constitutes a causal mechanism" beyond its positioning in explaining how some set of initial conditions in one or more contexts generates some set of outcomes or variations.

8. This "intermediary process" view of causation and mechanisms is quite common in political science and sociology (e.g., Mahoney 2001, 581; 2008, 413) and in the philosophy of social science (e.g., Bunge 1997, 414; 2004, 191; Mayntz 2004, 241, 253).

9. As a philosophy of social science, critical realism's understanding of causal mechanisms is consistent with the social mechanisms literature (e.g., Gorski's 2009; 2013 reprise of critical

realism for sociology and political science). In fact, several key social mechanisms papers (e.g., Stinchcombe 1991; Hedström and Swedberg 1996; 1998b; Demetriou 2007; and Hedström and Ylikoski 2010) have explicitly referred to the case for causal mechanisms in critical realist work by philosophers (Roy Bhasker and Rom Harré) and social scientists (e.g., Andrew Sayer). As noted by Gorski (2013, 667), "Bhaskar was already making this case by the early 1970s, well ahead of Boudon, Elster, or Hedström" (see also Gerring 2005, 164, 189). See Yeung 1997; 2003 for my methodological take on critical realism and the process-based abstraction method.

10. The inducement of industrialization through large-scale state-led investment in East Asian economies provided the initial "big push" akin to the industrialization of European nations in the nineteenth century. As described by Gerschenkron (1962, 11), "only when industrial development could commence on a large scale did the tension between the preindustrialization conditions and the benefits expected from industrialization become sufficiently strong to overcome the existing obstacles and to liberate the forces that made for industrial progress." To induce such rapid industrialization, the state worked with investment banks to finance large-scale plants and enterprises. The real threshold for rapid industrialization was the degree of backwardness or relative backwardness, such that the more backward economy tended to industrialize in "the form of a big spurt, during which for a fairly considerable length of time the development proceeded at an unusually rapid pace" (36).

11. As noted by Dedrick and Kraemer (1998, 26–27), "the U.S. success in PCs is driven mostly by U.S. companies, which invented the PC and have maintained their lead in the industry. However, there has been more government policy involved than many would suspect, starting with heavy military procurement and R&D during the Cold War and continuing with support for research at universities and national laboratories and the serendipitous decision to create the Internet." See also Zysman and Newman 2006; Block 2008; Block and Keller 2011; Mazzucato 2013; Wade 2014a; and Weiss 2014 for related studies of the hidden role of the state in the industrial transformation of the United States.

12. For recent reinterpretations of such a strategy of industrial transformation in development economics, see Cimoli et al. 2009c; Lin 2012a; and Salazar-Xirinachs et al. 2014.

13. Some important exceptions are available in the early pioneering studies, such as Haggard 1990 and Woo 1991, but their lessons on historical circumstances seem to have been forgotten or ignored by most subsequent followers of their ideas. Recent exceptions are Kohli 2004 and Greene 2008. In their paper on the historical origin of the developmental state in East Asia, Doner et al. (2005) point to the systemic vulnerability arising from the interaction among three separate but difficult circumstances of a severe (external) security threat, a scarce resource endowment, and a severe threat of domestic mass unrest. See also Haggard 2015 for an overview.

14. See Mkandawire and Yi 2014 for such an example. For a recent debate on the applicability of the developmental state concept to Africa, see Edigheji 2010; and Routley 2014. Other studies of China have also examined its state role in relation to development (Pei 2006; Hsueh 2011).

15. Summing up this complex scenario of state involvement, geopolitics, and internationalism in the American influence on the East Asian electronics industry, Dedrick and Kraemer (1998, 26–27) point out that "investment of the U.S. military in computers helped establish the country's leadership in the industry, and in turn, American strengths in electronics and computers encouraged the military to emphasize technology as a key strategic element in the Cold War. More directly, the interaction of government policy and business decisions helped Japan, Taiwan, Korea, and Singapore establish and enhance their competitive positions in computers and semiconductors."

16. See a recent interpretation of an "order transition" toward East Asian states and their macroregional institutions in Goh's (2013) *The Struggle for Order.*

17. For a specific application of Gerschenkron's perspective to East Asian technological change, see Hobday 2003; 2011.

18. See Wong's (2011) argument for the declining role of such state function in the biotech industry because of its inherent uncertainty.

19. In his cogent critique of Gerschenkron's idea of the state, as the operators, steering accurately this relative backwardness through a big spurt, Hirschman (1958, 9) points out

that "the underdeveloped country is thus pictured in the role of an Oblomov who can bring himself to leave his beloved bed and room only if the outside weather is irresistibly splendid. The implication here is that the operators really know all the time what needs to be done to shed backwardness and to achieve development and are therefore able to weigh the costs against the expected benefits of development."

20. To Greene (2008), Gerschenkron's "big push" theory might fit the initial experience of industrializing South Korea and, perhaps, even Singapore, but certainly not so much Taiwan. Measured in terms of debt-to-equity ratios, Taiwan had ratios since the 1970s similar to, and often lower than, those of the United States, partly due to the KMT's preference for military expenditure. But Taiwan failed to foster powerful, independent associations of producers with a broad scope to produce craft products, not just niche products, in ways that Germany and Italy did in their craft production. The role of formal and informal training institutions in both Germany and Italy was critical (Piore and Sabel 1984; Herrigel 1996), but absent in the case of Taiwan.

21. This weakness of "bracketing" out and being "thin" on the state's other institutions is mainly due to my lack of rich primary material. The importance of these nonstate institutions in state-led development has also received relatively little discussion in the early version of the developmental state literature. A few exceptions are Fields (1995) and Noble (1998) who have brought out some of these institutional influences of business associations and public-private groups in Taiwan prior to the 1990s.

22. See Aoki et al. 1997 for a collection of such thought in economics and development studies. Wade (1990, chap. 3) also offers a clear summary and critique of such a neoclassical explanation of East Asian industrialization. Smith's (2000) study of the effectiveness of industrial policy in Taiwan and South Korea in the 1980s represents such a neoclassical approach to economic development.

23. See Hall and Soskice 2001 and Hancké 2009 for the core analytics of this VoC framework, and Yeung 2004; 2007b, Walter and Zhang 2012, and Witt and Redding 2013 for diverse varieties of East Asian capitalisms.

24. See Y. Chu 2007; and Haggard and Zheng 2013. This phenomenon was also confirmed in my interviews with various bureaus and departments in Taiwan's Ministry of Economic Affairs. See the Appendix for more details on my interviews and interviewees.

25. In the earlier phase of state-led industrialization prior to 1990, these industry associations were described by Wade (1990, 282) as "the government's hand-maidens" who "do not provide significant inputs into policy-making" and "have too little independence to constrain the actions of government, and in few cases do they have much power to regulate the behavior of members."

26. In 1992, Hyundai's founder Ju-yung Chung ran for the presidency but lost to Kim Young-Sam (1993–1998). In 1994, several chaebol chairmen publicly acknowledged their illicit contributions of political funds to Presidents Chun and Roh between 1980 and 1993.

27. For in-depth analyses of labor in these three East Asian economies, see Y. Lee 2011 on South Korea and Taiwan, D. Chang 2008 and Deyo 2012 on South Korea, and Sung 2006 on Singapore.

28. See a recent example of such an analysis of South Korea's telecommunications sector in S. Y. Kim 2012 (158–60).

29. In an earlier study of this catching up of South Korean and Taiwanese display producers with Japan, Linden et al. (1998, 32) argue that "in both countries, firm capabilities, corporate strategies and a blistering pace of change overwhelmed government initiatives." See also Pack and Saggi 2006; Cimoli et al. 2009c; Stiglitz and Lin 2013; Salazar-Xirinachs et al. 2014; and Coe and Yeung 2015 for critical assessments of the case for new industrial policy in a world of global production networks.

30. See also Cimoli et al. 2009a and Hobday 2011 for cautions against "lesson making" based on the achievement of past industrializers, such as East Asian economies.

31. As argued succinctly by Gereffi and Sturgeon (2013, 330), "there can be no return to the ISI [import substitution industrialization] and EOI [export oriented industrialization] policies of old. Domestic industries in both industrialized and developing countries no longer stand alone and compete mainly through arms-length trade; instead, they have become deeply intertwined through complex, overlapping business networks created through recurrent

waves of foreign direct investment (FDI) and global sourcing. Companies, localities and entire countries have come to occupy specialized niches within GVCs. For these reasons, today's industrial policies have a different character and generate different outcomes from before. Intentionally or not, governments currently engage in GVC-oriented industrialization when targeting key sectors for growth." See also Milberg et al. 2014; and Wade 2014b.

32. To this policy effect, UNCTAD (2013, 175) recommends that "active promotion of GVCs and GVC-led development strategies imply the encouragement and provision of support to economic activities aimed at generating exports in fragmented and geographically dispersed industry value chains, based on a narrower set of endowments and competitive advantages. And they imply active policies to encourage learning from GVC activities in which a country is present, to support the process of upgrading toward higher value added activities and diversifying into higher value added chains." Other related policy frameworks developed by various international organizations to promote participation in global value chains and global production networks are found in OECD 2011; 2013; Elms and Low 2013; and OECD-WTO-UNCTAD 2013. See Coe and Yeung 2015 and Yeung 2015 for a critical assessment of these policy frameworks in the context of subnational regional development.

33. Even then, there were significant "bottlenecks" in the implementation of industrial policy in, for example, South Korea (see Westphal 1990).

34. This discussion is based on Levy et al.'s (2006) analysis of France and Japan since the early 1980s.

35. See also the debate between Lin and Chang (2009), and Lin's (2012b) clarification of Wade's (2010) critique and his own neoclassical argument for the facilitating role of the state in industrial upgrading. A critical review of this market-state impasse can be found in Wade 2014b.

References

Aiginger, Karl, and Susanne Sieber. 2006. "The Matrix Approach to Industrial Policy." *International Review of Applied Economics* 20(5): 573–601.

Amsden, Alice H. 1989. *Asia's Next Giant: South Korea and Late Industrialization.* New York: Oxford University Press.

——. 2001. *The Rise of "The Rest": Challenges to the West from Late-Industrializing Economies.* New York: Oxford University Press.

——. 2007. *Escape from Empire: The Developing World's Journey through Heaven and Hell.* Cambridge, MA: MIT Press.

Amsden, Alice H., and Wan-Wen Chu. 2003. *Beyond Late Development: Taiwan's Upgrading Policies.* Cambridge, MA: MIT Press.

Amsden, Alice H., and Takashi Hikino. 1994. "Project Execution Capability, Organizational Know-How and Conglomerate Corporate Growth in Late Industrialization." *Industrial and Corporate Change* 3: 111–47.

Amsden, Alice H., and Ted Tschang. 2003. "A New Approach to Assessing the Technological Complexity of Different Categories of R&D." *Research Policy* 32(4): 553–72.

Angel, David P. 1994. *Restructuring for Innovation: The Remaking of the U.S. Semiconductor Industry.* New York: Guilford Press.

Antràs, Pol, and Davin Chor. 2013. "Organizing the Global Value Chain." *Econometrica* 81(6): 2127–2204.

Antràs, Pol, and Elhanan Helpman. 2004. "Global Sourcing." *Journal of Political Economy* 112: 552–80.

Aoki, Masahiko, Hyung-Ki Kim, and Masahiro Okuno-Fujiwara, eds. 1997. *The Role of Government in East Asian Economic Development: Comparative Institutional Analysis.* Oxford: Clarendon Press.

Arnold, Walter. 1989. "Bureaucratic Politics, State Capacity, and Taiwan's Automobile Industrial Policy." *Modern China* 15(2): 178–214.

Bae, YoungJa. 2011. "Global Value Chains, Industry Structure, and Technology Upgrading of Local Firms: The Personal Computer Industry in Korea and Taiwan during the 1980s." *Asian Journal of Technology Innovation* 19(2): 249–62.

Bair, Jennifer, ed. 2009. *Frontiers of Commodity Chain Research.* Stanford, CA: Stanford University Press.

Bartlett, Christopher A., and Sumantra Ghoshal. 1989. *Managing Across Borders: The Transnational Solution.* London: Century Business.

Bell, Martin, and Paulo N. Figueiredo. 2012. "Innovation Capability Building and Learning Mechanisms in Latecomer Firms." *Canadian Journal of Development Studies* 33(1): 14–40.

Bello, Walden. 2009. "States and Markets, States versus Markets: The Developmental State Debate as the Distinctive East Asian Contribution to International Political Economy." In Mark Blyth (ed.), *Routledge Handbook of International Political Economy: IPE as a Global Conversation*. New York: Routledge, 180–200.

Bello, Walden, and Stephanie Rosenfeld. 1990. *Dragons in Distress: Asia's Miracle Economies in Crisis*. San Francisco, CA: Food First Books.

Bengtsson, Bo, and Nils Hertting. 2014. "Generalization by Mechanism: Thin Rationality and Ideal-Type Analysis in Case Study Research." *Philosophy of the Social Sciences* 44(6): 707–32.

Berger, Suzanne, and Richard K. Lester, eds. 2005. *Global Taiwan: Building Competitive Strengths in a New International Economy*. Armonk, NY: M. E. Sharpe.

Block, Fred. 2008. "Swimming against the Current: The Rise of a Hidden Developmental State in the United States." *Politics and Society* 36(2): 169–206.

Block, Fred, and Mathew R. Keller, eds. 2011. *State of Innovation: Technology Policy in the United States*. Boulder, CO: Paradigm.

Borrus, Michael, Dieter Ernst, and Stephan Haggard, eds. 2000. *International Production Networks in Asia*. London: Routledge.

Bowen, John T. Jr., and Thomas R. Leinbach. 2006. "Competitive Advantage in Global Production Networks: Air Freight Services and the Electronics Industry in Southeast Asia." *Economic Geography* 82(2): 147–66.

Boyd, Richard, and Tak-Wing Ngo, eds. 2005a. *Asian States: Beyond the Developmental Perspective*. London: RoutledgeCurzon.

——. 2005b. "Emancipating the Political Economy of Asia from the Growth Paradigm." In Richard Boyd and Tak-Wing Ngo (eds.), *Asian States: Beyond the Developmental Perspective*. London: RoutledgeCurzon, 1–18.

Boyer, Robert, Hiroyasu Uemura, and Akinori Isogai. 2012. "Conclusion: the Evolving Diversity of Asian Capitalisms, from the Asian Crisis to the Subprime Crisis." In Robert Boyer, Hiroyasu Uemura, and Akinori Isogai, (eds.), *Diversity and Transformations of Asian Capitalisms*. London: Routledge, 330–49.

Brahmbhatt, Milan, and Albert Hu. 2010. "Ideas and Innovation in East Asia." *World Bank Research Observer* 25(2): 177–207.

Breznitz, Dan. 2005. "Innovation and the Limits of State Power: Integrated Circuit Design and Software in Taiwan." In Suzanne Berger and Richard K. Lester (eds.), *Global Taiwan: Building Competitive Strengths in a New International Economy*. Armonk, NY: M. E. Sharpe, 194–227.

——. 2007. *Innovation and the State: Political Choice and Strategies for Growth in Israel, Taiwan, and Ireland*. New Haven, CT: Yale University Press.

Brodsgaard, Erik Kjeld, and Susan Young, eds. 2000. *State Capacity in East Asia*. Oxford: Oxford University Press.

Bunge, Mario. 1997. "Mechanisms and Explanation." *Philosophy of Social Sciences* 27(4): 410–65.

——. 2004. "How Does It Work? The Search for Explanatory Mechanisms." *Philosophy of the Social Science* 34(2): 182–210.

Bunker, Stephen, and Paul S. Ciccantell. 2007. *East Asia and the Global Economy*. Baltimore, MD: Johns Hopkins University Press.

Büthe, Tim, and Walter Mattli. 2011. *The New Global Rulers*. Princeton, NJ: Princeton University Press.

Cabestan, Jean-Pierre, and Jacques deLisle, eds. 2014. *Political Changes in Taiwan under Ma Ying-Jeou*. London: Routledge.

Castells, Manuel. 1992. "Four Asian Tigers with a Dragon Head." In Richard P. Appelbaum and Jeffrey Henderson (eds.), *States and Development in the Asian Pacific Rim.* Newbury Park, CA: Sage, 33–70.

Castells, Manuel, L. Goh, and Reginald Yin-Wang Kwok. 1990. *The Shek Kip Mei Syndrome: Economic Development and Public Housing in Hong Kong and Singapore.* London: Pion.

Cattaneo, Olivier, Gary Gereffi, and Cornelia Staritz. 2010a. "Global Value Chains in a Postcrisis World." In Olivier Cattaneo, Gary Gereffi and Cornelia Staritz (eds.), *Global Value Chains in a Postcrisis World.* Washington, DC: World Bank, 3–20.

——, eds. 2010b. *Global Value Chains in a Postcrisis World.* Washington, DC: World Bank.

Chan, Chin Bock, ed. 2002. *Heart Work: Stories of How EDB Steered the Singapore Economy from 1961 into the 21st Century.* Singapore: EDB.

——, ed. 2011. *Heart Work 2: EDB and Partners.* Singapore: Straits Times Press.

Chandler, Alfred D. 1984. "The Emergence of Managerial Capitalism." *Business History Review* 58(4): 473–503.

——. 1990. *Scale and Scope: The Dynamics of Industrial Capitalism.* Cambridge, MA: Harvard University Press.

——. 2000. *Paths of Learning: The Evolution of High-Technology Industries.* New York: The Free Press.

Chang, Dae-oup. 2008. *Capitalist Development in Korea.* London: Routledge.

Chang, Ha-Joon. 2002. *Kicking Away the Ladder? Economic Development in Historical Perspective.* London: Anthem.

——. 2003. *Globalisation, Economic Development, and the Role of the State.* London: Zed Press.

Chang, Ha-Joon, Antonio Andreoni, and Ming Leong Kuan. 2013. *International Industrial Policy Experiences and the Lessons for the UK.* Working Paper No. 450. Centre for Business Research, University of Cambridge.

Chang, Ha-Joon, Hang-Jae Park, and Chul Gyue Yoo. 1998. "Interpreting the Korean Crisis." *Cambridge Journal of Economics* 22: 735–46.

Chang, Kyung-Sup, Ben Fine, and Linda Weiss, eds. 2012. *Developmental Politics in Transition.* Houndmills, Basingstoke: Palgrave Macmillan.

Chang, Sea-jin. 2003. *Financial Crisis and Transformation of Korean Business Groups.* Cambridge: Cambridge University Press.

——, ed. 2006a. *Business Groups in East Asia.* Oxford: Oxford University Press.

——. 2006b. "Korean Business Groups: The Financial Crisis and the Restructuring of Chaebols." In Sea-jin Chang (ed.), *Business Groups in East Asia.* Oxford: Oxford University Press, 52–69.

——. 2008. *Sony versus Samsung.* Singapore: Wiley.

Chang, Sea-Jin, Chi-nien Chung, and Ishtiaq P. Mahmood. 2006. "When and How Does Group Affiliation Promote Firm Innovation." *Organization Science* 17(5): 637–56.

Checkel, Jeffrey T. 2006. "Tracing Causal Mechanisms." *International Studies Review* 8(2): 362–70.

Chen, Liang-Chih. 2009. "Learning through Informal Local and Global Linkages: The Case of Taiwan's Machine Tool Industry." *Research Policy* 38(3): 527–35.

Chen, Tain-Jy. 2014. *Taiwan's Industrial Policy since 1990.* Unpublished manuscript. National Taiwan University.

Chia, Siow Yue. 1997. "Singapore: Advanced Production Base and Smart Hub of the Electronics Industry." In Wendy Dobson and Chia Siow Yue (eds.), *Multinationals and East Asian Integration.* Canada: IDRC, 31–61.

Chibber, Vivek. 2002. "Bureaucratic Rationality and the Developmental State." *American Journal of Sociology* 107: 951–89.

Cho, Dong Sung, and Michael E. Porter. 1986. "Changing Global Industry Leadership: The Case of Shipbuilding." In Michael E. Porter (ed.), *Competition in Global Industries.* Boston: Harvard Business School Press, 539–67.

Chong, Alan. 2007. "Singapore's Political Economy, 1997–2007." *Asian Survey* 47(6): 952–76.

Chou, Chia-Chan, and Pao-Long Chang. 2004. "Core Competence and Competitive Strategy of the Taiwan Shipbuilding Industry." *Maritime Policy and Management* 31(2): 125–37.

Chu, Wan-wen. 2009. "Can Taiwan's Second Movers Upgrade via Branding?" *Research Policy* 38(6): 1054–65.

Chu, Yin-wah. 2009. "Eclipse or Reconfigured? South Korea's Developmental State and Challenges of the Global Knowledge Economy." *Economy and Society* 38(2): 278–303.

Chu, Yun-han. 1989. "State Structure and Economic Adjustment of the East Asian Newly Industrializing Countries." *International Organization* 43: 647–72.

——. 2007. "Re-engineering the Developmental State in an Age of Globalization Taiwan's Quest for High-Tech Industries." In Robert Ash and J. Megan Greene (eds.), *Taiwan in the 21st Century*. London: Routledge, 154–76.

Chua, Beng Huat. 1997. *Political Legitimacy and Housing: Stakeholding in Singapore*. New York: Routledge.

Chuang, Ya-Shisu. 2008. *The Development of Absorptive Capacity in Latecomer Firms: Case Studies from the Taiwanese TFT-LCD Industry*. Ph.D. thesis, University of Sussex.

Chung, Chi-Nien, and Ishtiaq P. Mahmood. 2006. "Taiwanese Business Groups: Steady Growth in Institutional Transition." In Sea-jin Chang (ed.), *Business Groups in East Asia*. Oxford: Oxford University Press, 70–93.

——. 2010. "Business Groups in Taiwan." In Asli M. Colpan, Takashi Hikino, and James R. Lincoln (eds.), *The Oxford Handbook of Business Groups*. Oxford: Oxford University Press, 180–209.

Chung, Young-Iob. 2007. *South Korea in the Fast Lane*. New York: Oxford University Press.

Chyi, Yih-Luan, Yee-Man Lai, and Wen-Hsien Liu. 2012. "Knowledge Spillovers and Firm Performance in the High-Technology Industrial Cluster." *Research Policy* 41(3): 556–64.

Cimoli, Mario, Giovanni Dosi, Richard Nelson, and Joseph E. Stiglitz. 2009a. "Institutions and Policies Shaping Industrial Development." In Mario Cimoli, Giovanni Dosi, and Joseph E. Stiglitz (eds.), *Industrial Policy and Development*. Oxford: Oxford University Press, 19–38.

Cimoli, Mario, Giovanni Dosi, and Joseph E. Stiglitz. 2009b. "The Political Economy of Capabilities Accumulation." In Mario Cimoli, Giovanni Dosi, and Joseph E. Stiglitz (eds.), *Industrial Policy and Development*. Oxford: Oxford University Press, 1–18.

Cimoli, Mario, Giovanni Dosi, and Joseph E. Stiglitz, eds. 2009c. *Industrial Policy and Development*. Oxford: Oxford University Press.

Coe, Neil M., and Martin Hess. 2011. "Local and Regional Development: A Global Production Network Approach." In Andy Pike, Andrés Rodríguez-Pose, and John Tomaney (eds.), *Handbook of Local and Regional Development*. London: Routledge, 128–38.

Coe, Neil M., Martin Hess, and Peter Dicken, eds. 2008. "Theme Issue on Global Production Networks." *Journal of Economic Geography* 8(3): 267–440.

Coe, Neil M., Martin Hess, Henry Wai-chung Yeung, Peter Dicken, and Jeffrey Henderson. 2004. "'Globalizing' Regional Development: A Global Production Networks Perspective." *Transactions of the Institute of British Geographers* n.s. 29(4): 468–84.

Coe, Neil M., and Henry Wai-chung Yeung. 2015. *Global Production Networks: Theorizing Economic Development in an Interconnected World*. Oxford: Oxford University Press.

Cole, David C., and Yung Chul Park. 1983. *Financial Development in Korea, 1945–1978*. Cambridge, MA: Harvard University Press.

Coleman, James S. 1986. "Social Theory, Social Research, and a Theory of Action." *American Journal of Sociology* 91(6): 1309–35.

——. 1990. *Foundations of Social Theory*. Cambridge, MA: Harvard University Press.

Colpan, Asli M., Takashi Hikino, and James R. Lincoln, eds. 2010. *The Oxford Handbook of Business Groups*. Oxford: Oxford University Press.

Costello, Sam. 2015. "How Many iPhones Have Been Sold Worldwide." http://ipod.about.com/od/glossary/f/how-many-iphones-sold.htm, accessed on May 14, 2015.

Cowhey, Peter, and John Richards. 2006. "Building Global Service Markets." In Jonah D. Levy (ed.), *The State after Statism: New State Activities in the Age of Liberalization.* Cambridge, MA: Harvard University Press, 301–39.

Crotty, James, and Kang-Kook Lee. 2007. "From East Asian "Miracle" to Neoliberal 'Mediocrity.' " In Jang-Sup Shin (ed.), *Global Challenges and Local Responses.* London: Routledge, 73–94.

Cumings, Bruce. 1987. "The Origins and Development of Northeast Asian Political Economy." In Frederic C. Deyo (ed.), *The Political Economy of the New Asian Industrialism.* Ithaca, NY: Cornell University Press, 44–83.

——. 1999. "Webs with No Spiders, Spiders with No Webs: The Geneology of the Developmental State." In Meredith Woo-Cumings (ed.), *The Developmental State.* Ithaca, NY: Cornell University Press, 61–92.

Cunningham, Edward, Teresa Lynch, and Eric Thun. 2005. "A Tale of Two Sectors: Diverging Paths in Taiwan's Automotive Industry." In Suzanne Berger and Richard K. Lester (eds.), *Global Taiwan: Building Competitive Strengths in a New International Economy.* Armonk, NY: M. E. Sharpe, 97–136.

Cyhn, Jin W. 2002. *Technology Transfer and International Production: The Development of the Electronics Industry in Korea.* Cheltenham, UK: Edward Elgar.

Dean, Jason. 2007. "The Forbidden City of Terry Gou." *The Wall Street Journal,* August 11.

Dedrick, Jason, and Kenneth Kraemer. 1998. *Asia's Computer Challenge.* New York: Oxford University Press.

Demetriou, Chares. 2007. "The Realist Approach to Explanatory Mechanisms in Social Science: More Than a Heuristic?" *Philosophy of the Social Sciences* 39(3): 440–62.

Demeulenaere, Pierre, ed. 2011. *Analytical Sociology and Social Mechanisms.* Cambridge: Cambridge University Press.

De Meyer, Arnoud, Pamela C.M. Mar, Frank-Jürgen Richter, and Peter Williamson, eds. 2005. *Global Future: The Next Challenge for Asian Business.* Singapore: John Wiley.

Deyo, Frederic C., ed. 1987. *The Political Economy of the New Asian Industrialism.* Ithaca, NY: Cornell University Press.

——. 2012. *Reforming Asian Labor Systems.* Ithaca, NY: Cornell University Press.

Dhanabalan, S. 2001. *Role of Government Ownership of Business in the Era of Globalisation and Role of Temasek.* Speech to Foreign Correspondents Association. Singapore, December 12, Singapore.

Diamond, Larry, and Gi-Wook Shin, eds. 2014. *New Challenges for Maturing Democracies in Korea and Taiwan.* Stanford, CA: Stanford University Press.

Dicken, Peter. 2015. *Global Shift.* 7th ed. London: Sage.

Dicken, Peter, Philip Kelly, Kris Olds, and Henry Wai-chung Yeung. 2001. "Chains and Networks, Territories and Scales: Towards an Analytical Framework for the Global Economy." *Global Networks* 1(2): 89–112.

Di Maio, Michele. 2009. "Industrial Policies in Developing Countries." In Mario Cimoli, Giovanni Dosi, and Joseph E. Stiglitz (eds.), *Industrial Policy and Development.* Oxford: Oxford University Press, 107–43.

Dittmer, Lowell. 2007. "The Asian Financial Crisis and the Asian Developmental State—Ten Years After." *Asian Survey* 47(6): 829–33.

Doner, Richard F., Bryan K. Ritchie, and Dan Slater. 2005. "Systemic Vulnerability and the Origins of Developmental States." *International Organization* 59(2): 327–61.

Duhigg, Charles, and David Barboza. 2012. "In China, Human Costs Are Built into an iPad." *New York Times,* January 25.

Duhigg, Charles, and Keith Bradsher. 2012. "How the U.S. Lost Out on iPhone Work." *New York Times,* January 21.

Dunning, John H., and Sarianna M. Lundan. 2008. *Multinational Enterprises and the Global Economy*. 2nd ed. Cheltenham, UK: Edward Elgar.

Edigheji, Omano, ed. 2010. *Constructing a Democratic Developmental State in South Africa*. Cape Town: HSRC Press.

Elms, Deborah K., and Patrick Low, eds. 2013. *Global Value Chains in a Changing World*. Geneva: World Trade Organization.

Elster, Jon. 1989. *Nuts and Bolts for the Social Sciences*. Cambridge: Cambridge University Press.

Ernst, Dieter. 2005. "Complexity and Internationalisation of Innovation: Why Is Chip Design Moving to Asia?" *International Journal of Innovation Management* 9(1): 47–73.

——. 2009. *A New Geography of Knowledge in the Electronics Industry? Asia's Role in Global Innovation Networks*. Policy Studies No. 54. Honolulu: East-West Center.

——. 2010. "Upgrading through Innovation in a Small Network Economy: Insights from Taiwan's IT Industry." *Economics of Innovation and New Technology* 19(4): 295–324.

——. 2013. *Industrial Upgrading through Low-Cost and Fast Innovation—Taiwan's Experience*. Working Papers Economics Series No.133. Honolulu: East-West Center.

Ernst, Dieter, and Linsu Kim. 2002. "Global Production Networks, Knowledge Diffusion, and Local Capability Formation." *Research Policy* 31 (8–9): 1417–29.

Evans, Peter. 1995. *Embedded Autonomy: States and Industrial Transformation*. Princeton, NJ: Princeton University Press.

——. 2008. "Is an Alternative Globalization Possible?" *Politics and Society* 36(2): 271–305.

——. 2010. "Constructing the 21st Century Developmental State." In Omano Edigheji (ed.), *Constructing a Democratic Developmental State in South Africa*. Cape Town: HSRC Press, 37–58.

——. 2014. "The Korean Experience and the Twenty-First-Century Transition to a Capability-Enhancing Developmental State." In Thandika Mkandawire and Il-cheong Yi (eds.), *Learning from the South Korean Developmental Success*. New York: Palgrave, 31–53.

Falleti, Tulia G., and Julia F. Lynch. 2009. "Context and Causal Mechanisms in Political Analysis." *Comparative Political Studies* 42(9): 1143–66.

Feenstra, Robert C. 1998. "Integration of Trade and Disintegration of Production in the Global Economy." *Journal of Economic Perspectives* 12(4): 31–50.

Ferrarini, Benno, and David Hummels, eds. 2014. *Asia and Global Production Networks*. Cheltenham, UK: Edward Elgar.

Fields, Karl J. 1995. *Enterprise and the State in Korea and Taiwan*. Ithaca, NY: Cornell University Press.

Fine, Ben. 2013. "Beyond the Developmental State." In Ben Fine, Jyoti Saraswati, and Daniela Tavasci (eds.), *Beyond the Developmental State*. London: Pluto Press, 1–32.

Fine, Ben, Jyoti Saraswati, and Daniela Tavasci, eds. 2013. *Beyond the Developmental State: Industrial Policy into the 21st Century*. London: Pluto Press.

Forbes, Naushad, and David Wield. 2002. *From Followers to Leaders: Managing Technology and Innovation in Newly Industrializing Countries*. London: Routledge.

Frangie, Samer. 2011. "Post-Development, Developmental State and Genealogy." *Third World Quarterly* 32(7): 1183–98.

Fröbel, Folker, Jurgen Heinrichs, and Otto Kreye. 1980. *The New International Division of Labour*. Cambridge: Cambridge University Press.

Fuller, Douglas B. 2005. "Moving along the Electronics Value Chain: Taiwan in the Global Economy." In Suzanne Berger and Richard K. Lester (eds.), *Global Taiwan: Building Competitive Strengths in a New International Economy*. Armonk, NY: M. E. Sharpe, 137–65.

——. 2007. "Globalization for Nation-Building: Taiwan's Industrial and Technology Policies for High-Technology Sectors." *Journal of Interdisciplinary Economics* 18(2/3): 203–24.

——. 2008. "The Cross-Strait Economic Relationship's Impact on Economic Development in Taiwan and China." *Asian Survey* 48(2): 239–64.

Fuller, Douglas B., Akintunde I. Akinwande, and Charles G. Sodini. 2005. "Leading, Following, or Cooked Goose? Explaining Innovation Successes and Failures in Taiwan's Electronics Industry." In Suzanne Berger and Richard K. Lester (eds.), *Global Taiwan: Building Competitive Strengths in a New International Economy.* Armonk, NY: M. E. Sharpe, 76–96.

Gambetta, Diego. 1998. "Concatenations of Mechanisms." In Peter Hedström and Richard Swedberg (eds.), *Social Mechanisms: An Analytical Approach to Social Theory,* 102–24.

Gereffi, Gary. 1994. "The Organization of Buyer-Driven Global Commodity Chains." In Gary Gereffi and Miguel Korzeniewicz (eds.), *Commodity Chains and Global Capitalism.* Westport, CT: Praeger, 95–122.

——. 1999. "International Trade and Industrial Upgrading in the Apparel Commodity Chain." *Journal of International Economics* 48(1): 37–70.

——. 2014. "Global Value Chains in a Post-Washington Consensus World." *Review of International Political Economy* 21(1): 9–37.

Gereffi, Gary, John Humphrey, and Timothy Sturgeon. 2005. "The Governance of Global Value Chains." *Review of International Political Economy* 12(1): 78–104.

Gereffi, Gary, and Miguel Korzeniewicz, eds. 1994. *Commodity Chains and Global Capitalism.* Westport, CT: Praeger.

Gereffi, Gary, and Timothy Sturgeon. 2013. "Global Value Chain-Oriented Industrial Policy." In Deborah K. Elms and Patrick Low (eds.), *Global Value Chains in a Changing World.* Geneva: World Trade Organization, 329–60.

Gerring, John. 1999. "What Makes a Concept Good?" *Polity* 31(3): 357–93.

——. 2004. "What Is a Case Study and What Is It Good For?" *American Political Science Review* 98(2): 341–54.

——. 2005. "Causation: a Unified Framework for the Social Sciences." *Journal of Theoretical Politics* 17(2): 163–98.

——. 2008. "The Mechanismic Worldview: Thinking inside the Box." *British Journal of Political Science* 38(1): 161–79.

——. 2010, "Causal Mechanisms: Yes, but . . ." *Comparative Political Studies* 43(11): 1499–1526.

——. 2012. *Social Science Methodology.* 2nd ed. Cambridge: Cambridge University Press.

Gerschenkron, Alexander. 1962. *Economic Backwardness in Historical Perspective.* Cambridge, MA: Belknap Press.

Gills, Barry K. 1996. "Economic Liberalization and Reform in South Korea in the 1990s." *Third World Quarterly* 17(4): 667–88.

Glassman, Jim, and Young-Jin Choi. 2014. "The Chaebol and the US Military–Industrial Complex: Cold War Geopolitical Economy and South Korean Industrialization." *Environment and Planning A* 46(5): 1160–80.

Goh, Evelyn. 2013. *The Struggle for Order: Hegemony, Hierarchy, and Transition in Post-Cold War East Asia.* Oxford: Oxford University Press.

Gold, Thomas B. 2000. "The Waning of the Kumintang State on Taiwan." In Kjeld Erik Brodsgaard and Susan Young (eds.), *State Capacity in East Asia.* Oxford: Oxford University Press, 84–113.

Gorski, Philip S. 2009. "Social "Mechanisms" and Comparative-Historical Sociology: A Critical Realist Proposal." In Peter Hedström and Björn Wittrock (eds.), *Frontiers of Sociology.* Leiden: Brill, 147–96.

——. 2013. "What Is Critical Realism? And Why Should You Care?" *Contemporary Sociology* 42(5): 658–70.

Gourevitch, Peter. 2008. "Containing the Oligarchs: The Politics of Corporate Governance Systems in East Asia." In Andrew Macintyre, T. J. Pempel, and John Ravenhill (eds.), *Crisis as Catalyst: Asia's Dynamic Political Economy.* Ithaca, NY: Cornell University Press, 70–92.

Gray, Kevin. 2011. "Taiwan and the Geopolitics of Late Development." *Pacific Review* 24(5): 577–99.

Graziano, Dan. 2012. "IDC: Samsung Passes Apple to become No.1 in Smartphones." http://www.bgr.com/2012/05/01/apple-samsung-idc-market-share, accessed on July 7, 2012.

Greene, J. Megan. 2007. "Taiwan's Knowledge-Based Economy." In Robert Ash and J. Megan Greene (eds.), *Taiwan in the 21st Century*. London: Routledge, 128–53.

———. 2008. *The Origins of the Developmental State in Taiwan*. Cambridge, MA: Harvard University Press.

Gross, Neil. 2009. "A Pragmatist Theory of Social Mechanisms." *American Sociological Review* 74(3): 358–79.

Guillén, Mauro F. 2010. "Capability Building in Business Groups." In Asli M. Colpan, Takashi Hikino and James R. Lincoln (eds.), *The Oxford Handbook of Business Groups*. Oxford: Oxford University Press, 743–62.

Gulati, Ranjay. 2007. *Managing Network Resources*. Oxford: Oxford University Press.

Haggard, Stephan. 1990. *Pathways from the Periphery*. Ithaca, NY: Cornell University Press.

———. 2015. "The Developmental State Is Dead: Long Live the Developmental State!" In James Mahoney and Kathleen Thelen (eds.), *Comparative Historical Analysis in Contemporary Political Science*. Cambridge: Cambridge University Press, 39–66.

Haggard, Stephan, and Robert R. Kaufman. 2008. *Development, Democracy, and Welfare States*. Princeton, NJ: Princeton University Press.

Haggard, Stephan, and Yu Zheng. 2013. "Institutional Innovation and Investment in Taiwan." *Business and Politics* 15(4): 435–66.

Hahm, Joon-Ho. 2003. "The Government, the *Chaebol*, and Financial Institutions before the Economic Crisis." In Stephan Haggard, Wonhyuk Lim, and Euysung Kim (eds.), *Economic Crisis and Corporate Restructuring in Korea*. Cambridge: Cambridge University Press, 79–101.

Hall, Peter A., and David Soskice, eds. 2001. *Varieties of Capitalism*. Oxford: Oxford University Press.

Hamilton-Hart, Natasha. 2000. "The Singapore State Revisited." *Pacific Review* 13(2): 195–216.

———. 2002. *Asian States, Asian Bankers*. Ithaca, NY: Cornell University Press.

———. 2008. "Banking Systems a Decade after the Crisis." In Andrew Macintyre, T. J. Pempel, and John Ravenhill (eds.), *Crisis as Catalyst: Asia's Dynamic Political Economy*. Ithaca, NY: Cornell University Press, 45–69.

Hancké, Bob, ed. 2009. *Debating Varieties of Capitalism*. Oxford: Oxford University Press.

Harbert, Tam. 2010. "Hon Hai Plans on Becoming LCD Powerhouse." *EDN*, July 6, 2010. www.edn.com, accessed on September 18, 2012.

Harrison, Bennett. 1994. *Lean and Mean: The Changing Landscape of Corporate Power in the Age of Flexibility*. New York: Basic Books.

Hart-Landsberg, Martin. 1993. *The Rush to Development: Economic Change and Political Struggle in South Korea*. New York: Monthly Review Press.

Hatch, Walter. 2010. *Asia's Flying Geese: How Regionalization Shapes Japan*. Ithaca, NY: Cornell University Press.

Hatch, Walter, and Kozo Yamamura. 1996. *Asia in Japan's Embrace*. Cambridge: Cambridge University Press.

Hedström, Peter, and Richard Swedberg. 1996. "Social Mechanisms." *Acta Sociologica* 39(3): 281–308.

———, eds. 1998a. *Social Mechanisms: An Analytical Approach to Social Theory*. Cambridge: Cambridge University Press.

———. 1998b. "Social Mechanisms: An Introductory Essay." In Peter Hedström and Richard Swedberg (eds.), *Social Mechanisms: An Analytical Approach to Social Theory*. Cambridge: Cambridge University Press, 1–31.

Hedström, Peter, and Björn Wittrock, eds. 2009. *Frontiers of Sociology*. Leiden: Brill.

Hedström, Peter, and Petri Ylikoski. 2010. "Causal Mechanisms in the Social Sciences." *Annual Review of Sociology* 36: 49–67.

Henderson, Jeffrey. 1986. "The New International Division of Labour and American Semi-conductor Production in South-East Asia." In Chris Dixon, David Drakakis-Smith, and Douglas Watts (eds.), *Multinational Corporations and the Third World*. Boulder, CO: Westview Press, 91–117.

——. 1989. *The Globalisation of High Technology Production*. London: Routledge.

——. 2011. *East Asian Transformation*. London: Routledge.

Henderson, Jeffrey, Peter Dicken, Martin Hess, Neil M. Coe, and Henry Wai-chung Yeung. 2002. "Global Production Networks and the Analysis of Economic Development." *Review of International Political Economy* 9(3): 436–64.

Herrigel, Gary. 1996. *Industrial Constructions: The Sources of German Industrial Power*. Cambridge: Cambridge University Press.

Hess, Martin, and Henry Wai-chung Yeung, eds. 2006. "Theme Issue on Global Production Networks." *Environment and Planning A* 38(7): 1193–1305.

Hirschman, Albert O. 1958. *The Strategy of Economic Development*. New Haven, CT: Yale University Press.

Hobday, Michael. 1995. *Innovation in East Asia*. Cheltenham, UK: Edward Elgar.

——. 1998. "Latecomer Catch-Up Strategies in Electronics: Samsung of Korea and Acer of Taiwan." *Asia Pacific Business Review* 4(2/3): 48–83.

——. 2000. "East versus Southeast Asian Innovation Systems." In Linsu Kim and Richard R. Nelson (eds.), *Technology, Learning, and Innovation*. Cambridge: Cambridge University Press, 129–69.

——. 2001. "The Electronics Industries of the Asia-Pacific." *Asian-Pacific Economic Literature* 15(1): 13–29.

——. 2003. "Innovation in Asian Industrialisation: A Gerschenkronian Perspective." *Oxford Development Studies* 31(3): 293–314.

——. 2011. *Learning from Asia's Success beyond Simplistic "Lesson-Making."* UNU-WIDER Working Paper No. 2011/42.

Hobday, Michael, and Asli M. Colpan. 2010. "Technological Innovation and Business Groups." In Asli M. Colpan, Takashi Hikino, and James R. Lincoln (eds.), *The Oxford Handbook of Business Groups*. Oxford: Oxford University Press, 763–81.

Hobday, Michael, Andrew Davies, and Andrea Prencipe. 2005. "Systems Integration: A Core Capability of the Modern Corporation." *Industrial and Corporate Change* 14(6): 1109–43.

Hobday, Michael, Howard Rush, and John Bessant. 2004. "Approaching the Innovation Frontier in Korea." *Research Policy* 33(10): 1433–57.

Hsu, Jinn-Yuh, Jessie P. Poon, and Henry Wai-chung Yeung. 2008. "External Leveraging and Technological Upgrading among East Asian Firms in the United States." *European Planning Studies* 16(1): 99–118.

Hsueh, Roselyn. 2011. *China's Regulatory State*. Ithaca, NY: Cornell University Press.

Hu, Albert Guangzhou. 2009. "The Regionalization of Knowledge Flows in East Asia." *World Development* 37(9): 1465–77.

Hu, Mei-Chih. 2012. "Technological Innovation Capabilities in the Thin Film Transistor-Liquid Crystal Display Industries of Japan, Korea, and Taiwan." *Research Policy* 41(3): 541–55.

Hu, Mei-Chih, and John A. Mathews. 2009. "Estimating the Innovation Effects of University-Industry-Government Linkages: The Case of Taiwan." *Journal of Management and Organization* 15(2): 138–54.

Huff, W. Gregg. 1994. *The Economic Growth of Singapore*. Cambridge: Cambridge University Press.

Humphrey, John, and Hubert Schmitz. 2002. "How Does Insertion in Global Value Chains Affect Upgrading in Industrial Clusters?" *Regional Studies* 36(9): 1017–27.

Hundt, David. 2009. *Korea's Developmental Alliance*. London: Routledge.

——. 2014. "Economic Crisis in Korea and the Degraded Developmental State." *Australian Journal of International Affairs* 68(5): 499–514.

Hung, Shiu-Wan, and Ruei-Hung Tang. 2008. "Factors Affecting the Choice of Technology Acquisition Mode: An Empirical Analysis of the Electronic Firms of Japan, Korea and Taiwan." *Technovation* 28(9): 551–63.

Hwang, Hye-Ran, and Jae-Yong Choung. 2014. "The Co-evolution of Technology and Institutions in the Catch-Up Process." *Journal of Development Studies* 50(9): 1240–60.

Jayasuriya, Kanishka. 2005. "Beyond Institutional Fetishism: From the Developmental to the Regulatory State." *New Political Economy* 10(3): 381–87.

Jessop, Bob. 1990. *State Theory*. Cambridge: Polity Press.

Jho, Whasun. 2007. "Liberalization as a Development Strategy: Network Governance in the Korean Mobile Telecom Market." *Governance* 20(4): 633–54.

Johnson, Chalmers. 1982. *MITI and the Japanese Economic Miracle*. Stanford, CA: Stanford University Press.

——. 1995. *Japan: Who Governs?* New York: W. W. Norton.

——. 1999. "The Developmental State: Odyssey of a Concept." In Meredith Woo-Cumings (ed.), *The Developmental State*. Ithaca, NY: Cornell University Press, 32–60.

Kalinowski, Thomas. 2008. "Korea's Recovery since the 1997/98 Financial Crisis." *New Political Economy* 13(4): 447–62.

Kalinowski, Thomas, and Hyekyung Cho. 2009. "The Political Economy of Financial Liberalization in South Korea." *Asian Survey* 49(2): 221–42.

Kang, David C. 2002. *Crony Capitalism: Corruption and Development in South Korea and the Philippines*. Cambridge: Cambridge University Press.

Kang, Myung-koo. 2009. "The Sequence and Consequences of Bank Restructuring in South Korea, 1998–2006: Too Fast to Adjust." *Asian Survey* 49(2): 243–67.

Kang, T. W. 1989. *Is Korea the Next Japan?* New York: The Free Press.

Kawakami, Momoko. 2009. "Learning from Customers Growth of Taiwanese Notebook PC Manufacturers as Original Design Manufacturing Suppliers." *China Information* 23: 103–28.

Keller, William W., and Louis W. Pauly. 2003. "Crisis and Adaptation in Taiwan and South Korea: The Political Economy of Semiconductors." In William W. Keller and Richard J. Samuels (eds.), *Crisis and Innovation in Asian Technology*. Cambridge: Cambridge University Press, 137–59.

Khan, Mushtaq H., and Stephanie Blankenburg. 2009. "The Political Economy of Industrial Policy in Asia and Latin America." In Mario Cimoli, Giovanni Dosi, and Joseph E. Stiglitz (eds.), *Industrial Policy and Development*. Oxford: Oxford University Press, 336–77.

Khanna, Tarun, and Yishay Yafeh. 2007. "Business Groups in Emerging Markets." *Journal of Economic Literature* 45: 331–72.

Kim, Byung-Kook. 2003. "The Politics of *Chaebol* Reform, 1980–1997." In Stephan Haggard, Wonhyuk Lim, and Euysung Kim (eds.), *Economic Crisis and Corporate Restructuring in Korea*. Cambridge: Cambridge University Press, 53–78.

Kim, Eun Mee. 1997. *Big Business, Strong State: Collusion and Conflict in Korean Development, 1960–1990*. Albany, NY: SUNY Press.

Kim, Hicheon. 2010. "Business Groups in South Korea." In Asli M. Colpan, Takashi Hikino, and James R. Lincoln (eds.), *The Oxford Handbook of Business Groups*. Oxford: Oxford University Press, 157–79.

Kim, Jiyoon. 2014. "The Party System in Korea and Identity Politics." In Larry Diamond and Gi-Wook Shin (eds.), *New Challenges for Maturing Democracies in Korea and Taiwan*. Stanford, CA: Stanford University Press, 71–105.

Kim, Linsu. 1997. *Imitation to Innovation: The Dynamics of Korea's Technological Learning.* Boston, MA: Harvard Business School Press.

——. 1998. "Crisis Construction and Organisational Learning: Capability Building in Catching-Up at Hyundai Motor." *Organization Science* 9(4): 506–21.

——. 2000. "Korea's National Innovation System in Transition." In Linsu Kim and Richard R. Nelson (eds.), *Technology, Learning, and Innovation.* Cambridge: Cambridge University Press, 335–60.

——. 2003. "Crisis, Reform, and National Innovation in South Korea." In William W. Keller and Richard J. Samuels (eds.), *Crisis and Innovation in Asian Technology.* Cambridge: Cambridge University Press, 86–107.

Kim, Linsu, and Richard R. Nelson, eds. 2000a. *Technology, Learning, and Innovation.* Cambridge: Cambridge University Press.

——. 2000b. "Introduction." In Linsu Kim and Richard R. Nelson (eds.), *Technology, Learning, and Innovation.* Cambridge: Cambridge University Press, 1–9.

Kim, Samuel S., ed. 2003. *Korea's Democratization.* Cambridge: Cambridge University Press.

Kim, Sung-Young. 2012. "Transitioning from Fast-Follower to Innovator: The Institutional Foundations of the Korean Telecommunications Sector." *Review of International Political Economy* 19(1): 140–68.

Kim, Wan-Soon, and You-il Lee. 2007. *The Korean Economy: The Challenges of FDI-Led Globalization.* Cheltenham, UK: Edward Elgar.

Kim, Yongyul. 2011. "From Catch-Up to Overtaking: Competition and Innovation in the Semiconductor Industries of Korea and Japan." *Asian Journal of Technology Innovation* 19(2): 297–311.

Kohli, Atul. 2004. *State-Directed Development.* Cambridge: Cambridge University Press.

——. 2009. "Nationalist versus Dependent Capitalist Development." *Studies in Comparative International Development* 44(4): 386–410.

Kor, Kian Beng. 2010. "Shipyards Set Example for Productivity." *Straits Times*, August 30. http://www.pmo.gov.sg, accessed on September 15, 2014.

Krugman, Paul. 1994. "The Myth of the Asia Miracle." *Foreign Affairs* 73(6): 62–78.

Kwon, Huck-ju, ed. 2004. *Transforming the Developmental Welfare State in East Asia.* Houndmills, Basingstoke: Palgrave Macmillan.

Kwon, Hyeong-ki. 2012. *National Globalization: Korean-Style Globalization from a Comparative Perspective.* Unpublished manuscript.

Lansbury, Russell D., Chung-Sok Suh, and Seung-Ho Kwon. 2007. *The Global Korean Motor Industry.* London: Routledge.

Lee, Jaeho, and Jim Slater. 2007. "Dynamic Capabilities, Entrepreneurial Rent-Seeking, and the Investment Development Path: The Case of Samsung." *Journal of International Technology Management* 13(3): 241–57.

Lee, Keun. 2013. *Schumpeterian Analysis of Economic Catch-up.* Cambridge: Cambridge University Press.

Lee, KongRae. 2000. "Technological Learning and Entries of User Firms for Capital Goods in Korea." In Linsu Kim and Richard R. Nelson (eds.), *Technology, Learning, and Innovation: Experiences of Newly Industrializing Economies.* Cambridge: Cambridge University Press, 170–92.

Lee, Kuan Yew. 2000. *From Third World to First: The Singapore Story: 1965–2000.* Singapore: Times Editions.

Lee, Kuen, and Chaisung Lim. 2001. "Technological Regimes, Catching-Up and Leapfrogging: Findings from the Korean Industries." *Research Policy* 30(3): 459–83.

Lee, Kuen, Chaisung Lim, and Wichin Song. 2005. "Emerging Digital Technology as a Window of Opportunity and Technological Leapfrogging: Catch-Up in Digital TV by the Korean Firms." *International Journal of Technology Management* 29(1/2): 40–63.

Lee, Kwon-Hyung. 2013. "An Alternative Perspective on Industrial Policy: The Case of the South Korean Car Industry." In Ben Fine, Jyoti Saraswati, and Daniela Tavasci (eds.) *Beyond the Developmental State*. London: Pluto Press, 61–84.

Lee, Namhee. 2007. *The Making of Minjung: Democracy and the Politics of Representation in South Korea*. Ithaca, NY: Cornell University Press.

Lee, Wei-chin, ed. 2010. *Taiwan's Politics in the 21st Century*. Singapore: World Scientific.

Lee, Yong-Sook. 2009. "Balanced Development in Globalizing Regional Development? Unpacking the New Regional Policy in South Korea." *Regional Studies* 43(3): 353–68.

Lee, Yong-Sook, Inhye Heo, and Hyungjoo Kim. 2014. "The Role of the State as an Inter-Scalar Mediator in Globalizing Liquid Crystal Display Industry Development in South Korea." *Review of International Political Economy* 21(1): 109–29.

Lee, Yoonkyung. 2011. *Militants or Partisans: Labor Unions and Democratic Politics in Korea and Taiwan*. Stanford, CA: Stanford University Press.

Leftwich, Adrian. 2008. *Developmental States, Effective States and Poverty Reduction*. United Nations Research Institute for Social development (UNRISD).

Leibfried, Stephan, Frank Nullmeier, Evelyne Huber, Matthew Lange, Jonah Levy, and John D. Stephens, eds. 2013. *Oxford Handbook of Transformations of the State*. Oxford: Oxford University Press.

Leou, Chia-feng. 2011. *Democratisation and Financial Governance: The Politics of Financial Reform in Taiwan (1988–2008)*. Ph.D. diss., SOAS, University of London.

Levy, David L. 2008. "Political Contestation in Global Production Networks." *Academy of Management Review* 33(4): 943–63.

Levy, Jonah D., Mari Miura, and Gene Park. 2006. "Exiting Etatisme? New Directions in State Policy in France and Japan." In Jonah D. Levy (ed.), *The State after Statism: New State Activities in the Age of Liberalization*. Cambridge, MA: Harvard University Press, 93–136.

Lim, Haeran. 2009. "Democratization and the Transformation Process in East Asian Developmental States: Financial Reform in Korea and Taiwan." *Asian Perspective* 33(1): 75–110.

———. 2010. "The Transformation of the Developmental State and Economic Reform in Korea." *Journal of Contemporary Asia* 40(2): 188–210.

Lim, Youngil. 1999. *Technology and Productivity: The Korean Way of Learning and Catching Up*. Cambridge, MA: MIT Press.

Lin, Justin Yifu. 2012a. *The Quest for Prosperity*. Princeton, NJ: Princeton University Press.

———. 2012b. *New Structural Economics*. Washington, DC: The World Bank.

Lin, Justin Yifu, and Ha-Joon Chang. 2009. "Should Industrial Policy in Developing Countries Conform to Comparative Advantage or Defy It?" *Development Policy Review* 27(5): 483–502.

Linden, Greg, Jeffrey Hart, Stefanie A. Lenway, and Thomas P. Murtha. 1998. "Flying Geese as Moving Targets: Are Korea and Taiwan Catching Up with Japan in Advanced Displays?" *Industry and Innovation* 5(1): 11–33.

Liu, John S., and Chyan Yang. 2008. "Corporate Governance Reform in Taiwan." *Asian Survey* 48(5): 816–38.

Liu, Tzu-Hsin, Yee-Yeen Chu, Shih-Chang Hung, and Shien-Yang Wu. 2005. "Technology Entrepreneurial Styles: A Comparison of UMC and TSMC." *International Journal of Technology Management* 29(1/2): 92–115.

Low, Linda. 1998. *The Political Economy of a City-State*. Singapore: Oxford University Press.

———. 2001. "The Singapore Developmental State in the New Economy and Polity." *Pacific Review* 14(3): 411–41.

Low, Linda, Mun Heng Toh, Teck Wong Soon, Kong Yam Tan, and Helen Hughes. 1993. *Challenge and Response: Thirty Years of the Economic Development Board*. Singapore: Times Academic Press.

Lundvall, B-Å, ed. 1992. *National Systems of Innovation*. London: Pinter.

Lüthje, Boy, Stefanie Hürtgen, Peter Pawlicki, and Martina Sproll. 2013. *From Silicon Valley to Shenzhen: Global Production and Work in the IT Industry*. Lanham, MD: Rowman & Littlefield.

MacKinnon, Danny. 2012 "Beyond Strategic Coupling: Reassessing the Firm-Region Nexus in Global Production Networks." *Journal of Economic Geography* 12(1): 227–45.

Mahmood, Ishtiaq P., and Will Mitchell. 2004. "Two Faces: Effects of Business Groups on Innovation in Emerging Economies." *Management Science* 50(10): 1348–65.

Mahmood, Ishtiaq P., and Weiting Zheng. 2009. "Whether and How: Effects of International Joint Ventures on Local Innovation in an Emerging Economy." *Research Policy* 38(9): 1489–1503.

Mahoney, James. 2001. "Beyond Correlational Analysis: Recent Innovations in Theory and Method." *Sociological Forum* 16: 575–93.

———. 2008. "Towards a Unified Theory of Causality." *Comparative Political Studies* 41(4/5): 412–36.

Malerba, Franco, and Richard Nelson. 2011. "Learning and Catching Up in Different Sectoral Systems." *Industrial and Corporate Change* 20(6): 1645–75.

———, eds. 2012. *Innovation and Learning for Economic Development*. Cheltenham, UK: Edward Elgar.

Manners, David. 2010. "Top 25 Fabless Companies." *ElectronicsWeekly.com*. January 19. http://www.electronicsweekly.com, accessed on September 20, 2014.

Manzo, Gianluca, ed. 2014. *Analytical Sociology*. New York: Wiley.

Mardon, Russell. 1990. "The State and the Effective Control of Foreign Capital: The Case of South Korea." *World Politics* 43(1): 111–37.

Market Intelligence and Consulting Institute. 2008. *Annual Report on Taiwan's Information Industry 2008* (in Chinese). Taipei: MIC.

Mathews, John A. 2002. *Dragon Multinational: A New Model for Global Growth*. Oxford: Oxford University Press.

———. 2006. *Strategizing, Disequilibrium and Profit*. Stanford, CA: Stanford University Press.

———. 2007. "How Taiwan Built an Electronics Industry." In Henry Wai-chung Yeung (ed.), *Handbook of Research on Asian Business*. Cheltenham, UK: Edward Elgar, 307–32.

Mathews, John A., and Dong-Sung Cho. 2000. *Tiger Technology: The Creation of a Semiconductor Industry in East Asia*. Cambridge: Cambridge University Press.

Mattlin, Mikael. 2011. *Politicized Society: The Long Shadow of Taiwan's One-Party Legacy*. Copenhagen: NIAS Press.

Mauzy, Diane K., and Robert S. Milne. 2002. *Singapore Politics under the People's Action Party*. London: Routledge.

Mayntz, Renate. 2004. "Mechanisms in the Analysis of Social Macro-Phenomena." *Philosophy of the Social Sciences* 34(2): 237–59.

Mazzucato, Mariana. 2013. *The Entrepreneurial State: Debunking Public vs. Private Sector Myths in Innovation*. London: Anthem Press.

McAdam, Doug, Sidney Tarrow, and Charles Tilly. 2001. *Dynamics of Contention*. Cambridge: Cambridge University Press.

———, 2008. "Methods for Measuring Mechanisms of Contention." *Qualitative Sociology* 31(3): 307–31.

McGrath, Dylan. 2012. "AMD Relinquishes Stake in Global Foundries." *EETimes*. March 4. http://www.eetimes.com/electronics-news/4237431/AMD-relinquishes-stake-in-Globalfoundries, accessed on November 5, 2014.

McKendrick, David G., Richard F. Doner, and Stephan Haggard. 2000. *From Silicon Valley to Singapore: Location and Competitive Advantage in the Hard Disk Drive Industry*. Stanford, CA: Stanford University Press.

Milberg, William, Xiao Jiang, and Gary Gereffi. 2014. "Industrial Policy in the Era of Vertically Specialized Industrialization." In José M. Salazar-Xirinachs, Irmgard Nübler, and Richard Kozul-Wright (eds.), *Transforming Economies: Making Industrial Policies Work for Growth, Jobs and Development*. Geneva: ILO, 151–80.

Milberg, William, and Deborah Winkler. 2013. *Outsourcing Economics: Global Value Chains in Capitalist Development*. Cambridge: Cambridge University Press.

Ministry of Trade and Industry. 1998. *Committee on Singapore's Competitiveness*. Singapore: MTI.

Minns, John. 2001. "Of Miracles and Models: The Rise and Decline of the Developmental State in South Korea." *Third World Quarterly* 22(6): 1025–43.

Mitchell, Timothy. 1991. "The Limits of the State: Beyond Statist Approaches and Their Critics." *American Political Science Review* 85(1): 77–96.

Mkandawire, Thandika, and Ilcheong Yi, eds. 2014. *Learning from the South Korean Developmental Success*. New York: Palgrave.

Mo, Jongryn. 2008. "The Korean Economic System Ten Years after the Crisis." In Andrew Macintyre, T. J. Pempel, and John Ravenhill (eds.), *Crisis as Catalyst: Asia's Dynamic Political Economy*. Ithaca, NY: Cornell University Press, 251–70.

Nathan, Andrew. 1993. "The Legislative Yuan Election in Taiwan." *Asian Survey* 33(4): 424–38.

Neilson, Jeffrey, Bill Pritchard, and Henry Wai-chung Yeung, eds. 2014. "Special Issue on Global Value Chains and Global Production Networks in the Changing International Political Economy." *Review of International Political Economy* 21(1): 1–274.

——, eds. (2015), *Global Value Chains and Global Production Networks*. London: Routledge.

Nelson, Richard R., ed. 1993. *National Systems of Innovation*. Oxford: Oxford University Press.

——. 2005. *Technology, Institutions and Economic Growth*. Cambridge, MA: Harvard University Press.

Nelson, Richard R., and Sidney G. Winter. 1982. *An Evolutionary Theory of Economic Change*. Cambridge, MA: Harvard University Press.

Ngo, Tak-Wing. 2005. "The Political Bases of Episodic Agency in the Taiwan State." In Richard Boyd and Tak-Wing Ngo (eds.), *Asian States: Beyond the Developmental Perspective*. London: RoutledgeCurzon, 83–109.

Nicholas, Katrina, and Andrea Tan. 2009. "Temasek's Chartered Semi sale Speeds Up Chip Industry Exit." *Bloomberg*. September 7. http://www.bloomberg.com, accessed on September 27, 2014.

Noble, Gregory W. 1998. *Collective Action in East Asia*. Ithaca, NY: Cornell University Press.

Nübler, Irmgard. 2014. "A Theory of Capabilities for Productive Transformation: Learning to Catch Up." In José M. Salazar-Xirinachs, Irmgard Nübler, and Richard Kozul-Wright (eds.), *Transforming Economies: Making Industrial Policies Work for Growth, Jobs and Development*. Geneva: ILO, 113–49.

OECD. 2011. *Global Value Chains: Preliminary Evidence And Policy Issues*. Paris: Organisation for Economic Co-operation and Development, DSTI/IND(2011)3. http://www.oecd.org/dataoecd/18/43/47945400.pdf, accessed on September, 12 2014.

——. 2013. *Interconnected Economies: Benefiting from Global Value Chains*. http://www.oecd.org/sti/ind/global-value-chains.htm.

OECD-WTO-UNCTAD. 2013. *Implications of Global Value Chains for Trade, Investment, Development and Jobs*. Report Prepared for the G-20 Leaders Summit, September 2013. http://unctad.org/en/PublicationsLibrary/unctad_oecd_wto_2013d1_en.pdf, accessed on September 9, 2013.

O'Riain, Sean. 2004. *The Politics of High-Tech Growth*. Cambridge: Cambridge University Press.

Ouyang, Hongwu Sam. 2006. "Agency Problem, Institutions, and Technology Policy: Explaining Taiwan's Semiconductor Industry Development." *Research Policy* 35(9): 1314–28.

Pack, Howard. 2000. "Research and Development in the Industrial Development Process." In Linsu Kim and Richard R. Nelson (eds.), *Technology, Learning, and Innovation: Expe-*

riences of Newly Industrializing Economies. Cambridge: Cambridge University Press, 69–94.

Pack, Howard, and Kamal Saggi. 2006. "Is there a Case for Industrial Policy? A Critical Survey." *World Bank Research Observer* 21(2): 267–97.

Parrilli, Mario Davide, Khalid Nadvi, and Henry Wai-chung Yeung. 2013. "Local and Regional Development in Global Value Chains, Production Networks and Innovation Networks." *European Planning Studies* 21(7): 967–88.

Peck, Jamie, and Henry Wai-chung Yeung, eds. 2003. *Remaking the Global Economy.* London: Sage.

Pei, Minxin. 2006. *China's Trapped Transition.* Cambridge, MA: Harvard University Press.

Pempel, T. J. 1999. "The Developmental Regime in a Changing World Economy." In Meredith Woo-Cumings (ed.), *The Developmental State.* Ithaca, NY: Cornell University Press, 137–81.

Pereira, Alexius A. 2008. "Whither the Developmental State? Explaining Singapore's Continued Developmentalism." *Third World Quarterly* 29(6): 1189–1203.

Perraton, Jonathan. 2005. "What's Left of 'State Capacity'? The Developmental State after Globalization and the East Asian Crisis." In Graham Harrison (ed.), *Global Encounters: International Political Economy, Development, and Globalization.* Houndmills, Basingstoke: Palgrave Macmillan, 95–114.

Perry, Martin, and Boon Hui Tan. 1998. "Global Manufacturing and Local Linkage in Singapore." *Environment and Planning A* 30(9): 1603–24.

Pietrobelli, Carlo, and Roberta Rabellotti. 2011. "Global Value Chains Meet Innovation Systems." *World Development* 39(7): 1261–69.

Pike, Andy. 2015. *Origination: The Geographies of Brands and Branding.* Oxford: Wiley-Blackwell.

Piore, Michael J., and Charles F. Sabel. 1984. *The Second Industrial Divide.* New York: Basic Books.

Pirie, Iain. 2008. *The Korean Developmental State.* London: Routledge.

——. 2013. "Globalisation and the Decline of the Developmental State." In Ben Fine, Jyoti Saraswati, and Daniela Tavasci (eds.), *Beyond the Developmental State.* London: Pluto Press, 146–68.

Pisano, Gary P., and Willy C. Shih. 2009. "Restoring American Competitiveness." *Harvard Business Review* (July–August): 114–25.

——. 2012. "Does America Really Need Manufacturing?" *Harvard Business Review* (March): 94–102.

Ponte, Stefano, Peter Gibbon, and Jakob Vestergaard, eds. 2011. *Governing through Standards.* Basingstoke: Palgrave Macmillan.

Ponte, Stefano, and Tim Sturgeon. 2014. "Explaining Governance in Global Value Chains." *Review of International Political Economy* 21(1): 195–223.

Poon, Jessie, Jinn-Yuh Hsu, and Jeongwook Suh. 2006. "The Geography of Learning and Knowledge Acquisition among Asian Latecomers." *Journal of Economic Geography* 6: 541–59.

Porter, Michael E. 1990. *The Competitive Advantage of Nations.* London: Macmillan.

Prahalad, C. K., and Yves Doz. 1987. *The Multinational Mission.* New York: The Free Press.

Ravenhill, John. 2003. "From National Champions to Global Partners: Crisis, Globalization, and the Korean auto Industry." In William W. Keller and Richard J. Samuels (eds.), *Crisis and Innovation in Asian Technology.* Cambridge: Cambridge University Press, 108–36.

Reiss, Julian. 2007. "Do We Need Mechanisms in the Social Sciences?" *Philosophy of the Social Sciences* 37(2): 163–84.

Rigger, Shelley. 2014. "Political Parties and Identity Politics in Taiwan." In Larry Diamond and Gi-Wook Shin (eds.), *New Challenges for Maturing Democracies in Korea and Taiwan.* Stanford, CA: Stanford University Press, 106–32.

Rodan, Garry. 1989. *The Political Economy of Singapore's Industrialization.* London: Macmillan.

Rodan, Garry, and Kanishka Jayasuriya. 2009. "Capitalist Development, Regime Transitions and New Forms of Authoritarianism in Asia." *Pacific Review* 22(1): 23–47.

Rodrik, Dani. 1995. "Getting Interventions Right: How South Korea and Taiwan Grew Rich." *Economic Policy* 10(1): 55–107.

Routley, Laura. 2014. "Developmental States in Africa? A Review of Ongoing Debates and Buzzwords." *Development Policy Review* 32(2): 159–77.

Salazar-Xirinachs, José M., Irmgard Nübler, and Richard Kozul-Wright, eds. 2014. *Transforming Economies: Making Industrial Policies Work for Growth, Jobs and Development.* Geneva: International Labor Organization.

Saxenian, AnnaLee. 2002. "Transnational Communities and the Evolution of Global Production Networks: The Case of Taiwan, China and India." *Industry and Innovation* 9(3): 183–202.

———. 2006. *The New Argonauts: Regional Advantage in a Global Economy.* Cambridge, MA: Harvard University Press.

Saxer, Carl J. 2002. *From Transition to Power Alternation: Democracy in South Korea, 1987–1997.* New York: Routledge.

Sayer, Andrew. 2000. *Realism and Social Science.* London: Sage.

Schein, Edgar H. 1996. *Strategic Pragmatism: The Culture of Singapore's Economic Development Board.* Cambridge, MA: MIT Press.

Schmitz, Hubert, ed. 2004. *Local Enterprises in the Global Economy.* Cheltenham, UK: Edward Elgar.

Schneider, Ben Ross. 2010. "Business Groups and the State." In Asli M. Colpan, Takashi Hikino, and James R. Lincoln (eds.), *The Oxford Handbook of Business Groups.* Oxford: Oxford University Press, 650–69.

Schumpeter, Joseph A. 1934. *The Theory of Economic Development.* Cambridge, MA: Harvard University Press.

Scott, Allen J. 1988. *New Industrial Spaces.* London: Pion.

Scott, David. 1999. *Refashioning Futures: Criticism after Postcoloniality.* Princeton, NJ: Princeton University Press.

Shin, Jang-Sup. 2015. "A Dynamic Catch-Up Strategy in the Memory Industry and Changing Windows of Opportunity." *Research Policy*, forthcoming.

Sil, Rudra, and Peter J. Katzenstein. 2010. "Analytic Eclecticism in the Study of World Politics: Reconfiguring Problems and Mechanisms across Research Traditions." *Perspectives on Politics* 8(2): 411–31.

Skully, Michael T., and George Viksnins. 1986. *Financing East Asia's Success.* New York: St. Martin's Press.

Slater, Dan, and Joseph Wong. 2013. "The Strength to Concede: Ruling Parties and Democratization in Developmental Asia." *Perspectives on Politics* 11(3): 717–33.

Smith, Heather. 2000. *Industrial Policy in Taiwan and Korea in the 1980s.* Cheltenham, UK: Edward Elgar.

Sohn, Eunhee, Sung Yong Chang, and Jeayong Song. 2009. "Technological Catching-Up and Latecomer Strategy: A Case Study of the Asian Shipbuilding Industry." *Seoul Journal of Business* 15(2): 25–57.

Steers, Richard M. 1999. *Made in Korea: Chung Ju Yung and the Rise of Hyundai.* London: Routledge.

Stiglitz, Joseph E., and Justin Y. Lin, eds. 2013. *The Industrial Policy Revolution.* Basingstoke: Palgrave Macmillan.

Stinchcombe, Arthur L. 1991. "The Conditions of Fruitfulness of Theorizing about Mechanisms in Social Science." *Philosophy of the Social Sciences* 21(3): 367–88.

Stopford, Martin. 2004. *Shipbuilding World Overview 2004.* Clarksons Shipping Intelligence Network. http://www.clarksons.net, accessed on December 27, 2014.

Straits Times. Various issues. Singapore.

Stubbs, Richard. 2009. "What Ever Happened to the East Asian Developmental State?" *Pacific Review* 22(1): 1–22.

Sturgeon, Timothy J. 2002. "Modular Production Networks: A New American Model of Industrial Organization." *Industrial and Corporate Change* 11(3): 451–96.

Sturgeon, Timothy J., and Momoko Kawagami, eds. 2011. *Local Learning in Global Value Chains: Experiences from East Asia.* Basingstoke: Palgrave Macmillan.

Suh, Chung-Sok, and Seung-Ho Kwon. 2014. "Whither the Developmental State in South Korea?" *Asian Studies Review* 38(4): 676–92.

Sung, Johnny. 2006. *Explaining the Economic Success of Singapore.* Cheltenham, UK: Edward Elgar.

Tan, Kenneth Paul. 2012. "The Ideology of Pragmatism: Neo-Liberal Globalisation and Political Authoritarianism in Singapore." *Journal of Contemporary Asia* 42(1): 67–92.

Tan, Qingshan. 2000."Democratization and Bureaucratic Restructuring in Taiwan." *Studies in Comparative International Development* 35(2): 48–64.

Teece, David J. 2009. *Dynamic Capabilities and Strategic Management.* Oxford: Oxford University Press.

Teece, David J., Gary Pisano, and Amy Shuen. 1997. "Dynamic Capabilities and Strategic Management." *Strategic Management Journal* 18(7): 509–33.

Temasek Review. Various issues. Singapore: Temasek Holdings.

Thomas, Daniel. 2014. "Nokia Partners with Foxconn to Take On Apple with Tablet Device." *Financial Times.* November 18. http://www.ft.com, accessed on May 15, 2015.

Thurbon, Elizabeth. 2003. "Ideational Inconsistency and institutional Incapacity: Why Financial Liberalisation in South Korea Went Horribly Wrong." *New Political Economy* 8(3): 341–61.

———. 2007. "The Developmental Logic of Financial Liberalization in Taiwan." In W. R. Garside (ed.), *Institutions and Market Economies: The Political Economy of Growth and Development.* Houndmills, Basingstoke: Palgrave, 87–111.

———. 2011. *Why the Declinists Are Wrong: Misconstructing the 1970s Korean State as the Developmental State Model.* Paper presented at the ISA Asia-Pacific Regional Section Inaugural Conference, 29–30 September. University of Queensland, Brisbane.

Tien, Hung-mao. 1989. *The Great Transition: Political and Social Change in the Republic of China.* Stanford, CA: Hoover Institution Press, Stanford University.

Tilly, Charles. 2001. "Mechanisms in Political Processes." *Annual Review of Political Science* 4: 21–41.

Tremewan, Christopher. 1994. *The Political Economy of Social Control in Singapore.* London: Macmillan.

Tso, Chen-Dong. 2004. "State-Technologist Nexus in Taiwan's High-Tech Policymaking: Semiconductor and Wireless Communications." *Journal of East Asian Studies* 4(2): 301–28.

Tsui-Auch, Lai Si. 2004. "Bureaucratic Rationality and Nodal Agency in a Developmental State: The Case of State-Led Biotechnology Development in Singapore." *International Sociology* 19(4): 451–77.

Tsui-Auch, Lai Si, and Toru Yoshikawa. 2010. "Business Groups in Singapore." In Asli M. Colpan, Takashi Hikino, and James R. Lincoln (eds.), *The Oxford Handbook of Business Groups.* Oxford: Oxford University Press, 267–93.

UNCTAD. 2013. *World Investment Report 2013: Global Value Chains.* New York: United Nations.

Underhill, Geoffrey R.D., and Xiaoke Zhang. 2005. "The State-Market Condominium Approach." In Richard Boyd and Tak-Wing Ngo (eds.), *Asian States: Beyond the Developmental Perspective.* London: RoutledgeCurzon, 43–66.

Wade, Robert. 1988. "State Intervention in "Outward-Looking" Development: Neoclassical Theory and Taiwanese Practice." In Gordon White (ed.), *Developmental States in East Asia*. New York: St. Martin's Press, 30–67.

——. 1990. *Governing the Market: Economic Theory and the Role of Government in East Asia Industrialization*. Princeton, NJ: Princeton University Press. Paperback Edition with New Introduction in 2003.

——. 2010. "After the Crisis: Industrial Policy and the Developmental State in Low-Income Countries." *Global Policy* 1(2): 150–61.

——. 2014a. "The Mystery of US Industrial Policy." In José M. Salazar-Xirinachs, Irmgard Nübler, and Richard Kozul-Wright (eds.), *Transforming Economies: Making Industrial Policies Work for Growth, Jobs and Development*. Geneva: ILO, 379–400.

——. 2014b. "Market versus State or Market with State." *Development and Change* 45(4): 777–98.

Waldner, David. 1999. *State Building and Late Development*. Ithaca, NY: Cornell University Press.

Walter, Andrew, and Xiaoke Zhang, eds. 2012. *East Asian Capitalism*. Oxford: Oxford University Press.

Wang, Jason H. J., and Henry Wai-chung Yeung. 2000. "Strategies for Global Competition: Transnational Chemical Firms and Singapore's Chemical Cluster." *Environment and Planning A* 32(5): 847–69.

Webber, Harry R. 2011. "BP Sues Rig Owner for $40B." *Pittsburgh Post-Gazette*. April 21, 2011. http://www.post-gazette.com, accessed on September 15, 2014.

Weiss, Linda. 1998. *The Myth of the Powerless State*. Cambridge: Polity Press.

——, ed. 2003a. *States in the Global Economy*. Cambridge: Cambridge University Press.

——. 2003b. "Guiding Globalisation in East Asia." In Linda Weiss (ed.), *States in the Global Economy*. Cambridge: Cambridge University Press, 245–70.

——. 2005. "Global Governance, National Strategies: How Industrialized States Make Room to Move under the WTO." *Review of International Political Economy* 12(5): 723–49.

——. 2014. *America Inc.? Innovation and Enterprise in the National Security State*. Ithaca, NY: Cornell University Press.

Westphal, Larry. 1990. "Industrial Policy in an Export-Propelled Economy: Lessons from South Korea's Experience." *Journal of Economic Perspectives* 4(3): 41–59.

Whang, Yun-kyung, and Michael Hobday. 2011. "Local "Test Bed" Market Demand in the Transition to Leadership: The Case of the Korean Mobile Handset Industry." *World Development* 39(8): 1358–71.

White, Gordon, ed. 1988. *Developmental States in East Asia*. New York: St. Martin's Press.

White, Gordon, and Robert Wade. 1988. "Developmental States and Markets in East Asia: An Introduction." In Gordon White (ed.), *Developmental States in East Asia*. New York: St. Martin's Press, 1–29.

Whitley, Richard. 1992. *Business Systems in East Asia*. London: Sage.

Whittaker, D. Hugh, Tianbiao Zhu, Timothy Sturgeon, Mon Han Tsai, and Toshie Okita. 2010. "Compressed Development." *Studies in Comparative International Development* 45(4): 439–67.

Witt, Michael A., and Gordon Redding, eds. 2013. *The Oxford Handbook of Asian Business Systems*. Oxford: Oxford University Press.

Wittenstein, Jeran, and Katrina Nicholas. 2009. "Abu Dhabi to Buy Chartered for S$2.5 Billion, Challenging UMC." September 7. *Bloomberg*. http://www.bloomberg.com, accessed on September 27, 2014.

Womack, James P., Daniel T. Jones, and Daniel Roos. 1990. *The Machines That Changed the World*. New York: Rawson Associates.

Wong, Joseph. 2004. *Healthy Democracies: Welfare Politics in Taiwan and South Korea*. Ithaca, NY: Cornell University Press.

——. 2011. *Betting on Biotech: Innovation and the Limits of Asia's Development State*. Ithaca, NY: Cornell University Press.

Wong, Poh Kam. 1995. "Competing in the Global Electronics Industry: A Comparative Study of the Innovation Networks of Singapore and Taiwan." *Journal of Industry Studies* 2(2): 35–62.

Woo, Jung-en. 1991. *Race to the Swift: State and Finance in Korean Industrialization*. New York: Columbia University Press.

Woo-Cumings, Meredith, ed. 1999a. *The Developmental State*. Ithaca, NY: Cornell University Press.

——. 1999b. "Introduction: Chalmers Johnson and the Politics of Nationalism and Development." In Meredith Woo-Cumings (ed.), *The Developmental State*. Ithaca, NY: Cornell University Press, 1–31.

Worthington, Ross. 2003. *Governance in Singapore*. London: RoutledgeCurzon.

Wu, Ching-Yan, and John A. Mathews. 2012. "Knowledge Flows in the Solar Photovoltaic Industry: Insights from Patenting by Taiwan, Korea, and China." *Research Policy* 41(3): 524–40.

Wu, Yongping. 2005. *Political Explanation of Economic Growth: State Survival, Bureaucratic Politics, and Private Enterprises in the Making of Taiwan's Economy, 1950–1985*. Cambridge, MA: Harvard University Asia Center.

Wu, Yu-Shan. 2007. "Taiwan's Developmental State after the Economic and Political Turmoil." *Asian Survey* 47(6): 977–1001.

Yang, Chyan, and Shiu-Wan Hung. 2003. "Taiwan's Dilemma across the Strait: Lifting the Ban on Semiconductor Investment in China." *Asian Survey* 43(4): 681–96.

Yang, You-Ren, and Chu-Joe Hsia. 2007. "Spatial Clustering and Organizational Dynamics of Trans-Border Production Networks: A Case Study of Taiwanese IT Companies in the Greater Suzhou Area, China." *Environment and Planning A* 39(6): 1382–1402.

Yeung, Henry Wai-chung. 1997. "Critical Realism and Realist Research in Human Geography: A Method or a Philosophy in Search of a Method?" *Progress in Human Geography* 21(1): 51–74.

——. 2000. "State Intervention and Neoliberalism in the Globalising World Economy: Lessons from Singapore's Regionalisation Programme." *Pacific Review* 13(1): 133–62

——. 2002. *Entrepreneurship and the Internationalisation of Asian Firms*. Cheltenham, UK: Edward Elgar.

——. 2003. "Practicing New Economic Geographies: A Methodological Examination." *Annals of the Association of American Geographers* 93(2): 442–62.

——. 2004. *Chinese Capitalism in a Global Era*. London: Routledge.

——. 2007a. "From Followers to Market Leaders: Asian Electronics Firms in the Global Economy." *Asia Pacific Viewpoint* 48(1): 1–25.

——, ed. 2007b. *Handbook of Research on Asian Business*. Cheltenham, UK: Edward Elgar.

——. 2009a. "Regional Development and the Competitive Dynamics of Global Production Networks." *Regional Studies* 43(3): 325–51.

——. 2009b. "Transnationalizing Entrepreneurship." *Progress in Human Geography* 33(2): 210–35.

——, ed. 2010. *Globalizing Regional Development in East Asia*. London: Routledge.

——. 2011. "From National Development to Economic Diplomacy? Governing Singapore's Sovereign Wealth Funds." *Pacific Review* 24(5): 625–52.

——. 2014. "Governing the Market in a Globalizing Era: Developmental States, Global Production Networks, and Inter-Firm Dynamics in East Asia." *Review of International Political Economy* 21(1): 70–101.

——. 2015. "Regional Development in the Global Economy: A Dynamic Perspective of Strategic Coupling in Global Production Networks." *Regional Science Policy and Practice* 7(1): 1–23.

Yeung, Henry Wai-chung, and Neil M. Coe. 2015. "Toward a Dynamic Theory of Global Production Networks." *Economic Geography* 91(1): 29–58.

Yun, Jong-Yong. 2005. "Samsung Electronics." In Arnoud De Meyer, Pamela C.M. Mar, Frank-Jürgen Richter, and Peter Williamson (eds.), *Global Future: The Next Challenge for Asian Business*. Singapore: John Wiley & Sons (Asia), 54–73.

Zaheer, Srilata. 1995. "Overcoming the Liability of Foreignness." *Academy of Management Journal* 38(2): 341–63.

Zhang, Xiaoke. 2002. "Domestic Institutions, Liberalization Patterns, and Uneven Crises in Korea and Taiwan." *Pacific Review* 15(3): 409–42.

Zhou, Yu. 2008. *The Inside Story of China's High-Tech Industry*. Lanham, MD: Rowman and Littlefield.

Zürn, Michael, and Jeffrey T. Checkel. 2005. "Getting Socialized to Build Bridges: Constructivism and Rationalism, Europe and the Nation-State." *International Organization* 59(4): 1045–79.

Zysman, John, and Abraham Newman. 2006. "The State in the Digital Economy." In Jonah D. Levy (ed.), *The State after Statism: New State Activities in the Age of Liberalization*. Cambridge, MA: Harvard University Press, 271–300.

Index

Tables are indicated by *t* following the page number.